GW01086979

Translation played a crucial role in the emergence of vernacular literary culture in the Middle Ages. This is the first book to consider the rise of translation as part of a broader history of critical discourses. Rita Copeland shows how ideas about translation from antiquity to the Middle Ages were generated within the theoretical systems of rhetoric and hermeneutics, textual production and textual interpretation. She discusses the importance of these systems in ancient and medieval education, showing how they shaped the practice of translation in the medieval schools and in literary culture at large. Translation became a site of opposition between learned Latin and vernacular cultures, and as a form of cultural appropriation exploited the models of textual invention supplied by rhetorical theory and exegetical practice. The book illuminates this critical history through close readings of German, French, and English translations of Latin texts, including works by Jean de Meun, Chaucer, and Gower.

Rita Copeland's innovative study has important implications for the understanding of medieval literary theory and throws light on wider developments in European learning in the Middle Ages.

CAMBRIDGE STUDIES IN MEDIEVAL LITERATURE

Rhetoric, Hermeneutics, and Translation in the Middle Ages

CAMBRIDGE STUDIES IN MEDIEVAL LITERATURE

This series of critical books seeks to cover the whole area of literature written in the major medieval languages – the main European vernaculars, and medieval Latin and Greek – during the period *c.* 1100–*c.* 1500. Its chief aim is to publish and stimulate fresh scholarship and criticism on medieval literature, special emphasis being placed on understanding major works of poetry, prose and drama in relation to the contemporary culture and learning which fostered them.

Recent titles in the series include

14 *Dreaming in the Middle Ages*, by Steven F. Kruger
15 *Chaucer and the Tradition of the 'Roman Antique'*, by Barbara Nolan
16 *The 'Romance of the Rose' and its Medieval Readers: Interpretation, reception, manuscript transmission*, by Sylvia Huot
17 *Women and Literature in Britain, 1150–1500*, edited by Carol M. Meale
18 *Ideas and Forms of Tragedy from Aristotle to the Middle Ages*, by Henry Ansgar Kelly
19 *The Making of Textual Culture: Grammatica and literary theory, 350–1100*, by Martin Irvine
20 *Narrative, Authority, and Power: The medieval exemplum and the Chaucerian tradition*, by Larry Scanlon
21 *Medieval Dutch Literature in its European Context*, edited by Erik Kooper
22 *Dante and the Mystical Tradition: Bernard of Clairvaux in the 'Commedia'*, by Steven Botterill

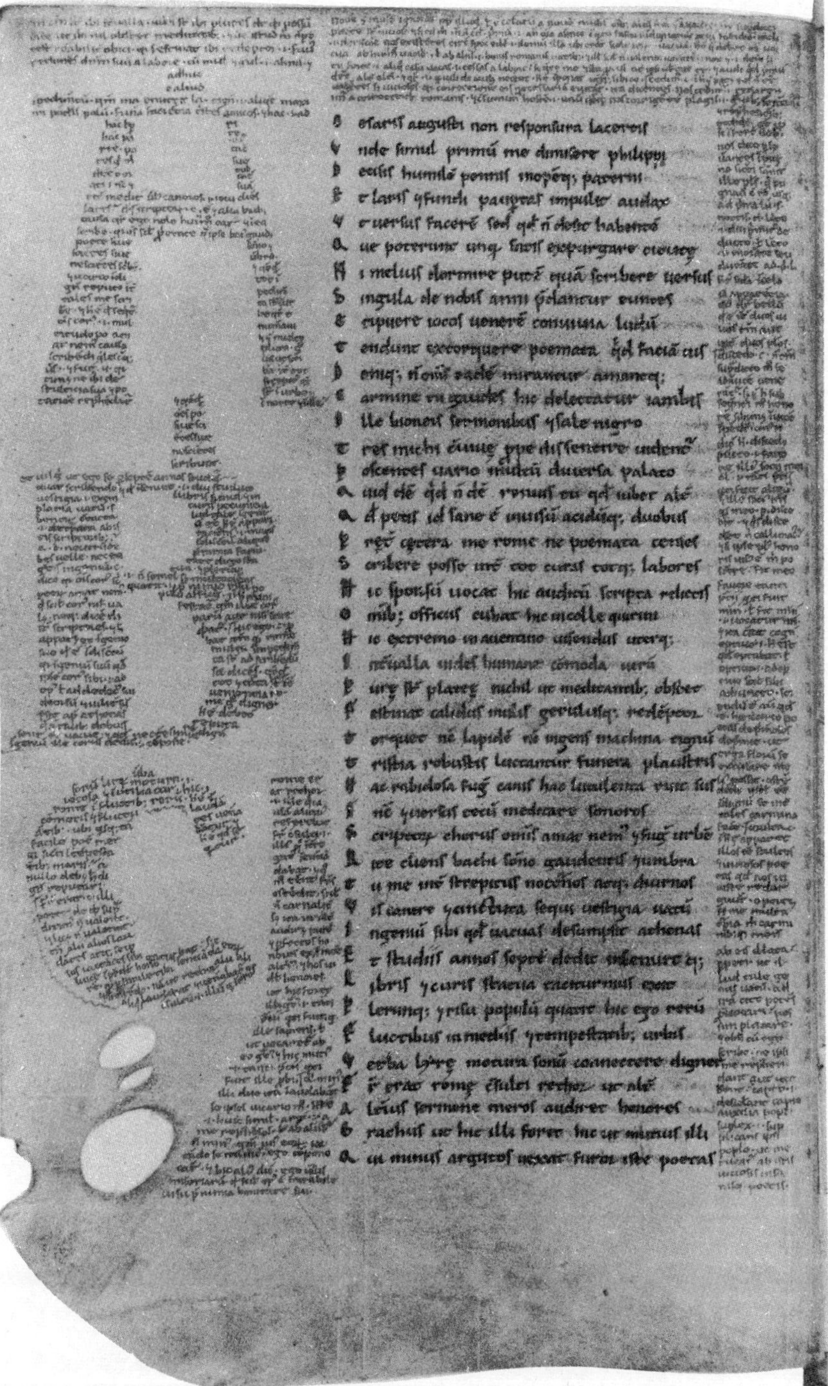

Trinity College, Cambridge, MS o.3.57 (fol. 67v), Horace, *Epistles* 2.2 with marginal commentary shaped into an alphabet.

Rhetoric, Hermeneutics, and Translation in the Middle Ages

Academic traditions and vernacular texts

RITA COPELAND

CAMBRIDGE
UNIVERSITY PRESS

Published by the Press Syndicate of the University of Cambridge
The Pitt Building, Trumpington Street, Cambridge CB2 1RP
40 West 20th Street, New York, NY 10011-4211, USA
10 Stamford Road, Oakleigh, Melbourne 3166, Australia

First published 1991
First paperback edition 1995

Printed in Great Britain at the University Press, Cambridge

British Library cataloguing in publication data

Copeland, Rita
Rhetoric, hermeneutics, and translation in the Middle Ages: academic traditions and vernacular texts. Cambridge studies in medieval literature; 11
I. Medieval literature.
Rhetoric
Translation, history
I. Title II. Series
870

Library of Congress cataloguing in publication data

Copeland, Rita.
Rhetoric, hermeneutics, and translation in the Middle Ages: academic traditions and vernacular texts / Rita Copeland.
p. cm. – (Cambridge studies in medieval literature; II)
Include bibliographical references and index.
ISBN 0 521 38517 2 (hardback)
ISBN 0 521 48365 4 (paperback)
1. Latin literature. Medieval and modern – Translations into foreign languages – History and criticism.
2. Latin literature – Translations into foreign languages – History and criticism.
3. Literature. Medieval – Translations from Latin – History and criticism.
4. Latin language – Translating – History.
5. Rhetoric. Medieval. 6. Hermeneutics.
I. Title. II. Series.
PA8035.C6 1991
478′.02′0902 – dc20 90–2036 CIP

ISBN 0 521 38517 2 (hardback)
ISBN 0 521 48365 4 (paperback)

CE

To my mother and to the memory of my father

Contents

Acknowledgments

In the course of writing this book I have incurred many debts to those who have shared their learning and wisdom with me. I want to thank, first of all, three colleagues in the English department at Texas, Thomas M. Cable, Ernest N. Kaulbach, and James I. Wimsatt, for their friendship, generosity, and dedication to all aspects of medieval studies. Their intellectual integrity and broad interests have made this a rich environment for scholarship. Many members of the wider community of medievalists contributed to this book. Ralph Hanna III read and commented on the entire manuscript with enthusiasm and acuity, and kindly provided me with his transcripts of some Lollard materials on translation. Karin Margareta Fredborg and Marjorie Curry Woods gave me advice on finer aspects of medieval rhetoric and graciously furnished copies of their own work on rhetorical commentaries. Writing this book would not have been possible without the recent efflorescence of scholarship on medieval literary theory. For their contributions to this field, their interest in this particular study, and their advice on specific questions, I want to thank Martin Camargo, Martin Irvine, Ian R. Johnson, Glending Olson, Nigel Palmer, Richard H. Rouse, and the late Judson Allen. Here I wish particularly to mention the generosity of Alastair Minnis, who provided invaluable help and information at early stages of this project, and later gave the manuscript a very perceptive reading. William W. Kibler lent his expertise on medieval French; Hubert Heinen and T. A. Shippey gave advice on Old High German. I owe some of my oldest debts to Phillip Damon, Anne Middleton, Joseph J. Duggan, and Derek Brewer, and it is a pleasure to record them here. Many colleagues outside of medieval studies have also contributed to this book. Two colleagues in classics, David Konstan and Patricia Rosenmeyer, read substantial portions of an earlier draft. Gudni Elisson kindly translated an article from Danish. From my friendships with Susan Shapiro and Barbara Harlow I have learned how crucial is the intersection of medieval studies with the work of other critical and historical discourses: I am grateful to them for many personal kindnesses and for their commitment to defining the common grounds of intellectual inquiry. I also want to thank Kevin Taylor, Katharina Brett, Josie Dixon, and Iris Hunter of Cambridge University Press for their care and efficiency in guiding this book through to publication.

The research for this study and time for writing were enabled by support from the American Council of Learned Societies, the National Endowment for the Humanities, and the Research Institute of the University of Texas. A Special Research Grant from the University of Texas provided funds for producing the frontispiece. I have received much help from the librarians of the Perry-Casteneda Library and the Harry Ransom Humanities Research Center of the University of Texas, Cambridge University Library, the Library of Trinity College, Cambridge, the Bodleian Library, Oxford, and the Bibliothèque Nationale, Paris. Section 2 of chapter 2 was published separately, in slightly different form, as an essay in *The Medieval Translator: The Theory and Practice of Translation in the Middle Ages*, ed. Roger Ellis (Cambridge: D. S. Brewer, 1989). I thank the publishers for permission to reprint. The photograph on the frontispiece and brief extracts from the same manuscript are reproduced by permission of the Master and Fellows of Trinity College, Cambridge.

My greatest debts, personal and intellectual, are to my family. My parents, to whom this book is dedicated, have given me their love of learning and their own devotion to *translatio studii*, to remembering and preserving the past. As always, my husband David has been my best reader and critic, and my most valued interlocutor and friend.

Abbreviations

CSEL	*Corpus scriptorum ecclesiasticorum latinorum*
CFMA	*Classiques français du moyen âge*
CCSL	*Corpus christianorum, series latina*
EETS, e.s.	Early English Text Society, extra series
EETS, o.s.	Early English Text Society, original series
MGH	*Monumenta germaniae historica*
PL	*Patrologia latina*, ed. J.-P. Migne (Paris, 1844–64)

Introduction

This book has a twofold purpose. First, it seeks to define the place of vernacular translation within the systems of rhetoric and hermeneutics in the Middle Ages. In serving this aim, its concern is not with a narrow pragmatics or theory of translation in the Middle Ages. Rather, it seeks to show how translation is inscribed within a large disciplinary nexus, a historical intersection of hermeneutical practice and rhetorical theory. These investigations, however, have much broader implications than the question of translation itself, and here lies the second purpose of this book: to examine the way that rhetoric and hermeneutics in the Middle Ages define their status in relation to each other as critical practices, to make these practices visible as discourses on their own terms. These two purposes go hand in hand. In order to define the place of vernacular translation within the systems of rhetoric and hermeneutics, it has been necessary to account for the disciplinary history and discursive character of rhetoric and hermeneutics themselves and to show how the features of these systems are carried over into certain kinds of vernacular literary production. Thus in its broadest implications this study points beyond the question of translation to the more fundamental question of medieval critical practices, the ideological force that these practices carried as textual institutions of learned culture in the Middle Ages. In studying vernacular translation I am also asking how the discourse of criticism defines the status of both Latin and vernacular textuality in the Middle Ages.

These two related purposes require individual comment here, and I begin with the historical problem of vernacular translation. A theoretical history of translation in the Western Middle Ages cannot be written as if translation represents a semi-autonomous development of stylistics. Considered in this way, medieval vernacular translation is little more than a collection of disparate practices, united by a few inherited commonplaces which center on the distinction between word for word and sense for sense, and useful for diachronic source study, stylistic analysis, or the study of particular literary or historical relationships. But the earliest theories of translation which the Latin West received from Cicero, Horace, and Quintilian did not emerge as critically transparent and historically portable reflections on practice. These theories of translation were formulated at Rome within a certain academic environment and in response to a certain disciplinary agenda. They emerged as a by-product of a conflict between the claims of rhetoric and grammar.

Rhetoric sought to establish itself as the master discipline by limiting the province of grammar to that of language usage and *enarratio poetarum*, that is, glossing and interpretation of the poets. Rhetoric asserted as its own province the powerful activity of textual (or oratorical) production. This contest between the disciplines had wide implications within Roman culture and long-reaching implications for the medieval inheritors of the Roman arts curriculum. This contest is also inscribed in the most famous of all Roman pronouncements on translation, Cicero's "non verbum pro verbo" (*De optimo genere oratorum* 5.14–15), which Jerome (among others) mediated to the Middle Ages. In describing how he has translated some models of Attic oratory, Cicero states: "I did not translate them as an *interpreter* but as an *orator*." This opposition between ways of translating is really part of a much larger issue, the conflict over disciplinary hegemony. From Cicero's position, to translate like an "interpreter" is to practice within the restricted competence of the textual critic whose duty is to gloss word for word; and this is a restriction that the profession of rhetoric (Cicero's profession) historically imposed on the profession of grammar. To translate as an "orator" is to exercise the productive power of rhetoric, a power which rhetoric asserted and maintained by purposefully distinguishing itself from grammar. As we can see from even this cursory view of Cicero's pronouncement, the real underlying issue is not how to define the terms of good translation, but rather how to define the disciplinary status and cultural privilege of rhetoric. Translation was only one of the sites on which this larger conflict was played out, and a theory of translation did not come into being except as an instrument of this disciplinary contest.

At the heart of this contest is the fact that the functions of rhetoric and grammar could not be so easily distinguished, and indeed that the two disciplines overlapped in the character of their most fundamental procedures, rhetorical *inventio* and grammatical or hermeneutical *enarratio*. It is in the domain of this overlap that the character of translation had to be defined. This disciplinary overlap was carried over into the Middle Ages, although, as I shall show, under somewhat different curricular and ideological conditions. And in the Middle Ages it was in this disciplinary overlap that vernacular translation achieved some of its most definitive characteristics.

Thus the idea of translation as an identifiable practice was not inaugurated in critical isolation, but was formed within a system of academic discourse. But while almost every modern historical and stylistic study of translation draws on Ciceronian theory (or some later form of it) as a *locus communis*, there has been little recognition and no sustained examination of the disciplinary context in which this theory was formulated. In other words, the modern historiography of translation, and especially of medieval translation, has treated it as a practice susceptible to theoretical regulation without taking into account the historical causalities through which translation could achieve this status, that is, the historical discourses which articulated the terms of translation. If translation could be theorized or conducted under the aegis of certain academic disciplines and could be shaped by the fortunes of those disciplines, then we need to write the history of translation through an account of these disciplines.

This brings me to the second purpose of this study. This book does not proceed so much as a history of translation than as an account of the relationship between rhetoric and hermeneutics, a nexus within which the character of medieval vernacular translation was largely defined. Medieval translation reflects the larger contours of the academic discourses which contain and shape it, and my concern is to show how these disciplinary formations also define the relationship between vernacular culture and Latin academic culture, a relationship most broadly articulated through vernacular translations of the classical *auctores*. To see how vernacular translation is grounded in certain critical discourses allows us to see how those discourses function within vernacular textual culture. The title of the book is intended to designate these related issues. The main title, "Rhetoric, Hermeneutics, and Translation in the Middle Ages," indicates that medieval translation cannot be understood without reference to the traditional systems of rhetoric and hermeneutics which so much defined its practice. The subtitle, "Academic traditions and vernacular texts," points to the way that translation, shaped and informed by the academic systems of rhetoric and hermeneutics, was also a primary vehicle for vernacular participation in, and ultimately appropriation of, the cultural privilege of Latin academic discourse.

The thesis that translation is a vehicle for vernacular appropriation of academic discourse is predicated on arguments about the nature of medieval commentary itself and about the relationship of translation to the commentary tradition. A chief maneuver of academic hermeneutics is to displace the very text that it proposes to serve. Medieval arts commentary does not simply "serve" its "master" texts: it also rewrites and supplants them. In this study I will devote considerable attention to the textual strategies of displacement that are displayed in medieval commentary. But for an intriguing, graphic image of such displacement we can look to the frontispiece of this volume. This page of text and commentary reflects, with vivid immediacy, the tension between authoritative text and its exegetical "servant." The page is from a collection of Horace's works, probably from the later twelfth century. Throughout this manuscript the text of Horace is accompanied by two columns of commentary, and in one of these columns the commentary is shaped into a dazzling series of geometric forms which vary from page to page (taking either abstract shapes, such as a checkerboard, or pictorial shapes, such as anvils or fish).[1] On the page reproduced here, showing a passage from *Epistles* 2.2 towards the end of the collection, the column of commentary takes the shape of the letters of the alphabet, the fundamental elements of grammatical teaching and exposition of the *auctores*. Here the commentary announces its own presence, as if offering an iconographic emblem of its own textuality, competing with, and indeed visually overtaking, the text of the *auctor* which it accompanies. This is, of course, an extreme image of displacement, notable because it is unusual. This book will be concerned with some of the more routine and familiar textual characteristics of medieval commentary, and will show how these features actually constitute mechanisms for displacing the authoritative text. One important step in the argument here will be to show that displacement of the source is a maneuver that medieval hermeneutics takes over from ancient rhetoric, which represents the ideal of oratorical discourse as a form of aggressive rivalry with a source or an opponent. Medieval vernacular translation of the classical *auctores* emerges from this historical intersection of rhetoric and hermeneutics, and carries the chief features of the academic practice from which it arises. It takes over the function of commentary on the *auctores*, and in so doing replicates the characteristic move of academic exegesis, that of displacing the very text that it proposes to serve. Like commentary, translation tends to represent itself as "service" to an authoritative source; but also like commentary, translation actually displaces the originary force of its models.[2] For vernacular translation, however, the source to be appropriated is not just the text of the *auctor*, but the academic criticism that mediates that text.

It is important to foreground the conditions and implications of medieval critical practice. During the last two decades a number of important studies of medieval literary theory have helped us to revaluate this period in the history of criticism, and I see my task here as that of continuing some of the discussions inaugurated in this recent body of scholarship.[3] Such scholarship has enabled us to understand medieval literary criticism in a different light. It has begun to correct a tendency – which nevertheless persists – to see medieval academic theory in an instrumental way, as a static repository of information about the sources and contexts of canonical "literary" texts, as a historical body of ideas that supplied the interpretive conventions out of which Chaucer, Dante, and others wrote. The best example of this is the way that mythography has traditionally been read, as a set of learned footnotes to what are then designated as "primary" texts, for example, the works of Chaucer. Once these theoretical structures and exegetical "data banks" have yielded up satisfactory readings of canonical authors they can recede into invisibility. In this traditional positivist way of reading, medieval critical theory and practice would become visible to us only in their application to something else. Rhetorical theory has also been a notable victim of this kind of positivism. It has been viewed as a neutral preceptive system, a descriptive taxonomy of style, or as an academic discipline whose history is constituted by its manifest meanings and whose claims to truth about the nature of language and discourse are accepted on their own terms. But rhetoric as a system, like philosophy, is itself a discursive construct; its language and strategies of self-representation are themselves susceptible of rhetorical explication.[4] My purpose here is to extend the corrective readings of recent scholarship on medieval literary theory. I propose to consider some of the ulterior structures of certain critical practices, rhetoric and hermeneutics, by examining what they disclose about themselves as mechanisms of discursive and institutional control. In other words, I want to explore what is at stake in the ways that these practices, as signifying systems, constitute themselves.

This book does not propose itself as a "key" to all vernacular translation. My arguments do not necessarily extend to the emergence of "popular" translation in genres such as the *lai* or the metrical romance from one vernacular language into another, nor to hagiographical or devotional writings, nor to translation of scientific or technical works. The important question of biblical translation also lies outside the scope of this study. My chief concern here is the question of academic critical discourse in Latin and vernacular traditions; therefore my focus is on texts that make these theoretical problems most visible, vernacular translations that are significantly linked with academic study and reception of the ancient *auctores*. While the book considers many aspects of the transmission of classical literary and rhetorical traditions, the treatment of vernacular translation focuses on receptions of Ovid, Martianus Capella, and Boethius.

A more difficult problem to address in terms of the scope of this book is that of medieval traditions of classifying the sciences. This is an important historical inquiry whose parameters are still being defined in modern scholarship. My study of rhetoric and hermeneutics acknowledges the force of traditional medieval constructions of disciplinary relations, but does not attempt to produce a history of such classifying systems in the Middle Ages or to account for their nature. My concern is to suggest how medieval critical practice operates in ways that are not always acknowledged within official models of knowledge, to account for some of the discursive conditions through which these practices regulate themselves. The very term "hermeneutics," meaning a system or science of interpretation, is problematic if we consider it only in the light of official academic classifications of the sciences in the Middle Ages, whereby the relationship between the trivium arts of grammar, rhetoric, and dialectic can be variously configured under different schemes (for example, Hellenistic divisions into logic, ethics, and physics, or Aristotelian divisions into practical, theoretical, and productive). While hermeneutical practice, or exegesis, derives its essential methods of textual commentary from the grammatical art of *enarratio poetarum*, it is certainly not a practice confined to the official parameters of *grammatica* as a study or an art. Rather, exegesis is the method that defines the whole project of *translatio studii* which is trans-disciplinary in its very conception and hence almost infinite in its potential coverage. The term "hermeneutics" is not one that we find in medieval discussions of *ordo scientiarum*, but certain codes and conventions of hermeneutical tradition are everywhere present as a "macro-discourse" that regulates all disciplinary inquiries.[5] In this sense, as I will argue, grammar itself becomes a master discourse, providing the means of access to all other knowledge in the insistently textual culture of the Middle Ages, and providing the method of retrieving the learning of the ancient *auctores*. But I am less concerned here with the actual scope of *grammatica* as it would have been represented in the Middle Ages, that is, as the study of grammatical usage and language theory, than with the interpretive methods derived from the grammarians. The term "hermeneutics" is thus more inclusive than the term "grammar," and it is used here to imply the range of interpretive mechanics and assumptions that are brought to bear upon textual production. But because hermeneutical practice across all the disciplines operates according to certain established, learned conventions, it itself constitutes a discursive domain, an identifiable system of language use, for it represents a way of codifying knowledge. My intention here is to trace how the relationship between rhetoric and hermeneutics was defined, not in the metacritical discussions of medieval academic theory on the relations between the sciences, but in the actual strategies of academic practice. In this way I can bring to the foreground some of the ideological conditions that governed and legitimized certain forms of academic discourse.

The book begins by constructing a history of the interaction of the disciplines of rhetoric and hermeneutics from late antiquity through the Latin Middle Ages. Modern work on hermeneutics, especially that of Gadamer, provides some valuable models for theorizing the way in which exegesis appropriates the tools of rhetoric. In the first chapter I consider how Roman disciplinary debates and practice created a space in which a rhetorical theory of translation could emerge; and the second chapter considers how that space could be redefined in the early Middle Ages by the force of new disciplinary directives. The rhetorical value of translation is lost in the very discourses that carry over Ciceronian theories of translation; but hermeneutical practice itself takes over the functions of rhetoric and creates a new context in which a rhetorical model of translation can emerge. In order to establish the terms of this argument it is necessary to examine the character of medieval hermeneutics, and in the third chapter I show how exegesis assumes the force of rhetorical performance and in fact supplants rhetoric as the master discourse. My concern here and throughout is with commentaries from the arts curriculum, not scriptural exegesis.

Chapters 4–5 show how vernacular translation of classical texts emerge from Latin commentary traditions which carry the force and imprint of rhetoric. These chapters examine Notker III of St. Gall, the *Ovide moralisé*, Old French translations of the *Consolatio*, Chaucer's *Boece*, and Walton's Boethius. The translations considered here function largely as commentaries, and I argue that by taking over the textual strategies of academic exegesis, vernacular writing can insert itself into the privileged cultural sphere of Latin learning. These chapters raise several new theoretical problems. First, I introduce a distinction between what I have called "primary" translation and "secondary" translation. These terms have only a relative value, denoting the degree to which the translation identifies itself with the exegetical practice of the schools, which is the "primary" point of departure for translation as a form of academic discourse. Primary translations, such as the work of Notker III of St. Gall, exhibit a close alliance with the aims and methods of exegetical practice, and like exegesis define their purpose in terms of service to a source text. Secondary translations (considered in chapter 7) derive their essential methods and motive from exegesis, but stand in a "secondary" relationship to the exegetical tradition of the schools: they do not define themselves through exegetical models of service or supplementation, but rather through rhetorical models of invention, that is, discovery of one's own argument or subject out of available topics or commonplaces. The second issue raised in these chapters is the distinction between interlingual reception, in which a vernacular translation stands in a direct relationship to Latin sources, and intralingual reception, in which a group of vernacular translations in the same language (such as the Old French Boethius translations) draw as much from one another as from the Latin tradition. The model of intralingual reception demonstrates how vernacular translation can function in much the same way as exegesis, working to supplant the very source that it proposes to serve. In the case of intralingual reception, a group of vernacular translations of a single *auctor* generates its own textual tradition which effectively displaces the Latin source tradition. This leads to the third problem raised in these chapters: the status of vernacularity within medieval academic culture. Vernacular translation emerges out of exegetical practice and replicates the major features of that practice, including the tendency to displace the source which it proposes to serve; and this paradigm extends to the relationship between vernacular translation-commentary and its sources in Latin academic discourses. Vernacular productions displace their Latin sources, and vernacularity inserts itself into the privileged sphere of academic culture. The analysis of these moves entails an analysis of the ideology of academic criticism, and specifically of its Latinity, in order to understand the implications of vernacular embodiments of these privileged discourses.

Chapter 6 returns to a history of disciplinary relationships, tracing the way that rhetoric comes to be redefined as a hermeneutical procedure. Rhetoric's key function, *inventio*, is identified, first in Augustine and later in rhetorical commentaries and *artes poetriae*, with the *modus interpretandi*. This picture of the historical transformation of *inventio* is developed largely through a study of commentaries on Horace's *Ars poetica*. The famous lines in the *Ars poetica*, "difficile est proprie cummunia dicere" (128) and "nec verbum verbo curabis reddere fidus interpres" (133–4), were variously interpreted in medieval commentaries, sometimes as precepts for translation, and sometimes in terms of exegetical practice. But in the rhetorical poetics of Matthew of Vendôme and Geoffrey of Vinsauf, these lines are used in the context of inventional theory. The purpose of this analysis is to show how ideas about commentary and about translation intersected with theoretical modifications of rhetorical invention.

Chapter 7 takes up some examples of what I have called "secondary" translation. Translation comes to be perceived as a form of rhetorical *inventio*, which has in turn been redefined as exegetical performance on a text or textual *topos*. The main texts considered here are Chaucer's *Prologue* to the *Legend of Good Women* and Gower's *Confessio amantis*. These texts have demonstrable relations with exegetical traditions, not simply in terms of content, but in terms of the character of exegesis, which works by displacing and appropriating the materials it proposes to serve. These translations represent an extension of exegetical procedures, and show how vernacular writing can authorize itself by taking over the function of academic discourse. These texts claim the prestige of a certain canonical authority within English writing; but they achieve this authority, not as "literary" productions, but as academic products. They define themselves through an identification with academic discourse, and "invent" themselves through the traditional textual strategies of hermeneutics.

In sum, my purpose here is to discover and trace out the ways in which translation articulates the relationship between academic and vernacular cultures in the Middle Ages. My method is to define the relationship between certain academic discourses, rhetoric and hermeneutics, and to consider how these critical relations are instantiated in vernacular translation of the *auctores*.

I

Roman theories of translation: the fusion of grammar and rhetoric

The Middle Ages inherited from Latin antiquity not only some commonplaces of translation theory, but also the academic framework for that theory. Roman theories of translation represented only one aspect of a much larger debate, within academic and critical circles, about the relationship between the study of grammar and the study of rhetoric. The familiar precepts about translation, which the Middle Ages borrowed from antiquity, center on the idea that translation may be literal (word for word) or loose (sense for sense); we find variations on this standard theme throughout medieval translators' prologues.[1] But it is not by tracing the fortunes of these commonplaces that we can evaluate the theoretical conditions under which ideas about translation were mediated from antiquity to the Middle Ages. In Latin antiquity, it was the framework of rhetoric and grammar, and of the relationship between these two disciplines, that gave meaning to ideas about translation. For the Middle Ages as well, it was through the tradition of academic discourse, inherited from the Romans, that ideas about translation took shape. In both antiquity and the Middle Ages, these systems of academic discourse had profound implications for the organization of textual culture as a whole. By examining the changing role of translation within these academic systems we can gain insight into the historical redefinitions of the systems themselves. Thus we begin here with the earliest formulations of these problems in antiquity.

In both Greek and Roman schools, the discipline of grammar comprised not only the technical study of language, but also textual commentary or criticism, the ancestor of what we today would call literary criticism. Rhetoric, on the other hand, represented the study of how to produce persuasive arguments, primarily public speeches. But between these two academic disciplines, the one concerned with textual commentary, the other with textual (or oratorical) production, there was much contested ground, for the concerns of these two disciplines overlapped and intersected in a variety of ways. In the Roman schools, translation was a practice common to both disciplines: in grammatical study it was an exercise; in rhetorical study it was considered both an exercise and an art form. The theories of translation contained in the writings of Cicero and Quintilian were formulated, not with the express aim of defining the practice of translation itself, but rather as a way of defining the status of rhetoric in relation to grammar. Translation theory was one way of clarifying the difference between the two disciplines. The practice of translation represented one point of reference, in this large academic debate, for distinguishing between the domains of grammar and of rhetoric. But, as I will argue here, the theory and practice of translation in the Roman schools also reflected the troublesome overlap between the concerns of grammar and rhetoric.

In Roman pedagogical and critical theory, translation was closely linked with the theory and practice of literary imitation (that is, the imitation of literary models). Like translation, literary imitation was a component of both grammatical and rhetorical study, although theories of imitation received much of their impetus from the rhetorical concerns of oratorical education, at least in the Rome of the late Republic and early Empire. One of the chief questions to be considered in this chapter is the theoretical relationship between translation and imitation, especially as these two practices were identified with the disciplines of grammar and rhetoric. Within grammatical study, translation was considered to be a special aspect of textual commentary; within rhetorical study, translation was seen as a special form of imitation. Thus distinctions between translation as a form of commentary and translation as a form of imitation lead back, as we will see, to larger disciplinary questions, that is, the distinction between the domain of grammar and the domain of rhetoric.

The terms of Roman translation theory are very complex and need to be unravelled carefully. When used as an exercise in grammatical study, translation represented a form of commentary; when associated with rhetorical study and the production of speeches, translation constituted a form of imitation. Yet, as we will consider, there was much overlap between the practices of commentary, translation, and imitation, just as there was much overlap between the study of grammar and of rhetoric. It is also important to note the relatively limited significance of translation within Roman pedagogy. Translation was only a small component of grammatical exercises in commentary and of rhetorical exercises in imitation. The scope of ancient textual commentary far exceeded that of translation as an educational practice; and similarly, theories of imitation comprehended much more than simply precepts about translation. Indeed, translation had a relatively restricted importance in Roman criticism and literary practice, if the rarity of theoretical articulations about translation and the absence of important translations within the Roman literary canon, are any indications. In the Golden Age, translation was mainly an exercise.[2] Unlike medieval vernacular literatures, Roman literature did not constitute itself largely by direct translation. It is a paradox of history, then, that the few scattered theoretical formulations about translation that survive in the extant corpus of Roman criticism should have come so much to dominate later European thought about translation, and especially to form the authorizing premises for the enormous role of translation in the vernacular Middle Ages.

The express interest in translation, manifest both in theory and in a variety of educational practices, was a natural product of the bilingualism of Roman culture of the late Republic and the early Empire, that is, from approximately the later second century B.C to the later second century A.D.[3] Within this historical context of Hellenized Latinity, especially from the first century B.C through the beginning of the second century A.D., the period of Cicero and Horace to the end of the career of Quintilian and of his student, Pliny the Younger, Latin translation from Greek operates according to a vertical hierarchy of prestige. The Romans acknowledge Greek as the more illustrious language, and translation from Greek into Latin can be described as a vertical movement from greater to lesser prestige.[4] As Marrou has pointed out, the Romans are the first people in the European West to exploit another language in order to achieve mastery over their own; and this systematic use of foreign resources is most important in regard to the formation of a literary culture.[5] The self-conscious fashioning of a Latin literary tradition out of the models of a hegemonic Greek culture is especially a Golden Age phenomenon, and no one articulates better than Cicero the Roman ambivalence about their position as debtors to Greek literary culture. In *De finibus*, Cicero expresses this ambivalence in terms of a deep contradiction: Latin must be made a fitting linguistic instrument for the transmission of Greek philosophical texts and thought, so that it can rival the suppleness of the Greek language; yet the purpose of such refinements is to render Latin adequate to serve the Greek texts which it will carry over to Roman literary culture. Even in this express aim of linguistic rivalry, the idea of service to a superior culture is implicit.[6] But it is precisely this deep ambivalence that creates a place for translation in the Roman curriculum and also in the higher reaches of Latin rhetorical and literary theory.

THE DISCIPLINARY STATUS OF GRAMMAR AND RHETORIC

In ancient Greece, grammatical study arose as a concomitant of systematic literary hermeneutics or exegesis. The grammarian taught reading and writing, and especially in the Alexandrian period, the sphere of grammar enlarged to include the full critical study of the poets. The title *kritikos*, or critic, became synonymous with *grammatikos*, and the aims of literary criticism became inseparable from the aims of a codified philology which could classify the poetic texts and regulate the study of them through the teaching of correct linguistic usage.[7] Early on this dual exegetical motive came into contact with rhetorical interests in describing the terms and distinguishing the parts of the oratorical – and by extension literary – text.[8] In Greece, the distinction between exegetical and rhetorical purposes does not seem to have been drawn as sharply as it came to be in Rome. Although the express purpose of Greek rhetoric was to determine means of persuasion, and rhetorical studies certainly occupied a highly practical and prescriptive sphere, the terms of rhetoric were not so insistently separated from those of literary analysis, as came to be the case in Rome of the late Republic, where the distinction was maintained in theory (although, as we will see, hardly sustained in the practice of literary criticism). Thus, for example, Aristotle's enterprise of poetic classification in the *Poetics* was that of delineating and interpreting the affective functions of poetry, which is directly associated with rhetorical analysis of the means of persuasion.[9]

After the middle of the second century B.C, the integration of grammatical with literary studies followed much the same path in Rome as it had in Greece.[10] But even by the first century B.C, when rhetoric had finally gained an established place in the official Roman curriculum, rhetorical concerns were, at least in theory, separated from those of grammar and literary exegesis by virtue of a hierarchical division of studies which placed rhetoric at the top of all fields of inquiry as the synthetic fulfillment of disparate kinds of knowledge. Contrary to the Platonic and Aristotelian tradition, Cicero gives rhetoric, as a praxis, a certain priority over philosophy, so that at the beginning of the *De inventione*, he offers a vision of primordial social development in which rhetoric activated a wisdom that was mute and socially inoperative (1.2.3). Cicero's Stoic training leads him to locate reason in both speech and thought, and to reconcile rhetoric and dialectic; but he goes even further by representing eloquence as a controlling framework, of which philosophy is an integral part.[11] Thus in the *Brutus* he called intelligence the glory of man and eloquence the lamp of that intelligence (15.59); and in *De oratore* he points to oratory as the summit of achievement:

> Sed nimirum maius est hoc quiddam, quam homines opinantur, et pluribus ex artibus studiisque collectum . . . Quam ob rem mirari desinamus, quae causa sit eloquentium paucitatis, cum ex eis rebus universis eloquentia constet, quibus in singulis elaborare permagnum est. (*De oratore* 1.4.16–5.19)

> [But the truth is that this oratory is a greater thing, and has its sources in more arts and branches of study, than people suppose . . . Let us therefore cease to wonder what may be the cause of the rarity of orators, since oratory is the result of a whole number of things, in any one of which to succeed is a great achievement.][12]

Even in the interdependence of rhetoric and philosophy (eloquence and wisdom), rhetoric or oratory is figured as the natural fulfillment of the aims of philosophy. Thus for Quintilian:

> Sed ea et sciet optime et eloquetur orator . . . Sit igitur orator vir talis, qualis vere sapiens appellari possit . . . (*Institutio oratoria* 1.Pr. 17–18)

> [But it is surely the orator who will have the greatest mastery of all such departments of knowledge and the greatest power to express it in words . . . Let our ideal orator then be such as to have a genuine title to the name of philosopher . . .][13]

In Rome, grammatical study defined itself as comprising *scientia* (or *ars*) *recte loquendi*, correct speaking and reading, and *enarratio poetarum*, study of the poets (*Institutio oratoria* 1.4.2). The order of these two concerns was, in practice, largely interchangeable, as mastery of language came through study of the poets, and the poets could be subjected to ever more sophisticated commentary through the refinement of linguistic skills. From Greek to Roman academic contexts, the definition of grammar and of the grammarian's duty remained relatively stable. From *scholia* on Dionysius Thrax comes a fourfold division of duties: correction of the text, accurate reading, exposition, and judgment (*kritikon*).[14] Among Greek teachers, the last of these duties, "judgment," seems to have implied largely the discovery of moral *exempla* in the poets.[15] In Rome, however, perhaps through the influence of Alexandrian philology, this critical faculty seems mainly to have implied the work of authenticating texts and drawing up a canon of authors (see *Institutio oratoria* 1.4.3). It is clear, however, that by the Roman period, the province of the *grammaticus* was strictly defined in terms of mastery of language (*methodicē*), textual criticism (emendation and usage), and poetic exposition, including the explanation of mythological references. Seneca makes an emphatic case for such a restricted sphere of activity:

Grammaticus circa curam sermonis versatur et, si latius evagari vult, circa historias, iam ut longissime fines suos proferat, circa carmina. (*Epistulae morales* 88.3)

[The scholar busies himself with investigations into language, and if it be his desire to go farther afield, he works on history, or, if he would extend his range to the farthest limits, on poetry.][16]

The sphere of grammatical studies at Rome was even further restricted by its exclusive attention, at least in policy, to poetic texts. Whereas in Greece the grammarian commented on both the poets and the prose-writers,[17] in Rome the teaching of prose texts, that is, the Greek and Latin historians and orators, seems to have been the special reserve of the *rhetor*. In Quintilian, as in Cicero (*De oratore* 1.41.187), the grammatical stage of learning is associated specifically with the study of poetry, whereas the study of prose authors is assigned to rhetorical studies. It is in the latter, more advanced stage of the curriculum, that the students are actively engaged in discovering models for their own oratorical style. Such restrictions on the scope of grammatical study in Rome would seem to suggest that rhetoric defined itself against grammar by reserving for itself a heuristic privilege, that is, the particular rhetorical privilege of invention, the discovery of one's own argument in order to render one's cause plausible. It was only with the study of the orators that teaching took on a fully preceptive character aimed at result and persuasion, that is, effective oratory.

The character of grammar at Rome may best be understood by the way that it was differentiated from rhetoric or, more accurately, the way that rhetoric imposed the terms of this difference. Tzvetan Todorov, writing of the history of Western semiotics and poetics, has drawn a valuable picture of the conception of rhetoric in antiquity:

The object of rhetoric is eloquence, defined as effective speech that makes it possible to act on others. Rhetoric grasps language not as form – it is not concerned with utterances as such – but as action; the linguistic form becomes an ingredient of a global act of communication (of which persuasion is the most characteristic type). Rhetoric deals with the functions of speech, not its structure. Its one constant is the objective it seeks to achieve: to persuade . . . Linguistic means are taken into account to the extent that they may be used to reach this objective.[18]

Todorov's insights into the historical relationship between rhetoric and linguistic study are also applicable to the question of how rhetoric defined itself against the discipline of grammar. On these terms we might say that, in Roman rhetorical theory at least, rhetoric concerns itself with discourse, that is, with a whole domain of language use or a whole system of communication; grammar, on the other hand, is concerned with linguistic form, with language as an instrument of discourse. It is to grammar that rhetoric assigns the purpose of describing and elucidating the formal components of the text and of language usage – the linguistic, syntactic, and tropological elements of correct speech. Because, according to this disciplinary construct, grammar is concerned only with language as form, its authority is limited to usage, to the structure of linguistic signifiers (or, on Todorov's model, "language as form," or "utterances"). Only rhetoric grasps language and text as totality – as action, function, result. Grammatical concerns are confined within the structure of the given text. Rhetoric deals with the text as a totality of audience, speaker, language, meaning, and persuasion or affect. For rhetoric, the totality of the text incorporates an area wider than the actual text itself: from compositional inception, that is, the speaker's (or writer's) invention of argument, to the effect upon its audience, or the result achieved after the text's formal closure. Rhetoric thus constructs its own disciplinary privilege as the art that can complete the partial or limited textual concerns of grammar: rhetoric unites the linguistic signifier with meaning and action. Rhetoric is itself metalinguistic, concerning itself, as Nancy Streuver has remarked, with discourse about discourse.[19] For the Romans, who draw upon the precedent of Sophistic rhetorical theory, it is a directive discipline. In Roman theory, rhetoric is the highest discipline, the culmination of all philosophy: it is thus rhetoric that claims within its domain the most important questions of language, meaning, and interpretation.

On what grounds did rhetoric so delimit the competence of grammar? To understand this problem, we must examine the theoretical models out of which ancient rhetoric defined its own disciplinary status and upon which Roman rhetoric in particular established its special privilege as the highest of the arts. These considerations will lead us to the question of how rhetoric defined the task of interpretation, or hermeneutics: was that task to be the proper office of grammar or of rhetoric?

Rhetoric, according to Aristotle and according to Roman practitioners and academic theorists, is a praxis. Aristotle's division of the fields of knowledge into the theoretical (or speculative), practical, and productive sciences builds on distinctions not just between the methods of the various sciences, but also between the aims of each kind of science.[20] It is the distinction between theoretical and practical science that most concerns us here. In *Nicomachean Ethics*, Aristotle distinguishes between theoretical knowledge, also called "scientific" knowledge, or *episteme*, and "practical wisdom," or *phronesis*. *Episteme* and *phronesis* are not themselves sciences or bodies of knowledge; rather they are "states by virtue of which the soul possesses truth" (6.3, 1139b15).[21] But these distinctions between "virtues" or "states of the soul" correspond to distinctions between the various kinds of science.

"Scientific" knowledge, or *episteme*, represents a concern with necessary and unchanging rules and principles: scientific knowledge is "a state of capacity to demonstrate" (6.3, 1139b32); it is a "belief about things that are universal and necessary . . . for that which can be known can be demonstrated" (6.6, 1140b31). This principle of knowledge is associated with the sciences that Aristotle calls speculative or theoretical: mathematics, physics, and theology (the last of these, which deals with the nature of being itself, is really the domain of metaphysics).[22] These are the sciences that deal, at various levels of abstraction, with universal and absolute truths: their method is exact, their aim is knowledge itself (*Metaphysics* 1.2, 892a30).

"Practical wisdom" or *phronesis* is a capacity or "virtue" by which one deals with matters that are changing and variable. According to Aristotle, the man of practical wisdom will be "able to deliberate well about what is good and expedient for himself, not in some particular respect . . . but about what sorts of things conduce to the good life in general . . . Thus in general the man who is capable of deliberating has practical wisdom" (*Nicomachean Ethics* 6.5, 1140a26–31). Moreover, there is no deliberation about absolute truths, which require a demonstration. Practical wisdom, therefore, is not scientific knowledge. Rather, "it is a true and reasoned state of capacity to act with regard to the things that are good or bad for man" (*NE* 6.5, 1140b5). The sciences associated with practical wisdom deal with relative questions such as human ethics, actions, means and ends. Their aim is not just knowledge, but action: to act or make others act on the basis of judgment and knowledge.[23] The pre-eminent practical science is, of course, politics, of which ethics is a part; under politics, which is the most comprehensive of the practical sciences, Aristotle lists also military strategy, economics, and rhetoric (*NE* 1.2, 1094b3).

Within Aristotle's system, the status of rhetoric as a practical science is a matter of debate. While at the opening of the *Nicomachean Ethics* he seems to imply that rhetoric, along with economics and strategy, is a practical science comprehended by politics, his position at the opening of the *Rhetoric* is quite different. Here he states clearly: "Rhetoric is the counterpart of dialectic. Both alike are concerned with such things as come, more or less, within the general ken of all men and belong to no definite science (*Rhetoric* 1.1, 1354a1).[24] By this he means that rhetoric, like dialectic, is an instrument of all sciences, rather than a particular kind of science.[25] But however rhetoric is to be classified among the sciences, its association with the intellectual virtue of practical wisdom, *phronesis*, is clear.[26] Rhetoric calls for an ability to deliberate about the contingent and the variable, about human actions and ethics, for which there are no fixed, necessary principles. "The duty of rhetoric is to deal with such matters as we deliberate on without arts or systems to guide us . . . The subjects of our deliberation are such as seem to present us with alternative possibilities . . . For it is about our actions that we deliberate and inquire, and all our actions have a contingent character; hardly any of them are determined by necessity" (*Rhetoric* 1.2, 1357a2–5, 25–7).

The identification of rhetoric and *phronesis*, and of both with the praxis of political science, was of course the keystone of Roman rhetorical theory. In Quintilian's disciplinary conception of rhetoric, we find a firm identification of rhetoric, not just with practical wisdom (as in Aristotle), but also with the practical sciences (a link which Aristotle does not clearly make). Quintilian draws on Aristotelian divisions of the sciences into theoretical, practical, and productive.[27] He defines practical sciences in terms of their aim, which is action, and he locates rhetoric within this scheme:

> . . . quarum in hoc finis est et ipso actu perficitur nihilque post actum operis relinquit, quae *praktikē* dicitur, qualis saltatio est . . . fere iudicandum est, rhetoricen in actu consistere; hoc enim quod est officii sui, perficit. Atque ita ab omnibus dictum est. Mihi autem videtur etiam ex illis ceteris artibus multum assumere . . . Si tamen una ex tribus artibus habenda sit, quia maxime eius usus actu continetur atque est in eo frequentissima, dicatur activa vel administrativa, nam et hoc eiusdem rei nomen est.
>
> (*Institutio oratoria* 2.18.1–5)

> [This is their end, which is realised in action, so that, the action once performed, nothing more remains to do: these arts we style *practical*, and dancing will provide us with an example . . . In view of these facts we must come to the conclusion that, in the main, rhetoric is concerned with action; for in action it accomplishes that which it is its duty to do. This view is universally accepted, although in my opinion rhetoric draws largely on the two other kinds of art {theoretical and productive}. Still, if rhetoric is to be regarded as one of these three classes of art, since it is with action that its practice is concerned, let us call it an active or administrative art, the two terms being identical.]

Within Roman theory we also find a connection between rhetoric as a practical science (a view which Quintilian tells us is "universally accepted") and as an exercise of practical wisdom. If the practical sciences are those that aim at result or action, so does Cicero also define practical wisdom itself, as the virtue that aims at results in the sphere of social and political interests:

> Placet igitur aptiora esse naturae ea officia, quae ex communitate, quam ea, quae ex cognitione ducantur . . . ea {i.e., sapientia} si maxima est, ut est certe, necesse est, quod a communitate ducatur officium, id esse maximum. Etenim cognitio contemplatioque naturae manca quodam modo atque inchoata sit, si nulla actio rerum consequatur. Ea autem actio in hominum commodis tuendis maxime cernitur; pertinet igitur ad societatem generis humani; ergo haec cognitioni anteponenda est.
>
> (*De officiis* 1.43.153)

> [My view, therefore, is that those duties are closer to Nature which depend upon the social instinct than those which depend upon knowledge . . . If wisdom is the most important of the virtues, as it certainly is, it necessarily follows that that duty which is connected with the social obligation is the most important duty . . . for the study and knowledge of the universe would somehow be lame and defective, were no {action} to follow. Such results, moreover, are best seen in the safeguarding of human interests. It

is essential, then, to human society; and it should, therefore, be ranked above speculative knowledge.][28]

Just as the practical sciences should aim at result or action, so the highest wisdom is that which has its end in result, in social and political action. It is worth noting that in this passage in *De officiis*, Cicero ranks the virtue of practical wisdom above that of "scientific" knowledge; by the same token, as we have seen, Roman academic theory ranks rhetoric (as a practical science) above all other sciences, even philosophy.

How then did Roman academic theory define the place of grammar in relation to rhetoric? The Romans represented grammar as a mere mastery of rules. If rhetoric is a praxis, grammar is a kind of *episteme*, theoretical or scientific knowledge in the most restrictive sense (as opposed to the sense in which Aristotle defines such knowledge as a grasp of universal, ontological truths). Seneca in this regard poses a loaded question about the aims of grammar, asking whether it can partake of the ethical concerns which rhetoric, along with philosophy, has arrogated as its own domain:

Quid horum ad virtutem viam sternit? Syllabarum enarratio et verborum diligentia et fabularum memoria et versuum lex ac modificatio? Quid ex his metum demit, cupiditatem eximit, libidinem frenat? . . . Quaeritur utrum doceant isti virtutem an non; si non docent, ne tradunt quidem.[29] (*Epistulae morales* 88.3–4)

[But which of these paves the way to virtue? Pronouncing syllables, investigating words, memorizing plays, or making rules for the scansion of poetry – what is there in all this that rids one of fear, roots out desire, or bridles the passions? The question is: do such men teach virtue, or not? If they do not teach it, then neither do they transmit it.]

And Quintilian, the consummate rhetorician, protective of the claims of rhetoric inscribed into its very conceptual system, denounces overweening grammarians:

Et grammatice (quam in Latinum transferentes litteraturam vocaverunt) fines suos norit, praesertim tantum ab hac appellationis suae paupertate, intra quam primi illi constitere, provecta; nam tenuis a fonte assumptis historicorum criticorumque viribus pleno iam satis alveo fluit, cum praeter rationem recte loquendi non parum alioqui copiosam prope omnium maximarum artium scientiam amplexa sit; et rhetorice, cui nomen vis eloquendi dedit, officia sua non detrectet nec occupari gaudeat pertinentem ad se laborem, quae, dum opere cedit, iam paene possessione depulsa est. (*Institutio oratoria* 2.1.4–5)

[*Grammatice*, which we translate as the science of letters, must learn to know its own limits, especially as it has encroached so far beyond the boundaries to which its unpretentious name should restrict it and to which its earlier professors actually confined themselves. Springing from a tiny fountain-head, it has gathered strength from the historians and critics and has swollen to the dimensions of a brimming river, since not content with the theory of correct speech, no inconsiderable subject, it has usurped the study of practically all the highest departments of knowledge. On the other hand, rhetoric, which derives its name from the power of eloquence, must not shirk its peculiar duties nor rejoice to see its own burdens shouldered by others. For the neglect of these is little less than a surrender of its birthright.]

Quintilian also provides a model of the theoretical or exact sciences, whose end lies in knowledge and understanding alone:

Cum sint autem artium aliae positae in inspectione, id est cognitione et aestimatione rerum, qualis est astrologia, nullum exigens actum sed ipso rei, cuius studium habet, intellectu contenta, quae *theoretikē* vocatur. (*Institutio oratoria* 2.18.1)

[Some arts, however, are based on examination, that is to say on the knowledge and proper appreciation of things, as for instance astronomy, which demands no action, but is content to understand the subject of its study: such arts are called *theoretical*.]

Here Quintilian uses the example of astronomy. But as James J. Murphy has pointed out, what Quintilian says of astronomy is quite comparable to what he says elsewhere of grammar, that its end is "objective" understanding of the rules of correct speech rather than dynamic result or action.[30] In the same way, grammar demands no action but rather *cognitio et aestimatio rerum*. Grammatical exercises did not involve memory, delivery, or imitation of full speeches,[31] for these are part of the active, productive, practical province of rhetoric. The analogy between grammar and the natural sciences in terms of the target of understanding as object, as form or structure, becomes clearer when we consider how the competence of grammar is constricted to *methodicē* or rules, and *enarratio* (or *historicē*), which means strictly analysis or description, not interpretation in the active sense of moral judgment or deliberation (*Institutio oratoria* 1.9.1).

This brings us to the question of the status of hermeneutics or interpretation in relation to the discipline of rhetoric. In his treatise on interpretation, *Peri hermeneias*, Aristotle had defined hermeneutics as a concern with linguistic action on things.[32] For the Romans, it is rhetoric that fulfills this interpretive directive: rhetoric as a discipline deals with meaning as action or result, and it is not surprising that rhetorical theory encompassed hermeneutical concerns within its own realm. Even though the discipline of grammar dealt with certain questions of interpretation, the analysis of language and texts, Roman rhetoric imposed such limits on grammar, so restricted its competence to matters of form and usage, that the concerns of grammar could not possibly extend to the dynamic questions of hermeneutics, that is, the conditions and implications of signification.

To understand how hermeneutics could properly be the domain of rhetoric, we must consider how hermeneutics itself can be defined according to the same theoretical model as rhetoric, that is, as a praxis. Here we may find some important insights from modern philosophical hermeneutics. The work of Hans-Georg Gadamer is particularly relevant for our investigation here, because he uses Aristotle's analysis of practical wisdom as a model for the basic theoretical problems of hermeneutics.[33] Gadamer locates the question of hermeneutics, moreover, not just in Aristotle's notion of practical wisdom, but also in the association of ancient rhetoric with the ideal of practical wisdom. Gadamer has formulated the theme of ancient rhetoric in terms of the aim of understanding "the whole in terms of the detail and the detail in terms of the whole."[34] We might add that whole and detail involve the grasp not only of the text itself, but also of a spectrum of circumstances surrounding the text, from the text's initial conception to its execution, and to its reception and interpretation. This is analogous to Todorov's excellent insight into the dynamic economy of ancient rhetoric, that it grasps language as action and function, rather than as static form.

But in the same way that rhetoric uses language to *produce* meaning and thus to act on others, so it is also concerned with *interpreting* language and meaning in a way that is appropriate to changing and variable circumstances of human behavior and actions. In other words, the art of interpretation, or hermeneutics, may be seen as a function of practical wisdom, for the interpretation of discourse is not simply a mastery of rules, but a judicious response to the contingent or changing circumstances which can determine different responses to that discourse. Here we can look to Gadamer's model of hermeneutics as the integration of understanding, interpretation, and application. For Gadamer, the fundamental hermeneutical problem is that these three faculties cannot be distinct activities of the hermeneutical process: interpretation is the explicit form of understanding, and understanding is always application.[35] Gadamer defines "application" as the historical "situatedness" (*Situationsgebundenheit*) of interpretation (not application in the sense of applying a theorem): it means that the historical situation of the interpreter cannot be separated from what is to be interpreted or from the act of interpretation itself. Gadamer thus draws from Aristotle's model of *phronesis*, practical wisdom, which requires deliberation over the changeable rather than scientific, "objectified" knowledge of fixed principles: "For moral being, as Aristotle describes it, is clearly not objective knowledge, i.e. the knower is not standing over against a situation that he merely observes, but he is directly affected by what he sees. It is something that he has to do."[36] This dialectical integration of understanding, interpretation, and application makes hermeneutics into an action, an event. Hermeneutics can be defined as a praxis, that is, in Aristotelian terms, the activity of practical wisdom.[37]

This notion of hermeneutics as application, that is, that the historical situation or circumstances of the interpreter must be part of the act of understanding, has its counterpart in ancient rhetorical theory in the principle of *kairos*, of fitting persuasion to the right and appropriate circumstances of subject, audience, and moment.[38] *Kairos* is a doctrine of good judgment about variable circumstances, and is fundamental to rhetoric's self-definition as a dynamic engagement with all the conditions of signification. The rhetorical concept of *kairos* applies to the production of texts; but within ancient rhetoric, the principle that *kairos* implies, that of practical wisdom, also extends to judgment of texts and discourse, as we will see when we consider Roman critical theories of imitation and translation. The model of hermeneutics that Gadamer presents is one that is already contained in Roman rhetorical theory; indeed, it is the very principle by which Ciceronian rhetoric defined its own power and place, Aristotelian notions of practical wisdom and understanding (or judgment).[39] As Gadamer has noted, any theoretical examination of understanding must turn to rhetoric, for both hermeneutics and rhetoric derive from praxis: like rhetoric, hermeneutics involves a productive attitude which supersedes the merely competent force of mastering rules.[40] The interpretive relationship of the "reader," in Gadamer's terms, to the text mirrors then the writer's creative power over the text: understanding itself takes on the character of event, of an "independent productive act," as the powers of cognition and explanation unite with the power of application.[41]

The idea that hermeneutical activity, in its highest form, is really a function of rhetoric, manifests itself in a variety of ways in Roman academic thought. Within the educational system, the aim of grammar is that of understanding the text as object, in the manner of an exact science. As the rhetoricians describe it, the object of grammar is passive absorption, understanding of language as occurrence or as formal given. Quintilian thus describes the work of interpretation to be carried on in the grammar schools:

Ideoque optime institutum est, ut ab Homero atque Vergilio lectio inciperet, quanquam ad intelligendas eorum virtutes firmiore iudicio opus est . . . Interim et sublimitate heroi carminis animus adsurgat et ex magnitudine rerum spiritum ducat et optimis imbuatur. (*Institutio oratoria* 1.8.5)

[It is therefore an admirable practice which now prevails, to begin by reading Homer and Vergil, although the intelligence needs to be further developed for the full appreciation of their merits . . . In the meantime let his mind be lifted by the sublimity of heroic verse, inspired by the greatness of its theme and imbued with the loftiest sentiments.]

Here the text itself may produce a preliminary, affective understanding, but it is not within the scope of the grammarian to shape this understanding into moral judgment. Such is the task, rather, of rhetorical instruction. Rhetoric will cultivate these gardens of affective response that the grammarians prepare, by moving that response from passive inspiration to intellection, to dynamic application. By supplying the precepts by which the orator actually produces such affective response in others, rhetoric resituates the student in relation to the text, giving him power over both the given and the future text. Grammar positions the reader (student) in a pre-critical surrender to the text; rhetoric gives the reader the preceptive and critical tools with which to understand the terms of such surrender and hence to master them. Rhetoric, as an exercise of practical wisdom, also supplies a model of hermeneutics: the reader is engaged in a dialectical relationship with the text, as interpretation is fused with application.

The discipline of grammar seems to have submitted to the territorial "rhetoric" of rhetoric, and to have thrived in accepting the definition imposed upon it so as to constrain its power. Neither the Latin grammarians nor their professional descendants, the scholiasts of late antiquity, produced a comprehensive system of literary aesthetics.[42] As late as the fourth century A.D., Tiberius Claudius Donatus could begin his commentary on the *Aeneid* with some sharp remarks about the limitations of grammatical studies of Virgil. According to Donatus, the writers of commentaries do not teach Virgil with any zeal, but use it as model of stylistic instruction. Donatus, however, proposes to read the *Aeneid* with a view to its *rhetorical* composition. It exemplifies the oratorical genre of praise (epideictic), and in it one sees not only the sublime artistry and structural unity of the text, but large thematic concerns, treatments of nature, morality, knowledge, customs, and experience, all comprehended under the discipline of rhetoric. A careful reading of the *Aeneid* will discover the high rhetoric of the poem, and will produce an understanding of such profound matters as orators, rather than grammarians, teach.[43] The grammatical programs of the Roman schools observed the restrictions placed on the discipline of grammar. In policy (if not necessarily in practice), grammatical study remained preliminary to oratorical study, confining its prescriptive energies to *scientia recte loquendi*, or the principles of usage, and for the rest exercising only descriptive authority in the work of *enarratio poetarum*: elucidating mythological and historical references, providing correct readings, glossing difficult words, and explaining meter.

Thus for the most part, it was the rhetoricians who produced comprehensive systems of literary theory, whether as preceptive guides, as in the *Rhetorica ad Herennium* or even Horace's rhetorically based *Ars poetica*, or as interpretive dicta, as in Cicero's *De oratore* or in Quintilian's *Institutio*. This is consistent with the basic premises of ancient rhetorical theory: from Aristotle to Cicero and Quintilian, rhetoric reserved much of the function of textual criticism for itself, building its system of invention and its precepts for decorum around principles of interpreting documentary evidence and literary canons.[44]

MODELS OF TRANSLATION AND IMITATION

Translation played a limited role in the grammatical program, which is to be expected, both because of the preliminary, foundational nature of grammatical training, and because of the restrictions placed upon interpretive activity within grammar. The most obvious function of translation is its role in the bilingual context of Roman education. Here Greek was originally taught side by side with Latin, and exercises in converting Greek texts into Latin and vice versa were commonplace.[45] With the decline in Roman bilingualism during the second and third centuries of the Empire, it became necessary to teach Greek as a foreign language, a necessity which is recorded in the survival, from the beginning of the third century A.D., of bilingual school manuals known as the *Hermeneumata pseudodositheana*.[46] These manuals provided

Latin–Greek vocabulary, as well as historical, mythological, narrative, and legal texts in a dual-language format. Thus elementary Greek came to be taught through basic translation techniques.

Another obvious context for translation was in the introductions to the poets in the form of the *praelectiones*, undertaken as one of the tasks of the *enarratio poetarum*. The *praelectio*, or preliminary reading, would involve some form of an *accessus ad auctorem* or formal introduction to the author, as well as explanations of sense, syntax, and lexicon sometimes derived from *scholia* on the given text. While this practice of exegetical reading along with schematic introduction to the text provides an invaluable source of information on the relationship between commentary and translation when we come to it in its medieval vernacular avatar, our actual knowledge of this procedure in Rome is restricted to intralingual examples. Here we have a clear and elaborate picture of the practice of commenting on Latin authors, from the extensive *enarrationes* of Servius on Virgil, Donatus on Terence, and even Priscian on Virgil. While these commentaries date from very late antiquity, and certainly in the case of Servius and Donatus have taken on an encyclopaedic character, they nevertheless reflect the major components of the exegetical techniques among the classical grammarians. They offer an indication of an early connection between paraphrase and literary exegesis, as the explication often takes the form of verbal recasting to deliberate on sense as well as on usage.[47] Such relatively late *scholia* (fourth through sixth century) on Latin authors register the norms of earlier practice, and are useful indicators in the absence of comparable records from the periods of Cicero and Quintilian.[48] The same strategy of collapsing interpretation and paraphrase is evident in Alexandrian *scholia* on Greek texts: once again this gives an intralingual situation which nevertheless suggests a parallel for commentary conducted through interlingual paraphrase.[49] But we seem to have no substantial records detailing the practice of commenting, in Latin, on Greek texts. Throughout antiquity, the *scholia* on Greek texts appear to have been produced in Greek, largely by Alexandrian and Hellenistic grammarians, and we have thus no real records of the form that oral, classroom *praelectiones* on Greek authors by Latin grammarians might have taken. Of course, many of the grammar teachers in Rome were themselves Greek, and grammar teachers, whether Greek or Roman, would typically have been bilingual and thus might have conducted such literary expositions in either language: it is also probable that Greek texts were sometimes subjected to exposition in Latin, thus providing an obvious context for the merging of translation and exegetical practice. But our only records of such interlingual exposition – Greek text accompanied by Latin commentary and sometimes translation – date from the early Middle Ages or occur in the more specialized context of patristic scholarship.

In Quintilian, however, we do find an exact account of the role of translation in the grammatical program. But here translation seems to be poised just on the boundary between grammar and rhetoric. In fact it is in terms of the functions that translation is designed to serve in Quintilian's program that the boundary between grammar and rhetoric comes under some dispute.[50] In setting out the *officia grammatici* (*methodicē* and *historicē*), he adds to these instruction in the rudiments of oratory as preliminary to rhetorical schooling:

Igitur Aesopi fabellas, quae fabulis nutricularum proxime succedunt, narrare sermone puro et nihil se supra modum extollente, deinde eandem gracilitatem stilo exigere condiscant; versus primo solvere, mox mutatis verbis interpretari, tum paraphrasi audacius vertere, qua et breviare quaedam et exornare salvo modo poetae sensu permittitur. (*Institutio oratoria* 1.9.2)

[Their pupils should learn to paraphrase Aesop's fables, the natural successors of the fairy stories of the nursery, in simple and restrained language and subsequently to set down this paraphrase in writing with the same simplicity of style: they should begin by analysing each verse, then give its meaning in different language, and finally proceed to a freer paraphrase in which they will be permitted now to abridge and now to embellish the original, so far as this may be done without losing the poet's meaning.]

On the one hand, this program specifies restraint in paraphrase and simplicity of analysis, as if to accord with the strictures imposed upon grammar of dealing with textual ingredients rather than with totalities, with form rather than with function, and of remaining within descriptive, theoretical spheres (predicated on the aim of understanding the given, the unchangeable). But on the other hand, Quintilian's program also calls for exercise in *abbreviatio* and *amplificatio*, which are in fact elements of *elocutio* or style, one of the five parts of rhetoric. More importantly, however, Quintilian continues by indicating how this exercise in paraphrasing prepares the way for exercises in more extended commentary:

Sententiae quoque et chriae et ethologiae subiectis dictorum rationibus apud grammaticos scribantur, quia initium ex lectione ducunt. (*Institutio oratoria* 1.9.3)

[He should also be set to write *aphorisms*, *moral essays* (*chriae*) and *delineations of character* (*ethologiae*), of which the teacher will first give the general scheme, since such themes will be drawn from their reading.]

Such exercises, drawing upon a measure of personal invention, look towards the kinds of rhetorical exercises which Quintilian prescribes in 2.4.18–24, refutation and confirmation of the narrative, praise and blame of character, and comparisons of character, which lead, of course, to declamatory exercise.

Indeed, Quintilian registers an awareness of how his grammatical program of paraphrase and extended textual analysis (*abbreviatio*, *amplificatio*, *aphorism*, *chria*, *ethologia*) threatens to invade the territory of rhetoric. Directly after describing this program, he enforces once again the distinction between the spheres of grammar and rhetoric:

Cetera maioris operis ac spiritus Latini rhetores relinquendo necessaria grammaticis fecerunt; Graeci magis operum suorum et onera et modum norunt.
(*Institutio oratoria* 1.9.6)

[Other more serious and ambitious tasks have been also imposed on teachers of literature by the fact that Latin rhetoricians will have nothing to do with them. Greek rhetoricians have a better comprehension of the extent and nature of the tasks placed on their shoulders.]

Such a protest needs to be registered here, because Quintilian's grammatical program for translation, exercise in textual adaptation, is essentially rhetorical in orientation, despite his attempts to segregate grammar from rhetoric. The practice in *abbreviatio* and *amplificatio* points towards (indeed, is no less than) the elements of *elocutio*, the discovery and mastery of language and style through experimentation. Thus even at this preliminary stage, the program of translation partakes of the active rhetorical system, by involving the application of what has been interpreted, and by building towards textual product and result in the proto-declamatory exercises of *aphorism*, *chria*, and *ethologia*.

Quintilian's program for translation here provides a ready perspective on the intersection of grammar and rhetoric. First, the terms of such exercises can hardly be separated from those of *declamatio*. Suetonius, describing rhetorical training, mentions the analysis of rhetorical texts, and exercises in narration, translation, praise and blame, as well as evaluation of customs and myths, a series which virtually mirrors the grammatical program.[51] Quintilian, introducing the theory of declamation or mock-oration, remarks on the value for the rhetor of adopting the expository methods of the *grammaticus*. Poetic narrative is the property of the teacher of literature, or *grammaticus*, whereas historical narrative, founded on *gesta res*, is the proper concern of the rhetorician (2.4.2). But the exegetical methods of the grammarians may be brought to serve the aims of rhetoric:

Sed de ratione declamandi post paulum. Interim, quia prima rhetorices rudimenta tractamus, non omittendum videtur id quoque, ut moneam, quantum sit collaturus ad profectum discentium rhetor, si, quemadmodum a grammaticis exigitur poetarum enarratio, ita ipse quoque historiae atque etiam magis orationum lectione susceptos a se discipulos instruxerit. (*Institutio oratoria* 2.5.1)

[I will speak of the theory of declamation a little later. In the mean time, as we are discussing the elementary stages of a rhetorical education, I think I should not fail to point out how greatly the rhetorician will contribute to his pupils' progress, if he imitates the teacher of literature whose duty it is to expound the poets, and gives the pupils whom he has undertaken to train, instruction in the reading of history and still more of the orators.]

Thus, as in book 1.9, where the description of proto-declamatory exercises of textual adaptation, moral essays, and character analysis is preceded by a program of simple textual *enarratio* and paraphrase (of Aesop), so here in book 2, Quintilian introduces the *declamatio* proper with a similar grammatical program of textual exegesis, borrowing the methods of grammar while at the same time protesting its intrusion into rhetoric. But in the act of appropriating for rhetoric the methods of grammar, Quintilian attributes to grammar – by implication – an active hermeneutical property whose end is a dynamic understanding rather than an objective (or "theoretical") explanation.

The second way in which Quintilian's grammatical program for translation suggests the intersection of grammar and rhetoric is that the grammatical paradigm for translation is essentially grounded in the terms of rhetorical imitation. It is also within the larger concerns of imitation that rhetorical theories of translation are articulated. There are many dimensions to the question of textual imitation in Roman rhetorical and literary theory. In order to situate translation in its proper position as an aspect of imitation, it will be necessary here to consider imitation from at first a broad perspective, and by degrees to narrow the discussion to translation itself.

The pervasive bilingualism and biculturalism of educated Romans produced the competing senses of continuity with and disjunction from the hegemony of Greek culture. Hellenistic Greek culture within Rome produced certain landmarks in theories of literary or rhetorical imitation, notably in the work of Dionysius of Halicarnassus and in the *Peri hypsos* of "Longinus." But these texts, drawing as they do upon the monolithic and highly self-referential terms of Greek culture, offer a coherent vision of the aims of imitation, coherent because uncomplicated by any deep sense of cultural rupture. In Dionysius of Halicarnassus, the most complicating factor is a yearning for continuity with the Greek past, produced by a sense of temporal – but not cultural – distance from the Attic ideal.[52] In both Dionysius and "Longinus," historicity is the most consistent informing perspective on the ideal of imitation. In both the *Epistle to Pompeius*, which quotes a large section of the second book of his lost treatise *De imitatione*, and in the series of studies on Attic orators, Dionysius is largely concerned with the recovery of rhetorical (or stylistic) decorum and skill through the judicious use of Attic models.[53] In Dionysius' classicism, the rift with an earlier, pre-eminent culture, or perhaps the sense of decline, is figured in temporal terms, which admits also the possibility of the rightful recovery of the Attic legacy. The corruption of Greek eloquence by Asianism can be reversed by a return to Attic standards, and such a return can be achieved in Latin as well as in Greek eloquence.[54] "Longinus'" discussion of the decline of contemporary standards is similarly cast in terms of temporal difference and moral decay through generational decline.[55] While some recognition of intercultural movement finds a place in the comparison between Demosthenes and Cicero in an appraisal of Atticism,[56] the better part of this discussion is given over to comparisons between Plato and Demosthenes, and leads into the famous chapter on imitation of earlier writers as a means to sublimity.[57] In both Dionysius and "Longinus," an acknowledgment of the standards of the dominant Roman culture which they inhabit can be absorbed without conflict into a larger concern for continuity through imitation, as Greek texts are perceived as natural models for contemporary Roman as well as Hellenistic writers. The assumed hegemony of Greek literary culture –

even in the decline of that culture – offsets any conflict between the claims of contemporary Greek and Latin culture, as Latin can only make claims to recognition through its cultivation of Atticist principles.

In the hands of Roman theorists, the question of imitation is immediately complicated by a bifurcation into intralingual and interlingual forms.[58] The few intercultural references in Dionysius and "Longinus" do not amount to a revaluation of the principles of imitation. But in the Roman context, intercultural or interlingual imitation often invites the question of translation in addition to that of transmission, and the theory of imitation must be adjusted to legitimize and account for this specialized procedure.

The ideal of imitation in Roman rhetoric is often figured in intracultural terms. Cicero's *De oratore* 2 and Quintilian's *Institutio oratoria* 10 argue from the assumption that the aspiring orator will nourish his talent by following the models of his own teachers and of his own culture. Quintilian clearly prefers exercises in paraphrasing Latin models over interlingual paraphrase (*Institutio oratoria* 10.5.5–8); and Cicero's paradigm for the ideal of evolution through imitation, arising from the question "Quid enim causae censetis esse, cur aetates extulerint singulae singula propre genera dicendi?" ("Why now is it, do you suppose, that nearly every age has produced its own distinctive style of oratory?"), is the emergence of Isocrates' style from the progress of rhetoric among antecedent Greek generations (*De oratore* 2.22.92–6).[59]

In the intracultural context, imitation is figured in terms of an organic growth from one generation to the next, so that the *genus dicendi* of one age finds new forms in successive ages.[60] Such transmission can be represented in terms of direct pedagogical influence, as a form of agricultural nurturing, as in *De oratore* 2.21.88:

nam sicut facilius, in vitibus, revocantur ea, quae sese nimium profuderunt, quam, si nihil valet materies, nova sarmenta cultura excitantur: ita volo esse in adolescente, unde aliquid amputem; non enim potest in eo sucus esse diuturnus, quod nimis celeriter est maturitatem assecutum.

[. . . for, as with vines it is easier to cut back the branches which have shot out too riotously than to produce new growths by cultivation from a feeble stock, even so in a young man I want something to prune, because the sap can never live long in anything which has ripened too early.]

Just as commonly, however, such generational growth is attributed to the zeal of students to emulate their immediate predecessors while also surpassing them, so that such growth is the product of direct experience of greatness within a single epoch:

quem nunc consummari potissimum oporteat, cum tanto plura exempla bene dicendi supersint quam illis, qui adhuc summi sunt, contigerunt. Nam erit haec quoque laus eorum, ut priores superasse, posteros docuisse dicantur. (*Institutio oratoria* 10.2.28)

[. . . and it is now above all times that such perfection should be attained when there are before us so many more models of oratorical excellence than were available for those who have thus far achieved the highest success. For this glory also shall be theirs, that men shall say of them that while they surpassed their predecessors, they also taught those who came after.][61]

Imitation can also take the form of reworking one's ancient predecessors, as in Cicero's advice to Brutus to "modernize" the elder Cato (*Brutus* 27.68), so that eloquence is revitalized from one epoch to the next.

In all of these intracultural contexts, imitation is figured as a patriarchal pattern of transmission through kinship and legacy, through proximity or contiguity, rather than through difference. As Thomas Greene has suggested, the relationship between model and copy may be represented as "metonymic" or "syntagmatic," in the same sense in which the linguistic function of metonymy signifies a combination of related elements.[62] The differences that intervene between model and copy are the products of inventional force, without which imitation is a barren act, for "nihil autem crescit sola imitatione" ("indeed nothing grows from imitation alone," *Institutio oratoria* 10.2.9). The relationship between model and copy, like the relationship of lineage, is predicated on the act of invention: the model, or ancestor, discovers and posits the ground for future invention. Such an evolutionary pattern is enabled or sustained by the very interpretive community which it creates. Hence, to justify the imitative enterprise, the copy produces, not conspicuous likeness of the original, but rather what is understood and revalued in the original. Dionysius of Halicarnassus had defined imitation (*mimesis*) as an "activity receiving the impression of a model by inspection of it."[63] This idea of receiving an "impression" or impress is expressed figuratively in Roman theory as the quality of paternal–filial resemblance, so that likeness, or "impress," is that which is perceived or understood to inhere in both original and new, a paternal legacy of quality rather than of mere shape or form. Thus Seneca remarks:

Hoc faciat animus noster: omnia, quibus est adiutus, abscondat, ipsum tantum ostendat, quod effecit. Etiam si cuius in te comparebit similitudo, quem admiratio tibi altius fixerit, similem esse te volo quomodo filium, non quomodo imaginem; imago res mortua est . . . Puto aliquando ne intellegi quidem posse, si imago vera sit; haec enim omnibus, quae ex quo velut exemplari traxit, formam suam inpressit, ut in unitatem illa conpetant. (*Epistula* 84.8–9)

[This is what our mind should do: it should hide away all the materials by which it has been aided, and bring to light only what it has made of them. Even if there shall appear in you a likeness to him who, by reasons of your admiration, has left a deep impress upon you, I would have you resemble him as a child resembles his father, and not as a picture resembles its original; for a picture is a lifeless thing . . . I think that sometimes it is impossible for it to be seen who is being imitated, if the copy is a true one; for a true copy stamps its own form upon all the features which it has drawn from what we may call the original, in such a way that they are combined into a unity.]

Thus in the act of inspecting a model and receiving its impress, the imitator in turn stamps or impresses his own features upon the model.[64] This hermeneutical movement, from exegesis (inspection) to appropriation (the copy imposing its impress upon the model), ensures lineal continuity and passes onto successive generations the grounds for interpretive consensus. The need for conspicuous resemblance between model and copy is obviated by the larger framework of interpretive consanguinity: imitations are joined by metonymy to their antecedents.

Interlingual, intercultural imitation can also take such metonymic form; but here the ideal of generational transmission is complicated by the impulse to rival not only the model, but the very literary culture that the model represents. Dionysius of Halicarnassus had defined emulation (*zelos*) as an "activity of the soul impelled towards admiration of what seems to be fine";[65] and *zelos*, the desire to vie with the object of admiration, is recognized throughout Roman theory of imitation as a factor that ensures excellence and cultural evolution through new achievement:

Namque et consummati iam patroni veteribus aemulantur et eos iuvenum ad optima tendentium imitatur ac sequitur industria. (*Institutio oratoria* 10.1.122)[66]

[Indeed, the consummate advocates of the present day are serious rivals of the ancients, while enthusiastic effort and lofty ideals lead many a young student to tread in their footsteps and imitate their excellence.]

In the context of intralingual imitation, such rivalry exercises itself within the larger framework of consanguinity and hence of continuity. Interlingual imitation, on the other hand, may yearn for continuity, but it must also recognize cultural disjunction, for the Romans are less the inheritors than the mediators of the Greek past. Even the Roman proponents of Atticism in the first century B.C must argue in terms of cultural transposition rather than of unmediated transmission. Theories of rhetorical (or literary) imitation comprehend both intra- and interlingual forms: indeed, Quintilian's list of literary, historical, and rhetorical models is distributed almost equally between Greek and Latin authors (10.1.46–131). But interlingual imitation can hardly be theorized without reference to conquest as a component of contestation, or aggressive supremacy as a factor in the challenge to Greek hegemony. Of course, this is not a fast rule: the perspective on Greek culture and its Latin beneficiaries changes somewhat from the late Republic and early Augustan age to the Imperial age, with the sense of aggressive confrontation becoming more pronounced in the latter period.[67] Seneca the Elder (A.D. 37) writes of Roman eloquence in the time of Cicero rivaling or surpassing "insolent Greece";[68] but even in an earlier period, during the Augustan age, Horace equates literary with military supremacy over Greece in a well-known passage of the *Ars poetica*:

Nil intemptatum nostri liquere poetae,
nec minimum meruere decus vestigia Graeca
ausi deserere et celebrare domestica facta,
vel qui praetextas vel qui docuere togatas.
nec virtute foret clarisve potentius armis
quam lingua Latium, si non offenderet unum
quemque poetarum limae labor et mora. (lines 285–91)

[Our own poets have left no style untried, nor has least honor been earned when they have dared to leave the footsteps of the Greeks and sing of deeds at home, whether they have put native tragedies or native comedies upon the stage. Nor would Latium be more supreme in valour and glory of arms than in letters, were it not that her poets, one and all, cannot brook the toil and tedium of the file.][69]

It is in this framework of cultural rivalry that we should also place the famous passage on imitation from the *Ars poetica*:[70]

> Aut famam sequere aut sibi convenientia finge . . .
> Difficile est proprie communia dicere; tuque
> rectius Iliacum carmen deducis in actus,
> quam si proferres ignota indictaque primus.
> publica materies privati iuris erit, si
> non circa vilem patulumque moraberis orbem
> nec verbo verbum curabis reddere fidus
> interpres, nec desilies imitator in artum
> unde pedem proferre pudor vetet aut operis lex.
>
> (*Ars poetica* 119 and 128–35)

[Either follow traditional subjects or invent things that are self-consistent . . . It is difficult to treat common matter in a way that is particular to you; and you would do better to turn a song of Troy into dramatic acts than to bring forth for the first time something unknown and unsung. Public material will be private property if you do not linger over the common and open way, and if you do not try to render word for word like a faithful translator, and if, as an imitator, you do not throw yourself into narrow straights from which shame or poetic law will not let you escape.][71]

Horace's understanding of poetic composition as a rhetorical program proceeding from invention of material to style and arrangement (*inventio*, *elocutio*, and *dispositio*) informs the theory of agonistic imitation set forth here.[72] These lines of the *Ars poetica* constitute an imperative to appropriate that which is *publica materies* through the reinventive faculties of *dispositio* and *elocutio*. Here translation is merely conservation (the aim of the *fidus interpres*), a debased form of imitation, perhaps recalling grammatical exercises in close paraphrase (cf. *Institutio oratoria* 1.9.2, "mox mutatis verbis interpretari"). As C. O. Brink observes, Horace is concerned "with the effect on the poet's subject (i.e. his invention of material) if the new work remains tied to the wording of an older."[73] Horace proposes a theory of rhetorical imitation where the force of invention intervenes between model and copy, just as Quintilian remarks that "nothing grows from imitation alone."

For Horace, as for other Roman theorists, the impulse to displace Greek literary culture is felt as strongly as the impulse to mediate and preserve its values. Whereas the same rules may apply to interlingual as to intralingual imitation so that the external picture of metonymic relationships remains much the same for either context, interlingual imitation carries with it the knowledge of cultural disjunction rather than the security of patrimony, as the relationship is not that of kinship, but of difference. Greek texts can be transposed, Romanized, even naturalized, but in effect they must be also displaced. There are few ready formulas in Roman theory of imitation for this paradox of metonymic intent and disjunctive reality. But it is perhaps this very paradox and the anxiety that it produced that accounts for the power of the greatest Roman achievements in intercultural imitation.

The issue of disjunction does, however, find expression in Roman theorizing about translation. Although translation is recognized as a version of imitative practice, it is never figured in the metonymic terms of both intralingual and interlingual imitation. Theoretical discussions of translation do not even propose an ideal of kinship or lineal continuity. The act itself of translation (as apart from the beneficial effects of such exercise upon future Roman eloquence) does not participate in the evolutionary scheme of imitation (especially intralingual imitation), for it is an act of transference rather than of transmission. Translation offered a perfect platform for contesting the pre-eminence of Greek culture, as its theoretical terms derived from the model of disjunction and difference from the Greeks.

Unlike other forms of rhetorical (and sometimes literary) imitation, translation in Roman theory is figured as a pattern of transference, substitution, and ultimately displacement of the source. Thomas Greene describes this pattern of transference from Greek to Roman culture as "metaphoric" or "paradigmatic," in the sense in which the linguistic function of metaphor signifies a substitution of one element by a similar term.[74] To understand interlingual translation as essentially substitutive in its aim also clarifies how Roman theory conceives translation as a rhetorical activity: the object of translation is difference with the source, and the act of translating is comparable to the act of inventing one's own argument out of available topics. The aim of translation is to reinvent the source, so that, as in rhetorical theory, attention is focused on the active production of a new text endowed with its own affective powers and suited to the particular historical circumstances of its reception. Thus in translation, the force of rhetorical invention should produce difference with the source. As a rhetorical act, literary translation seeks to erase the cultural gap from which it emerges by contesting and displacing the source and substituting itself: it forges no synthetic links with its source. Thus in terms of an interior anatomy, translation can be distinguished from imitation.

In terms of exterior form, the difference between translation and imitation is more accessible, but no less complicated. The ideal of imitation, as we have seen, is that of organic recreation from an earlier text, in the sense of formal or substantive adaptation. Translation, on the other hand, is recognized as necessarily replicative, as it aims to match form and substance in a different language. But also essential to the replicative function of rhetorical translation is the aim of differentiation from the original. This aim has two causes: first, translation arises from an acknowledgment of difference; and second, the Roman reverence for Greek culture was simply a corollary of the desire to displace that culture, and eliminate its hegemonic hold, through contestation and hence difference. The paradox of difference through replication is registered clearly in Roman rhetorical theories of translation. Thus while both translation and imitation aim to reinvent the source, the similarity between these two acts is only superficial. The imitative aim of "making different," of re-creation, rests on an ideal of familial continuity with a real or (in the case of Greek sources) naturalized past; the aim of inventive difference in the replicative project of translation, however, emerges from a disturbing political agenda in which forcibly substituting Rome for Greece is a condition of acknowledging the foundational status of Greek eloquence for *Latinitas*. The replicative principles of translation are not founded on a dream of patriarchal continuity or evolutionary progress, but on a historical agenda of conquest and supremacy through submission, or in Horace's famous words, "Graecia capta ferum victorem cepit et artis / intulit agresti Latio" (captive Greece captured the savage victor and brought the arts into rustic Latium).[75]

How is this sense of difference to be achieved in a task which defines at least its material boundaries in terms of sameness, of matching text for text, albeit across a linguistic gap? In histories of Western translation theory, the primary contribution of the Romans is generally regarded to be the inaugural formulation of the terms of the debate about literal as opposed to loose translation, that is, about the translator's responsibility to the source.[76] The "literal–loose" polarity is certainly present as an issue in Roman theory, but this alone does not explain the complexity of Roman assumptions, and on its own it is nothing more than a simple commonplace, even for the Romans who inaugurated it. It is what lies behind this commonplace that merits attention here. The idea of difference in Roman translation is theorized in terms that bear upon the intersection of grammar and rhetoric, and specifically of *enarratio* and *inventio*.

The orbit of Roman interests in translation is elegantly encompassed in a letter of Pliny the Younger in which he recommends translation as *exercitatio*, practice in composition that develops literary technique:

> Quaeris quemadmodum in secessu, quo iam diu frueris, putem te studere oportere. Utile in primis, et multi praecipiunt, vel ex Graeco in Latinum vel ex Latino vertere in Graecum. Quo genere exercitationis proprietas splendorque verborum, copia figurarum, vis explicandi, praeterea imitatione optimorum similia inveniendi facultas paratur; simul quae legentem fefellissent, transferentem fugere non possunt. Intellegentia ex hoc et iudicium adquiritur. (*Epistulae* 7.9.1–3)
>
> [You ask me what course of study I think you should follow during your present prolonged holiday. The most useful thing, which is always being suggested, is to translate Greek into Latin and Latin into Greek. This kind of exercise develops in one a precision and richness of vocabulary, a wide range of metaphor and power of exposition, and moreover, imitation of the best models leads to a like aptitude for original composition. At the same time, any point which might have been overlooked by a reader cannot escape the eye of a translator. All this cultivates perception and critical sense.][77]

Five elements in this passage form the grammatical–rhetorical nexus for translation. For clarity I will treat them slightly out of the order which Pliny gives. The passage moves basically from *exercitatio* to *enarratio*. Translation develops first a lexical command, "proprietas splendorque verborum," which falls within the grammatical domain of *scientia recte loquendi*; and second, we find the grammatical function of *enarratio* in the observation about close reading, "quae legentem fefellissent, transferentem fugere non possunt." Third, the development of "copia figurarum" and "vis explicandi" hovers on the boundary between knowledge (or *scientia*) of the rules of speech (the figures, rules for exposition) and active experience (*peritia*) in intelligent interpretation and presentation of the material. Fourth, the comment "inveniendi facultas paratur," introducing the concept *invenire*, brings us into the rhetorical center of the activity of translation, as we have now, in abbreviated form, the theory of enabling the future text, that is, the grounds of invention. Finally, "intellegentia" and "iudicium" ("perception" and "critical sense") introduce a hermeneutical dimension as complementary to the exegetical and heuristic functions of translation. This linear exposition of Pliny's terms is deceptive, for it might suggest that there is a discernible progress or crossing of boundaries from grammatical exercise to active rhetorical discovery. On the contrary, Pliny's account suggests a simultaneity of these various operations (for instance, in the connectives "praeterea" and "simul"), so that the faculties of grammar and rhetoric seem to merge in the act of translation. Thus grammatical *exercitatio* in style, usage, and exposition becomes a rhetorical discovery of one's power over language. Even as as one scrutinizes the given text one is pointed towards the future text.

Another way to formulate the terms of this intersection is that in Pliny we see a merging of commentary and imitation. Commentary, or *enarratio*, falls within the domain of grammar, and as such represents a passive response whose aim, as in the terms of natural sciences, is reception of a fixed quantity of information. Imitation, on the other hand, is a function of the active rhetorical faculty, and is explicitly perceived in heuristic terms. Thus Pliny's association of *imitatio* with "inveniendi facultas" recalls Quintilian's insistence that it is the force of invention that intervenes to differentiate model from copy (*Institutio oratoria* 10.2.9). We should also recall how Quintilian's grammatical program of translation threatens to take on rhetorical dimensions because it is inherently heuristic, becauses it is so much grounded in the principles of imitation theory. What is implicit in Quintilian's program, as in Pliny's account, is that the act of commentary itself forms the ground for inventional departures from the original text. But it is also the inventional faculty of rhetoric that allows rhetoric to be so closely associated with the hermeneutical model of practical wisdom, for both are occupied with concrete, but changing (hence indeterminate) realities. Rhetoric is the faculty that attempts "to make the world of language intelligible."[78] For the Sophist Gorgias as for Cicero and Quintilian, rhetoric embodies all other systems that engage the particular and ever-changing circumstances of human affairs – e.g., ethics and politics – because rhetoric is the mastery of the equally changeable conditions of persuasion that lead to ethical or social action.[79] It is thus appropriate that the act of commentary, whether in imitation or in translation, should be "rhetoricized" as an inventional act, and that rhetoric itself should provide a hermeneutical directive for translation.

Throughout Cicero's scattered remarks on translation, the question of active differentiation from the original text is theorized in the much more aggressive terms of contestation and displacement. The most famous formulation, which has achieved dubious status as the foremost commonplace in translation theory, comes from the late treatise *De optimo genere oratorum*. In order to mediate to Roman students the nature of Attic oratory, Cicero has translated the most famous speeches of Demosthenes and Aeschines:

nec converti ut interpres, sed ut orator, sententiis isdem et earum formis tamquam figuris, verbis ad nostram consuetudinem aptis. In quibus non verbum pro verbo necesse habui reddere, sed genus omne verborum vimque servavi. Non enim ea me adnumerare lectori putavi oportere, sed tamquam appendere. Hic labor meus hoc assequetur, ut nostri homines quid ab illis exigant, qui se Atticos volunt, et ad quam eos quasi formulam dicendi revocent intellegant. (*De optimo genere oratorum* 5.14–15)

[And I did not translate them as an interpreter, but as an orator, keeping the same ideas and the forms, or as one might say, the "figures" of thought, but in language which conforms to our usage. And in so doing, I did not hold it necessary to render word for word, but I preserved the general style and force of the language. For I did not think I ought to count them out to the reader like coins, but to pay them by weight, as it were. The result of my labor will be that our Romans will know what to demand from those who claim to be Atticists and to what rule of speech, as it were, they are to be held.][80]

This passage has come to be celebrated for the formula "non verbum pro verbo," often associated with Horace's similar injunction "nec verbo verbum curabis reddere fidus interpres." But its real force and interest derives, I believe, from the concluding sentence, in which Cicero announces the intention of his labor: to provide an "accurate" *Roman* model, using the full resources of *Latinitas*, of the principles of Attic Greek oratory. The intention in part is to mediate Attic principles by matching them with their Latin correspondents. But there is a greater sense that Cicero has arrogated for his texts a seminal status for future students, so that his translations of the Greek orators will replace and hence displace the Greek speeches as reference points for Atticist style in Latin oratory. In this way, "nostri homines" will know precisely what constitutes Atticism and will be able to judge these Roman orators who claim to be Atticists ("qui se Atticos volunt"). Thus at the end of the *De optimo* Cicero offers his translation as a rule ("regula") by which future Latin orators will measure their own efforts in the Atticist style (7.23).

In light of this substitutive move we can judge the more familiar themes of this and related passages in Cicero's writings. The injunction to translate "non verbum pro verbo," but rather preserving the force and figures of the language and the general *sententiae*, represents a principle of conservation directed, not to service of the source text, but to the benefit of the target language. Moreover, this injunction against literalism is not framed in a context that favors meaning above language or that directs attention to the preservation of the signified, despite the way that this precept was later interpreted within the patristic tradition of translation theory.[81] For Cicero, the rhetorical framework of translation would not allow any differentiation between the claims of *verba* and *sententia*: to reconstitute the text verbally and stylistically represents an act of resignification.[82] Form and style are subjected to interpretive force, bent "ad nostram consuetudinem," transplanted and naturalized to generate Latin models of eloquence. All elements of the original text – *sententiae*, *formae*, *figurae* – are reined in by "verbis ad nostram consuetudinem aptis"; and the metaphor of monetary exchange, "adnumerare" / "appendere," suggests that the source text, once transferred into the system of Latin currency, takes on a new value of its own. Once converted into Latin currency, the text takes on a kind of primary status, so that the translation can virtually supplant the original as a rhetorical model. The discovery of one's own literary language through translation carries within it inventional implications.

Similar expressions of the inventional and contestative nature of translation are to be found in somewhat less celebrated remarks of Cicero, notably in *De oratore* 1.34.155 and *Tusculan Disputations* 2.11.26. The example from *Tusculan Disputations* suggests in more aggressive terms how Latin may lay claim to primacy: ". . . verti etiam multa de Graecis, ne quo ornamento in hoc genere disputationis careret Latina oratio" (". . . I have often translated from the Greek poets as well, that Latin eloquence might not lack any embellishment in this kind of discussion").[83] In *De oratore* 1.34.155, Cicero has Crassus advocate translation as an exercise in coinage ("sed etiam exprimerem quaedam verba imitando, quae nova nostris essent"). Quintilian cites this passage from *De oratore* in his long discussion of imitation in *Institutio oratoria* 10, adding that the exercise of translation is justified by the vast difference between the Greek and Roman idioms, so that the great number and variety of figures must be rediscovered ("excogitandi," thought out) in Latin (10.5.2–3).

Yet even such ordinary pedagogical rationales are not without paradox. The unavoidably replicative nature of translation finds a variety of rationalizations in Roman theory. As we have seen, translation is figured as an aggressive hermeneutics: it reinvents Greek *eloquentia*, it generates new models, it displaces its Greek sources, and in general is described in the active terms of a rhetorical project. Yet this "active" or rhetorical model of translation necessarily contains in its functioning a form of "passive" receptiveness, that which is associated with grammatical training and thus officially segregated from the rhetorical sphere. The translator aspires to enter the language of the original by acute understanding (cf. Pliny's "intellegentia ex hoc et iudicium adquiritur"); but once it has been opened through this active understanding, the language of the original is expected to inform, to shape the target language. The force of the original language, its "figurae multae et variae," is somehow to infuse or penetrate the translator's native medium. Only thus can translation be justified as enabling linguistic reception and the increase of *Latinitas*, whether figured in terms of verbal coinage, or monetary exchange (conversion), or even as transplanting and naturalization. Thus the translator performs an act of aggressive interpretation so as to lay open his language and usage to receive a formative influence. We might recall here the paradox in imitation theory whereby the copy both stamps its impress upon the model and receives that model's impress upon its own features. We might also recall how Quintilian allows grammar the subsidiary or partial hermeneutical function of inspiring the student with the loftiness and power of epic poetry, so that such preparatory readings will infuse the mind with desire for the more mature understanding that is promised by rhetoric. In a sense, translation asks for a similar moment of appreciative desire and receptiveness.

The tension between the explicit agenda of aggression and the ulterior necessity of pliancy to formative influences is most acutely apparent in Cicero's *De finibus*. Throughout this treatise Cicero defends the value of Latin translations of Greek philosophical texts on the grounds that Latin can rival Greek for linguistic suppleness and lexical richness (e.g., 1.3.10). Yet the ulterior premise of such a defense is that Latin should be recognized as adequate to the task of serving Greek philosophical texts, so that more Romans should be acquainted with the primary philosophical tradition of Greece (1.2.4–6; 1.3.8; 1.4.10). In other words, then, the theorizing of translation as an aggressive contestation and displacement of the source is predicated on a contrary impulse to yield to and receive a formative influence; that influence can then be appropriated and naturalized in Roman terms. Thus this rhetorical circle of translation moves from hermeneutical aggression to a process of absorption, best figured in grammatical terms, and finally to a heuristic appropriation or reinvention of the informing influence.[84]

The Roman interest in translation establishes a certain theoretical nexus which reappears, with some modifications, in the Middle Ages. The principal element here is the link between grammar and rhetoric, which manifests itself in the intersection of *enarratio* and *inventio*, exegetical and heuristic functions. Through this merging of grammar and rhetoric, invention itself takes on the character of a hermeneutical movement, as it is through the principles of commentary that the translation reinvents its source and appropriates it for *Latinitas*. The merging of exegetical and rhetorical functions will provide, in the vernacular literary cultures of the Middle Ages, the primary theoretical framework for translation as a hermeneutical practice. The Romans also inaugurate a distinction between imitation and translation, through a powerful antithesis between intralingual evolution along metonymic lines and interlingual displacement or metaphoric substitution. This differentiation between intralingual imitation and interlingual translation will not have the same force in the Middle Ages that it does for the Romans, as it will not carry quite the same political agenda of cultural disjunction and aggressive contestation figured in the historical terms of military supremacy. But the essential paradox of the enterprise of translation as replication through difference, through displacement, substitution, and cultural or canonical appropriation, will gain new importance in the Middle Ages. The medieval practice of translation as a form of appropriation and substitution will be conditioned, as in Roman contexts, by rhetorical theories of invention; but these inventional theories will have been redefined according to medieval notions of textuality.

2

From antiquity to the Middle Ages I: the place of translation and the value of hermeneutics

In Roman contexts, as we have seen, it is rhetoric that supplies a hermeneutical model for translation. Rhetoric here is a coherent praxis in which eloquence conditions meaning and in which reason is internal to both thought and discourse.[1] Thus translation, as a problematic of discourse, is necessarily bound up with the deepest questions of interpretation, signification, and reception. This rhetorical model of translation descended to the vernacular Middle Ages, but only by very indirect routes. The theoretical channels that mediate Roman ideas of translation to later periods so refigure or suppress the underlying rhetorical principles that the framework for translation which emerges in later medieval vernacular contexts is less a recovery of Roman ideas than a new formulation along similar lines. The forms of medieval vernacular translation that we will consider here are still grounded in models of hermeneutics and rhetoric: but the hermeneutical model re-emerges in medieval textual practices associated with grammatical studies; and the rhetorical directive is newly established through medieval redefinitions of the *modus inveniendi*. In this chapter and the next I will address the theoretical and practical conditions out of which new hermeneutical formulations arose in the Middle Ages. This present chapter has two purposes: to reconsider the transmission of Roman translation theory to the medieval West, and to sketch out a historical relationship between rhetoric and hermeneutics in the earlier Middle Ages. As we will see, it is through the alliance of these two academic discourses that medieval vernacular translation defines its own practice.

In order to understand the circumstances that give rise to the vast project of vernacular literary translation, we must trace the fortunes of the Roman model of translation, its revaluation in the hands of late classical and early Christian theorists. There are two routes by which Roman principles are transmitted: the rhetorical compendia of late antiquity and patristic writings on translation. The latter of these routes, the patristic transmission, is usually the better known, as it figures significantly in histories of translation theory in the West. But it does not supply an unproblematic continuity between Roman and later traditions, as such histories have tended to suggest.[2] Its terms are specific to certain kinds of translation practice in which a rhetorical directive plays only a restricted role; and here Jerome's reception of Cicero and Horace does provide an important legacy. But it is to the lesser known of these two routes of transmission, the late antique rhetorical manuals, that a more generalized force might be attributed, if only because these manuals contribute so importantly to a thorough reorganization of rhetorical systems for the early Middle Ages and onwards. In these manuals the competence of rhetoric is narrowed to what seems often a purely academic or propaedeutic enterprise. Here the scope of translation is similarly constricted, its role diminished to that of service to *elocutio*.

THE PLACE OF TRANSLATION IN THE RHETORICS OF LATE ANTIQUITY

The period from the first to the fourth century A.D. produced few Latin works on rhetoric, and it is generally recognized that nothing in this period offered a significant advance upon the comprehensive rhetorical system of Quintilian. Moreover, the continuing bilingualism of the Empire, at least through the third century, permitted Hellenistic technical manuals to maintain a certain currency in the Latin West, so that these, rather than parallel Latin *technai*, could supplement the important theoretical texts of Cicero and Quintilian.[3] But there was, nevertheless, a growing linguistic rupture between East and West, and the extent of this break by the third century is evidenced by the emergence of bilingual school manuals, the *Hermeneumata pseudodositheana*.

The revival in the fourth century of Latin rhetorical *technai* and theoretical accounts points in two ways to the eclipse of the Greek language in the West.[4] First, these rhetorical surveys of the fourth and fifth centuries seem to suggest, by their sudden profusion, that such Latin works were needed to replace the technical Greek manuals which students in the West could no longer read.[5] Second, the considerable dependence of these rhetorics on the *De inventione* suggests that this youthful and incomplete work of Cicero also achieved new currency in the fourth century as a substitute for the Greek manuals which were no longer linguistically accessible to students in the Latin West.[6] For this reason as well, the commentaries of Victorinus and Grillius on the *De inventione* became widely influential in mediating classical doctrine; Victorinus' commentary, in fact, remained a primary reference on Cicero through the twelfth century.

The nature of these rhetorical manuals and commentaries indicates the new circumstances of rhetorical theory and teaching in late antiquity. The most commonly noted feature of these rhetorics is the stress that they lay upon *inventio*, while *elocutio* commands somewhat less attention, and the remaining three parts of rhetoric (*dispositio*, *memoria*, *pronunciatio*) are virtually suppressed.[7] This may be explained in part by the reliance of these rhetorics on the *De inventione* whose disproportionate devotion to invention is simply a factor of its unfinished state. But the structural and substantive influence of the *De inventione* on these later texts is itself symptomatic of a deeper change in the situation of rhetoric in late antiquity. The incomplete picture of rhetoric that the *De inventione* draws, the prominence of inventional matters and the subordination or neglect of the other divisions of rhetoric which serve to activate invention and bring rhetoric into the domain of public concerns, was in a certain way congenial to the interests of late antiquity. The structure of civic life that had supported the ideal of oratory in Republican and early Imperial Rome had essentially disappeared by the fourth century A.D. Procedures in the law courts now debarred the comprehensive opening and closing addresses which had so much shaped earlier Roman theories of public delivery. Thus while judicial rhetoric, as a study of legal procedure, that is, identifying the correct issues (*status*) of a case and the argumentative topics to be used, remained important, training in judicial oratory, that is, presentation, lost its place in the rhetorical curriculum. While in the Greek East epideictic rhetoric actually dominated in the oratory of the Second Sophistic, in the Latin West, epideictic and deliberative rhetoric seem to have been subordinated to forensic rhetoric, as the primacy of topical theory in these manuals and commentaries suggests. In Victorinus' commentary especially we can see the transformation of rhetoric into a textbook application of the rules of the system: the disputational and philosophical aspects of rhetoric take on increasing importance as the discipline loses its practical relevance to public and civic structures.[8] Thus the importance of the *De inventione* for these late rhetorics is not only a factor in, but also a symptom of, a general reorienting of rhetorical attitudes.

The primacy of inventional theory without commensurate attention to composition and presentation produces, in these manuals, a rarefied sense of rhetoric and a loss of the force of application and praxis. This is particularly notable in the *artes* of Julius Victor and Fortunatianus and in the commentary of Victorinus, and the influence of this abstraction or theorization of rhetoric carries over to early medieval *artes*, especially those of Boethius, Martianus Capella, Cassiodorus, Isidore of Seville, and Alcuin.[9] Perhaps because of the influence of the schematic *Rhetorica ad Herennium*, the question of *elocutio*, which still commands some attention, is often represented among the *rhetores latini minores* as a theory of figures; it may have retained a theoretical relevance because of the mannerism of contemporary prose styles.[10] There is a tendency among these fourth-century texts to turn in on themselves, to reify invention as a system without discernible relevance to external, public affairs. The presentation of topics of argumentation and of the issues of the case becomes a virtual taxonomy, an end in itself, an autonomous exercise in disputation and distinction.[11] In Victorinus' commentary, this sense of a self-referential rhetorical system manifests itself in the rejection of Cicero's distinction between the *officium oratoris* and the *finis oratoris* (*De inventione* 1.5.6): Victorinus would conflate the two as the *finis officii*, seeing the end or result of eloquence as internal to its very tasks (*officia*), as if the result (persuasion) were internal to the intention or duty itself.[12]

This reification of rhetoric, its divorce from external, circumstantial referents, brings rhetoric much closer to Quintilian's model of theoretical knowledge, such as the natural sciences or the system of grammar. The system of topical invention remains coherent, but its application to material issues become increasingly obscure. Rhetoric would thus seem to have lost its distinction as a hermeneutical model based upon *phronesis* and praxis. Invention, separated from the other components of eloquence, effectively separates itself from the concerns of linguistic communication, and thus from the very terms of signification as Roman rhetoric would define it. While rhetoric strengthens its affiliation with dialectic, its practical engagement with discourse, and hence with the ethics of human performances, has seemingly weakened, and it verges upon becoming a textbook art. The divorce between invention and the rhetorical performance signals in effect a divorce between meaning and language, as rhetoric ceases to grapple with discourse as totality, from discovery to mediation to determination of meaning. Cut off from application to such issues, rhetoric's orientation seems to shift almost to that of a fixed science such as mathematics or even grammar, from which it had so purposefully distinguished itself in the past.[13]

One of the more influential of these fourth-century compendia, the *Artes rhetoricae libri III* of Fortunatianus, contains a reference to translation (*conversio*) in the section on *elocutio* in book 3. As in other contemporary manuals, the treatment of *elocutio* here is schematic, brief, and substantively disconnected from the treatment of inventional doctrine which occupies books 1 and 2. Book 3 constitutes only about one-fifth of the whole treatise; but it covers four-fifths of the parts of rhetoric: *dispositio*, *elocutio*, *memoria*, and *pronunciatio*. *Elocutio* is defined here, in the opening of the section devoted to it, as consisting in "quantitate verborum et structurae qualitate," verbal amplitude and stylistic decorum. Most of the exposition is given over to *copia verborum* and the means of achieving it. "Copia quo modo gignitur," asks the *discipulus*; the answer, "legendo, discendo, novando, exercando," in reading, learning by observation, in coinage, and in exercise.[14] Following Quintilian and Cicero, Fortunatianus presents translation as one method of coinage and as one aspect of exercise, along with intralingual imitation (paraphrase):

> Verba quibus modis novantur? primo Graeca transferimus, ut nova ex his Latina confingamus . . . Quae igitur summa est exercitationis, id est quot partibus constat? quattuor. Quibus? ut Graeca in Latinum convertas, ut difficilia scribas, ut μετάφρασιν facias, ut de tempore adsidue dicas.[15]

> [In what ways are words coined? First we carry over Greek words, so that from them we can invent new Latin words . . . What is the chief point of exercise, that is, what does it consist of? Four things. What are they? That you translate Greek into Latin, write challenging compositions, practice paraphrasing {from verse into prose and prose into verse}, and diligently practice speaking *ex tempore*.]

Under coinage, the transferring of *lexica* from Greek to Latin probably refers less to translation (although it involves a form of this) than to direct importation of Greek words. Translation is properly one of the functions of elocutionary *exercitatio*.

Elocutio here has been equated essentially with *copia verborum*, and translation, as a form of *exercitatio*, provides one means of achieving this quantitative aim. Roman theoretical concerns, the integration of all the five parts of rhetoric under the double aegis of wisdom and ethics, seem to have been eclipsed here by a prioritizing of the mechanics of eloquence. *Copia verborum*, which for Quintilian is one of the aspects of eloquence, has effectively become here the aim of eloquence: the means has become the end. Indeed, Quintilian's discussion of the relationship between *exercitatio* and *eloquentia* in *Institutio oratoria* 10 on imitation (which corresponds to the above discussion in Fortunatianus) begins with a formulation about the resources of eloquence: "eae constant copia rerum ac verborum" (10.1.5). Similarly Cicero's *De oratore* enlarges on the relationship between eloquence and philosophy, or simply *verba* and *sententia* (3.6.24; 3.14.56). But here in Fortunatianus we find only a truncated version of this classical formula: *copia rerum* has disappeared, and we are left only with *copia verborum* as the aim of *elocutio*, *exercitatio*, and hence of translation.

In this context, in which eloquence has been divorced from *res* or *sententia*, that is, from the question of meaning, translation necessarily loses its heuristic or inventional capacity. It has become, rather, a mechanism of style, which in turn has lost its productive application to the determination of meaning in language. *Elocutio* has virtually assumed the character of its debased stereotype, merely external ornamentation. Along these lines we also see that Fortunatianus defines *exercitatio* as an activity which does not generate new features of style but which rather maintains the knowledge already achieved ("quod non quidem generat verba, sed alit ac tuetur").[16] Here *elocutio*, along with its component, translation, has narrowed its competence to that which, for Quintilian, would befit the program of grammar. Any productive, hermeneutical application seems to be reserved here for invention, which as we have seen, occupies its own atomized sphere. This dissociation between invention and the other parts of rhetoric, which we have noted as typical of late antiquity, seems to have led to a kind of grammaticization of *elocutio*, along with *dispositio*, *memoria*, and *pronunciatio*. As invention becomes an increasingly rarefied and autotelic study, unlikely to actualize itself in civic disputation, so the other parts of eloquence have atrophied in terms of their original rhetorical purpose and have taken on very much the pedagogical function of *progymnasmata*, the preliminary exercises in declamation used in rhetorical study. *Elocutio* could readily avail itself to such service; it could easily be schematized to supplement the *progymnasmata* for teaching *Latinitas* in the increasingly vernacular culture of the late Empire and early Middle Ages. Invention has gravitated into the orbit of dialectic (anticipating Ramistic developments) and as a textbook art of disputation has ceased to exercise any influence over the other parts of rhetoric. These remaining parts, especially *elocutio*, gravitate into the orbit of grammar. As a part of the program of *elocutio*, translation would return to its restricted grammatical function, stripped of its hermeneutical and inventional powers.

The *Artes rhetoricae* of Fortunatianus is the only rhetorical manual from late antiquity to mention translation at all. The reason for the lack of attention to translation in this late context probably lies in the fact that knowledge of Greek was itself disappearing in the West, and the conservation of *Latinitas* against vernacular encroachments became the primary instructional purpose. Without the knowledge of Greek, and thus without the sense of Greek cultural hegemony, the entire purpose of vertical translation, as the Romans understood it (and as Fortunatianus also seems to understand it) would be lost. Fortunatianus' manual exerts a considerable influence on later rhetorical theory. Cassiodorus refers directly to it as one of the works transcribed for the use of his monks at Vivarium, and bases much of his own discussion of invention on it, although in the *Institutiones* he suppresses information about *elocutio*.[17] Martianus Capella similarly relies extensively on Fortunatianus for treatments of invention, memory, and delivery.[18] Through the Carolingian period, the treatise remains an authoritative supplement to the basic texts of Cicero and the Auctor ad Herennium, and like the other fourth-century *technai* as well as the works of Cassiodorus and Martianus Capella, it is used as a propaedeutic to general studies. Its importance for the history of translation theory may lie precisely in its diminution of the terms of translation along with the delimiting of the competence of *elocutio* to that of external ornamentation.

THE PATRISTIC MODEL OF TRANSLATION AND ITS INFLUENCE[19]

There is a strong tradition of translation theory that derives from patristic writings which are roughly contemporary with the rhetorical *technai* of late antiquity. Patristic criticism provides a positive link between classical theory and certain varieties of medieval practice: its assumptions underlie the criteria of learned and religious translation from Boethius and John Scotus Eriugena to Bacon and Aquinas. But despite its classical borrowings, the patristic premise for translation does not really harmonize with the interests of Roman theory; and despite its long-lived authority, the patristic model does not account for much of the actual character of vernacular literary translation in the later Middle Ages. It inherits and bequeaths a rhetorical language about translation while rejecting the assumptions behind that language.

Patristic theory uses some of the classical commonplaces about translation and lends its own authority to these formulations so that they survive in the Christian West. But this terminological continuity between Roman and early Christian theory actually disguises a dramatic difference between the two. The Roman ideal of translation as a rhetorical project locates the problem of signification in linguistic performance itself, in the tropological force of eloquence, in the "turning" of meaning through the signifier. As translation is a rhetorical procedure, its conceptual field is discourse itself, that is, human control of signification, and its explicit object is the valorization of *Latinitas*. Roman translation theory, like rhetoric, grapples with linguistic heterogeneity as its principal concern, and it establishes the problem of meaning as something within rather than beyond discourse.[20] This is consistent with the way in which Roman rhetoricians subordinate philosophy to rhetoric. Roman translation serves the target text and target language in a project of displacement and appropriation which foregrounds cultural difference through linguistic difference. Patristic criticism borrows the terminological apparatus of Cicero and Horace, but in order to generate a theory of translation directed almost entirely at meaning and at signification outside the claims of either source or target language. As I will argue here, patristic theory effectively rejects the rhetorical rationale inscribed in the Roman formulas that it uses, and thus rejects the motives of contestation, displacement, and appropriation. As early Christian semiology accords human language a secondary, although necessary, role in relation to the primacy and stability of divine signification, so patristic translation theory is concerned mainly with recuperating a truthful meaning beyond the accidents of human linguistic multiplicity.[21] It addresses particular textual conditions only in so far as these aid or impede access to supra-textual meaning. The problem of difference, of linguistic and literary heterogeneity, is of course a central theme in patristic theory; but whereas Roman theory seeks to erase difference (even as it recognizes it) by foreclosing the originary claims of the source and substituting Latin for Greek, patristic criticism seeks more to resolve difference by pointing towards a communality of source and target in terms of the immanence of meaning. Because the patristic position is articulated largely with reference to translation of the Bible and of theological texts, the question of displacement, so much a motive in Roman theory, is naturally ruled out here as an ideal.

The concerns of the patristic tradition of translation are not those of generating a distinct literary culture. In this respect, then, it can take over the formulas of Roman theory, based on the formula of literal as opposed to loose translation, without accepting the heuristic, rhetorical motives for which those formulas stand. Instead, it can supply a supra-linguistic teleology, so that even contradictory readings can be resolved through an inspired exegesis.[22] This is Augustine's epistemological premise in considering the discrepancies between Hebrew Scripture and the Greek Septuagint, where both the Hebrew text and the Greek translation can legitimately claim originary authority through inspiration:[23]

Quae autem non praetermissa uel addita, sed aliter dicta sunt, siue alium sensum faciant etiam ipsum non abhorrentem, siue alio modo eundem sensum explicare monstrentur, nisi utrisque codicibus inspectis nequeunt reperiri. Si ergo, ut oportet, nihil aliud intueamur in scripturis illis, nisi quid per homines dixerit Dei Spiritus, quidquid est in Hebraeis codicibus et non est apud interpretes septuaginta, noluit ea per istos, sed per illos prophetas Dei Spiritus dicere. Quidquid uero est apud Septuaginta, in Hebraeis autem codicibus non est, per istos ea maluit quam per illos idem Spiritus dicere, sic ostendens utrosque fuisse prophetas . . . Quidquid porro apud utrosque inuenitur, per utrosque dicere uoluit unus atque idem Spiritus; sed ita ut illi praecederent prophetando, isti sequerentur prophetice illos interpretando; quia sicut in illis uera et concordantia dicentibus unus pacis Spiritus fuit, sic et in istis non secum conferentibus et tamen tamquam ore uno cuncta interpretantibus idem Spiritus unus apparuit.

[However, it is impossible, without examining both the Hebrew and the Greek texts, to discover passages not omitted or added but put in different words, whether they give another meaning, though one not conflicting with the original, or whether they can be shown to express the same meaning, though in a different way. If then we see, as we ought to see, nothing in those Scriptures except the utterances of the Spirit of God through the mouths of men, it follows that anything in the Hebrew text that is not found in that of the seventy translators {of the Septuagint} is something which the Spirit of God decided not to say through the prophets. Conversely, anything in the Septuagint that is not in the Hebrew texts is something which the same Spirit preferred to say through the translators, instead of through the prophets, thus showing that the former and the latter alike were prophets . . . Moreover, anything that is found in both the Hebrew and the Septuagint, is something which the one same Spirit wished to say through both, but in such a way that the former gave the lead by prophesying, while the latter followed with a prophetic translation. For just as the one Spirit of peace was present in the prophets when they spoke the truth with no disagreement, so the same one Spirit was manifestly present in the scholars when without collaboration they still translated the whole in every detail as if with one mouth.][24]

Under such a teleological hermeneutic, even the signified is subordinated to the ultimate referents, sacred history and the economy of salvation.[25] Any progression towards meaning through the diversity of languages must, in fact, constitute a return to original meaning. Hence the role of literal translation in Augustine's system (as well as in that of Jerome) is that of recovering a kind of originary certitude which the human conventions of rhetoric have not vitiated or obscured:

Sed quoniam et quae sit ipsa sententia, quam plures interpretes pro sua quisque facultate atque iudicio conantur eloqui, non apparet, nisi in ea lingua inspiciatur quam interpretantur, et plerumque a sensu auctoris devius aberrat interpres, si non sit doctissimus, aut linguarum illarum ex quibus in latinam scripturam pervenit, petenda cognitio est aut habendae interpretationes eorum qui se verbis nimis obstrinxerunt, non quia sufficiunt, sed ut ex eis libertas vel error dirigatur aliorum, qui non tam verba quam sententias interpretando sequi maluerunt.

[Since the meaning which many interpreters, according to their ability and judgment, seek to convey is not apparent unless we consult the language being translated, and since many translators err from the sense of the original authors unless they are very learned, we must either seek a knowledge of those languages from which Scipture is translated into Latin or we must consult the translations of those who translate word for word, not because they suffice but because by means of them we may test the {laxity} or falsity of those who have sought to translate meanings as well as words.][26]

The emphasis upon transcendent meaning, from which no version, despite its linguistic peculiarities, is exempt, argues for a metonymic picture of translation. Its force in this framework is reconstitutive, to recover a kinship or wholeness of meaning beyond the circumstance of individual languages.[27] This is antithetical to the disjunctive picture of translation drawn by Roman rhetoric. The notion of such continuity, at once transcendent and immanent, that we see in Augustine, is inevitable for questions of Scripture, where translation performs a teleological office of revelation and prophecy. While Jerome contested the conception of the biblical translator as prophet, arguing that even this sacred task was achieved through technical expertise ("hic eruditio et verborum copia, ea quae intelligit, transfert"), he also saw the integrity of Scripture as immune to the accidents and errors of human language which may only obscure (but not change) its meaning.[28] Yet such an assumption about the inviolability of textual meaning defines even Jerome's purpose in his non-scriptural projects of translation from the Greek Church Fathers. It is this principle that actually grounds his theories of translation, although he articulates them in terms drawn from Roman rhetoric.

It is conventional to identify Jerome as a Ciceronian, as his theoretical writings on translation form a tissue of classical quotation and allusion. As Louis Kelly has suggested, this identification with Cicero is appropriate for Jerome's own practice in translating non-scriptural texts.[29] But his theoretical statements belie the rhetorical motives inscribed in the sources whose authority he invokes. In the preface to his translation of Eusebius' *Chronicles*, he founds his arguments upon the theoretical precedents of Cicero and Horace. In Epistle 57 to Pammachius (often known as *De optimo genere interpretandi*), written about twenty years after the translation of Eusebius, he quotes Cicero, *De optimo genere oratorum* 14–15, along with Horace, *Ars poetica* 133–4. He also quotes from and draws on his earlier preface to the translation of Eusebius. In Epistle 57 he marshals the authority of Cicero and Horace to advocate saving and serving the source text, its meaning and force, by accepting the necessity of linguistic difference. He certainly recognizes the claims of eloquence, of *proprietas verborum*, and in his own translations achieves a certain "dynamic equivalence" with the style of his originals.[30] But in these theoretical statements he speaks of meaning and discourse as if they constitute separate functions, the latter not be served at the expense of the former.

Before we turn to the texts of Jerome's arguments, let us recall the historical value of his classical references. The passage from Cicero's *De optimo genere oratorum* argues, not for conserving the source, but for appropriating and displacing the authority of the original so as to invent a model of Atticism within *Latinitas*. For Cicero, to iterate is not to conserve, but to resignify, in the sense of a currency exchange, where to achieve equivalence is also to enforce difference through transposition into a new system. Value is determined through language, as Cicero's metaphor of currency exchange suggests. It is precisely this rhetorical valuation of words that Augustine rejects when he resigns his post in Milan as a *rhetor*, as a "venditor verborum" in the "speech-markets" (*Confessiones* 9.5 and 9.2). Jerome's use of this passage to authorize his own arguments against the claims of language is an act of brilliant misquotation. His use of Horace in this context is even more transgressive, for the Horatian dictum "nec verbum verbo curabis reddere fidus interpres" is actually part of an argument in the *Ars poetica* against the very kind of conservation of the source which, as we will see, Jerome favors.

In translation of learned (that is, non-scriptural) texts, Jerome eschews literalism as clumsy and as an obstacle to the meaning. In certain respects, this position recalls the ideas that Cicero sets forth in *De finibus*, where he promotes the sense-for-sense method in philosophical translation. For Cicero, clarity of meaning is naturally a priority:

Nec tamen exprimi verbum e verbo necesse erit, ut interpretes indiserti solent, cum sit verbum quod idem declaret magis usitatum. (3.4.15)

[Though all the same it need not be a hard and fast rule that every word shall be represented by its exact counterpart, when there is a more familiar word conveying the same meaning. That is the way of a clumsy translator.][31]

It would seem that Cicero exempts philosophical discourse from his policy of rhetorical contestation, and that Jerome might find grounds here for his own rejection of literalism as an impediment to clarity. But Cicero undercuts this very argument by his more urgent agenda of countering the cultural and intellectual hegemony of the Greek tradition: even here, Cicero's sense-for-sense policy represents an assertion of the linguistic independence of Latin from Greek, as well as of the critical independence of Latin philosophical inquiry from its Greek sources. Thus he advocates augmenting and challenging the Greek source as part of the project of translation:

Quid si nos non interpretum fungimur munere, sed tuemur ea quae dicta sunt ab iis quos probamus, eisque nostrum iudicium et nostrum scribendi ordinem adiungimus? quid habent cur Graeca anteponant iis quae et splendide dicta sint neque sint conversa de Graecis? Nam si dicent ab illis has res esse tractatas, ne ipsos quidem Graecos est cur tam multos legant quam legendi sunt . . . Quodsi Graeci leguntur a Graecis, iisdem de rebus alia ratione compositis, quid est cur nostri a nostris non legantur? (1.2.6)

[And supposing that for our part we do not fill the office of a mere translator, but, while preserving the doctrines of our chosen authorities, add thereto our own criticism and our own arrangement: what ground have these objectors for ranking the writings of Greece above compositions that are at once brilliant in style and not mere translations from Greek originals? Perhaps they will rejoin that the subject has been dealt with by the Greeks already. But then what reason have they for reading the multitude of Greek authors either that one has to read? . . . If Greek writers find Greek readers when presenting the same subjects in a differing setting, why should not Romans be read by Romans?]

Thus even in this philosophical context, Cicero's sense-for-sense method, ostensibly directed to serving meaning, actually leads to a rhetorical contest in which the re-creative and interpretive powers of discourse play an important role.

Jerome models his own norms of translation upon such a precedent without registering any of the conflict inherent in the Ciceronian rhetorical stance. For Cicero the aim of textual transfer – *translatio* – expresses itself in terms of the motive of textual transgression, in terms of the heuristic capacities of eloquence itself.[32] In Jerome, the aggressive force of this motive has virtually disappeared, to be replaced by a sense of eloquence as instrumental or conductive rather than as affective in itself. Jerome's testament to the claims of eloquence has more the flavor of an *apologia* than of a prescriptive program. In the preface to Eusebius' *Chronicle*, in a passage that he will take up later in Epistle 57 to Pammachius, he refers to Cicero and echoes Horace only to reverse their priorities, by theorizing language as an impediment to fidelity rather than as a facilitator of difference:

> . . . unde et noster Tullius Platonis integros libros ad uerbum interpraetatus est, et cum Aratum iam Romanum exametris uersibus edidisset, in Xenofontis Oeconomico lusit, in quo opere ita saepe aureum illud flumen eloquentiae quibusdam scabris et turbulentis obicibus retardatur, ut qui interpraetata nesciunt, a Cicerone dicta non credant: difficile est enim alienas lineas insequentem non alicubi excedere, arduum ut quae in alia lingua bene dicta sunt eundem decorem in translatione conseruent. Significatum est aliquid unius uerbi proprietate: non habeo meum quo id efferam, et dum quaero implere sententiam, longo ambitu uix breuis uiae spatia consummo. Accedunt hyperbatorum anfractus, dissimilitudines casuum, uarietas figurarum, ipsum postremo suum et ut ita dicam uernaculum linguae genus. Si ad uerbum interpraetor absurde resonat; si ob necessitatem aliquid in ordine, in sermone mutauero, ab interpraetis uidebor officio recessisse . . . Quorsum ista? uidelicet ut non uobis mirum uideatur si alicubi offendimus, si tarda oratio aut consonantibus asperatur aut uocalibus hiulca fit aut rerum ipsarum breuitate constringitur, cum eruditissimi homines in eodem opere sudauerint et ad communem difficultatem quam in omni interpraetatione causati sumus, hoc nobis proprium accedat, quod historia multiplex est, habens barbara nomina, res incognitas Latinis, numeros inextricabiles, uirgulas rebus pariter ac numeris intertextas, ut paene difficilius sit legendi ordinem discere quam ad lectionis notitiam peruenire. Unde praemonendum puto ut, prout quaeque scripta sunt, etiam colorum diuersitate seruentur, ne quis inrationabili aestimet uoluptate oculis tantum rem esse quaesitam et, dum scribendi taedium fugit, labyrinthum erroris intexat.[33]

> [Thus Cicero translated the whole corpus of Plato, and when he had produced a Latin Aratus in hexameter verses, he amused himself with Xenophon's *Oeconomicus*, in which work his golden flood of eloquence is so often hindered by rough and turbulent obstacles that those who do not know that it is a translation do not believe that it was written by Cicero. It is difficult, when following another's path, not to overstep somewhere; it is only with difficulty that the elegant idiom of another language retains its own decorum in translation. A meaning may be conveyed by a single word: but in my vocabulary I have no comparable word; and when I try to accommodate the full sense, I take a long detour around a short course. There are other matters to consider: the prolixity of *hyperbaton*, difference in grammatical cases, the varieties of rhetorical figures, and finally what I might call the particular native character of the language. If I translate word for word it sounds silly; if by necessity I change some aspect of word order or diction, I will seem inadequate to the task of the translator . . . The point of all this is that it should not seem strange to you if our translation offends, if its hesitant speech is uneven with consonants and its vowels open with hiatus, or if it is constrained by the summary treatment of the subject. Learned men will have sweated over this work; and along with the difficulty which we allege to be common to all

translation there is an additional problem for us: historical writing is complex, with names foreign and matters unfamiliar to Latin speakers, with inextricable measures and diacritical marks interspersed equally among facts and figures, so that it is almost more difficult to determine how it is to be read than to understand the meaning of the passage. Whence I think it should be borne in mind that writing is served – in proportion – by wide diversity of rhetorical figures, as long as one does not mistake, through an unreasonable delight in the senses, the artifice of eloquence for the subject-matter itself so that, until one flees the tedium of writing, one weaves a web of errors.]

Here the reference to Cicero's practice echoes Cicero's own frequent self-reference, although Jerome denies him the very success that Cicero claims for his own translations. More notable is that the sentence "difficile est enim alienas lineas insequentem non alicubi excedere," with its theme of following the path of a predecessor, seems to be an allusion to *Ars poetica* 119, "Aut famam sequere aut sibi convenientia finge," and 128, "Difficile est proprie communia dicere." The likelihood that Jerome is deliberately alluding to these lines in Horace is borne out in Epistle 57 to Pammachius, where Jerome quotes *Ars poetica* 133–4 and follows almost immediately by quoting the passage "difficile est enim alienas lineas insequentem non alicubi excedere" from his own preface to Eusebius. But in alluding to this section of the *Ars poetica*, both in the Eusebius preface and, as we shall see, in Epistle 57, Jerome inverts the Horatian principle of licensed transgression (winning private rights over public property, diverging from the public pathway), and offers, as if through Horace's distant authority, a principle of conformity and fidelity. The difficulty of achieving difference becomes, in Jerome, the difficulty of conserving likeness, of not overstepping ("excedere"); here, delight in eloquence leads to betrayal of the matter, to a labyrinth of error. To render word for word is to risk obstructing or straying from the predecessor's path, the "aliena linea," rather than, as in Horace, to risk too easy an access. There is some degree of inconsistency in Jerome's precept: at times, he seems to equate a word-for-word translation with sheer clumsiness, as Cicero does, and at other times he equates it with an improper delight in reproducing verbal artifice. But in either case, such verbal fidelity is seen as textual betrayal and hence is proscribed. For Jerome, the "native genius" of a language represents at best an opportunity to seek dynamic equivalence, not dynamic difference.

In the more famous Epistle 57, Jerome lines up his authorities, quoting from Cicero (*De optimo genere oratorum* 14–15), from the *Ars poetica*, and from his own preface to Eusebius:

ego enim non solum fateor, sed libera uoce profiteor me in interpretatione Graecorum absque scripturis sanctis, ubi et uerborum ordo mysterium est, non uerbum e uerbo, sed sensum exprimere de sensu. habeoque huius rei magistrum Tullium, qui Protagoram Platonis et Oeconomicum Xenofontis et Aeschini et Demosthenis duas contra se orationes pulcherrimas transtulit . . . sufficit mihi ipsa translatoris auctoritas, qui ita in prologo earundem orationum locutus est: *putaui mihi suscipiendum laborem utilem studiosis, mihi quidem ipsi non necessarium. conuerti enim ex Atticis duorum eloquentissimorum nobilissimas orationes inter seque contrarias, Aeschini et Demosthenis, nec conuerti ut interpres, sed ut orator, sententiis isdem et earum formis tam quam figuris, uerbis ad nostram consuetudinem aptis. in quibus non pro uerbo uerbum necesse habui reddere, sed genus omnium uerborum uimque seruaui. non enim me ea adnumerare lectori putaui oportere, sed tamquam adpendere* . . . sed et Horatius, uir acutus et doctus, hoc idem in Arte poetica erudito interpreti praecipit: *nec uerbum uerbo curabis reddere fidus interpres* . . . cum Eusebii *Chronikon* in Latinum uerterem, tali inter cetera praefatione usus sum: *difficile est alienas lineas insequentem non alicubi excedere* . . .[34]

[In fact I not only admit but openly declare that in translation from Greek texts (except in the case of sacred Scripture, where the very order of the words is a mystery) I render the text, not word for word, but sense for sense. For this I have the authority of Cicero, who translated Plato's *Protagoras* and Xenophon's *Oeconomicus* and the two most beautiful orations of Aeschines and Demosthenes which they delivered against each other . . . Cicero's authority will suffice for me; in the prologue to those orations he remarked: "I thought it my duty to undertake a task which will be useful to students, though not necessary for myself. That is to say I translated the most famous orations of the two most eloquent Attic orators, Aeschines and Demosthenes, orations which they delivered against each other. And I did not translate them as an interpreter, but as an orator, keeping the same ideas and the forms, or as one might say, the 'figures' of thought, but in language which conforms to our usage. And in so doing, I did not hold it necessary to render word for word, but I preserved the general style and force of the language. For I did not think I ought to count them out to the reader like coins, but to pay them by weight, as it were." . . . Moreover Horace, a shrewd and learned man, similarly advised the skilled translator: "Do not attempt to render word for word like a faithful interpreter." . . . When I translated Eusebius' *Chronicle* into Latin, among other matters in the preface I said: "It is difficult, when following another's path, not to overstep somewhere."

Here the quotations from Cicero and Horace, as authorizing premises, nest incongruously with a final invocation of another translator, Evagrius of Antioch, from whom Jerome quotes the preface to a rendering of the life of St. Anthony:

ex alia in aliam linguam ad uerbum expressa translatio sensus operit et ueluti laeto gramine sata strangulat. dum enim casibus et figuris seruit oratio, quod breui poterat indicare sermone, longo ambitu circumacta uix explicit. hoc igitur ego uitans ita beatum Antonium te petente transposui, ut nihil desit ex sensu, cum aliquid desit ex uerbis. alii syllabas aucupentur et litteras. tu quaere sententias.[35]

[A translation given word for word from one language to another conceals the sense, even as an overgrown field chokes the seeds. Given that speech conforms to cases and figures, a close translation sets forth at tedious length what might be expressed concisely. I have rendered this life of Saint Anthony, at your request, and I have avoided such literalism; in changing the language I have not changed the sense. Let others strive after letters and syllables; you seek after the meaning.]

Then referring to Hilary the Confessor as a translator, Jerome concludes,

nec adsedit litterae dormitanti et putida rusticornm [*sic*] interpretatione se torsit, sed quasi captiuos sensus in suam linguam uictoris iure transposuit.[36]

[Neither did he bother himself with the sleepy letter, nor did he wrench himself with an unnatural rendering of vulgar matters; rather, by right of victory he led away the sense captive into his own language.]

The point of the quotation from Evagrius of Antioch is clear: literal translation is rejected as a hindrance to meaning, and discourse is reduced to an instrumental, mediative function. For this authorizing precedent to be invoked along with those of Cicero and Horace effectively neutralizes the agonistic imperative of the Roman theorists. Jerome's own image of the translator leading meaning captive into his own language seems perhaps a distant echo of Horace's captive Greece who captured her savage conqueror and introduced eloquence into Rome. For Jerome as well, the translator's conquest is his servitude; but it is, however, a service outside the rhetorical claims of intention and effect.

For the heuristic motivation behind the dicta of Cicero and Horace, Jerome has substituted a rhetoric which has more in common with that of his contemporaries among the *rhetores latini minores*, where the connection between discovery and affective discourse has been virtually severed. With the atomization of invention, the question of meaning has lost its dynamic relationship with the acts of signifying, that is, structure, eloquence, and delivery, which embody and actualize meaning as intention. Jerome's rhetoric of translation suggests a similar divorce, a priority of the claims of meaning over and apart from language as the vehicle of intention.

It is not at all remarkable that we should find such a shift of emphasis in Jerome's theory of translation, given the religious parameters of his enterprise. Even apart from his main preoccupation with scriptural translation, in which he advocates a strict literalism so as to preserve the very mystery of the divine logos, and in which the Ciceronian dictum has no place, his priorities are always doctrinal.[37] But despite the inevitability of the teleological repositioning that we find in his theory, it is useful to revaluate here his reception of classical doctrine, for several related reasons. Histories of translation theory have generally taken at face value Jerome's use of classical authorities, so that his relationship with the Ciceronian position has been seen in terms of continuity rather than recognized as a rupture. The critical willingness to accept what seems at the surface to be a genuine continuity in the proscription of literalism may be a result of the way in which the historical terms of translation have commonly been treated as a system separate from other critical conditions or rules.[38] Thus the rhetorical grounding and application of translation theory in its early classical avatar has remained largely unexplored; and the transition from classical to early Christian and later medieval has thus been written as a history of dicta which can be extracted from their original frameworks and readily inserted into new contexts. But the deeper systems that govern the discourse of translation are also subject to change; and if Jerome mediates classical theories to the Christian Middle Ages, he transposes them without the rhetorical grounding that integrates translation with other norms of classical literary and critical practice. What the Christian West receives, through Jerome, as classical authority for translation is in fact a counter-rhetorical model. The theoretical legacy of Jerome is to remove from translation the agonistic hermeneutic of rhetoric, and to substitute a hermeneutic of access through language to a communality of meaning. By evaluating not only what is present but also what is absent in Jerome's classical transpositions, we can see that the terms of the *fidus interpres* have been so reconstituted as to promote rather than to proscribe textual fidelity. Through Jerome the Middle Ages inherits the formula "non verbum pro verbo" as a model of textual fidelity rather than of difference, as a theory of direct conservation of textual meaning without the impediment of linguistic multiplicity.

Jerome leaves a double theoretical legacy to the Middle Ages. The terms of the Ciceronian dictum, inverted to give privilege to signified meaning, recur most commonly in such formulations as that of Gregory the Great on the error and confusion that literal translators produce:

Indicamus praeterea quia gravem hic interpretum difficultatem patimur. Dum enim non sunt qui sensum de sensu exprimunt, sed transferre verborum semper proprietatem volunt omnem dictorum sensum confundunt. Unde agitur ut ea quae translata fuerint nisi cum gravi labore intellegere nullo modo valeamus.[39]

[Let us note, moreover, that we suffer this grave difficulty of translators: as long as none of them translate according to sense, but insist on transferring the property of every word, they confuse the meaning of every statement. The point is that without great labor we cannot in any way understand the things that have been translated.]

This utilitarian notion is registered with little change in academic and ecclesiastical circles throughout the Middle Ages, especially during periods of increased textual transmission, such as the thirteenth century. We find Bacon quoting Jerome to this effect, and similar statements in Aquinas.[40] It is also worth noting that Jerome's directive to translate according to sense rather than word so as to achieve unimpeded access to an absolute meaning could be taken up, perhaps somewhat surprisingly, in late medieval theories of biblical translation. The General Prologue to the Wycliffite Bible (*c.* 1395), usually attributed to John Purvey, uses the Hieronymian arguments against literalism as part of a larger effort to ensure the "openness" of the sacred text, to protect its meaning from the interference of verbal clutter:

First it is to knowe that the beste translating is, out of Latyn into English, to translate aftir the sentence and not oneli aftir the wordis, so that the sentence be as opin either openere in English as in Latyn, and go not fer fro the lettre; and if the lettre mai not be suid in the translating, let the sentence euere be hool and open, for the wordis owen to serue to the entent and sentence, and ellis the wordis ben superflu either false.[41]

This theoretical statement has taken Jerome's hermeneutic of access which gives priority to sense over word, and has applied it to translating the Bible, for which Jerome himself advocated the strictest literalism so as not to violate the sacred mystery immanent in the very words of Scripture. The Wycliffite mis-appropriation of Jerome's formula represents another chapter in the legacy of Jerome's own mis-appropriation of Cicero and Horace. Jerome's conceptual intervention in the transmission of Roman rhetorical ideas of translation had its own long history; and in this example we can see how far that intervention has come: the Ciceronian precept of translating according to sense so as to efface the authority of the original can be transmuted, over the course of a millennium, into a defense against scriptural transgression, to ensure the open presence of the most authoritative of all texts.

But Jerome's inversion of the *fidus interpres* formula to advocate fidelity to the textual signified could also be inverted again to represent a standard for literalism. Boethius, in the prologue to his second commentary on Porphyry's *Isagoge*, and John Scotus Eriugena, in the preface to his translation of the *De caelesti hierarchia* of the Pseudo-Dionysius, refer to the *fidus interpres* to characterize their own translative strategies. W. Schwarz has suggested that Boethius draws his formulation from Jerome, and that Eriugena is in turn dependent upon Boethius;[42] and indeed, there are clear echoes from the earlier to the later author:

Secundus hic arreptae expositionis labor nostrae seriem translationis expediet, in qua quidem uereor ne subierim fidi interpretis culpam, cum uerbum uerbo expressum comparatumque reddiderim. cuius incepti ratio est quod in his scriptis in quibus rerum cognitio quaeritur, non luculentae orationis lepos, sed incorrupta ueritas exprimenda est. quocirca multum profecisse uideor, si philosophiae libris Latina oratione compositis per integerrimae translationis sinceritatem nihil in Graecorum litteris amplius desideretur. [Boethius, *In Isagogen Porphyrii*][43]

[This second work, a readily accessible exposition, will clarify the text of my translation, in which I fear that I have incurred the blame of the "faithful translator," as I have rendered it word for word, plainly and equally. And here is the reason for this procedure: that in these writings in which knowledge of the matter is sought, it is necessary to provide, not the charm of a sparkling style, but the uncorrupted truth. Wherefore I count myself very successful if, with philosophical texts rendered into the Latin language through sound and irreproachable translations, there be no further need of Greek texts.]

Sin vero obscuram minusque apertam praedictae interpretationis seriem iudicaverit, videat me interpretem huius operis esse, non expositorem. Ubi valde pertimesco, ne forte culpam fidi interpretis incurram.
[John Scotus Eriugena, preface to translation of *De caelisti hierarchia*][44]

[If someone should find the text of the aforesaid translation obscure or impenetrable, let him consider me the translator of this work, not its expositor. Indeed, I fear that I have incurred the blame of the faithful translator.]

These patterns of multifold quotation (Horace–Jerome–Boethius–Eriugena) represent as many layers of "misquotation" or redefinition. In prizing the strategy of literal translation as the only means of certifying the "uncorrupted truth" of the original text, Boethius is in fact transposing Jerome's program for literalism in translating Scripture, "where the order of the words is itself a mystery," to the project of translating philosophical texts.[45] In doing so, he conflates the debased term of secular translation – *fidus interpres* – with the approved *modus* of sacred translation, also that of literal fidelity, and in this way rehabilitates *fida interpretatio* for secular translation.

This rehabilitation is by no means unqualified. By willfully committing the fault of the *fidus interpres*, Boethius has assigned a certain rhetorical priority to discourse itself, recognizing it not only as cognitive intermediary but also as the locus of intention and hence meaning. This is not to suggest that Boethius holds ontologically that language is constitutive of truth.[46] Rather, it is to suggest that Boethius returns this particular commonplace of translation theory to its original force as a rhetorical precept wherein linguistic usage does have the power to shape truth because it has the power to persuade or to induce belief. It is in the very language of the text that the translator is to find its uncorrupted truth; and any departure from the linguistic directive of the source represents a departure from its substantive directive. Thus to compensate for the inevitable loss of meaning in translation, the margin of difference must be as small as possible. Depending on one's position, this is either a rhetorical or an incarnational view of discourse; in the secular oratory of antiquity, and in the sacred writing of Christianity, discourse is itself constitutive of meaning. In Roman rhetoric, the rationale for an aggressive and contestative translation against the word of the original is precisely that of reinventing the text by resignifying it, to change its language and therefore its significance. Thus for Cicero, the aim of translation is to critique – interpret – and thereby reconstitute the original text. Conversely, in sacred contexts, the idea of divine speech as constitutive serves as the rationale for literal translation; for Jerome, the very order of the words in the Bible is a mystery, and the meaning of Scripture is not to be falsified by the linguistic liberties of a translator.[47] In Boethius' program, in his imposition of Jerome's *modus* for sacred translation on to a secular project, there is inevitably a trace of the sacramental view of speech which is still present in the secularized theory; for indeed, it is Jerome's authority as the translator of the Vulgate that enables the rehabilitation of *fida interpretatio* in the secular sphere.[48]

But Boethius' invocation of Jerome's authority validates a rhetorical motive for translation in order to reject that motive. In alluding to Jerome as a precedent for his own position, he is rehearsing Jerome's own pattern of "mis-allusion" to Horace, that of citing an earlier authority to justify what is, in fact, a counter-position to that authority. Boethius' citation of Horace through Jerome has a twofold implication: while Boethius has reaccorded secular discourse a certain constitutive claim which Jerome would deny it, he has not reinstated the priority of language over meaning that Horace and Cicero would assert. In one sense, Boethius' position is even more anti-rhetorical than Jerome's, for the quest for "knowledge of the matter" rather than "the charm of a sparkling style" is taken here to justify the very kind of clogged literalism that Jerome would censure as obscurantist and incommensurate with the aims of taking meaning captive. By justifying literalism as the only certain access to meaning in a philosophical text, Boethius diametrically inverts the ideal of philosophical translation that begins with Cicero's *De finibus*: for Cicero's policy of sense-for-sense translation aimed at shaping Latin into a philosophical language (and at setting the new Latin against the older Greek tradition), Boethius has substituted a rule of word-for-word translation aimed at conserving the signified of the source intact.

But as this last inversion should suggest, there is one respect in which Boethius' position is highly consonant with that of Cicero, although Boethius' purposes are contrary to the Ciceronian perspective. In effect, Boethius has reinscribed a rhetorical motive in the sense-for-sense method by rejecting rhetoric on grounds more definitive than those of Jerome. In a move counter to Jerome, and by default commensurate with Cicero and Horace, Boethius implies that translation according to sense introduces the rhetorical mode of signifying by transposition or indirection, and thus introduces the linguistic capacity to multiply meanings through ambiguity and tropological difference. This is to attribute a heuristic potential to eloquence, so that the translator's language would become, not the instrument of meaning, but rather a constitutive and affective force itself. Like Cicero, Boethius would see this method as producing dynamic difference between texts. But precisely because it threatens to betray the source by functioning as rhetorical transposition and substitution, Boethius rejects it. Over this, then, Boethius chooses literalism as a counter-rhetorical method.

That this inversion of Jerome and negative validation of the Ciceronian-Horatian position has its own medieval legacy is attested in John Scotus Eriugena, whose own formulations (in the passage quoted above) seem to derive from those of Boethius. Eriugena in fact defends himself against charges of insufficient literalism in the *De divisione naturae*;[49] and elsewhere he expounds the transgressive dangers of rhetorical indirection:

> Quisquis rhetorico verborum syrmate gaudet,
> Quaerat grandiloquos, Tullia castra petens;
> Ast mihi sat fuerit, si planos carpere sensus
> Possem tardilocus pragmata sola sequens.
> Interior virtus sermonum rite tenenda:
> Verborum bombi fallere saepe solent.[50]

[Whoever rejoices in the rhetorical cloak of words, let him seek grandiloquence, striving for the Ciceronian camp; but it will be enough for me if I can cull the plain sense, with slow, deliberate speech, following only the matter of the text. The internal value of the text is duly to be grasped; the bombast of words is often deceptive.]

Boethius' rejection of eloquence on the grounds of its heuristic potentials has resolved itself here, in Eriugena's verse, into a commonplace prioritizing of matter over form. Yet taken together with Eriugena's other defenses of literalism for the sake of accuracy, this commonplace should not be seen simply as a continuation of Hieronymian formulas. While Eriugena echoes Jerome's overriding concern for matter, his understanding of this principle actually represents a transformation of Jerome's arguments against literalism into an apology for literalism. There is some evidence that Eriugena knew and worked with Boethius' commentaries, for Boethius' commentaries on Porphyry's *Isagoge* were coming to be known in monastic and palace schools in the ninth century.[51] Boethius's preface to his translation-commentary may thus have had a certain influence in the later reception of patristic ideas about translation, and in Eriugena, what appears to be a patristic commonplace about the priority of meaning over language may in fact be understood in terms of Boethius' mediation of these earlier arguments. Behind Eriugena's use of a traditional formula lies a distrust of the sense-for-sense method as that which can introduce rhetorical ambiguity and reinvention rather than recuperation of meaning. As this pattern of reception suggests, the transmission of classical and patristic theories of translation is not a history of continuity but of a series of ruptures. Despite the superficial similarity of certain commonplaces about translation (word-for-word vs. sense-for-sense, the *fidus interpres*, the priority of meaning over form), medieval understandings of translation are far from homogeneous, and we must look to particular lines of transmission to understand how the rules of translation are conditioned and applied.

The *rhetores latini minores* and the patristic tradition carry over rhetorical formulas about translation *via* non-rhetorical or anti-rhetorical programs. In neither case does translation achieve an explicitly interpretive or affective status in the mediation of meaning; in neither case does translation open the possibility for textual appropriation and change according to the particular circumstances of reception. Neither tradition constructs the act of translation in terms of a hermeneutical praxis involving language as action. Fortunatianus places translation under the aegis of *elocutio*. But like his contemporaries, he tends to atomize the parts of the rhetorical system, so that *elocutio* no longer activates *inventio* and its interpretive claims. For the patristic tradition (that is, the double legacy of Jerome that extends through the later Middle Ages in learned and doctrinal translation), the hermeneutical motive is teleological, emphasizing the supra-verbal unity and continuity of meaning; and despite their differences in method and principle, both Jerome and Boethius aim at recuperating meaning beyond the particular and differentiating accidents of language.

But alongside these articulated theoretical traditions, the vernacular Middle Ages does develop a norm of translation whose hermeneutical motive is directed at textual appropriation and at the shaping and persuasive powers of discourse. The Middle Ages discovers – or reclaims – this model of translation in the very term which, in Roman theory, occupied a debased and restricted position: grammar.

THE TRIVIUM ART OF GRAMMAR: HERMENEUTICS AS THE MASTER DISCOURSE

In book 3 of *De nuptiis Philologiae et Mercurii*, Martianus Capella has Grammar address the assembly with an account of her duties:

Officium uero meum tunc fuerat docte scribere legereque; nunc etiam illud accessit, ut meum sit erudite intellegere probareque, quae duo mihi [uel] cum philosophis criticisque uidentur esse communia. ergo istorum quattuor duo actiua dicenda sunt, duo spectatiua, si quidem impendimus actionem, cum quid conscribimus legimusue, sequentum uero spectaculo detinemur, cum scripta intellegimus aut probamus [et] licet inter se quadam cognatione coniucta sint, sicut ceteris artibus comprobatur . . . Partes autem meae sunt quattuor; litterae, litteratura, litteratus, litterate. litterae sunt quas doceo, litteratura ipsa quae doceo, litteratus quem docuero, litterate quod perite tractauerit quem informo. profiteor autem de orationis natura usuque tractare.[52]

[My duty in the early stages was to read and write correctly; but now there is the added duty of understanding and criticizing knowledgeably. These two aspects seem to me to be shared with the philosophers and the critics. Two of these four functions may be called active, and two contemplative, since indeed we are active when we write or read anything, but we are engaged in the contemplation of the result when we understand or assess what has been written, although these four functions are all linked by a certain affinity, just as is shown to happen in other studies also . . . I have four parts: letters, literature, the man of letters, and literary style. {Letters are what I teach, literature is I who teach, the man of letters is the person whom I have taught, and literary style is the skill of a person whom I form.} I claim to speak also about the nature and practice of poetry.][53]

This passage from Martianus' early fifth-century text represents a moment of transition from the academic norms of the late Empire to those of the early Middle Ages. Grammar here is explicitly associated with interpretation and criticism, and indeed with literary studies in general. Exegesis is represented as a passive (or "contemplative") activity, a characterization which recalls the Roman distinction between the passive acquisition of knowledge, which is the purpose of grammar and its subsidiary, *enarratio*, and the active pursuit of eloquence, which is the interest of rhetoric. But on the other hand, Grammar claims for herself the whole compass of literary activity, from language to text to writer to style; and by emphasizing her role as exegete, she implies that the concern with the reception of texts, that is, their affective power, also comes under her aegis. Moreover, she says of her role, "profiteor autem de orationis natura usuque tractare," that is, she covers the nature and use of *oratio*. Where the English translators of this passage have rendered *oratio* as "poetry" (which is historically consistent with the classical restrictions on grammatical studies), the term "discourse" would more accurately indicate the way in which, during the late Empire, the concerns of the grammarian have broadened to include varieties of writing, both prose and poetry, as grammar takes up the literary subjects increasingly neglected by the rhetoricians.

In late antiquity, the need to reconstruct the meanings and contexts of a historically distant classical literature has afforded the grammarian's activity a new prominence.[54] Classical antiquity could restrict the exegetical services of the grammarian to an elementary application, largely because the Latin texts studied in the Roman schools were more or less contemporary cultural products. But even by the late fourth century, the exhaustive commentaries of Servius on Virgil met a very real need for elucidating a linguistic and literary usage already archaic and unfamiliar.[55] The increasing necessity for such reconstructive commentary on the ancient *auctores* brought greater prestige to this aspect of grammatical study. By the time of Isidore of Seville, such *enarratio* is no longer a simple propaedeutic, but has in fact attained the intellectual status of a comprehensive, recuperative inquiry which enables the most advanced textual study and becomes, in turn, a model for literary historians and scriptural exegetes. Isidore thus elevates the gloss to the status of philosophical investigation.[56]

The old debate about the boundary between grammar and rhetoric recurs in the *De nuptiis*, but in such a way as to suggest that its urgency as a question of disciplinary definition is by this point slipping. When Grammar has completed her account of letters, syllables, parts of speech, and usage, and proposes to take up other topics, Minerva interrupts her and pre-empts any remarks that Grammar may have on metaplasms, tropes, schemata, and figures, or the permissable "improper" usages:

quae si ab scholaribus inchoamentis in senatum caelitem ducis, decursae peritiae gratiam deflorabis . . . formam igitur praedictae praeceptionis absolueris, si praecipuis memoratis iam te ab inchoamentorum uulgarium uilitatibus uindicaris.

[If you bring such matters from the elementary school before the celestial senate, you will nip in the bud the goodwill you have won by this display of knowledge . . . The teaching you have given us will be well-proportioned and complete if you keep to your own particular subjects and do not cheapen them by commonplace and elementary instruction.][57]

There is some ambiguity here as to how Grammar is actually overstepping her limits. First, it is Minerva, not Grammar, who suggests that Grammar will next speak of tropes and figures. This may be interpreted as an attempt to register a pre-emptive protest against disciplinary encroachments, after the fashion of Quintilian's emphatic warnings. To be sure, Minerva's restriction of Grammar's coverage to elementary concerns reflects classical constraints on the competence of grammar; but there is also an implication that study of the tropes and figures is itself one of the elementary concerns of grammar, and as such should not be paraded before the celestial senate as advanced learning. It is not entirely clear from this passage whether the *figurae* are properly beyond the province of the grammarian or whether the grammarian's proper treatment of them is only as a propaedeutic to the fully prescriptive analysis of them by the rhetorician. But the old contest between grammar and rhetoric over the teaching of the figures, and thus the old division of the figures into those of speech and those of thought (respectively the province of the grammarian and of the rhetorician, although even this distinction was never absolute), has lost much of its edge by this period.[58] In the previous century Donatus had considered the tropes and figures of speech at some length in the *Ars maior*. While Martianus' discussion of the *figurae* in book 5 is closely modelled after a short treatise by the third-century rhetorician Aquila Romanus,[59] some of the material, such as irony, covered here under "figures of thought" had been covered by Donatus under the tropes; and similarly, some of the terms treated here under rhetoric, such as *isocolon*, *homoeoteleuton*, *paronomasia*, and *epanalepsis*, would have been understood, by the fifth century, as largely the business of the grammarian.[60] But Martianus' rather equivocal stance on the territory of grammar looks forward to a period, about a century later, when such notions of disciplinary "purity" will have lost much of their relevance to structures of learning. Minerva's interruption of grammar thus foretokens another way in which the *officia* of grammar gain a new intellectual primacy. Not only does the recuperative function of grammatical *enarratio* come to represent a new hermeneutical imperative; but as rhetorical study loses its direct application to the particular circumstances of discourse and gravitates into the orbit of dialectic, so the task of critical interpretation of the rhetoricity of texts, of authorial intention and affective devices, comes under the increasingly privileged aegis of grammar.

Indeed, the line between descriptive and prescriptive analysis of tropes is already beginning to blur in Servius.[61] In the sixth century, the grammarian Priscian models his *Praeexercitamina* after the declamatory exercises (*Progymnasmata*) of the Alexandrian rhetorician Hermogenes, thus transferring a rhetorical text into a grammatical sphere. By the early seventh century, Isidore of Seville distinguishes the *figurae* of grammar and rhetoric in terms of those which appear frequently in poetry and those which are more common in prose, and in the chapter on rhetoric refers his reader back to the grammar chapter for the account of *schemata* derived from Donatus. In other words, the external disciplinary distinctions have seemingly disappeared, to be replaced by internal generic distinctions.[62] On the question of the levels of style, Isidore also combines classical rhetorical precept with the authority of grammatical commentary on Virgil.[63] In the early eighth century, Bede's treatise *De schematibus et tropis* seems to witness a final breakdown of the older, "purist," distinctions between the disciplinary domains of grammar and rhetoric: his definitions derive from Donatus, but his discussion of scriptural allegory, in which he distinguishes between *allegoria in factis* and *allegoria in verbis*, shifts the analysis onto a hermeneutical plane concerned with discursive totalities rather than local usages.[64] Grammar and its attendant offices of textual commentary and analysis of discourse become central to the curriculum, and Donatus, Servius, and Priscian the major mediators of classical antiquity.[65] Grammatical *enarratio* thus takes on the double function of historical recuperation and rhetorical interpretation of texts, and the grammarians provide the paradigm for the art of textual exposition in all intellectual fields.

There is little homogeneity to early medieval education, nor is it properly continuous with Roman academic practices. The nature of education differs from region to region, from "humanist" to Christian "rigorist" milieux, from clerical to monastic circles, and from monastic to episcopal to presbyterial schools.[66] Despite the heterogeneity of pre-Carolingian education, however, there is a basic continuity with ancient methods: elementary training consists of grammatical usage, reading, and *enarratio*, whether of secular or sacred texts. But the Roman educational system, already partially transformed in late antiquity, undergoes a thorough reprioritizing in the Middle Ages. Late antiquity had seen the divorce of rhetoric from the arts of discourse, which became, in large part, the province of grammar. But in patristic and medieval programs of education, theology supplants rhetoric as the summit of curricular study.

As an intellectual inquiry within the curriculum, rhetoric retains its importance as a counterpart of dialectic, its position since late antiquity, as witnessed in Boethius' *De differentiis topicis* and in Isidore's double chapter on rhetoric and dialectic (book 2). But in terms of its extrinsic rationale, rhetoric's office is revalued in terms of service to theology. Cassiodorus discovers rhetoric, along with the other human arts, planted in Scripture, to be cultivated for the elucidation of Scripture.[67] Similarly, Isidore affirms the ethical directives of rhetoric, defining eloquence as persuasion to *iusta et bona*.[68] In Alcuin's *Disputatio de rhetorica et de virtutibus*, the ethical application of rhetoric to civil issues has its complement in a definition of the virtue of moral philosophy (prudence, justice, courage, temperance) whose authority is grounded, not in social convention, but in divine revelation. Alcuin also illustrates the three kinds of rhetoric (demonstrative, deliberative, and judicial) through reference to their use in Scripture.[69] The inventional aspects of rhetoric remain a training ground for legal and civic dispute, as witnessed by the definitions in Isidore and Alcuin, as well as for philosophical inquiry, as seen in the long influence of the Victorinus commentary.[70] But rhetoric no longer serves in a primary ethical or epistemological capacity. It has been subsumed by theology.

Where the oratorical function of rhetoric – that is, rhetoric as the art of eloquence – retains an authentic importance is, of course, in preaching. The application of rhetoric to preaching is a primary theme in patristic programs of education, as part of the general attempt to revalue pagan learning for Christian use. This justification of eloquence probably gains its firmest hold in the Carolingian period, when Rabanus Maurus resurrects the preaching program in book 4 of Augustine's *De doctrina christiana* as a practical guide for clerics.[71] As a theory of preaching, Augustine's work had somewhat less of an impact in early centuries than Gregory's popular ecclesiastical guide, *Cura pastoralis*, which put forward a theory of preaching without explicit reference to the system of rhetoric.[72] Thus the influence of Augustine's rhetorical definition of preaching entered into the curriculum somewhat later than the more general influence of his exegetical program.

But in the tradition of preaching, rhetoric is itself in the service of *enarratio*: for pulpit oratory is an elaborate medieval answer to the highly developed forms of textual exegesis of late antiquity. Here, in this nexus of rhetoric and the grammatical function of *enarratio*, lies a significant transposition of the ancient curricular hierarchy. In late antiquity, rhetorical theory, as we have seen, had moved away from a direct concern with the activation of meaning in discourse, and thus from the sphere of concern which it shared with such ancient hermeneutical theory as Aristotle's *Peri hermeneias*. While the study of figures nominally still belonged to rhetoric, such attention to the verbal arts fitted so well into the expanding interests of grammar that this area could be given over to the grammarian along with other techniques of elucidating usage, as illustrated by the "grammatical" treatment of figures in Donatus, Isidore, and Bede. In effect, rhetorical theory as a curricular discipline (rather than in the specific application of eloquence to preaching) had ceased to perform the very *officium* which it had reserved for itself in antiquity, that of providing a sophisticated and systematic analysis of signification as praxis, or to recall Todorov's terms, of the text as totality. As an area of study as well as a practice, it had ceased to function as a way of mediating the contingencies of human language and the need for moral action, or as a way of "making the world of language intelligible."[73] Its heuristic objectives, that is, the discovery of ideas in argumentative structures, had become increasingly separated from its discursive concerns, that is, the linguistic acts that give form and direction to those arguments discovered. It had become less and less a "discourse about discourse."[74]

As if to fill the space left open when rhetoric distanced itself from active application to discourse, grammar assumes an unprecedented importance for the systematic analysis of the text as a discursive system. The grammatical function of *enarratio* becomes itself a metadiscourse. It provides access to all fields of learning, and in many respects constitutes an application of that learning, as inquiry can advance itself through commentary. What Isidore says of the grammatical art in general, that it is "origo et fundamentum liberalium litterarum" (1.5.1) can be said especially of the exegete's activity for which the grammarians provided a model. In this way the once debased activity of the grammarians can now supply the paradigm for the exalted activity of biblical exegesis.

Preaching is a medieval answer to ancient civic oratory, but also, as I have noted, to ancient and late-classical systems of textual commentary. It is an act of mediating the divine Word through varieties of human interpretation. The conflation of these functions, the oratorical and the exegetical, is the theme of the *De doctrina christiana*. Augustine takes up the Ciceronian *officia* of *probare*, *delectare*, and *flectere* (*Orator* 20.69) and substitutes *docere* for *probare* (4.74), so that the orator's duty of proof towards persuasion becomes the preacher's duty of instruction towards conversion and salvation. But the preacher can take up these offices only after intensive study of the grounds and modes of signification, that is, after the interpretation of biblical discourse (books 1–3). To evangelize is to re-enact the Word through commentary on the Word: the oratorical office of re-enactment is achieved through – and on behalf of – the "grammatical" office of exegesis. The highest study is theology: the praxis of theology is instruction and evangelizing. The means of achieving these rhetorical aims is *enarratio* in all of its varieties.

Enarratio is not, as in classical education, a necessary preliminary to oratory; it is, here, a concomitant of oratory. *Lectio* and *praedicatio* are simply aspects of the same process.[75] In this way, also, the twofold program of scriptural reading, *lectio* and *praedicatio* could be enlarged to a threefold program of *lectio*, *disputatio*, *praedicatio*. The dialectical term *disputatio* could be adapted to this exegetical context to mean an active analysis of the questions raised and the cruces discovered in a reading of Scripture, an analysis which would find its way into preaching and thus praxis.[76] *Enarratio* thus embraces both exposition and argument.

In sacred studies, exegesis thus interprets – or mediates – the Word of God. In secular studies of all the liberal arts, *enarratio* interprets, reconstructs, revalorizes a world of ancient literature and learning from whose original intellectual and cultural framework the Middle Ages is increasingly distanced. *Enarratio* now assumes the role of "making the world of language intelligible" – that world of language now textualized as the corpus of ancient learning and as scriptural revelation. In its secular avatar, that intelligible access represents, now, not the public forum of civil dispute, but the goal of *translatio studii*, a goal which is akin to what Ricoeur has called "the struggle against the estrangement from meaning itself," or the goal of hermeneutical appropriation, "the struggle against cultural distance and historical alienation [which] actualises the meaning of the text for the present reader."[77] The commentator's concern with the language of the text, a legacy of the grammarian's *enarratio*, can also be seen in terms of Gadamer's definition of "application": ". . . understanding always involves something like the application of the text to be understood to the present situation of the interpreter."[78] *Enarratio* comes to represent a dynamic, re-creative, engagement with the language of tradition.[79]

In treatment of the liberal arts, and especially in literary exposition of ancient texts, medieval *enarratio* can assume the character of application because it makes the historical situation of the interpreter a condition rather than an accident of interpretation. Rather than simply piling encyclopaedic information upon the text, one way in which the methods of the grammarian have been characterized,[80] or erecting other meanings on top of the literal ones,[81] *enarratio* engages dialectically with the text, through critique, restatement, and refiguration "ad nostram consuetudinem," to borrow a phrase from Cicero. This is not to suggest that medieval exegetes operated with a self-reflexive model of historicity in which there is a recognized alterity between past and present, in the way that modern hermeneutics has constructed this problem. Since the work of Schleiermacher in the early nineteenth century, modern hermeneutics has struggled with the conflicting claims of historical consciousness, that is, the ideal of reconstructing the past on its own terms, and the historicity of the interpreter.[82] But the medieval exegete registers nothing of such a conflict: for the project of *translatio studii*, his own historicity, bringing the text forward to his own historical situation, is all that matters. The absence of such a conflict is itself the productive ground for medieval interpreters as appropriators of classical tradition.

The paradox of the ancient struggle between grammar and rhetoric is that the Middle Ages recovers – or reinvents – the rhetorical motive of cultural appropriation and displacement in the newly elevated practice of *enarratio poetarum*, that is, in the once debased and delimited activity of the grammarian. In late antiquity, rhetoric's force as a praxis diminishes, not because it comes to be identified with figures and tropes, but – just the opposite – because as a formal study it concentrates almost entirely on inventional theory, and leaves the practical problem of negotiating linguistic usage to the grammarians. In practice, grammatical *enarratio* comes to supplant rhetoric as the master discourse: in medieval preaching, rhetoric is in the service of sacred commentary, and in the arts curriculum, commentary performs the now privileged office of recuperating the *auctores*. Even more paradoxical, as we shall see, is that the rhetorical motive of translation would be recovered in the Middle Ages, not through the transmission of ancient rhetorical theory or through translation theory derived from the Roman rhetoricians, but rather through the medieval exegetical practice that came to fulfill the office that rhetorical study could no longer perform, that of giving access to a tradition of linguistic performance.

To understand how translation could define its practice out of exegetical traditions, it is necessary to consider first how commentary defined its own status as an academic discourse in relation to rhetoric. As hermeneutics supplanted rhetoric as the master curricular practice, it also assumed the character of rhetoric; and it is to this question that we now turn.

3

The rhetorical character of academic commentary

When Quintilian presents his version of Aristotle's division of the sciences into theoretical, practical, and productive, he identifies rhetoric chiefly with the practical sciences, which are concerned with action (*Institutio oratoria* 2.18.1–5). For Quintilian as for Cicero, rhetoric, as a mastery of political and social discourse, represents the highest art, the fulfillment even of philosophy.[1] Thus it is not surprising that Quintilian's model of the sciences should implicitly give precedence to the practical sciences, which demand action, rather than to the theoretical or exact sciences. For Quintilian, as we have seen, the theoretical sciences occupy a restricted sphere: they are concerned with a kind of knowledge "which demands no action, but is content to understand the subject of its study." It is in terms of this reckoning of theoretical sciences that Quintilian restricts the competence of grammar and of grammatical *enarratio poetarum*.

Quintilian's version of the classification of the sciences provides a good reference point for the discussion here of the change in the status of grammar from antiquity to the Middle Ages. If we see the value of rhetoric and grammar in the Middle Ages in terms of the inaugural formulations of their relationship in Roman models of the sciences, we can understand how *enarratio* exceeded the disciplinary restrictions that rhetoric imposed on it in antiquity. As hermeneutical appropriation of the materials of the past, medieval *enarratio* reaches beyond the limits of what Quintilian would have considered an exact science to constitute a form of a relative or practical science. It does not simply treat the text as a pre-given universal for which philological science can supply a fixed exposition. Rather, the text is the subject of continuous and changing interpretation according to the judgment of each generation of expositors. We should recall the ancient restrictions upon grammar, and especially Quintilian's pre-emptive protests against the overstepping of the grammarians into the dynamic realm of praxis which rhetoric claimed for itself. The work of the grammarians always threatened to achieve the force of praxis, that is, deliberation about the variable rather than simply inquiry into the necessary. Medieval *enarratio* seems to follow through on the threat that its classical counterpart had posed to rhetoric. Medieval exegesis replicates rhetoric's productive application to discourse: as the orator fitted a speech to the particular circumstances of persuasion, so in a certain sense the medieval exegete remodels a text for the particular circumstances of interpretation. Even though medieval commentary works around the text, alongside the text, as addenda to the text, it can take on a primary productive character: it continually refashions the text for changing conditions of understanding. It becomes an art whose end is realized in a kind of action.

To speak of medieval commentary assuming a rhetorical force is not just figurative: commentators use rhetorical systems and techniques as *modi interpretandi*. In interlinear, marginal and narrative commentary, the text can be the subject of re-creative exposition from lexical and tropic detail to comprehensive architectonics, from judgment of authorial intention to directives for reader-response (the realm of affectivity or persuasion). We can distinguish two levels in the application of rhetorical principles to textual commentary. First there is the analysis of rhetorical devices of style, structure, and argument in the text, those formal considerations which by the twelfth century were classified under *modus agendi*. This represents a direct extension of the grammarian's descriptive role: the grammarian's *enarratio* consists largely of pointing to the uses and effects of the compositional devices codified by the rhetoricians. But there is also a second level at which textual commentary appropriates rhetorical principles. Commentaries use rhetorical categories of argumentation or, more generally, heuristic strategies, to define and organize the exposition itself. In this respect then, commentaries do not simply discover and describe rhetorical elements in the texts they treat. Rather, the commentaries themselves are governed by rhetorical assumptions. Sometimes the rhetorical structure of the commentary is explicit, as in the case of some early forms of the *accessus ad auctores* in which the exposition is generated out of rhetorical *circumstantiae*, the topical categories associated with rhetorical invention. The theoretical implications of this *accessus* form will be considered here in some detail as an example of the rhetoricized commentary from which vernacular translation emerges. Often, however, the rhetorical assumptions that govern a commentary are only implicit. In the reception of classical authors, the goal of rationalizing the text as a coherent signifying system, an aim which is itself rhetorical, is sometimes achieved through sustained troping of the text, resignifying the text through meticulous rehearsing of its narrative. This expository method, often known as allegoresis, represents a productive challenge to the text; it does not simply impose meanings from without (which is what Rosemond Tuve's term "imposed allegory" implies), but, rather, patiently reconstructs (or, in effect, re-argues) the text according to directives that the text itself provides – plot, *materia*, *modus agendi*. In a sense, then, the commentator uses the plot, matter, and stylistic procedure of the text in the way that an orator uses rhetorical topics like the attributes of the person and the act, that is, to supply information out of which the exegetical narrative is constructed.

The rules by which orators compose have here become the rules by which grammarian-exegetes read. As grammarians turn rhetorical strategies of composition into strategies of reading, taxonomy, and interpretation, they effect a passage from a prescriptive to a descriptive realm. But in this transposition from composition to exposition, the prescriptive motive is still imprinted on these rhetorical strategies; conversely, the compositional, prescriptive context of ancient rhetorical teaching had used these strategies as the interpretive or expository models by which exemplary speeches might be analyzed and then imitated. The history of the distinction between the grammarian's descriptive and the rhetorician's prescriptive mode is actually one of mutual imprinting. Thus in medieval commentary the incorporation of rhetorical theories of argumentation into exegesis gives the hermeneutical function a heuristic force: commentary can act productively to effect a change on the text for new conditions of reading. Moreover, and importantly for the history of literary translation, this textual hermeneutic, carrying its heuristic and prescriptive imprint, enables *enarratio* to achieve a form of difference with the text, or to shift the terms slightly, to displace the text. Commentaries reproduce and resituate the text through paraphrase; or they subsume it, as commentaries are grafted on to the text and texts are inscribed in the commentaries. Commentaries themselves become texts to be appropriated by later exegetes and to be incorporated in later commentaries. Thus as grammatical *enarratio* becomes a privileged term in making the world of textualized knowledge intelligible and interpretable, its own procedures become increasingly rhetoricized, as it unites hermeneutical with heuristic motives. The rhetorical systems incorporated into exegetical structures do not lose their inventional and argumentative force when they are transplanted; rather, they exert a certain rhetorical power in their new exegetical environment, to transform commentary into a kind of praxis. The generative force of rhetoric finds itself here in the interpretive directive of the grammarian-exegete: here rhetoric becomes a discursively productive "grammar" of reading.

These considerations have direct bearing on the way that we can understand the emergence and status of vernacular translation of the *auctores*. As I shall demonstrate in chapters 4 and 5, vernacular literary translation develops out of exegetical procedures which carry the imprint of rhetorical procedures. We have seen that the Romans theorize translation as a rhetorical project of achieving difference with the original text. The Roman idea of translation finds its counterpart in medieval vernacular translation. Medieval translation emerges out of a tradition of rhetoricized *enarratio* in which exposition assumes the character of hermeneutical application and textual appropriation.

But it is necessary first to consider some aspects of that exegetical tradition out of which vernacular translation arises. The purpose of the present chapter is to explore the rhetorical dimension of medieval *enarratio*, to consider the textual character and function of commentary itself. The following discussion examines four different kinds of textual practice that exemplify the rhetorical character of academic commentary. First I will consider a form of academic prologue that uses the ancient rhetorical system of topical invention. Second,

I will consider how discussions of authorial *intentio* serve as exegetical structures. The third example here will be the practice of allegoresis. Finally I will consider some implications of textual paraphrase. My interest here is to offer an account, not of the conscious intentions of commentators, but rather of what the language and methods of commentary reveal about the status of hermeneutics in relation to rhetoric.

One early form of the *accessus ad auctores*, the prologues that accompany commentaries on sacred and secular texts, derives its structure from the classical rhetorical scheme of the *circumstantiae*, the specific questions that must be asked of a given case in order to formulate an argument about it. This prologue scheme offers some of the most direct evidence of the adaptation of rhetorical to exegetical systems. This particular form of the *accessus ad auctores* came into use during the Carolingian period, and is associated mainly with Remigius of Auxerre, the prolific commentator who flourished during the second half of the ninth century and the first decade of the tenth century.[2] As a way of organizing the exposition of the text, of setting out what is to be covered, this *accessus* scheme proposes all or some of the following questions: *quis*, *quid*, *cur*, *quomodo*, *ubi*, *quando*, and *unde* or *quibus facultatibus* (who, what, why, in what way, where, when, whence or by what means). Sometimes these questions appear in the form of topics: *persona*, *res*, *causa*, *tempus*, *locus*, *modus*, *facultas* (person, act, cause, time, place, manner, means). A good example of this scheme, using both the interrogative and the topical forms, occurs in an *accessus* to a commentary on Sedulius' *Carmen Paschale*:[3]

> VII sunt perioch[a]e, id est circumstanti[a]e, que constant in initio uniuscuiusque libri, id est quis quid cur quomodo quando ubi quibus facultatibus. In quibus continetur tempus, locus, persona, res, causa, qualitas, facultas. Videlicet quis fecit? Sedulius. Quid fecit? Paschale carmen de veteri et novo testamento. Cur fecit? Quia videbat, quod pauci essent, qui de humanitate et incarnatione salvatoris metrico opere aliquod opus facerent. Quomodo fecit? Metrico stilo, non prosaico. Quando fecit? Tempore Theodosii et Valentiniani imperatorum. Ubi fecit? In Achaia. Quibus facultatibus vel unde? De facultatibus eorum, quos imitatus est.[4]

> [There are seven summaries, that is circumstances, which are established at the beginning of every book: who, what, why, in what way, when, where, with what faculties (means). In these are comprised time, place, person, matter, cause, quality (nature), means. Thus, who produced it? Sedulius. What did he produce? A paschal song according to the Old and New Testaments. Why did he produce it? Because he noticed that there were few who had written poetry about the humanity and incarnation of the savior. In what way did he fashion it? In verse, not prose. When did he write it? In the time of the emperors Theodosius and Valentinian. Where did he write it? In Achaia. With what means did he write it? By means of those sources that he imitated.]

Sometimes the list of circumstances is reduced to three or four.[5] By the eleventh century this rhetorical framework for the *accessus* is rare; Bernard of Utrecht describes it as an "ancient" system.[6] It was superseded by a more widely used form which considered the title, the author's intention, the formal procedure, the utility of the work, and the part of philosophy to which the work belonged.[7] The obvious purpose of the circumstantial – or rhetorical – format is to provide information about the text and thereby to situate it; it shares this function with all the other prologue forms in use from late antiquity to the late Middle Ages. What, then, was especially appropriate about the circumstantial system of rhetoric, so that it was made to serve, in the *accessus* associated with Remigius, as an exegetical apparatus?[8]

To begin to answer this, we should consider the role of the *circumstantiae* in ancient and medieval rhetoric. In ancient rhetorics, the *circumstantiae* are an important component of argumentation, serving to define the specific attributes or circumstances of the case. But the position and function of this formula within rhetorical systems can vary. The theory of the seven circumstances derives originally from Hermagoras of Temnos, a Greek rhetorician of the second century B.C. Hermagoras' handbook is not extant, but the teaching contained in it can be reconstructed, as it was an influential and much-quoted manual. Much of Hermagoras' system survives in the compendium of the Pseudo-Augustine, one of the minor Latin rhetoricians of late antiquity.[9] Hermagoras recognized both the thesis and hypothesis, or the unlimited and limited question, as rhetorical controversies. In distinguishing between them, he delimited the hypothesis by seven attributes, which the Pseudo-Augustine lists as *quis*, *quid*, *quando*, *ubi*, *cur*, *quem ad modum*, and *quibus adminiculis*.[10] But in Hermagoras' system, the circumstances play only a preliminary definitional role: they are not central to Hermagoras' doctrine of invention, but serve only to introduce the argument by circumscribing it. Far more important for Hermagoras' analysis of the hypothesis is the doctrine of *status* or *stasis*. This represents the crucial issues or controversies upon which the case or hypothesis rests. The *staseis*, or *quaestiones rationales*, are conjecture, definition, quality, and legal procedure.[11] The Hermagorean system of invention, in which the circumstances play only a preliminary role, is found in the *Ars rhetorica* of C. Julius Victor, which was Alcuin's main source on the circumstances.[12]

It is from Cicero's *De inventione*, however, that classical and medieval rhetorical doctrine derives a standard theory of the circumstances.[13] In the *De inventione* Cicero both rejects and adopts Hermagoraean doctrine: he does not admit the thesis into the sphere of rhetoric, but he builds his theory of controversies or *constitutiones* upon Hermagoras' *status* theory (see *De inventione* 1.6.8; 1.8.10–1.11.16). Cicero also incorporates a version of Hermagoras' doctrine of circumstances into his own theoretical system, and at the same time assigns the circumstances a more significant role than Hermagoras seems to have done. In Hermagoras the circumstances represent a preliminary scheme for delimiting the hypothesis. But in the *De inventione*, Cicero reworks the circumstances into an elaborate system of topics, the attributes of the person and the act, to be used in formulating the part of the speech known as *confirmatio* or proof (1.24.34–1.28.43). The seven circumstances are actually imbedded here in a large topical scheme, covering eleven attributes of the person, and, under attributes of the action, comprising four categories: attributes coherent with the performance of the act, connected with the act, adjunct to the act, and consequent upon it (the latter three are external to the actual performance of the action). The many *attributa* correspond only partially to Hermagoras' tight formula of *circumstantiae*: the attributes of the person correspond to *quis*; the whole topic of the action (*negotium*) corresponds to *quid*; and under the performance of the act (*in gestione negotii*), the considerations *locus*, *tempus*, *occasio*, *modus*, and *facultas* correspond to the remaining five circumstances.[14]

Cicero has moved these circumstantial considerations from a definitional to a procedural position. In Cicero, the doctrine of *status* now represents the definitional point of departure, and the circumstances have become part of the core of topical invention itself, as they provide the argumentative framework for one of the six parts of the oration, *confirmatio* or proof. This topical canon of the *De inventione* became a mainstay of later rhetorical theory.[15] Through the influence of the *De inventione*, later rhetoricians used the circumstances as topics for invention under *confirmatio*, artificial proofs, or more generally, the *narratio* or statement of the case. Quintilian uses the circumstances as topics of argument under artificial proof; Fortunatianus uses them as the means of formulating the *narratio* after the *status* of the case has been determined, and as the materials for one of the sources of argument for artificial proof, the arguments "before the act" (*ante rem*). Martianus Capella follows Fortunatianus in using the seven circumstances as artificial proof *ante rem*. C. Julius Victor also uses them under artificial proof and credible narrative. Sulpitius Victor and Victorinus follow the scheme of the *De inventione* in treating the circumstances as an inventional formula under *confirmatio*.[16]

Boethius is probably the most important figure for transmitting a coherent rhetorical doctrine of the circumstances to the Middle Ages. In book 4 of *De differentiis topicis*, he carefully explains the differences between dialectical and rhetorical topics and thereby the difference between the two systems of dialectic and rhetoric. Like Cicero, Boethius assigns the thesis to dialectic; the hypothesis, however, is proper for the rhetorician, because "it examines questions that are limited by a multitude of circumstances."[17] He gives the circumstances as who, what, where, when, why, in what manner, and by what means. Working from the *De inventione*, he goes on to find the topics for invention in the attributes of the person and the act.[18] But he effects some important changes here. First, he does not address the attributes of the person and the act as the topics of *confirmatio*, the fourth part of the oration, as the *De inventione* does. Boethius is not concerned with the technicalities of the oration and its parts. Instead he finds in the topics of *confirmatio* a scheme which can be generalized to represent the art of rhetorical invention as a whole.[19] He elevates the scheme of the circumstances to a comprehensive position, to define rhetorical method and to represent the discipline of rhetoric itself. Thus he also conflates the theories of Hermagoras and of Cicero on the circumstances. In Hermagoras, the circumstances had a definitional function, to delimit the hypothesis; in Cicero, they have a procedural function, as an apparatus for topical invention under proof. But in Boethius, the circumstances are both definitional and procedural: they define the status of rhetoric itself, because they constitute its fundamental procedure, the invention of topics that ground the hypothesis in all of its particularity. According to one scholar, Boethius' concern to define the methods of rhetoric in relation to those of dialectic "led to a progression from a theory of topics to an implied theory of the status of rhetoric as an art."[20] Through Boethius, the circumstances become a cornerstone of rhetorical method.

This is the traditional value of the circumstantial scheme. Rhetoric properly deals with questions delimited by a multitude of circumstances, and topical invention based on the *circumstantiae* becomes a fundamental method of rhetoric. Rhetorical arguments are grounded in the particular circumstances of the case, that is, the person, the action, the time, and the place; but the argumentative performance itself, and by extension the whole art of rhetoric, is defined by the circumstantiality of its heuristic procedure. As a theory of topics the *circumstantiae* come to constitute, in Boethius, a definition of rhetoric itself.

But how may we account theoretically for the assimilation of this system into a hermeneutical scheme? The circumstances define rhetoric by delimiting the hypothesis; they also define rhetoric by constituting its basic procedure, topical invention. When this inventional structure is placed before a text and commentary, as in the case of the circumstantial *accessus*, it would seem to make of the text an act delimited by circumstances, and to make of the commentary an argument to be invented out of those circumstances. In other words, the heuristic formula of the circumstances can define the hermeneutical act itself.

The historical example of the circumstantial *accessus* raises the question of how the hermeneutical act can be represented and understood in rhetorical terms. This question, implicit in the textual methods of the medieval *accessus*, is also a central critical issue within modern work on hermeneutics. To articulate the historically specific terms of this problem for medieval hermeneutics, we can look to the broadly theoretical terms in which Gadamer explains the relationship between rhetoric and hermeneutical practice. Gadamer posits an alliance between rhetoric and hermeneutics in terms of the circumstantial or temporal "situatedness" of both:

> Rhetoric . . . is tied to the immediacy of its effect. Now the arousing of emotions, which is clearly the essence of the orator's task, is effectual to a vastly diminished degree in written expression, which is the traditional object of hermeneutical investigation. And this is precisely the difference that matters: the orator carries his listeners away with him; the convincing power of his arguments overwhelms the listener. While under the persuasive spell of speech, the listener for the moment

cannot and ought not to indulge in critical examination. On the other hand, the reading and interpretation of what is written is so distanced and detached from its author – from his mood, intention, and unexpressed tendencies – that the grasping of meaning of the text takes on something of the character of an independent productive act, one that resembles more the art of the orator than the process of mere listening. Thus it is easy to understand why the theoretical tools of the art of interpretation (hermeneutics) have been to a large extent borrowed from rhetoric.[21]

Let us use this model to explore how exegetical systems can operate in terms of rhetorical systems. First, as Gadamer suggests, interpretation is an act delimited by particular circumstances, by the historically particular situation of the interpreter and his community. This renders the text itself susceptible to circumstances of reception, just as rhetorical arguments are tailored to particular circumstances of time, event, and audience. This first principle leads to a second: the hermeneutical performance assumes a kind of inventional or heuristic force, and becomes an "independent productive act."

These two principles of hermeneutics correspond with the two principles of the rhetorical theory of the *circumstantiae*: first, that the circumstances define rhetoric by delimiting the hypothesis; and second, that they define rhetoric by constituting its basic procedure, topical invention. The twofold value of the circumstantial scheme in rhetoric is in a sense replicated in the hermeneutical context. The individual interpretive act is defined by its historicity, by the historical situatedness of understanding, and this circumstantiality of interpretation also defines the exegetical process in general, to render it something of "an independent productive act," on the order of rhetorical invention of argument. With this in view, we can see how the historicity of the hermeneutical act corresponds to the circumstantiality of the rhetorical act. The rhetorical task of persuasion involves the principle of *to prepon*, appropriateness, the suiting of discourse to the particular conditions of argumentation, to the specific receptivity of the audience to which it is directed. Rhetoric finds its proper end in action rather than in knowledge or product, as Quintilian tells us. Rhetoric's dynamic engagement with changeable conditions of persuasion can thus provide a paradigm for exegetical engagement with the particular circumstances of textual reception.

It is in this way, then, that we can account theoretically for the value of the rhetorical *circumstantiae* when they are taken over by an exegetical system. The circumstantial *accessus* dramatizes the way in which medieval hermeneutical performance can assume a kind of heuristic force, enabling argument in the form of textual exposition. The exegete can take possession of the text as a discursive totality in the way that the *rhetor* (or orator) can grasp the case as a circumstantial totality (the summation of attributes of the person and the act). Exegetical practice treats the text, not as a universal principle, but as an action situated in particular historical circumstances. In the Remigian prologue, the topical system of the *circumstantiae* functions as a kind of hermeneutical application: it allows the exegete to "invent" arguments about the text – or "action" – which are appropriate to new conditions of interpretation or reception, just as the orator invents a speech that is suited to the particular conditions of time, place, and audience.

We have, then, a kind of equation between historical rhetoric and a theory of hermeneutics. But in the circumstantial *accessus* we seem to have an intriguingly literal form of this equation. Let us now turn to a particular textual case from Remigius' own exegetical practice. Remigius' *accessus* to Martianus Capella's *De nuptiis Philologiae et Mercurii*, together with his commentary on it, exemplifies the way in which medieval hermeneutics appropriates the methods of rhetoric. The prologue offers a comprehensive model of the circumstantial formula:

Primo est transeundum per septem periochas, id est circumstantias, quae constant in initio cuiusque libri authentici . . .: quis quid cur quomodo ubi quando unde. Ergo ad illud quod interrogatur . . . quis, respondetur . . . persona auctoris, ut quis scripsit? Martianus. Secunda periocha est . . . quid. Ad quam interrogationem redditur . . . res, quae titulo ipsius operis declaratur. Scripsit enim de nuptiis Philologiae et Mercurii. Tertia periocha est . . . cur. Respondetur ei . . . causa quare de nuptiis Philologiae et Mercurii scripserit, videlicet quia volebat disputare de septem liberalibus artibus. Quarta periocha est . . . quomodo, ad quod redditur . . . modus. Modi autem locutionum aut prosaice aut metrice fiunt, quod utrumque iste in hoc executus est opere. Quinta periocha est . . . ubi. Respondetur ei . . . locus, ut ubi scripsit? Carthagini. Sexta periocha est . . . quando. Ad quam interrogationem respondetur . . . tempus, quod posteris indagandum reliquit et hactenus manet incertum. Septima periocha est . . . unde, ad quod respondetur . . . materies, ut unde scripsit? De nuptiis videlicet Philologiae et Mercurii et de VII liberalibus artibus.[22]

[First to be considered are the seven summaries, that is circumstances, which are established at the beginning of every authentic book: who, what, why, in what manner, where, when, by what faculties. Thus the question who refers to the person of the author: who wrote it? Martianus. The second summary is what, which refers to the matter at hand, which is announced by the title of the work itself. Martianus thus wrote of the marriage of Philology and Mercury. The third summary is why, which refers to the cause: why did he write about the marriage of Philology and Mercury? Clearly because he wanted to examine the seven liberal arts. The fourth summary is in what manner, which refers to the method. Literary discourses are created through the modes of either verse or prose: Martianus has used both in this work. The fifth summary is where, which refers to the place: where was it written? In Carthage. The sixth summary is when, which refers to the time at which it was written; this the author has left to be investigated by future generations and to this day the answer remains uncertain. The seventh summary is by what means, which refers to the materials used: by what means did he write it? Clearly by means of the marriage of Philology and Mercury and of the seven liberal arts.]

We know from internal evidence that Remigius would have associated the seven circumstances with the formulation of the *narratio* and with artificial proof *ante rem*, for he comments on Martianus' treatment of this scheme.[23] Martianus had relied for his information on no less an authority than Fortunatianus. Remigius simplifies Martianus by equating the sources of argument *ante rem* (i.e., the *circumstantiae*) with the elements of the *narratio* itself.[24] His own prologue to the commentary may be seen, according to such terms, as the skeletal construction of a *narratio*, or even as the formulation of a proof *ante rem*, in this case quite literally before the thing itself, the text and commentary. The *accessus ad auctorem*, as its name declares, is an introduction to the author; but we might say that its subtext is almost always an *accessus ad commentatorem*, an introduction to the interpretive strategies and interests of the exegete who takes possession of the text of the *auctor*. The *accessus*, with its rhetorical overtones, pre-empts authorial intentionality to lay the ground for exegetical intention. In Remigius' prologue to Martianus, this subtext of hermeneutical appropriation is implied in the answers to *cur* and *unde*, and in the exegetical argument that these topics produce.

In Boethius' account of the circumstances (which draws upon *De inventione* 1.26.37), *cur* and *quid* are connected with the performing of the action. *Unde* is one of the circumstances which are coherent with the performing of the action. In Remigius' prologue to Martianus, *cur* and *unde*, the cause of the action and the means of performing it, are essentially the same: Martianus wished to explain the seven liberal arts, and he achieved this by writing about the marriage of Mercury and Philology and the seven liberal arts. Cause and means are also identical with the action itself: the answer to *quid*, "id est res," is announced in the title of the work, *De nuptiis Philologiae et Mercurii*. We find a similar identification of cause and means in the Remigian prologue to the *Carmen Paschale* of Sedulius (quoted above), which presents the cause of the text as Sedulius' wish to produce a metrical work about the Incarnation, and identifies the means of achieving this purpose as the techniques that Sedulius borrowed from the poets whom he imitated ("Quibus facultatibus vel unde? De facultatibus eorum, quos imitatus est"). But such an identification of cause and means is not routine in this form of the *accessus*. In a Remigian commentary on the *Disticha Catonis*, for example, the instrumental question, here *quibus auxiliis*, is answered by a reference to historical context and the support of patrons.[25] A Remigian *accessus* to the *Aeneid* also distinguishes between cause, to praise Augustus, and means (here *materies*), which is identified as the plot or story line itself, the destruction of Troy, the wanderings of Aeneas, and his arrival in Italy.[26]

In Remigius' prologue to Martianus, the identification of the action performed (*res* or *quid*) with the cause and means of performing the action suggests a broad theoretical intention that the commentator shares with the *auctor*: to advance a theory of knowledge by teaching the individual disciplines which comprise knowledge. The *causa* of the text is to explain the fields of study. But as its unfolding in both Martianus' text and Remigius' commentary suggests, this *causa* or intention is not simply to set forth a body of given information about each of the liberal arts. The purpose for both Martianus and Remigius is to theorize the divisions of the arts, to define the system which can contain and balance the various disciplines. Thus they teach the individual disciplines and teach the theoretical system that divides knowledge into disciplines. Such a metadisciplinary interest accounts for the identification between *res*, *causa*, and *facultates* (*materies*). The purpose of the text or act is to expound a theory of knowledge: the text performs such an exposition by exemplifying and explaining the individual fields. This purpose, like its rhetorical counterpart (the *causa* or *cur* of Boethius) is external to (or connected with) the actual performance of the action, but it is realized in the very performance of the theorizing (*materies*) itself. As a connected function, cause here is virtually indistinguishable from the coherent function, means: both have a metadisciplinary application.

The *accessus* presents the commentator's picture of Martianus' purpose and achievements. But it also represents the commentator's purpose and product. Remigius' exegetical purpose is not just to expound the text but to theorize anew the system of the liberal arts. Such theorizing is constitutive of the commentator's text, not external to it; thus the means or material through which this purpose is realized are identical with the material of the commentary itself. In expounding the disciplinary contours of Martianus' system, Remigius advances his own conception of the arts, their intrinsic characters and extrinsic relationships. Remigius' conception of the arts serves to situate Martianus' text in a disciplinary context redefined according to the historical circumstances of interpretation, according to the historicity of the interpreter. We can see here how the role of the grammarian-exegete has expanded from simply exposition of fixed information to deliberation about the variable. Such metadisciplinary theorizing dramatizes the way in which medieval interpretation has assumed the rhetorical power of application.

Remigius uses Martianus' text to reclassify the seven liberal arts.[27] Early medieval encyclopaedists (Cassiodorus, Isidore, Alcuin, Rabanus Maurus) did not seek a comprehensive philosophical system for classifying knowledge; philosophy itself became simply a division of dialectic, and the liberal arts became propaedeutic to theology. The arts themselves served as a convenient scheme of knowledge.[28] But Remigius was heir, through Heiric of Auxerre (fl. 865), to the teachings of Eriugena, whose philosophical scheme for the branches of knowledge represented a radical departure from the thinking of earlier medieval expositors of the arts.[29] Remigius does not carry over the hybrid system that Eriugena presented in the *De divisione naturae*, in which philosophy is subdivided into logical, practical, natural, and theological knowledge.[30] Instead, Remigius returns to the traditional Hellenistic division of philosophy into physics, ethics, and logic, a system used by earlier encyclopaedists, notably Isidore of Seville.[31] But Remigius does retain Eriugena's notion that the arts are immanent in the soul, and he relies heavily on Eriugena's own commentary on Martianus, where this theme of the immanence of the arts finds expression. For the materials that he uses to develop this conceptual framework he also borrows from the "Dunchad" commentary on Martianus (now recognized as probably the work of Martin of Laon). Remigius clearly seeks to justify and rationalize the liberal arts in a way that was not urgent to Martianus working in late antiquity. For Remigius' educational context, the conditions of interpretation have been formed by the intellectual concerns of his predecessors. His efforts at conceptual reassessment often take the form of digressions from Martianus' text, and the work of his exegetical predecessors serves as the *materies* through which he realizes his own interpretive argument. Thus he uses earlier commentaries to actualize the text for present readers; and the meaning he discovers in those commentaries informs his own metadisciplinary approach to Martianus' text.

This process by which the interpretive performances of his predecessors become Remigius' own interpretive purpose (*causa*) as well as his means (*materies*) for executing that purpose can best be seen in some of the digressive explanations that he introduces in the chapter on dialectic. In the explanation of the term *accidens* (*De nuptiis* §347), one of the five terms or predicables of dialectic, he appropriates – through quotation and paraphrase – the *enarrationes* of the "Dunchad" and of Eriugena on this point. The passage quoted from the "Dunchad" begins by explaining *accidens*:

Accidens est quod substantiae accidit et substantiam deserit. Si ergo accidit, unde venit? Vel quo pergit postquam deserit? Quidam sic intelligunt: Quando venit non aliunde venit nec ad aliquid redit redeundo.[32]

[Accident is that which occurs in a substance and deserts a substance. If it thus occurs, whence does it come? To where does it proceed after it disappears? Certain people understand it thus: when it comes it does not come from elsewhere nor, in returning, does it return to something.]

But by way of the example of rhetoric as an *ars* that may or may not occur among men, the "Dunchad" commentary introduces a larger argument about the immanence of the arts, which Remigius closely paraphrases:

Igitur necesse est ut aliter atque melius intelligamus. Omnis igitur naturalis ars in humana natura posita et concreata est. Inde fit ut omnes homines naturaliter habeant naturales artes, sed quia poena primi hominis in animabus hominum obscurantur et in quandam profundam ignorantiam devolvuntur, nihil aliud agimus discendo nisi easdem artes quae in profundo memoriae repositae sunt in praesentiam intelligentiae revocamus, et cum aliis occupamur curis nihil aliud agimus artes negligendo nisi ipsas artes iterum dimittimus ut redeant ad id unde evocatae sunt.[33]

[Therefore we should understand this in a different and better way. Every natural art is placed in and created with human nature. Whence it happens that all men naturally possess natural arts. But because of the sin of the first man [the arts] are obscured in the minds of men and are sunk in a certain profound ignorance: so that in learning we do nothing more than recall into the presence of understanding those arts that are stored in the depth of memory; and when we are occupied with other cares we do nothing else in neglecting the arts than send them away so that they return to there from whence they were called forth.]

The commentary has diverted the *materies* of the text to the service of a new interpretive *causa*, as the discussion of a term within the discipline of dialectic becomes the grounds for a metadisciplinary argument. Eriugena's *Annotationes in Martianum* also provides an account of the immanence of the arts at this point in Martianus' text, and Remigius supplements his borrowing from the "Dunchad" by reworking Eriugena's *enarratio*:

Philosophi dicunt omnibus hominibus accidere disciplinas. Quod si ita est, ergo omnis homo rhetor vel dialecticus. Videmus tamen complures expertes esse rhetoricae et aliarum disciplinarum. Unde ergo verum est quod omni homini rhetorica accidat? Sed aliud est quod accidit secundum naturam, aliud quod secundum exercitium et experientiam. Ergo secundum naturam omni homini accidit disciplina, solis vero philosophis secundum exercitium et disciplinam.[34]

[The philosophers say that the disciplines (arts) occur in all men. But if this is so, then every man is a rhetor or a dialectician. However we see that many are devoid of rhetoric and other disciplines. Whence, therefore, is it true that rhetoric occurs in every man? In fact, there is one form of rhetoric that occurs through nature, and another kind that occurs through exercise and experience. Therefore an art occurs naturally in every man, but only by exercise and discipline in philosophers.]

We find similar moves elsewhere, especially in the chapter on dialectic: Remigius will incorporate – or more loosely apply – a reading from his sources which raises the discussion to a metadisciplinary level.[35] These appropriative moves assume a special importance in view of the way that throughout his commentary Remigius seeks to create a unifying "philosophy" of the arts. He achieves this conceptual order by consistently reallegorizing Martianus' text to accord with a notion of *philosophia* – that is, all the liberal arts – as *veritatis intelligentia* (287.23). Thus the goddess Philosophia "significat omnes artes" (287.23). In book 1, Athena's seven-rayed crown becomes a figure for the seven liberal arts:

Per CORONAM SEPTEM RADIORUM perfecta scientia septem artium designatur, quae idcirco liberales dicuntur quia liberaliter fruge veritatis animam pascunt, vel quod liberam et expeditam mentem a tumultibus saeculi requirant. Dicuntur etiam et perceptae eo quod propter se ipsas non propter aliud appetendae et percipiendae sunt.[36]

[By the seven-rayed crown perfect knowledge of the seven liberal arts is signified. These are called liberal because they liberally nourish the mind with the fruit of truth, or because they seek a mind that is free from and unencumbered by the commotions of the world. Likewise they are so called and known because they are desired and gathered in for their very own sake and not for the sake of something else.]

By appropriating the *materies* of previous commentators Remigius accomplishes his own conceptual restructing. This restructuring, however, serves to displace Martianus' text itself, a process of displacement already at work in the "Dunchad" and Eriugena commentaries. While Remigius' commentary contains and illuminates the primary text and the meanings built into that text by previous commentators, it also achieves a significant form of difference with that text.

The fact that in one of its forms the *accessus ad auctores* borrows an inventional structure is suggestive of how, in general, exegesis associates itself with rhetoric and how, in its own workings, it replicates some of the moves of rhetoric. We see how Remigius invents Martianus' text anew out of exegetical intermediaries and thereby displaces that text even as he proposes to illuminate its discursive coherence. He discloses the workings of the *De nuptiis* by disclosing a new rationale or *causa* for that text, a *causa* that derives from the circumstances of Carolingian reception of late classical learning.

This process in which the commentary reinvents the text through difference with it, proposing a counter-text even as it works through the given text, is significantly akin to the Roman idea of translation as displacement and substitution. The medieval exegete seems to achieve, in practice, a kind of metaphoric or substitutive relationship to the primary text; it is in similarly metaphoric terms that the process of translation is theorized in Roman rhetorical contexts. Roman translation theory offers explicit information about its substitutive and contestative aims; in contrast, medieval exegetical practice offers no such explicit theory of its own motives. But the substitutive force of exegesis is dramatized in such structures as the circumstantial *accessus*, where the argument of the commentary displaces that of the text. The agenda of aggressive political rivalry that underlies the Roman idea of translation as substitution has been transformed, in the medieval exegetical context, into an agenda of cultural recuperation: but this transformed motive nevertheless manifests itself as textual appropriation, which is also the objective of Roman translation.

Remigius' work thus supplies a paradigm for the ways in which medieval exegesis assimilates rhetorical motives and commentary assumes the dimensions of an independent productive act. In other exegetical frameworks where the rhetorical motive does not manifest itself so visibly, its force can nevertheless be recognized. In a sense, such rhetorical information is encoded in exegetical structures, so that the rhetorical motive manifests itself through procedure if not explicitly in format. There is, of course, historical evidence that medieval exegetes recognized a certain continuity between the circumstantial *accessus* and later forms of the *accessus* that superseded it. Several commentators from the eleventh and twelfth centuries remarked on the difference between the *antiqui*, who deemed it necessary to cover the seven circumstances when introducing a text, and the *moderni*, who investigate fewer and somewhat different topics.[37] Some later forms of the *accessus* from the eleventh century onwards preserve vestiges of the circumstantial format.[38] At the beginning of the twelfth century, a shortened form of the circumstantial *accessus* was still in use, especially by Hugh of St. Victor, who used the short scheme *persona*, *locus*, *tempus* as the basis of a prologue to a historical source-book for students.[39] Thus even in mechanical terms the newer exegetical structures bear the imprint of the earlier rhetorical form. But the rhetorical impress is clearest in the action that such exegesis takes upon texts.

One of the most important rhetorical actions that exegesis performs upon the text is to "rewrite" it according to the significance that the interpreter discovers for the text. In the Remigian prologue the significance of the text is determined with the answer to *cur* or *causa*, which is understood largely in terms of the author's *intentio*. In later exegetical structures, the positing of the author's *intentio* is often equivalent to a statement of the work's significance.[40] This discovery of significance in authorial *intentio* invites a revaluation of the work's structure according to the meaning that the interpreter has posited. In effect this represents a progression through rhetorical categories: from *inventio*, or the determination of the text's issues and their significance, to *dispositio*, the determination of how meaning provides the work with its structural coherence. At one level, these rhetorical strategies have been converted to descriptive terms, for the exegete claims only to expound the given, not to produce meaning and structure. But at another level these strategies retain their prescriptive force, as the structural coherence which the exegete discerns in the text is only made possible – and visible – by the significance posited. To construct authorial *intentio* out of the circumstances of the text is to rehearse the process of invention out of the circumstances of the case.

This process of discovering structure in intention or cause is exemplified in a twelfth-century *accessus* to Ovid's *Heroides*.[41] This uses the prologue form which was standard for the twelfth century, what R.W. Hunt has called the "type C" prologue: *vita poetae*, *titulus operis*, *intentio scribentis*, *materia*, *modus agendi* (or *modus tractandi*), *utilitas*, and *cui parti philosophiae supponitur* (life of the poet, title of the work, intention of the writer, style or mode of procedure, utility, and the part of knowledge to which the work belongs).[42] The topic *intentio scribentis* corresponds in function with the topic *cur* or *causa* of the earlier circumstantial *accessus*, although the actual ancestry of this twelfth-century prologue form lies, not in rhetorical, but in ancient philosophical terminology.[43] The prologue offers a range of related *intentiones scribentis*: to exemplify foolish, unchaste, and mad love; to commend chaste and to censure unchaste love; to accomplish here through the epistles what Ovid had neglected in the "precepts" of the *Ars amatoria*, that is, to show how one's passions may be stirred up through letters, to exhort to virtue and to discourage vice; and to respond to accusations that his writings had taught illicit love, so that here he propounds by example the kinds of love that Roman matrons should imitate, and the kinds they should reject. With all of these intentions in view, the book has two controlling intentions, one general and one specific. Its general intention is to delight and to work for the common profit; its specific intention, as manifested in the individual epistles, is to praise chaste and to censure unchaste love. In so far as there are various epistles there are various intentions: some mean to commend chastity and others mean to censure unchastity. This catalogue of the *intentiones speciales* announces the thematic diversity of the work. But it also provides a unifying structure for the text, that of its general moral significance. The problem of determining the structural coherence of a heterogeneous collection like the *Heroides* can be resolved by reading that heterogeneity as the specific manifestations of a general moral intention.[44] This program of reading which refigures structural coherence by disclosing intention or significance may be seen in rhetorical terms as progressing from invention (*inventio scribentis* performs the same function as the inventional topic *cur* or *causa*) to the actualizing of that argument in a coherent discursive structure (*dispositio*). The text can be "rewritten" as formally unified because its meaning or cause has been discovered.

Commentaries on the *Distichs of Cato* and on Geoffrey of Vinsauf's *Poetria nova* also exemplify the process by which the exegete's discussion of significance or *intentio* can disclose and thus impose structure. A Remigian prologue to the *Distichs of Cato* from an eleventh-century manuscript uses three *accessus* forms: a shortened circumstantial scheme (*persona*, *locus*, *tempus*, *causa scribendi*); the full scheme of the seven circumstances ("apud antecessores"); and a shortened "new" scheme ("apud modernos"), consisting of the poet's life, the title of the work, and the part of philosophy to which it belongs.[45] Under the second scheme, the answer to *cur* is given as "quaeritur an ad ipsius verterit utilitatem an ad omnium fecerit correctionem" (he seeks to turn himself to good or to bring about the improvement of all). In the section explaining the "modern" prologue, the commentary introduces an *intentio auctoris*: "reprehendere mores hominum qui tunc temporis credebant se posse per inanem gloriam pervenire ad veram beatitudinem" (to censure the ways of men who at that time believed they could arrive at true happiness through empty glory). From *causa* to *intentio scribentis*, the moral significance of the work remains the same.

But the *Distichs of Cato* presented a structural problem similar to that presented by the *Heroides*: both texts presented a collection of materials (a collection of *sententiae* or of verse epistles) whose immanent principle of structure had to be disclosed and articulated. Neither text offered an obvious system of arrangement. But in the case of the *Distichs of Cato* the moral *intentio* suggested a precise structural principle, that of the four cardinal virtues, justice, prudence, fortitude, and temperance.[46] The obvious division of the *Distichs* into four books justified this disclosure of its immanent structural rationale, so that each book treats a different virtue. This application of the four virtues to the four books of the *Distichs* is a commonplace of Cato commentaries in manuscripts of the thirteenth and fourteenth centuries.[47] The Stoic doctrine of the four virtues was a standard frame of reference for medieval ethical teaching; one of its important contexts for transmission to the Middle Ages was Ciceronian rhetorical theory. *De inventione* 2.53.159–65 gives an analysis of the virtues in relation to deliberative oratory, to define the moral framework and objectives of this type of speech, although as part of the principle of honor the system of the virtues is applicable to all the branches of rhetoric.[48] Victorinus and Alcuin carry forward the idea of the virtues as part of the moral structure of rhetoric, each in his own fashion equating the virtues with the wisdom which is the necessary counterpart of eloquence.[49] This ethical framework, associated by tradition with the moral grounds of rhetoric, is applied to the *Distichs of Cato* as the moral grounds for the arrangement of the text. Here the commentator's move from discovery of meaning to determination of structure, from *inventio* to *dispositio*, is accomplished through the application of a moral framework that is itself part of the tradition of rhetorical discourse.

A thirteenth-century commentary on the *Poetria nova* also exemplifies how the system of rhetoric is inscribed within the system of hermeneutics. The *accessus* defines the subject and significance of the book ("artificiosa eloquentia") through a definition of the book's structure. The book's structure represents its subject, for its parts are the five parts of rhetoric:

Materia autem huius libri est artificiosa eloquentia, scilicet rethorica, secundum quam docet poetas metrice [loqui]. Unde ex quinque partibus [eius] constat principaliter; sunt enim quinque partes rethorice que eam integraliter constituerunt, ita ut si desit una pars, rethorica non possit esse integra, sicut nec domus potest esse integra si desit fundamentum uel paries uel tectum. Sunt autem iste: inuentio, dispositio, elocutio, memoria, et pronunciatio . . .

[The subject of this book is artful eloquence, namely rhetoric, according to which art the book teaches poets to speak metrically. Whence the book principally consists of the five parts of rhetoric; the five parts of rhetoric constitute the whole in such a way that if one part is missing, rhetoric cannot be complete, just as a house cannot be complete if the foundation or the walls or the roof be missing. These are the parts: Invention, Arrangement, Style, Memory, and Delivery . . .][50]

This identification of significance with structure is a felicity of the particular metacritical character of this commentary: in expounding a rhetorical treatise, the commentary demonstrates the theoretical precepts that it proposes to explain. It actualizes these precepts as strategies of interpretation. According to the *accessus*, Geoffrey of Vinsauf writes both *de arte* and *ex arte*. He offers precepts while actually demonstrating them: he is both a rhetorician (teacher of rhetoric) and an orator.[51] But the commentator's strategy of discovery and organization derives from his positing of authorial *intentio* at the end of the *accessus*:

Intentio eius est ut instrvat lectorem quod sciat loqui rethorice, siue in metro siue in prosa, vt ibi hec nota tam prose seruit quam metro. Agit autem non solum de hac arte secundum quod in noticia habetur sed secundum quod in usu inuenitur.

[Its purpose is to teach the reader what he should know of speaking rhetorically, whether in verse or in prose, so that what is noted there serves prose as well as verse. Moreover, he writes about this art not only as it is held theoretically, but according to what is found in practice.][52]

The conjunction between theory and practice here would seem to refer to the preceding discussion of writing *de arte* and *ex arte*, as it also suggests the valuable illustrations of precepts throughout the *Poetria nova*. This *intentio* indicates how the commentator can discover a unifying structural principle in the significance of the text: if the intention of the book is to present both theory and application, then its purpose is embodied in its formal arrangement. The form of the book is its *materia*, the five parts of rhetoric. But the self-reflexiveness of the *Poetria nova* is mirrored in the strategy of the commentary, which also, in a way, speaks *de arte* by speaking *ex arte*. In exounding the *materia* and *intentio* of the text, the commentator writes about the art; but through this exposition he discovers the meaning of, and imposes a coherent structure on, the text. In so rehearsing the move from invention to disposition (discovery of argument and determination of structure) the commentary itself works *ex arte*, exemplifying through hermeneutical action the principles of rhetorical action.

Nowhere, however, does exegesis make a stronger claim to rhetorical control, to the power of *inventio* and *dispositio*, than in allegoresis of the ancient poets. Allegoresis submits the text to a thorough process of resignification, from the author's intention to his structural arrangement and stylistic procedure to particular verbal usage. The commentary on the *Aeneid* attributed to Bernardus Silvestris exemplifies the way in which hermeneutics can appropriate some of rhetoric's most sacred maneuvers.[53] The prologue establishes the argumentative grounds of the commentary by distinguishing between the philosophical import of the work and Virgil's poetic fictions: "et veritatem philosophie docuit et ficmentum poeticum non pretermisit" ([Virgil] taught the truth of philosophy and did not neglect poetic fiction).[54] The prologue then takes up some of the terms associated with earlier *accessus* forms:

Si quis ergo Eneida legere studeat, ita ut eius voluminis lex deposcit, hec in primis oportet demonstrare, unde agat et qualiter et cur, et geminam observationem in his demostrandis [*sic*] non relinquere.[55]

[Therefore, if anyone should desire to read the *Aeneid* according to the terms that this text requires, he must first show the means by which Virgil writes, the manner in which he writes, and why, and in showing these things he must not neglect the double aspect of the text {as both philosophy and poetry}.]

The terms *unde*, *qualiter*, and *cur* are later equated with the topics *intentio*, *modus agendi*, and *utilitas*. These terms are then applied to the narrative. In considering the *modus agendi* of the narrative fiction, the commentator observes that Virgil uses the artificial order, beginning his narration *a medio*. But having covered the *figmentum poeticum*, the prologue returns to take up the other half of the *gemina doctrina* posited for the work, the philosophical teaching:

Nunc vero hec eadem circa philosophicam veritatem videamus. Scribit ergo in quantum est philosophus humane vite naturam. Modus agendi talis est: in integumento describit quid agat vel quid paciatur humanus spiritus in humano corpore temporaliter positus. Atque in hoc describendo naturali utitur ordine atque ita utrumque ordinem narrationis observat, artificialem poeta, naturalem philosophus.
Integumentum est genus demostrationis [*sic*] sub fabulosa narratione veritatis involvens intellectum, unde etiam dicitur involucrum.[56]

[Now let us consider these matters in terms of the philosophical truth. In as much as he writes about the nature of human life, Virgil is a philosopher. This is his procedure: under an integument he describes what the human soul does and endures while it is

placed, for a time, in a human body. In depicting this he uses the natural order. In this way he follows either order of narration: as a poet he follows the artificial order, as a philosopher he follows the natural order.
An integument is a kind of exposition that wraps the understanding of truth under a poetic fiction, whence it is also called a "veil."]

By reading the narrative as an *integumentum*, as a "veil" or "wrapping" for a philosophical truth, the interpreter supplies an ulterior structure of meaning which can be exposed or discovered through a rehearsal of all the narrative particulars.[57]

But this act of supplying an ulterior structure is not equivalent to imposing a value from a position outside the text: it is for this reason that Rosemond Tuve's influential formulation "imposed allegory" is inadequate to describe the workings of allegoresis. To read the text as allegorical (which is what allegoresis does) is to propose a structure of reference which is presented as anterior to the text and from which the text is seen to emerge as if organically. While allegoresis figures itself – even modestly – as disclosure, it in fact operates as a deep recausing of the text as if from within the text. In supplying an anterior structure of reference the allegoresis radically changes the status of the text. The commentary inserts itself as the originary point of the text by exposing and rehearsing the ulterior aspect of the *intentio scribentis* ("et veritatem philosophie docuit"). But such exegesis does not discard the given text once its truths have been delivered up. Instead it invests the given text with a new tropological significance (as integument) and with a new structural rationale which makes the *modus agendi* the result of the exegete's own disclosive readings. The commentary on the *Aeneid* works systematically through the text, recasting the fiction according to the dictates of the text's own *modus agendi*. As the prologue indicates, the allegoresis proposes to save the text by a kind of pre-emptive move, by substituting itself as the dynamic intentionality or cause which acts, not on the text, but through it. The commentary attributed to Bernardus, like its predecessor by Fulgentius, allegorizes the *Aeneid* in terms of the human pilgrimage from birth to adulthood, from ignorance and errant passion to learning, wisdom, and virtue. The commentary establishes this moral architectonics by working within the *modus agendi* and *ordo* of the text, reading the artificial order of the given narrative, the *integumentum*, as the natural order of its "proper" meaning or reference. The very mechanics of composition have become part of the allegorical composition. The commentator inserts himself into the very *dispositio* of the text, not changing the order, but claiming that order as the result of his own correct, disclosive reading. By inserting itself this way into the *modus agendi* and producing a reading that complies with the alternate view of the text as observing natural order for its philosophical *déroulement*, Bernardus' allegoresis effectively claims for itself a role not only in the correct reading of texts, but in the correct production of texts.

Thus in its move to validate the text within the terms of the text's own formal system, allegoresis proposes itself as co-extensive with the text, as the realization, at the level of the text's "proper" (as opposed to "figurative") reference, of authorial intentionality. The point at which the exegete lays out the grounds of the text – the *unde*, *qualiter*, and *cur* – is the point at which he assumes a productive role in the formation of the text, generating its *intentio*, its *modus agendi*, and *utilitas*. The moves that we find in Bernardus' commentary have parallels in the work of other allegorizing exegetes. For example, William of Conches' prologue to his allegorizing commentary on the *Timaeus* distinguishes between reading Plato's text according to the letter (a gloss) and according to the sense (an exposition); and in his actual *accessus* to the text he provides a corrective "sense" exposition of the philosophical and scientific import of the *Timaeus* in terms of its cause or intention, its *modus agendi*, and its utility. The *modus agendi* of the text is to be understood as its disclosure of the efficient, formal, final, and material cause of the world. In this way the exegete discloses a comprehensive philosophical scheme through the formal constitution of the text.[58]

The *accessus* to the *Aeneid* commentary attributed to Bernardus offers another interesting emblem of the exegete's appropriation of affective control, of the historical and theoretical alliance of commentary with the office of rhetoric. The *accessus* contains a very odd turn. In the process of outlining the points about authorial responsibility to be covered in a prologue, the commentator applies the threefold scheme of *intentio*, *modus agendi*, and *causa* to the prologue itself:

Quoniam proemii officium in comparanda lectoris vel auditoris benevolentia, docilitate, attentione totum consistit, relictis septem que a pluribus in principiis librorum queruntur, hec tria nos considerasse sufficiat: scilicet unde agat actor ut docilis reddatur lector; qualiter ut benivolus; cur ut attentus.[59]

[Given that the duty of an introduction consists entirely in obtaining the reader's or listener's benevolence, willingness for instruction, and attention, we have not mentioned the seven items which are considered by many writers in the introductions of books. We have found it sufficient to treat these three items: by what means {whence} the author works, so that the reader may be rendered teachable; the author's style, which renders the reader benevolent; and the author's purpose, which renders the reader attentive.]

This curious slippage (in the first sentence) seems to make the commentator (the writer of the *accessus* and commentary) almost indistinguishable from the author (Virgil). In other words, prologues normally show how the *author* gains the benevolence and attention of his readers; but this prologue discusses *its own* duties, as a *prologue*, to achieve this readerly attention. This move – or slippage – seems to reassign the intentionality of the primary text to the commentary. By conflating the commentator's affective intentions with those of the author, it positions exegesis within a rhetorical frame. The *accessus ad auctorem* has become an *accessus ad commentatorem*.

Medieval *enarratio* or hermeneutics has assumed the power of rhetoric to grasp discourse as action, as totality, and to reunite the signifier with the newly signified. Hermeneutics, as we have seen, does not simply address and describe the terms of discourse or argument: it masters and applies these terms, rearguing the text by appropriating the prescriptive strategies of rhetoric. I have considered this in terms of the principles of cause or intention, and structure, which correspond roughly to the categories of invention and disposition. I have suggested that the effect of these rhetorical operations of exegesis corresponds closely with the object of translation proposed in Roman rhetorical writings, that is, the displacement of the original text and the investment of the new text with an originary authority.

But medieval commentaries achieve possibly the most forceful difference with texts through their most basic and characteristic practice: the systematic paraphrase of texts. Paraphrasing can encompass a range of practices, from glossing the individual word to reformulating sentences or larger blocks of text, to previewing or recapitulating whole sections or episodes by means of summaries. For the most part, paraphrase works by combining these practices, so that glossing of a single word will lead to rephrasing and explanation of a whole passage. Systematic paraphrase is the lowest common denominator of medieval exegesis; it is the most familiar, the most routine element of medieval commentary traditions, so much so that its basic character changes little from period to period, from late antiquity onwards. Its broad familiarity makes paraphrase the most difficult and least rewarding feature of medieval exegetical techniques to exemplify at large, that is, without reference to the fortunes of a particular text or problem at the hands of a series of commentators. For this reason I reserve most discussions of paraphrase for studies of vernacular translations in the next two chapters.

But some of the issues associated with exegetical paraphrase merit our attention here. Paraphrase is the most obvious feature of *enarratio* in classical and medieval practice; its pedagogical value is also self-evident. Perhaps for these reasons its hermeneutical status is less understood or recognized. It is through the mechanics of paraphrase that the text truly becomes the property of the commentary. Sometimes lemmata are absorbed into the text of the commentary in integral blocks. But just as often the lemma is broken up and redistributed through the exposition, so that the very word order of the lemma is recast within the syntactic and expository structure of the commentary. In this way marginal commentary achieves the same effect as interlinear gloss: it introduces itself into the text by breaking the text down into lemmata, which it surrounds and appropriates by quotation and restatement. Through paraphrase the commentary becomes container of, no longer supplement to, the original text, at least in terms of graphic, formal disposition.[60]

The point of recasting word order is often to loosen compressed syntax, to supply causal connections, to force hidden layers of signification to the surface and play them out there in a kind of illuminated foreground. The effect is to lay hold of what Gerald Bruns has called "indeterminate areas," to fix them by claiming verbal possession of them.[61] Gadamer has spoken of the ambiguities, the "open indeterminacy" by which the work of art, like myth, "is able to produce constant new invention from within itself." Its essence, like that of a game played, is its temporality, its "continually becoming a new event"; it achieves this through its very openness or "productive ambiguity."[62] Bruns has remarked on the value of Gadamer's formulation for our understanding of the framework within which the medieval exegete acts upon authoritative texts. For Bruns the grammarian's interventions – or "embellishments" – in the indeterminate areas of the text represent a form of rhetorical invention, "invention conceived as the art of finding what it is that can be said in any given case."[63] But this application of Gadamer's textual hermeneutics to the rhetoricity of medieval exegesis can be taken further and refined. What Bruns has called the medieval exegete's "sanction of embellishment" represents an inventional act only in the broadest sense. Much of the action of embellishment takes place at the level of verbal expression, as forms of paraphase in which the implicit or the ambiguous is rendered linguistically explicit. This seems to represent, not invention itself, but the actualization of invention in discourse, the bringing forward of what has been discovered to the event of discourse. Paraphrase gives verbal expression to that which may be silent in the text but which the interpreter has discovered, and in this its function corresponds with that of *elocutio*. In terms of the rhetorical model of exegesis offered by the circumstantial *accessus*, this attention to verbal expression corresponds to the examination of *qualitas* or *quomodo*. Paraphrase and related forms of linguistic embellishment that intervene in the "indeterminate areas" of the text constitute the stage after invention, the stage of discursive application, the domain of *elocutio*. It is appropriate that the characteristic mode of the grammarian exegete should be *elocutio*: this had been the sphere of competence traditionally associated with grammar since late antiquity, the area that rhetoric had come to neglect. But in the context of exegesis, paraphrase as *elocutio* works towards reuniting the primary parts of rhetoric, that is, invention with structure and style. In this hermeneutical framework, the directive of invention (the discovery of textual *causa*, *intentio*, or *facultas*) is fulfilled through the formal and discursive offices of *dispositio* and *elocutio*. Rather than constituting invention itself, paraphrase or embellishment constitutes what might be called linguistic application, the actual mediation and determination of meaning through language.[64]

The high Middle Ages recognized a difference between gloss and commentary in terms of a difference between the letter and the meaning (*sententia*) of the text.[65] But even explanation of *sententia* involves restatement and must work at the level of verbal expression. In its simplest application paraphrase serves as pedagogical tool: the glossing of unfamiliar words or the recasting of difficult syntax. Yet even so modest a purpose may lead to the most elaborate results, in which the text is encrusted with word-by-word glosses and clarifications. Remigian commentaries on the *Disticha Catonis*, for example, supply explanatory alternatives for nearly every word of the text, so that in effect the commentary verbally rebuilds the text through a close sequence of synonyms.[66]

But the commentary on Virgil attributed to Bernardus Silvestris, the purpose of which is clearly to expound the "meaning" rather than the "letter" of the text, also uses the technique of word-by-word gloss. This is especially the case with the treatment of book 6. At the beginning of this book Bernardus announces that since Virgil makes a more profound statement of philosophical truth here, the commentary will dwell longer on expositions of individual words.[67] The descent to the underworld is read as an allegory of the attainment of wisdom through knowledge of the arts and informed contemplation of human events. Here the commentary edges through the text, supplying words and phrases with a figurative value which can then be translated into their "proper" sense and hence into "direct" speech:

INTER TALIA: extirpationes vitiorum et insertiones virtutum. SOCIOS: philosophantes. ARMIS: Arma quibus hostes impugnantur et socii deffenduntur, sunt tres animi potentie, scilicet irascibilitas, concupiscentia, animositas. ACCINGITUR: Circummunitur. Cum enim circa Eneam hinc bona illinc mala, malis pretendit irascibilitatem, bonis apponit concupiscentiam utrisque animositatem; animositate enim appetit bona et impugnat mala. TRISTI: studioso et sollicito. ASPECTANS: ratione contemplans. PRECATUR: Preces sunt desideria eius. SI: utinam. HEU: Gemit pro morte Miseni quia eum comitatus erat, id est dolet pro debilitate caduce glorie quia eam secutus fuerat (6.183–9).[68]

[INTER TALIA: rooting out vices and putting in virtues. SOCIOS: philosophers. ARMIS: The weapons by which enemies are assailed and comrades are defended are three powers of the soul: irascibility, eagerness, and courage. ACCINGITUR: is secured. For when the good here and the evil there surround Aeneas, he presents irascibility to the evil forces, applies eagerness to the good, and courage to both. For with courage he strives after the good and assails the evil. TRISTI: with zeal and concern. ASPECTANS: contemplating with the reason. PRECATUR: prayers are his desires. SI: if only. HEU: He bewails the death of Misenus because he was his comrade; that is, he grieves for the frailty of fallen glory because he had followed after it.]

The context for this is the interpretation of the descent of Aeneas as a descent to the underworld through virtue, in which the wise man contemplates (descends to) worldly things so as to know their frailty and vanity, and thereby to reject them. Misenus has been interpreted (at line 149) as Greek for "fallen praise," or worldly glory, which Aeneas, representing the soul led by virtue and reason, must renounce or bury. Thus the felling of trees in the forest for the funeral pyre of Misenus is interpreted as the work of rational contemplation, uprooting vices and planting virtues. In mechanical terms this paraphrase is comparable to what we find in the more pedantic Remigian commentaries, for in similar fashion the Bernardus commentary rebuilds the text word by word. But it is also a reading that produces the tropes that it explicates, refiguring the text almost word by word. This linguistic application to the text, a form of attention to the *quomodo* of the text, works as a radical displacement of the text: the paraphrase itself takes on the originary authority of "proper" speech, of the meaning or truth that was concealed by the *integumentum* and was thus anterior to it. Here the paraphrase represents itself not as an alternative to the text, but as necessary to producing or completing the text.[69]

The purpose of this chapter has been to exemplify some of the ways in which medieval commentary assumes the character of rhetorical performance. We have seen how exegesis appropriates many of the tools and textual strategies of rhetoric. As an empowered critical practice it serves what was once rhetoric's function, the active production of discourse. In a sense, rhetoric recovers its force in medieval *enarratio*: it is exegesis that now activates the rhetorical principle of *kairos*, applying itself to changing circumstances of discourse. I have tried to demonstrate here how commentary can be read for its own textuality, for what it says about its own discursive action, rather than only for the kinds of readings it produces of other texts. In other words, I have tried to foreground the form and function of medieval interpretive acts, to consider the interpretive performance itself rather than the interpretation that the commentary produces. These are important distinctions to make, for as we will see in the next two chapters, vernacular translation of the curricular *auctores* emerges by identifying itself, not with "literary" performance, but with exegetical performance, with the discourse of academic culture. It is thus important to understand how that discourse represents itself: and as I have argued here, exegesis operates under the imprint of rhetoric. It is on the model of this transformed hermeneutics that medieval translation defines its own character.

4

Translation and interlingual commentary: Notker of St. Gall and the *Ovide moralisé*

In the medieval commentary tradition, *enarratio* assumes a rhetorical power of discursive production. It is not mere repetition and reproduction. Rather, it contests and remakes the primary text; it can take on a kind of originary force of its own, becoming a text to be appropriated by later exegetes, to be grafted on to the primary text, and thus to change the conditions of reception for that text. The most characteristic form of this rhetorical or productive action on the text is paraphrase: exegetical paraphrase consumes or envelops the text and can remake the text on many levels, from style to structure to conceptual orientation.

This defining characteristic of Latin hermeneutical practice carries over into the emergent tradition of vernacular commentary. Vernacular textual exegesis builds upon the model supplied by learned Latin precedent. But in vernacular commentary of the Latin *auctores*, the process of textual paraphrase is also an act of interlingual translation. Thus in some of its most important forms from its earliest history to its later development, vernacular translation maintains strong affinities with established exegetical practice. The association between Latin and vernacular exegesis is very close, and this association has profound implications for our understanding of vernacular translation from the Latin *auctores*. But before we turn to a consideration of vernacular texts, it will be helpful to offer some preliminary observations on the historical relationship between hermeneutics and translation, and to provide a theoretical model for classifying the kinds of translations to be treated here and in later chapters.

INTERPRETATIO AS SPEECH, EXEGESIS, AND TRANSLATION: SOME MODELS FOR VERNACULAR PRACTICE

As is well known, the imbrication of hermeneutics and translation is reflected in the historical links between the words associated with these two activities. The legacy of Aristotle and Philo is a basic meaning of the word *hermeneia* as expression, language, or production of discourse.[1] Philo uses the term *hermeneia* to mean something like "literal expression":

> They read the Holy Scriptures and seek wisdom from their ancestral philosophy by taking it as an allegory, since they think that the words of the literal text [*rhetes*

hermeneias] are symbols of something whose hidden nature is revealed by studying the underlying meaning.[2]

Elsewhere Philo uses *hermeneia* to mean speech as a conveyer of ideas.[3] Rhetoric, in turn, disciplines thoughts or ideas by channeling them into speech, or *hermeneia*.[4] Aristotle's *Peri hermeneias*, of course, investigates *hermeneia* as signification or logical predication, as the relationship of language to idea or thought. Philo's positioning of rhetoric with respect to *hermeneia* or expression suggests that in its earliest usage and meaning, *hermeneia* is the product of rhetoric's midwifery, but is also a primary rather than secondary or ancillary operation of language: indeed, it is rhetoric that serves *hermeneia*, that guides it to material realization.

It is thus an irony of the history of this term that it also comes to represent a supposedly supplementary or secondary kind of discourse, that of exegesis. It seems that early Christian writings tend to impose this meaning on *hermeneia* and its lexical family.[5] This is closely analogous with the more common meaning of the Latin equivalent for this term, *interpretatio*. While in antiquity *interpretatio* could be used to mean "signification," its broader usage was comparable to the modern English "interpretation."[6] It is also ironic that the base meaning of *hermeneia* as expression, the exteriorizing of the internal world of thought, could come to imply various intermediary activities: as exegesis it could mean a negotiation between the given text and its readers, but this could also be extended to the intermediary function of translation, a "going between" or "carrying over" between two languages.[7] This is even more the case in antiquity with the Latin term *interpretatio*: just as common as its meaning of "exegesis" is its meaning as "translation," which of course it shares with the words *conversio* and *translatio*.[8] Indeed, the basic meaning of *interpres* in classical Latin is a negotiator, an agent between two parties.[9] This would perhaps explain why the Latin term *interpretatio*, along with its lexical family, would be less likely to preserve the strict meaning of *hermeneia* as language or expression, and instead would most commonly designate such intermediary functions as explication and translation.

In the Latin Middle Ages, the term *interpretatio* preserves the three meanings it had acquired in antiquity, in much the same proportions of common and restricted usage that it had had in antiquity. Its meaning as signification (discourse) or *elocutio* seems to be attested mainly in the relatively restricted context of studies *de modis significandi* based on Boethius' translation of the *Peri hermeneias* (*De interpretatione*), and his two commentaries on it. Isidore of Seville assigns it this meaning only in the section on dialectic, in a summary of the *Peri hermeneias*:

Omnis enim elocutio conceptae rei mentis interpres est. Hanc Aristoteles, vir in rerum expressione et faciendis sermonibus peritissimus, Perihermeniam nominat, quam interpretationem nos appellamus; scilicet quod res mente conceptas prolatis sermonibus interpretetur per cataphasin et apophasin, id est ad firmationem et negationem.
[*Etymologiae* 2.27.2–3]

[Every expression is an "interpreter" of a concept of a thing in the mind. Aristotle, a man most skilled in expressing issues and in constructing arguments, calls this *{peri}hermeneia*, which we call *interpretatio*. This is because the mental concept of a thing – by means of statements set forth – may "signify" through *cataphasin* and *apophasin*, that is, through affirmation and negation.]

That this meaning of *interpretatio* as signification is found chiefly in the tradition of commentary on the *Organon* can be illustrated by the range of this term in Aquinas' writings. Outside his commentaries on Aristotle, Aquinas often uses *interpretatio*, *interpres*, *interpretor*, etc. in the broader sense of explanation, interpretation, mediation, or translation. But within his commentaries on Aristotle he assigns the meaning speech, expression, or signification to *interpretatio*, as roughly equivalent to *oratio* or *elocutio*. This is particularly the case with his commentary on the *Peri hermeneias*, where these seem to be the exclusive meanings for this term and its related forms.[10]

Interpretatio as a form of "gloss' is suggested in Isidore of Seville. Having defined the term "etymology" and noting that many words in Latin and Greek are obscure, Isidore proceeds to define "gloss": "Glossa Graeca interpretatione linguae sortitur nomen" (1.30.1) ["Gloss" gets its name in Greek from linguistic explanation.][11] Later grammarians found it necessary to refine and expand Isidore's treatment of etymology and gloss. In the twelfth century, Petrus Helias' commentary on Priscian distinguishes between *interpretatio* and other forms of exposition on the grounds that *interpretatio* is necessarily interlingual:

[Ethimologia] [d]iffert autem ab interpretatione que est translatio de una loquela in aliam. Ethimologia vero fit sepius in eadem loquela.[12]

[Etymology differs thus from *interpretatio*, which is a translation from one language into another. Most often an etymology is produced in the same language.]

An anonymous twelfth-century gloss on Priscian also insists on the point:

Sunt qui assignent differentiam inter ethimologiam et interpretationem [expositionem] et derivationem hanc: . . . Interpretatio est expositio unius lingue per aliam, ut antropos, i.e. homo.[13]

[There are those who posit a difference between etymology, *interpretatio* {exposition}, and derivation in the following ways: . . . *Interpretatio* is the exposition of one language by another, as in *anthropos*, that is, *homo*.]

Such pointed definitions suggest that the fortunes of *interpretatio* as commentary or explanation are to be bound inextricably with the idea of interlingual translation. We do find this collocation in Isidore as well, although in a different context of the *Etymologiae*, the book on the origin of words:

Interpres, quod inter partes medius sit duarum linguarum, dum transferet. Sed et qui Deum [quem] interpretatur et hominum quibus divina indicat mysteria, interpres vocatur [quia inter eam quam transferet]. [*Etymologiae* 10.123]

[Interpreter: because one is between the parts, midway between two languages, when one translates. But he is also called an interpreter who is placed between God, whom he interprets, and men, to whom he reveals the divine mysteries, because that which he carries over is between.]

Such a conflation of the act of translation with the office of interpreting divine discourse (carried out variously in prophecy, preaching, or biblical exegesis), suggests even more positively than the preceding examples how the two functions of translation and exegesis define one another in mutual terms.[14] The identification between translation, exegesis, and the interpretation of divine speech is preserved into the later Middle Ages. For example, we find these principles reflected with little change in the *Catholicon* (1286) of Joannes Balbus (John of Genoa), a widely used dictionary which was printed in the fifteenth century. The *Catholicon* defines *interpretatio* as either translation or exposition between two languages, and (echoing Isidore) conflates this twofold value with the idea of mediation, especially between God and man:

et dicitur interpres qui diversa genera linguarum novit. Scilicet quod unam linguam exponit per aliam vel unam linguam transfert per aliam. Et dicitur sic quia mediator est inter unam linguam seu loquelam et aliam . . . Quia interpres sit medius duarum linguarum [c]um transfert vel exponit unam linguam per aliam[.] Sed qui inter deum interpretatur et homines quibus divina indicat misteria interpres vocatur.[15]

[And one who knows diverse kinds of languages is called an interpreter. This is evident because he expounds one language through another or translates one language by means of another. And he is so called because he is a mediator between one language or speech and another . . . For an interpreter is in the middle of two languages when he translates or expounds one language through another. But he who mediates between God and men, to whom he reveals the divine mysteries, is also called an interpreter.]

It is also not surprising that this particular theme, translation as a form of exegesis, would surface in the most urgent medieval debates about translation, those of the Wycliffites. In 1401, an English writer, Richard Ullerston, must define the two functions in terms of their overlap rather than in terms of any positive difference between them:

Antequam enim ad questionem respondeatur, aut ad eius materiam descendatur, uidendum est quid nominis? huius quod dico transferri et interpretari, translator et interpres . . . Et ex hinc dicuntur translatores qui vnam lingwam alteri coaptant seu proporcionant, aut vnam per aliam exponunt. Et sic loquendo de transferre accipitur pro interpretari, quod est vnam lingwam per aliam exponere, et translator pro interprete sumitur. Vnde translatores dicuntur interpretes et e contra . . . Sumitur enim interpretari aliquando pro exponere, reuelare, explanare, seu reserare sensum in uerbis latentem.[16]

[Before we answer the question or move to considering {my opponent's} material, we must consider the question of what to call him. Since I say of this matter that it is "translated" {transferred} and interpreted, he is a translator and an interpreter . . . And for this reason they are called translators who take or apportion out one language to another, or who expound one language by another. And speaking in this way, it is evident that the verb "to translate" is taken to mean "to interpret," that is, to expound one language through another; and "translator" is taken to mean "interpreter." Whence translators are called interpreters and vice versa . . . Thus "interpret" is sometimes taken to mean "expound," "reveal," "explain," or "unlock" the sense hidden in the words.]

The notion of exegesis has so curious and consistent a power over the definition of *interpretatio* even in its application to translation that an instance of slippage in definition can be significant. In the prologue to his translation of the *De caelesti hierarchia* of the Pseudo-Dionysius (which I have considered in a different context in chapter 2 above), Eriugena is compelled to prise apart the two notions, to separate out the issue of translation from the interference of exegetical inquiry:

Si quis autem nimis tardae aut nimis inusitatae redarguerit elocutionis, attendat, non me tantum, sed et se ipsum nihil posse plus accipere, quam quod ipse distribuit, qui dividit singulis propria, prout vult. Sin vero obscuram minusque apertam praedictae interpretationis seriem iudicaverit, videat, me interpretem huius operis esse, non expositorem. Ubi valde pertimesco, ne forte culpam fidi interpretis incurram.[17]

[If someone should find the language {of this translation} too cumbersome or unfamiliar let him bear in mind that neither he nor I can have a greater capacity for understanding than what God, who doles out each person's given powers (as He wishes), has provided. If someone should find the text of the aforesaid translation obscure or impenetrable, let him consider me the *translator* of this work, not its *expositor*. Indeed I fear that I have incurred the blame of the faithful translator.]

The idea of exegesis, so commonly tied with the term *interpretatio*, has here been forcibly wrested away from the associated idea of translation and reconstituted as a separate entity in the term *expositio*. This is a curious move, given that elsewhere Eriugena uses the word *interpretare* to denote explanation or interpretation.[18] In this preface, the idea of interpretation or exegesis seems to pose an interpolative risk: the already supplementary act of translation cannot admit supplementation or interference from the allied process of explanation. But the need here to segregate and contain the act of exegesis in the word *expositio* suggests that exegesis would have more than merely supplementary power. It seems to represent the possibility of producing meanings independent of the text. The role of the *expositor* is implicitly contrasted with that of the *fidus interpres*, who respects the primary authority of the text by preserving even its obscurities; the *expositor*, however, asserts an independent productive authority over the text by achieving difference with it. In this case the exegete would assume the responsibility of resolving the obscurities and mysteries of the text. As we have seen, the character of medieval exegesis is to constitute a kind of primary discourse itself, to displace rather than simply to supplement the text. That Eriugena must call attention to a distinction between translation and exegesis suggests that the words *interpres* / *interpretatio* are otherwise ambiguous. But his impulse to force a distinction between the expositor and the translator and to clear the word *interpres* of any exegetical motive offers an interesting paradox. The very character of medieval exegesis suggests the meaning of *interpretatio* in the Aristotelian sense: medieval exegesis assumes the power of *interpretatio* as primary discourse, signification, expression. As *interpretatio (hermeneia)*, denoting discourse, is bound up with rhetoric, which allows discourse to realize itself effectively, so exegesis, as we have seen, takes over the productive force of rhetoric. It is this productive force of exegesis that threatens to interpose itself in Eriugena's ideal of the *fidus interpres*.

This slippage of the term *interpretatio* can serve as a paradigm for the way that rhetoric, hermeneutics, and translation are bound together as historical practices and in the history of theoretical discourse. In medieval vernacular practice, translation arises so much in the context of *enarratio* that it resists any effort to resolve the ambiguity or pry apart the double meaning of *interpretatio*. The reliance on *enarratio* is multifold. The vernacular translation may carry over Latin commentary along with the original text, or may use commentary to elucidate the text; at later historical stages the translation may rely on certain developed traditions of vernacular commentary which, in turn, have their roots in Latin *enarrationes*. We have also seen how Latin commentary is largely constituted by textual paraphrase, which takes over and surrounds the text; vernacular translation simply extends this model of exegesis to interlingual terms. It also doubles the process of interlingual paraphrase when it translates Latin commentary along with the text: here it produces paraphrase of what is already paraphrase. Thus at all levels vernacular translation defines itself through the established structures of hermeneutical activity.

But as a hermeneutical practice, vernacular translation also constitutes itself through rhetorical directives. As the conventions of medieval commentary operate through principles of rhetoric, so translation expresses this rhetorical motive as well. But it goes beyond exegesis to register another rhetorical motive, one which is not present in the intralingual tradition of exegesis. Vernacular translation allies itself with ancient rhetorical models of translation through its recovery and rehabilitation of *exercitatio*, using translation to develop and perfect literary skills in the native language. In Roman translation theory, of course, *exercitatio* represents a way of contesting and displacing the source through linguistic difference and cultural appropriation. In its rationale, *exercitatio* corresponds to the rhetorical office of *elocutio*, or more broadly to the aims of *eloquentia*. Its immediate object is to achieve *copia verborum*, but this stylistic enrichment, in turn, is conceived in tandem with *copia rerum*, and thus takes its place in the larger program of moral action and cultural interpretation, as the practice of rhetoric is defined. In late antiquity, as we have seen, the aim of *copia verborum* and the value of translation as a form of *exercitatio* lose their application to the political or cultural project of eloquence. The divorce of rhetorical argumentation from political engagement seems to lead to a divorce within rhetorical teaching between invention and the other components of *eloquentia*, and the competence of rhetoric narrows from practice to textbook art. *Elocutio* becomes a mechanical exercise of improving vocabulary; translation as *exercitatio* serves not to extend the cultural authority of *Latinitas*, but at best to preserve it from further shrinkage. But in medieval vernacular translation, *exercitatio* regains the productive force which it was accorded in Roman ideas of translation. In vernacular translation, *exercitatio* is constituted, not as an explicit theoretical principle, but as a practice: we see it in the continuing efforts of translators to define the range of vernacular literary languages and to generate a vernacular canon which will substitute itself for Latin models in the very process of replicating them. The rhetorical motive of displacing the source is already at work in the tradition of hermeneutics out of which vernacular translation arises; in the project of translation, however, the motive to contest and hence reinvent the text is also informed by the rhetorical directive of *exercitatio*. It achieves new force in its application to ever-changing conditions – or horizons – of vernacular literary discourse. Most importantly, however, the grounding of vernacular translation in hermeneutical practice ensures that *exercitatio* will not lapse into the arid, autotelic pursuit of *copia verborum*. The exegetical tradition had already rehabilitated rhetorical practice under a new guise, reintegrating the function of invention with the other parts of eloquence, in secular studies by "saving" the ancient *auctores*, and in sacred studies by mediating and proclaiming the scriptural text. Vernacular translation carries forward this recovery of rhetoric, reuniting *copia verborum* with *copia rerum*, using exegetical practices to generate new vernacular textual canons, and thereby also giving new force to *elocutio*.

In vernacular translation we see a merging of Roman rhetorical principles of translation with the rhetorically oriented program of medieval exegesis. In both Roman translation theory and medieval exegesis, rhetorical and hermeneutical principles are conjoined. But in the Roman system the rhetorical element dominates, because it is voiced as an explicit theoretical value; conversely, in medieval exegesis, the hermeneutical objective of serving the text is expressly articulated, and thus dominates as the obvious theoretical directive. In medieval vernacular translation as well, the rhetorical principle and the hermeneutical principle will alternately occupy the dominant position.

On this basis we can identify two forms of vernacular translation of the Latin *auctores*, although any distinctions must remain somewhat flexible, as there is much overlap between the forms. In general, the first form of translation gives prominence to its exegetical directives; the second form is closer to the Roman rhetorical model of translation, which stresses the inventional power of the translator, who can discover the text anew in his own language.

We can designate the first of these forms as an "early" or "primary" form of translation. In one respect, the term "early" does refer to the historical occurrence of this kind of translation, as this is the most characteristic form of the earliest examples of vernacular translation. But as we also find many examples of this form in later vernacular practice (we will consider texts of this type from as late as the later fourteenth century and early fifteenth century), the term "early," with its chronological connotations, is not sufficient. Thus I use the term "primary" to designate this form with respect to its affinities and innate characteristics rather than to its place in a diachronic order. There is also a certain "primacy" to this form in that, regardless of when it occurs, it has its most direct affinities with the exegetical tradition of the medieval schools. The most general characteristics of this form are that the translations announce themselves as translations by calling attention to their dependence upon – and service to – the original text. They typically also foreground their reliance upon exegetical materials, thus proposing to serve the text through *enarratio* as well as through interlingual translation. Thus they give prominence to an exegetical motive, by making obvious their recourse to commentaries (or exegetical strategies) and by according the original text an authoritative canonical status (most often by naming it and naming their enterprise as translation). Yet these translations exhibit the rhetorical tendencies of medieval exegetical practice: even as they proclaim themselves to be serving and supplementing the text, they work in effect to contest and supplant that text. It is in this "primary" form of translation that we most often encounter the medieval version of rhetorical *exercitatio*, the discovery and augmentation of a native literary language. Thus while this primary model of translation articulates its motive in terms of exegetical and perhaps didactic service, it orients its practice towards a self-sufficient or independent discourse, using the original as a model against which to discover and define new textual idioms. This and the following chapter will consider texts that exemplify the range of such "primary" translation.

The other form of vernacular translation can be designated here as a "later" or "secondary" form. These terms also refer both to chronological position and to the nature of the form itself. On the whole, this form of translation occurs in later stages of the development of vernacular textual traditions. I do not intend the term "secondary" to be a judgment on the literary "value" of this form; rather, I use it to denote a certain distance of this form from the medieval exegetical tradition, a distance that is mediated by the primary form of translation. This form typically instantiates itself as a product of the primary type of translation, and thus stands in a secondary relationship to the exegetical tradition of the schools. In this "secondary" form the rhetorical motive takes precedence so that the translations tend to define themselves as independent textual productions. The best concrete examples of this type of translation are those texts with which we are most familiar within our own literary historical canon, texts such as Chaucer's *Legend of Good Women* or *Knight's Tale*, or Gower's *Confessio amantis*. These "secondary" translations may use many of the procedures associated with exegesis and with the primary form of translation, including recourse to commentaries themselves or, frequently, interpolations on the part of the translator that take on an exegetical or even editorial character (as in the narrator's interpolations in *Troilus and Criseyde*); but they also tend to suppress the exegetical character of these moves by integrating them into a larger program of textual reinvention. Rather than representing themselves as translations in the service of authoritative sources, these texts tend to claim for themselves (either directly or implicitly, through the irony of disclaimers) a kind of originary discursive status, as if the translation, once achieved, displaces the source by assuming a certain canonical authority of its own. While they may acknowledge a source (as in the case of Chaucer's *Legend of Good Women* or even the fictive claims of the *Troilus*) and hence their own status of translations, they exploit the logic of exegetical supplementation to recontextualize their sources and so to efface them. This is one function of the *Prologue* to the *Legend of Good Women* or of Gower's extrinsic and intrinsic prologues to the *Confessio amantis*: the prologues provide a new fictional, generic, or structural context for the traditional materials or translations that have been assembled together, thereby claiming a certain originary status for the vernacular texts (although, of course, in Chaucer and Gower such claims are never unequivocal, but are always subject to their own internal dismantling). This model of translation needs to be understood in terms of changes in the idea of invention that occur in medieval rhetorical theory. In chapter 6 I will examine medieval transformations of inventional theory and in chapter 7 I will consider the implications of this for the "secondary" form of translation.

This distinction between "primary" and "secondary" forms of translation can serve, at best, as an approximate framework. "Primary" and "secondary" represent poles at either extreme of a continuum: few translations constitute pure instances of either model. It is for this reason that I have avoided using the terms "exegetical" and "rhetorical" to differentiate these forms, for such a designation would be misleading. These two models are constituted of the same elements and derive from the same conditions: both emerge from a nexus of hermeneutical and rhetorical practice, a nexus which has, as we have seen, its own long history. Neither of these models has exclusive claims to one or the other of these practices. These models differ only in the way that they direct their emphasis. Primary translation presents itself as a form of exegesis, but exegesis has already redefined its practice in rhetorical terms. Secondary translation presents itself as an independent discovery, or invention of material, but as I shall argue in chapter 6, rhetorical invention is redefined in the later Middle Ages as a form of textual hermeneutics.

These two poles of the continuum, or models of translation, correspond roughly to the distinction, in Roman translation theory, between the elementary translations produced under the guidance of the *grammaticus* and the more advanced or self-consciously aggressive translations to be carried out when the student reaches the stage of rhetorical training or expertise. In Roman theory the two forms of translation may be represented as distinct and mutually exclusive practices. But in actuality the boundary between them is unstable, as each carries the force of the other as an ulterior directive. The attempts of such theorists as Cicero or Pliny to force distinctions between the two forms are no more than critical fictions that serve certain ideological ends within the Roman academy, that is, to mark off the province of rhetoric from that of grammar and to conserve the status of rhetoric as the master discipline. In the Middle Ages, the ideological terms and theoretical formulations have changed, along with the structure and function of academic institutions, as we will consider later in this chapter. Nevertheless, the paradigm of two systems representing themselves as distinct, but in practice closely intertwined and drawing their force from the ulterior similarity of their motives, has remained strikingly the same.

What I have designated as the primary form of translation is by no means a static or unified practice. Along the continuum from primary to secondary translation there are various stages or forms of primary translation. This chapter will examine two very different instantiations of primary translation, representing either end of the "primary" range of this continuum. To illustrate the stage of this practice that is formally closest to the exegetical techniques of instruction in the schools we will consider a rendering of part of the *De nuptiis Philologiae et Mercurii* by Notker the German, in which we see how translation can offer itself almost purely as *enarratio* to give access to the original text. From this we will jump forward to consider the other extreme of what can still be called primary translation, to be exemplified here by the *Ovide moralisé*. This text of some 72,000 lines announces its motive as explication, but it takes that hermeneutical motive to its most contestative extreme by channeling its explicative energies into a wholesale vernacular *exercitatio* which challenges the privileged status of Latin as the language of academic discourse. The *Ovide moralisé* represents a stage of translation that is midway between the exegetical practice of the schools and the most extreme forms of secondary translation. In other words, it represents a transitional point on the continuum from primary to secondary translation.

This chapter will also introduce the question of the status of vernacular discourse within medieval academic culture. This raises new questions about the function of interlingual *exercitatio*. As we have seen, the issue of interlingual *exercitatio* is central to Roman theories of translation. In the Roman period this question is negotiated in terms of a rhetorical definition of translation which provides a theoretical framework for an explicit political agenda of rivalry with and appropriation of a prestigious and established literary culture. The structures of metaphoric and metonymic relations that define Roman ideas of translation and imitation remain relevant to the medieval context, but under transformed conditions. In the Middle Ages, the problem of translation as an interlingual movement between an established discourse and an emergent literary culture (Latin to vernacular) is defined through a more complex disciplinary sponsorship, the exegetical tradition which has co-opted and subsumed rhetoric. Moreover, the institutional and ideological framework of the interlingual movement between Latin and the medieval vernaculars differs significantly from that which informs the movement between Greek and Latin at Rome. In the Middle Ages, Latin as the established intellectual language does not represent a historically "foreign" culture to be absorbed, imitated, and appropriated, which is what Greek in effect represents in Republican and even Imperial Rome. In the Middle Ages, Latin culture is a privileged stratum *within* larger cultural communities, and its privilege rests on its symbolic and practical value as a force of continuity against both geographical and historical distance. Latin ties Western Europe together and links modernity with pagan and Christian antiquity. Vernacular translation is carried out under the expressed recuperative motives of the exegetical tradition, but in its very nature it threatens the notion of a recuperative coherence by opening a symbolically unified intellectual discourse to linguistic multiplicity. These are issues which will be explored at some length here; but let us turn now to a concrete textual study.

INTERLINGUAL *EXERCITATIO*: NOTKER THE GERMAN AND MARTIANUS CAPELLA

The necessity of teaching *utriusque linguae* after the time of the late Empire was almost universal, but the earliest extensive records of such vernacular-Latin instruction date only from the eighth century in German and the ninth century in Old English, in the form of paraphrases and continuous glosses. There are records of the use of the vernacular for preaching in the Germanic countries and Gaul from the Carolingian period and earlier.[19] The evidence for bilingual teaching throughout the Middle Ages is considerable, pointing of course to the production of grammars and glossaries as well as interlingual commentaries.[20] But the early English and Germanic monastic school traditions offer the best evidence for the affinity between vernacular glossing, exegetical paraphrase, and translation. The unusual amount of vernacular study material preserved in Old English and Old High German provides a tangible link between the production of full-scale vernacular translations and established exegetical practice in Latin.[21]

The work of Notker the German (known also as Notker III or Notker Labeo), a monk of St. Gall who lived from the mid-tenth century to 1022, closely records the strategies of teaching *utriusque linguae* in the monastic schools. His work thus provides some of the best examples that we have of "early" or "primary" translation, that is, of vernacular translation in its primary relationship with exegetical practice. The German tradition of vernacular glossing, whether interlinear, marginal, or contextual, and of paraphrases of mainly sacred texts, dates from as early as the eighth century. Thus Notker's work has some historical precedent in the schools of German-speaking areas. But in a letter that Notker wrote (*c.* 1015) to Bishop Hugo von Sitten, he registers a certain unease about crossing over the boundaries of Latin culture with his vernacular productions, treating this as if it were an unprecedented project. In this letter Notker lists his translations, discusses his rationales for translating, and offers to show his efforts to the Bishop (if the Bishop will only provide the parchment for copying them):

Sunt enim ecclesiastici libri – et praecipue quidem in scolis legendi – quos impossibile est, sine illis praelibatis ad intellectum integrum duci. Ad quos dum accessum habere nostros vellem scolasticos, ausus sum facere rem paene inusitatam, ut latine scripta in nostram [linguam] conatus sim vertere et syllogistice aut figurate aut suasorie dicta per Aristotelem vel Ciceronem vel alium artigr[aph]um elucidare.

Quod dum agerem in duobus libris Boethii – qui est de consolatione Philosophiae et in aliquantis de sancta trinitate – rogatus [sum], et metrice quaedam scripta in hanc eandem linguam traducere, Catonem scilicet ut Bucolica Virgilii et Andriam Terentii. Mox et prosam et artes temptare me voluerunt, et transtuli Nuptias Philologiae et Categorias Aristotelis et Periermenias et principia arithmeticae. Hinc reversus ad divina totum Psalterium et interpretando et secundum Augustinum exponendo consummavi; Iob quoque incepi, licet vix tertiam partem exegerim. Nec solum haec sed et novam rhetoricam et computum novum et alia quaedam opuscula latine conscripsi.

Horum nescio, an aliquid dignum sit venire in manus vestras. Sed si vultis ea – sumptibus enim indigent – mittite plures pergamenas et scribentibus praemia, et accipietis eorum exempla. Quae dum fuerint ad vos perlata, me praesentem aestimate. Scio tamen, quia primum abhorrebitis quasi ab insuetis, sed paulatim forte incipient se commendare vobis, et praevalebitis ad legendum et ad dinoscendum, quam cito capiuntur per patriam linguam, quae aut vix aut non integre capienda forent in lingua non propria.[22]

[There are Christian books – and principally those read in the schools – which cannot possibly be fully comprehended without introductory study. Since I wanted my students to have an introduction to these texts, I presumed to do something almost unprecedented: I ventured to translate them from Latin into our language, and to elucidate syllogistic, stylistic, and rhetorical precepts according to the teachings of Aristotle, Cicero, or other arts authors.

Because of what I had done with two books by Boethius – the *Consolation of Philosophy* and a good deal of *On the Trinity* – I was asked to translate some metrical texts into the same language: Cato's *Distichs*, Virgil's *Bucolics*, and Terence's *Andrias*. Soon they wanted me to try prose and arts texts, and I translated the *Marriage of Mercury and Philology*, the *Categories* of Aristotle, the *Peri hermeneias*, and the *Principles of Arithmetic*. From this, turning to divine subjects, I completed the whole Psalter, translating it and providing an exposition based on Augustine. I also began the Book of Job, although I scarcely completed the exposition of more than one third. Not only did I do these translations, but I also wrote a new rhetoric, a new computus, and certain other Latin works.

I don't know whether any of these things are worthy of your attention. But if you want to see them – they are costly to produce – send several skins of parchment and expenses for the scribes, and you will receive copies of them. When they have been delivered to you, think of me as present. I know that while at first you will recoil from them as if from things unfamiliar, nevertheless they will, by degrees, begin to commend themselves to you forcefully, and you will be able to read and construe them. Things which are understood only partially and with difficulty in a language that is not one's own are quickly grasped in one's native tongue.]

Notker calls his undertaking "paene inusitata," almost unprecedented. In historical terms this is a curious description of his work, since there is a strong tradition of German glossing from at least the eighth century, and of translation from the early ninth century onwards. But perhaps it is the range of genres included in his translations that he considers unprecedented, particularly the preponderence of classical arts texts among the translated items that he lists.[23] Notker perhaps suggests that the vernacular itself is an unlikely medium for the transmission of such curricular monuments when he anticipates the Bishop's initial shock upon seeing the translations ("I know that at first you will recoil as if from things unfamiliar"). But Notker also (strategically) anticipates an unfolding of the Bishop's more generous sensibilities: the translations will "commend themselves" to the Bishop, for upon reading them he will appreciate the value of the native language ("patria lingua") for making abstruse meanings in the "lingua non propria" more accessible.

Notker's address to the Bishop is a tissue of modest protestation and polite anticipation. These ironies allow the letter to register a strong sense of difference between Latin and the vernacular in terms of a hierarchy of prestige.[24] Notker assigns the vernacular a certain negative value of providing access to the curricular *auctores*. Presumably (to judge from the surface if not necessarily the ulterior meaning of Notker's statements) the vernacular can be superseded once it has enabled "proper" knowledge of the "lingua non propria." But Notker's actual practice belies such assumptions, in ways probably as invisible to him as to his exegetical predecessors and contemporaries. As we have seen, exegesis in the Middle Ages defines its practice in terms quite opposite to those by which it is understood in express theoretical terms. Notker's letter articulates a firm boundary between Latin and vernacular, at least in terms of intellectual status and literary propriety. But an analysis of Notker's work can show that the boundaries between commentary and text are not firmly fixed. While in terms of a hierarchy of prestige, Notker has claimed the "debased" role of vernacular translator, he in fact assumes the powerful role of commentator, and he performs this role most consistently in his vernacular writing. The vernacular text, accordingly, is empowered: it is the site from which Notker exerts his exegetical control.

Notker's translation of books 1 and 2 of Martianus Capella's *De nuptiis* provides an excellent paradigm for primary translation: it simply imposes interlingual terms on the standard text-commentary format.[25] Text and exegetical translation are intermingled without being synthesized; the text is quoted and the paraphrase follows or accompanies it. The paraphrase does not offer itself as something apart from or independent of the text, but in so serving the text the paraphrase both incorporates and annexes the text, relegating the original to a virtually dependent position. The paraphrase, despite its officially supplementary status, becomes the focal *lectio*. In the Latin academic tradition, commentary surrounds, absorbs, and dominates the text. Notker's interlingual format augments this process: the vernacular paraphrase takes over the text and in addition incorporates and restates glosses and commentaries that pertain to the text.

The Martianus translation opens with a reduced paraphrase of Remigius' introduction to book 1:

Remigius lêret únsih tísen auctorem in álenámen uuésen gehéizenen martianum . únde mineum úmbe sîna fáreuua . felicem úmbe héilesôd . capellam úmbe sînen uuássen sín . uuánda capra apud grecos dorcas a uidendo gehéizen íst.[26]

[Remigius teaches us that this author was called, as his first name, Martianus; and he was called Mineus because of his color; Felix for the sake of a good omen; and Capella because of his sharp wit, for *capra* {she-goat} is called by the Greeks *dorcas* {a roe} on account of its good eyesight.]

Notker's introduction continues along the lines suggested by Remigius' introduction, borrowing, as in the passage above, where Remigius in turn has borrowed from Eriugena.[27] Remigius' commentary is thus received as so much an integral component of the canonical text that its authoritative force is greater than that of framing device or means of entry: it has become part of the text to be translated. Here exegesis quite literally inscribes itself in translation and informs the translative act with its own power of discursive production.

Notker's translation practice recognizes no distinction between text and *enarratio*. The first German sentence corresponding to the Martianus text opens with a gloss to a rubric and then proceeds to render the text:

SATIRA IN HONORE HIMENEI HOS PRECINIT UERSUS. *Tu quem psallentem thalamis . quem matre camena progenitum perhibent . copula sacra* .i. nati per copula sacra . *deum*. Himenee chît tiu satira . dú bíst tér . dén diu chínt tero góto ságent síngenten . dáz chît quónen ze síngene in dien brûtechémanaton . únde dén síe chédent sîn dero sáng-cúttenno sún . uuánda dû sólih sángare bíst. Tû bíst ter dén uirgilius héizet amorem . filium ueneris. Fóne démo ér chît . omnia uincit amor. Tû tûost uuónên díngolih ze ándermo.[28]

[A "satire" in honor of Hymen introduces these verses. *You who make music for marriages, who, they say, were born of a Muse, by sacred union* – that is, born by sacred union – *of gods*. This satire is said {to be} of Hymen. You are the one whom the children of the gods say {is} singing, that is, {who} used to sing in these bridal chambers, and whom they say is the son of the song-goddesses, because you are such a singer. You are the one whom Virgil calls Amor, the son of Venus. Of him he says "love conquers all." You cause all things to dwell together.]

First we might note that in quoting the lemma from Martianus, Notker inserts a gloss ("*copula sacra* .i. nati per copula sacra . *deum*"). The translation of the first half-line "Tu quem psallentem thalamis") expands to become an explication of the hemistich ("dáz chît quónen ze síngene," [that is, used to sing]). The same is true of the second hemistich, where he glosses his own translation ("únde dén sie chédent sîn dero sáng-cúttenno sún . uuánda dû sólih sángere bist" [and whom they say is the son of the song-goddesses because you are such a singer]). For this hemistich Notker also provides an explication which seems to be inspired both by Remigius and by the Virgilian echoes in Martianus' text. On the phrase "quem matre camena progenitum,"

Remigius comments, "*Camena* quasi canena, a canendo, vel quasi canens melos, et est generale nomen omnium Musarum bene canentium."[29] Notker's response is to conflate Remigius' explanation of "mater camena" as Venus with Martianus' own association of Hymen with Venus several lines later ("O Hymenaee decens, Cypridis qui maxima cura es"), in which the phrase "maxima cura es" echoes Virgil, *Georgics* 4.354 and *Aeneid* 1.678.[30] Notker's version of Remigius' gloss registers the Virgilian connection: "Tû bíst ter dén virgilius héizet amorem . filium ueneris" (You are the one whom Virgil calls Amor, the son of Venus). But Notker extends his version of Remigius' gloss beyond any suggestion in Remigius by going on to gloss *Amor* with a quote from *Eclogues* 10.69, the commonplace "omnia uincit amor." This in turn requires an explanation which ties it back to Martianus' text: "Tû tûost uuónên díngolih ze ándermo" (you cause all things to dwell together). This anticipates Martianus' line 7, "semina qui arcanis stringens pugnantia uinclis" ([you who] bind together the warring seeds with sacred bonds).[31] Presumably the idea of Hymen as Amor, the son of Venus, leads Notker to the theme of conjugal love that can "conquer" and hence unite the warring elements of the universe. Notker's own mythographical excursions allow him to unite the themes of "hymn" (marriage song) and Hymen (marriage).

Thus within his vernacular domain, the translator assumes the multiple roles of glossator, exegete, and mythographer. The translation itself is generated out of *enarratio*, which is either a source for the translation or is invented within it. The passage just analyzed is a good paradigm for Notker's procedure throughout the Martianus translation: it happens to contain nearly the range of the strategies that he uses. It shows how the text is challenged and remade within the translation, but also how, in turn, that translation constructs itself as simply an extension of the commentator's forum. Notker exerts his power over the text through exegesis. Thus, for example, when quoting a lemma from the text he can insert a gloss, and then translate his own gloss rather than the original terms, as in the following example, where he prefers his literalized explanation to Martianus' more ambiguous image:

Atque auram mentis .i. spiritum uite . *corporibus socias* . Tû gîbest tien lîchamon lîbhafti.[32]

(*You share the breath of mind* – that is, the spirit of life – *with bodies*. You give life {the quality of being alive} to those bodies.]

When the translation takes over an existing *enarratio* it can break down the boundaries between explication and that which is to be understood or explicated, refusing a strict separation between the act of explication and meaning itself, and instead demonstrating their interrelatedness.[33] By translating text and existing commentary as one, the vernacular seams the two together to form a new textual organism. The following example comes from Martianus' first *prosa*:

dum crebrius istos Hymenaei uersiculos nescio quid inopinum intactumque moliens cano . . .[34]

([While I sing these verses of Hymen over and over devising I know not what unexpected and untried matter . . .]

Remigius comments on this passage:

Quid est quod dicit *Nescio quid inopinum cano* cum semper dicat, nisi quia secta Peripateticus fuit? Illi enim cum semper dicant se nescire fatentur asserentes siquidem sicut in profundo putei latere veritatem.[35]

[What does it mean when he says "I sing I know not what unexpected matter," as he always says, if not that he was a member of the Peripatetic sect? Whereas the Peripatetics always profess themselves to be ignorant, they acknowledge claiming, as it were, to hide truth in a deep pit.]

Notker's version mediates between the text and Remigius' commentary by restructuring the text around the gloss on Peripatetics:

Tô íh tícchost álso míh tiu satyra lêrta díse uérsa sáng fóne himeneo . ne-uuêiz .s. uuánda íh peripatheticus pín . uuáz únchundes fórderônde . únde úngehándelotes. Dáz chît er . uuánda peripathetici ne-uuéllen nîehtes quís sîn.[36]

[Then I repeatedly sang about Hymen as the satire taught me these verses, devising I know not – that is, because I am a Peripatetic – what unknown and unformed matters. He says this because Peripatetics do not claim to be certain of anything.]

Notker's reception of Martianus' text through Remigius' commentary elevates Remigius to a certain primary, authorial status. But Notker's editorial grafting of the two together has the effect of displacing them both: Notker's text instead occupies the focal position. Like the commentators before him, Notker incorporates canonical writings (here both Martianus and Remigius) into his own text, and through this grafting assumes one of the standard authorial functions associated with Latin exegetical practice, that of *compilator*. Given that his translations are, among other things, records of classroom practice, his frequent references to the authoritative book (*das puoch*) may signify as much the written text before his own readers, that is, the canonical text accompanied by Notker's vernacular paraphrase, as the unmediated original work itself.[37] His own interlingual compilation assumes in effect the status of an *auctoritas*.

Notker's work and the unease that he registers about its effect upon a clerical audience (Bishop Hugo) can serve here to raise some large questions about the status of the vernacular in relation to the official discourse of academic culture and the literary prestige of the Latin *auctores*. The motive of displacement within exegesis assumes a new importance when the vernacular enlarges its competence to become a new linguistic medium for *translatio studii*. The problems of an interlingual movement, as Latin literary and exegetical traditions are re-embodied in diverse emergent vernaculars, can be understood within the same structural terms that define Roman norms of imitation and translation: lineality as opposed to rupture, the metonymic structure of evolution as opposed to the metaphoric structure of substitution.

THE IDEOLOGICAL ASSUMPTIONS OF ACADEMIC CRITICISM: LATINITY AND VERNACULARITY

For Notker to characterize his vernacular exegesis and translation as something "paene inusitata" points to the uncertain or perhaps uncomfortable place of the vernacular in the high cultural project of *translatio studii*. For us to understand the curious status of vernacular exegesis and translation we should reconsider the principal structures of medieval Latin hermeneutics. Latin exegetical practice in the Middle Ages carries the rhetorical force of *hermeneia*, or primary or productive discourse: it works to displace the original text, materially by paraphrase, and conceptually by reconstituting the argumentative structure of the text. As a practice, exegesis thus operates through metaphoric principles, in terms similar to the model of rhetorical translation in Roman theory. Latin commentary substitutes itself for the text in question, inserting itself into the *auctoritas* of that text, hence appropriating that authority, and to varying degrees performing in lieu of the text. The dynamic effect of exegesis is to achieve a certain difference with the source.

But what are the ideological assumptions that condition and empower academic critical discourse in the Middle Ages? Unlike the Roman model of translation, medieval Latin exegesis has no acknowledged political agenda of rivalry with the tradition that it seeks to assimilate. Even the reading of pagan *auctores* in terms of philosophical or ethical allegory, or in terms of Christian doctrine, officially aims to recuperate, not to efface, the authority of the ancient and late classical legacy. Medieval hermeneutical practice defines its ideological relationship with antiquity in terms of continuity or of an organic and inevitable lineage: the pagan *imperium* can be subsumed within the larger compass of Christian culture.[38] This assumption of lineal continuity is directly expressed in the linguistic ties of medieval academic discourse with antiquity. The medieval *artes* curriculum devotes itself to nurturing and sustaining a textual culture of *Latinitas*.[39] Roger Wright has recently argued that medieval Latin as a textual language and Latinity as a cultural practice were the inventions of Carolingian grammarians – notably Alcuin – who sought to stabilize and regulate an official language of professional clerical education by introducing an archaized system of spelling and pronunciation into Latin usage, with the effect of distinguishing Latin from the Romance languages.[40] The result is to enforce a perceived link between the Latin cultures of the *moderni* and the *antiqui*, a perception which serves the professionalization of classical and Christian learning.

In the *De vulgari eloquentia* Dante identifies Latin with "grammar" ("Est et inde alia locutio secundaria nobis, quam Romani gramaticam vocaverunt" [And {in addition to our natural, vernacular language} we also have a second language, which the Romans call *grammatica*]);[41] and in the *Convivio* Dante explains that it is the very artifice or studied regulation of Latin that underwrites its superiority to native or vernacular usage:

onde, con ciò sia cosa che lo latino molte cose manifesta concepute ne la mente che lo volgare far non può, sì come sanno quelli che hanno l'uno e l'altro sermone, più è la vertù sua che quella del volgare . . . Dunque quello sermone è più bello ne lo quale più debitamente si rispondono [le parole; e più debitamente si rispondono] in latino che in volgare, però che lo volgare seguita uso, e lo latino arte: onde concedesi esser più bello, più virtuoso e più nobile.

[Thus, since it is a fact that Latin can express many things conceived by the human mind which the vernacular cannot, as anyone knows who has facility in both {languages}, its virtue is greater than that of the vernacular . . . That language is more beautiful, then, in which the words are to a greater extent related to each other as they ought to be; and they are so to a greater extent in Latin than in the vernacular, since the vernacular follows usage, while Latin follows {rules of} art. Thus it is granted that Latin is more beautiful, more virtuous, and more noble.][42]

The very enterprise of *translatio studii* is conducted in the language of the *antiqui* whose learning must be saved and transmitted. Giles of Rome in the late thirteenth century invents the illustrious "invention" of Latin as a tool for the dissemination of the sciences:

Videntes enim Philosophi nullum idioma vulgare esse completum et perfectum, per quod perfecte exprimere possent naturas rerum, et mores hominum, et cursus astrorum, et alia de quibus disputare volebant, invenerunt sibi quasi proprium idioma, quod dicitur latinum, vel idioma literale: quod constituerunt adeo latum et copiosum, ut per ipsum possent omnes suos conceptus sufficienter exprimere.[43]

[The philosophers, seeing that there was no complete and perfect native idiom by which they could articulate the nature of things, human laws, the course of the stars, and other subjects that they wanted to discuss, invented for themselves a language which was in effect their own, a literary language, which is called Latin. They made this language so profound and rich that they could adequately express all their meanings through it.]

Similarly, John of Salisbury's arguments for the continuing relevance of Aristotelian linguistic logic extend into an argument for the mastery of the language of transmission itself.[44] The Latin language, the writing and reading of that language, serves to link past with present. Latin constitutes its ideological power doubly: its linguistic presence signifies a symbolic order of history, and those who use it as a language participate in the myth of temporal and spatial coherence. Dante captures this double ideological force of Latin when he says in the *Convivio*:

. . . lo latino è perpetuo e non corruttibile, e lo volgare è non stabile e corruttibile. Onde vedemo ne le scritture antiche de le comedie e tragedie latine, che non si possono transmutare, quello medisimo che oggi avemo; che non avviene del volgare, lo quale a piacimento artificiato si transmuta.

[Latin is perpetual and not corruptible, while the vernacular is both unstable and corruptible. Thus we perceive that the language of ancient writings, both comedies and tragedies, is the same Latin we have today: no writer can modify it on his own.

This is not true of the vernacular, which can be modified at will by every writer who uses it.][45]

In *De vulgari eloquentia* 1.9.10 Dante uses the same reasoning about the mutability of languages that are subject to the conditions of use and circumstances of place ("qui nec natura nec consortio confirmantur, sed humanis beneplacitis localique congruitate nascuntur"), and proceeds with an argument, like that of Giles of Rome, about the invention of "grammar" as a stabilizing force that can resist the inevitability of historical difference:

Hinc moti sunt inventores gramatice facultatis; que quidem gramatica nichil aliud est quam quedam inalterabilis locutionis idemptitas diversis temporibus atque locis. Hec cum de comuni consensu multarum gentium fuerit regulata, nulli singulari arbitrio videtur obnoxia, et per consequens nec variabilis esse potest. Adinvenerunt ergo illam, ne propter variationem sermonis arbitrio singularium fluitantis, vel nullo modo vel saltim imperfecte antiquorum actingeremus autoritates et gesta, sive illorum quos a nobis locorum diversitas facit esse diversos.[46]

[The inventors of the art of grammar were motivated on this account: for indeed grammar is nothing other than a certain unalterable identity of speech through diverse times and places. Since grammar was regulated by the common consensus of many people, it does not seem to be subject to the will of any one person, and therefore it cannot be subject to variability. Thus they invented it lest, on account of the inconsistency of a language wavering at the will of individuals, we would have no, or at best imperfect, access to the ideas and the records of the ancient *auctores*, or of those whom geographical difference makes different from us.]

Dante, like Notker, straddles Latin and vernacular culture, so that for him, as for Notker, the urgent fact of historical difference must be acknowledged as a primary and compelling theme in any account of linguistic use. But even as late as the second half of the fourteenth century, when the fact of vernacularity as a historical force in textual culture can scarcely be suppressed or concealed under a myth of lineal continuity, one commentator on a grammatical text identifies Latin as the linguistic descendent of Greek and in turn of Hebrew, and thus of the divine language of God.[47]

This dialectic between symbolic order and linguistic-social practice underwrites the power of academic hermeneutics in the Middle Ages. The intralinguistic relationship between medieval exegesis and the *auctores* constitutes a metonymic structure, comparable to that which underlies Roman theories of imitation. Thus while at one level medieval Latin hermeneutical practice registers a motive of displacement, at another level the linguistic medium within which that practice is conducted proposes a structure of organic, evolutionary continuity with ancient texts. Medieval hermeneutical practice does not just participate in the privileged language of classical learning: it is a material embodiment of that myth of continuity. It is in this way that academic discourse can guarantee its own cultural privilege, and that of those who use that discourse. Thus in the Latin hermeneutical tradition, the motive of contestation expressed in exegetical practice is contained within a larger system, the linguistic structure that embodies exegesis and positions it within a certain ideological framework of historical and cultural continuity. The intralingual character of the tradition visibly affirms its sense of organic linkage with the textual culture of antiquity. Its Latinity serves to conceal both the inevitability of historical difference and the actual process of displacement that is played out in exegetical practice. As an ideological force Latinity works to contain and suppress the contradictions inherent in the very practices that it supports.

But vernacular exegesis and paraphrase introduces the factor of an interlingual movement, the rendering of text and commentary in a new language, or more precisely, in diverse new languages which are outside the official culture of academic discourse.[48] In formal or strategic terms, vernacular exegesis resembles its Latin counterpart, carrying over the motive of contestation that is inscribed in hermeneutical practice. But its language poses a disjunction in the linguistic continuity between *antiqui* and *moderni*. In a sense the vernacular inserts itself into the ideological project of *translatio studii* as a new linguistic medium for carrying over the learning of the ancients: as a practice, *translatio studii* means the carrying over of learning, but it works like the disjunctive act of translation itself. The vernacular substitutes itself for the linguistic – and implicitly cultural – authority of Latin, thus proposing to participate in the privileged academic discourse of hermeneutics. The vernacular challenges the symbolic order of continuity by breaching the very linguistic order that had suppressed historical difference and had contained the disruptive force of exegesis itself. When the vernacular co-opts the system of exegesis it co-opts the status of an academic institution, and it embodies itself within that powerful institutional discourse. But even as the vernacular takes over the discourse of official culture, it works to expose what had been the ideological fictions of that culture: it exposes the myth of historical continuity by embodying the inevitability of historical difference. It illuminates the discontinuity that had always been there. We shall see some implications of this in the *Ovide moralisé* as well as in the Boethian texts to be considered in the next chapter.

At both the level of its practice and the level of the linguistic system that embodies it, vernacular exegesis operates in substitutive terms. As exegetical practice it is also translation, and it empowers itself by appropriating the texts which it proposes to serve. In its very language it effects a rupture in linguistic ties with the Latin *auctores* and with the accumulated *auctoritas* of medieval Latin exegesis in the *artes* curriculum. But this act of substitution has much in common with the model of translation in Roman theory: vernacular exegetical translation forges new links with the Latin cultures of antiquity and the Middle Ages by replicating them at the same time that it registers profound difference with them. The links that it forges with the traditions of Latin textuality are, of course, those of appropriation. Its relationship with Latinity can be described as metaphoric in structure. But more importantly, this substitutive structure also constitutes a rhetorical act of *exercitatio*: it represents the mastery and appropriation of a privileged discourse. By inserting itself into the academic transmission of classical texts it reshapes itself as a medium of formal hermeneutical practice. The examples of primary translation considered in this and the next chapter record various aspects and stages of vernacular attempts to master and domesticate a discourse of high culture. Thus, the vernacular context carries one step further the motive of displacement that is inscribed in the practice of exegesis. Not only does the new hermeneutical performance displace text and antecedent commentary; now, with the factor of interlingual transference, vernacular can displace Latin as the linguistic system within which exegesis is practiced. Vernacular exegesis and translation register a visible sign of the disjunction that had always operated in exegetical practice.

When Notker expresses his discomfort about changing the language in which *translatio studii* is conducted, he is not simply affirming a commonplace that Latin is a technically superior language. His concern about appropriating a whole exegetical apparatus into German registers, perhaps at a level of a historical unconscious, a threat of disjunction within the project of *translatio studii*. To render text and commentary in a new or emergent literary language is to force an acknowledgment of the inevitability of historical difference within the project of *translatio studii*, to expose the internal contradiction of historical and cultural distance. It is to expose a difference that is already there in that exacting and seemingly self-sufficient system of cultural recuperation.

The uneasy newness registered in "paene inusitata" is also a tension that can express itself in the agonistic terms of *exercitatio*. Notker has appropriated, not just the *copia verborum* but also the *copia rerum* of exegesis: he has taken on the productive functions of exegesis, becoming glossator, expositor, mythographer, and compiler, authorial functions that will be the very source of power for later vernacular translators, as we shall see. Notker's work never announces its aims as substitutive and never proposes to appropriate and efface its source. This is the nature of primary translation. What we might call its "textual ideology" is to conceive of itself as performing exegetical service. But in the act of translating and thus registering difference, the vernacular begins to assimilate the *copia rerum* and *copia verborum* of its sources and so begins to constitute its own discursive identity within official academic culture.

THE *OVIDE MORALISÉ*

If for Notker in the eleventh century the use of the vernacular for the exegesis of the *auctores* is "paene inusitata," no traces of this discomfort remain to be registered in the *Ovide moralisé*, composed in the first quarter of the fourteenth century. With this vast vernacularization of the *Metamorphoses* and of the industry of mythography and Ovid commentary that had accumulated over a millenium, the tendencies of primary translation achieve their fullest and sometimes most extreme expression. In the *Ovide moralisé* we see how the vernacular can assimilate the traditional forms of academic commentary on the *auctores*, and how translation can be carried on under the aegis of *expositio*. By the fourteenth century in France, the legitimacy of the vernacular as an expository medium for academic and classical subjects is not in question: the late thirteenth century through the late fourteenth century sees an efflorescence of vernacular translations of texts from the university curriculum in France and in Italy.[49] Given this it should not be surprising that the *Ovide moralisé* represents its purpose almost entirely as exposition. But in the application of its expository purpose it also reveals the extent to which vernacular commentary can assume the rhetorical character of its medieval Latin counterpart.

The *Ovide moralisé* has usually been read as a source for other texts, as an inert repository of information about the sources of "canonical" vernacular works, or at best as an instantiation of late medieval mythographical interests. As a critical performance this text has remained largely invisible, in much the same way that the textuality or performative character of medieval Latin commentaries has remained invisible, so that these texts are relegated to the ancillary status of information-banks that retreat out of sight once they have enabled satisfactory readings of "major" authors and historical themes. But like the exegetical texts studied in the previous chapter, the *Ovide moralisé* has much to tell us about the status of the critical act in the Middle Ages and, in its particular case, about the genre of criticism within vernacular writing. While medieval critical discourse has occupied a provisional space in literary historiography, visible to literary historians only until it yields up its applications to other projects, the formal and ideological conditions of these discourses are by no means provisional: a text like the *Ovide moralisé* discloses as much information about its own hermeneutical status as it does about the texts that it reads or about its influence on subsequent readings of classical authors.

We have seen that Notker's translation of Martianus takes over the form, as well as the content, of Remigian expositions. It begins with an abbreviated *accessus* to Martianus which is based on Remigius' introductory remarks on the author's name and the title. When we compare Notker's work to the *Ovide moralisé* we jump forward to the other end of the continuum of primary translation. With this jump we can draw a very sharp contrast between the use of commentary in the two texts. The *Ovide moralisé* also provides an *accessus* of sorts in which it borrows the terminology of scholastic and pre-scholastic literary prologues. But whereas Notker's *accessus* introduces Martianus' text as received through Remigius' commentary, the *accessus* to the *Ovide moralisé* is almost completely self-referential. It introduces the *Ovide moralisé* itself.

Late medieval Latin *accessus* to Ovid's works, including the *Metamorphoses*, produce, as might be expected, a range of prologue forms. Arnulf of Orléans in the twelfth century uses the common *accessus* form (Hunt's "type C"), consisting of *vita*, *titulus*, *materia*, *utilitas*, *intentio*, *cui parti philosophiae supponitur*, and *modus tractandi*. This form seems to remain most popular for Ovid commentaries in subsequent centuries.[50] But some later writers also made use of scholastic terminology, adopting the fourfold causal scheme of the Aristotelian prologue: efficient, material, formal, and final cause.[51] Some prologues, however, combine the two forms, presenting such mixtures such as *materia*, *intentio*, *finalis causa*, *cui parte ethicae supponitur*, or more replete combinations which use both systems in their entirety. One successful combination of this sort is Giovanni del Virgilio's exposition of the *Metamorphoses* written in 1322–3, where the prologue gives lengthy discussions of each of the four cases, and then adds discussions of *titulus libri* and *cui parti philosophiae supponitur*.[52]

The opening seventy lines of the *Ovide moralisé* function much as an academic prologue, although they do not present the strict form of a traditional prologue with its careful progression from topic to topic. The discussion in these opening lines, however, presents what might be seen as a composite of topics from the "type C" and the scholastic or Aristotelian prologue, including some Romance equivalents for Latin exegetical terminology. The influence of academic prologues is most visible in the terms "espondre" and "exposicion" (lines 11, 48, 75; cf. Latin "exponere" and "expositio"), and in the terms "profitable" and "profiter" (lines 55 and 58; cf. Latin "utilitas").[53] The discussion in lines 44–6, "Qui le sens en porroit savoir, / La veritez seroit aperte, / Qui souz les fables gist couverte" (the truth that lies hidden beneath the fables will be clear to one who can discern the meaning of them) clearly depends on academic treatments of *integumentum*.[54] Even where the prologue does not offer a French equivalent for academic literary terms, the subject matter covered corresponds generally to *utilitas*, *unde* or *causa*, *intentio*, *auctor*, *causa efficiens*, and *modus tractandi* (or *modus agendi*). We will consider these correspondences in some detail.

But the *Ovide moralisé* registers an important difference with Latin academic practice. These terms and topics, translated now into their vernacular equivalents, are mainly directed to the vernacular translation and commentary itself, and not, as in standard academic prologues, to the Ovidian text under consideration. In the opening fourteen lines the author justifies the enterprise of exposition in terms of its ethical utility:

Se l'escripture ne me ment,
Tout est pour nostre enseignement
Quanqu'il a es livres escript,
Soient bon ou mal li escript.
Qui bien i vaudroit prendre esgart,
Li maulz y est que l'en s'en gart,
Li biens pour ce que l'en le face,
Et cui Dieus done eür et grace
De conquerre sens et savoir,
Il ne doit pas sa bouche avoir
Trop chiere au bien dire et espondre,
Quar nulz ne doit son sens repondre,

Quar ne vault sens que l'en enserre
Ne plus qu'avoirs repost en terre.

[If Scripture doesn't lie to me, all that is written in books, whether good or evil, is for our instruction. For anyone who really wants to pay attention, evil is presented there so that one may guard against it, and good so that one may imitate it. Anyone to whom God gives good fortune and grace to attain wisdom and knowledge ought not to refrain from speaking and expounding what is proper, for one ought not to hide wisdom, since wisdom kept under wraps is worth no more than riches buried underground.][55]

Whatever is written in books may profit us by exemplifying good and evil. Here the author takes what had become a traditional critical rationale borrowed from St. Paul (Romans 15.4). This formula was often applied, among other things, to the *Heroides*, which could be seen to offer illustrations of good and bad love, to be imitated or rejected. The nature and function of these contrasting illustrations could be discussed under the headings *intentio* and *utilitas*.[56] To the extent that these opening lines of the *Ovide moralisé* do reflect the thematic influence of *Heroides* prologues, the discussion of the moral value of texts that contain good and evil would seem to be governed by the idea of the utility of ethical exemplification. A prologue to the *Heroides* says that the text belongs to the field of ethics, "ethicae subponitur, quia de iusto amore instruit"; similarly, a prologue to the *Tristia* states that the text belongs to ethics, "quia de moribus tractat."[57] But the line "Tout est pour nostre enseignement" is also a commonplace appeal to the *utilitas* of *compilatio*, a convention that had its origins in the prologues to learned and scriptural compilations.[58] Its presence here in the prologue to the *Ovide moralisé* may be an echo to this exegetical convention validating the work of the compiler. It would suggest here that the author of the *Ovide moralisé* is pointing to the character of his own text, either as a collection of Ovidian materials or as a compilation of pagan and Christian narratives together with exegetical *auctoritates*, and that he himself is adopting the posture of the *compilator*. I will return to the implications of this posture later in this chapter.

The Ovidian text itself may contain examples of good and evil for our profitable instruction: but what occupies the foreground in these opening lines of the *Ovide moralisé* is the utility of the exposition that is about to be performed and the ethical responsibility of the expositor. The discussion of *utilitas* and ethics serves to introduce, not Ovid as *auctor*, but the expositor himself, and is directed to justify the expositor's own undertaking: "Il ne doit pas sa bouche avoir / Trop chiere au bien dire et espondre." The academic prologue doubles back on itself, introducing the very text that it generates rather than the Ovidian text that it proposes to explicate. If the standard *accessus ad auctorem* is always really an *accessus ad commentatorem*, the prologue to the *Ovide moralisé* renders this tendency explicit. Indeed, the explicitly auto-referential character of this prologue represents a departure from other vernacular assimilations of academic practice. A fourteenth-century French translation of Ovid's *Ars amatoria* presents a prologue which uses some standard academic devices and terminology, but the exegetical posture assumed here is quite conservative: the exposition is directed to service of the *auctor* rather than, as in the *Ovide moralisé*, to the text generated out of the commentator's privileged insight.[59]

The rest of the prologue to the *Ovide moralisé* also dramatizes this tendency, which was only implicit in the traditional academic *accessus*, of pointing to the commentator rather than the *auctor*. The section that would correspond to standard discussions of *causa* or *intentio* describes the engendering, not of the original work, but of the present text:

Pour ce me plaist que je commans
Traire de latin en romans
Les fables de l'ancien temps,
– S'en dirai ce que je entens –
Selonc ce qu'Ovides les baille. (lines 15–19)

[Thus I am pleased to commence my translation of the ancient stories from Latin into the vulgar tongue, just as Ovid presents them – and I will relate what I understand about them.]

This is the only reference in the prologue to the *auctor*, Ovid. But unlike conventional academic prologues to Ovid, the *Ovide moralisé* does not provide a *vita* of the poet. The absence of so conventional an element is suggestive: this prologue constitutes an act of auto-exegesis on the part of the translator-exegete, and while a naming of Ovid as the source is appropriate, there is no place here for a *vita* of Ovid.

It is for the same reason that the ensuing discussion, which appears to correspond roughly to the Aristotelian topic of efficient cause, allows the author of the *Ovide moralisé* to situate his own text in an exegetical tradition and to locate the cause of his undertaking in God:

Pluiseur ont essaié sans faille
A fere ce que je proupos,
Sans acomplir tout lor proupos,
Et ja soit ce qu'en moi n'ait mie
Plus sens ne plus philosophie
De ceulz qui ce cuidierent faire,
En Dieu me fi de cest afaire,
Qui aus sages et aus discrez
Repont et cele ses secrez,
Si les revele aus aprentis
Qui sont de l'enquerre ententis. (lines 20–30)

[Many others have made valid attempts to do what I propose without accomplishing their whole purpose; and although I am not endowed with more wisdom and knowledge than those others who believed they could do this, in undertaking this task I put faith in God, who hides and conceals his secrets from wise and knowing men, but reveals them to beginners who diligently seek Him.]

The precedent for his exegetical project lies with unsuccessful human attempts to achieve an authentic reading, which is to be distinguished from the true authorial and interpretive power of God, from which his own project can derive its success. In differentiating here between human and divine authorial power, the poet of the *Ovide moralisé* may be borrowing a commonplace from scholastic biblical commentary, the *duplex causa efficiens*.

Scholastic commentators used the Aristotelian category of efficient cause to describe the authorial engendering of a text. But the Bible required a particular refinement of this category: as a whole entity the authorship of the Bible lies with God, while its individual books were realized in human language by a succession of human authors. The category of efficient cause might thus be divided twofold: the primary, or "moving" authorship of God could be acknowledged and removed to the safety of unassailable privilege, while the exegete applied himself to the real problem of analyzing the human-produced discourse of the text's human author.[60] That this principle of biblical criticism should inform the construction of exegetical purpose in the *Ovide moralisé* does not represent an unlikely crossing of boundaries between sacred and secular commentary. At the very least, the historical precedent for an exchange of techniques between scriptural and arts commentary is considerable. Early biblical exegetes borrowed and built on the techniques of arts commentators, and in the later Middle Ages, the techniques of scholastic biblical exposition, including the Aristotelian or causal prologue, were widely applied to the exposition of pagan *auctores*. But the notion from scriptural criticism of a *duplex causa efficiens* has a special relevance to the *Ovide moralisé* given that the author considers himself as much a biblical exegete as an arts commentator. Throughout his text he uses the Bible to gloss Ovid, and conversely Ovid's text to expound the truths of Scripture. Thus, for example, to his rendering of Ovid's creation myth he adds matter from glosses on Genesis from the *Glossa ordinaria* and Peter Comester.[61]

Near the very end of his poem, in book 15, he takes up the theme of good reading, of the interpretive wisdom that can force texts to yield up their secret meaning. This is the theme that he broaches in his introduction, under the aegis of the *duplex causa efficiens*; but in book 15 this theme is applied to the methods of interpreting pagan *fabulae* and the Bible:

> Voirs est, qui Ovide prendroit
> A la letre et n'i entendroit
> Autre sen, autre entendement
> Que tel com l'auctors grossement
> I met en racontant la fable,
> Tout seroit chose mençognable,
> Poi profitable et trop obscure . . .
> Et qui la fable ensi creroit
> Estre voire, il meserreroit
> Et seroit bogrerie aperte,
> Mes sous la fable gist couverte
> La sentence plus profitable.
> Dont qui la tient à pure fable,

Ne li chaille quel qu'ele soit,
Et qui pense qu'en fables oit
Autre sens, autre entendement,
Ne doit trop embreveusement
Blasmer la fable ne reprendre
Por ce qu'il ne la puet entendre
Ou bon sens qu'ele puet avoir.
Bon sens et acordable à voir
Puet l'en en ceste fable metre,
Qui bien set exposer la letre.
Ensi est la Sainte Escripture
En pluisors leus trouble et obscure,
Et samble fable purement.
Qui n'i met autre entendement
Qu'en la letre ne samble avoir,
Et qui creroit, por non-savoir,
Qu'il n'i eüst autre sentence,
Il se decevroit, sans doutance,
Si metroit s'ame à dampnement.[62] (book 15, lines 2525–57)

[Certainly, whoever would take Ovid's texts at the literal level and not understand another sense, another meaning than what the author crudely presents in recounting the story, to this person everything would be a lie, of little profit and great obscurity, . . . and whoever would thus believe the fable to be true, would commit error and would clearly be a heretic. But beneath the fable, the most profitable meaning lies hidden. Thus whoever fixes on the fable alone doesn't care what it is really about; and he who believes that in the fable there is another meaning, another sense, ought not blame or condemn the fable rashly just because he cannot understand it or the good meaning that it can have. Whoever knows how to expound the letter can derive from the fable a meaning that is good and consistent with truth. Indeed, even sacred Scripture is difficult and obscure in many places and seems to be mere fable. He who cannot derive another meaning which Scripture does not seem to have at its literal level, and who would believe, through ignorance, that there is no other meaning there, would certainly deceive himself and place his own soul in damnation.]

This strong identification with the aims and methods of biblical exegesis creates a natural context for the principle of the *duplex causa efficiens* in the prologue. But the notion of God as the "first" author, the prime mover "Qui aus sages et aus discrez / Repont et cele ses secrez" (book 1, lines 27–8) is applied here to the inspiration of the exegete rather than of the *auctor*. In explaining the generation of his own exegetical text the author of the *Ovide moralisé* assumes the role of human *causa efficiens*, and as explicator of divine truths concealed within the *fabula* or integument, positions himself as the human beneficiary of God's interpretive direction. The exegete has so placed the original *auctor* as here to have entered into the privileged authorial hierarchy of *duplex causa efficiens*. The exegete adapts the tools of his trade to perform a complex act of auto-exegesis.

The lines in the prologue that correspond to *modus tractandi* and *utilitas*, with which the prologue concludes, are similarly auto-referential. The poet describes his method of exposition and its value or "profit." He will not produce an exposition for every *fable*, for this would weary his audience; he will confine himself, as briefly as he can, to expounding "les mutacions des fables / Qui sont bones et profitables" (lines 53–4).

The prologue to the *Ovide moralisé* suggests how much primary translation develops out of the conventions and interests of academic commentary. It shows, indeed, how vernacular translation emerges by extending and making visible the rhetorical principles and motives that are latent in academic hermeneutics. The prologue to the commentary on the *Aeneid* attributed to Bernardus Silvestris also suggests a kind of slippage between the authorial claims of Virgil and of the commentator: the prologue to Virgil threatens to turn into a prologue to the commentator, as academic terminology is applied to the *accessus* itself. But in the prologue to the *Ovide moralisé*, such slippage has now fixed or counterbalanced itself on the side of the commentator's authorial power. In the *Ovide moralisé* the rhetorical motive of appropriation, which governs so much medieval exegetical practice, has realized itself in the process of vernacular translation. First, the commentary has supplanted the text, in that the prologue provides an exposition of the forthcoming exposition itself. It is notable that the prologue refers mainly to the exegetical rather than translative functions of the *Ovide moralisé*, as if the status of the poem as a whole were bound up with its expository purpose. Its identity as a translation is subsumed within its dominant identity as an exposition, and the Ovidian text becomes the pretext for the proper work of exposition, upon which productive attention has now been refocused. But this process of displacement assumes another dimension here: the *Ovide moralisé* also exemplifies the vernacular appropriating Latin academic discourse which is applied, not to a privileged *auctor* (Ovid), but to its own engendering as a vernacular text. This represents both an extension of and a radical rupture with academic traditions of *translatio studii*. It carries over the tendency within academic hermeneutics to contest the priority of the text and to substitute the exegesis for the text. But in vernacularizing the critical apparatus of commentary and the commentary itself it ruptures the linguistic links that Latin exegesis preserves with ancient *studia*. In applying this vernacular apparatus to itself, a vernacular text, a vernacular translation and commentary, it effaces the linguistic presence of the Latin Ovid, and effectively breaks any remaining linguistic links with classical *auctoritas*. Thus a vernacular system of exegesis replaces its Latin precedent; and in a radical move of appropriation, a vernacular translation substitutes itself for the Latin original as the object of exegetical interest.

These appropriations and substitutions represent a form of translation as rhetorical *exercitatio*, the mastering and naturalizing of a non-native discourse to achieve *copia rerum* along with *copia verborum*. The vernacular appropriation and application of academic terminology and exegetical procedures demonstrates how this rhetorical procedure of *exercitatio* can be undertaken as part of a hermeneutical program. But the principle of *exercitatio* here can be broadened to include more than the use of certain academic terminologies: it can also be seen as the borrowing of certain authorial roles or postures. The poet of the *Ovide moralisé* so much conceives his role as that of exegete rather than translator that his initial approach to the actual text of Ovid, that is, his translation of *Metamorphoses* 1.1–2, becomes the point of entry to a debate about the limits of exegetical power. These opening lines of the *Metamorphoses* contain Ovid's statement of *intentio*: "In nova fert animus mutatas dicere formas corpora" ([My] heart moves [me] to tell of forms changed into new bodies). This becomes the occasion for the exegete's own statement of intention; or we might say that the exegete's *intentio* co-opts that of Ovid:

Or vueil comencier ma matire.
Ovides dist: "Mes cuers vieult dire
Les formes qui muees furent
En nouviaux cors". Aucun qui durent
L'autour espondre et declairier
S'entremistrent de l'empirier,
De l'auteur reprendre et desdire,
Disant que li autours dut dire:
"Les cors qui en formes noveles
Furent muez", mes teulz faveles
Ne doivent audience avoir:
Homs raisonables puet savoir
Que bien dist, ce croi, li autours,
Quar, ançois que li Creatours
Creast le monde, il n'iert encors
Ne ne pooit estre nul cors
Qui nove forme receüst.
Quel cors iert il dont Dieus deüst
Forme traire au comencement?
Il n'iert riens fors lui seulement,
Qui en sa devine pensee
Avoit toute forme pensee
Tele come il la donneroit
Au cors, que de noient feroit,
Sans aïde de nulle rien,
Sans point de present mairien.
Einsi croi je qu'il soit sans faille. (book 1, 71–97)

[Now I wish to begin my matter. Ovid said: "My heart wishes to tell of the forms that were changed into new bodies." Certain persons who should have expounded and elucidated the author took it upon themselves to blame him, to accuse and confound the author, stating that he ought to have said: "the bodies which were changed into new forms"; but such falsehoods don't deserve an audience. A reasonable man can understand, I believe, that the author spoke justly; for before the Creator made the world, there never was, nor could there be, any body which received a new form. What body was there from which God could create a form in the beginning? There was nothing besides Him alone, who, in his divine mind, imagined each form just as he would give it to the body, which he would create from nothing, with no help and no limitation of visible matter. Thus I believe this is the absolute truth.]

Having offered his literal rendering of Ovid's lines, the translator immediately resumes the role of exegete, by pointing to the risk of betraying an author when expounding him: certain expositors spoil and misrepresent the author when they propose emendations to his text. Having just inaugurated his own performance as translator, he conceives and represents that performance in terms of the responsibility of the exegete ("epondre" and "declairier").

He launches directly into a polemic against an earlier commentator, probably Arnulf of Orléans, who had supplied a correction to the first line.[63] Arnulf had suggested that Ovid's statement, "forms changed into new bodies," was unacceptable on philosophical grounds ("because qualities [forms] cannot become substance [bodies]"), but could be read as poetic "hypellage" for "corpora mutata in novas formas" (bodies changed into new forms).[64] The *Ovide moralisé* insists on the veracity of Ovid's statement, authorizing it through a fairly simplified account of the Neo-Platonic doctrine of forms and the perpetuity of God. What is significant here, however, is the way that the poet-commentator defines his exegetical purpose by authenticating Ovid's text and saving it from those falsifiers, whose misstatements "ne doivent audience avoir." He thus inaugurates his task of translation by contesting an earlier exegetical authority, by affirming the correct reading upon which his own translation depends, and so authorizes his own place in a kind of exegetical lineage.

The *Ovide moralisé* seems to contain and rehearse within its own boundaries the very practice and history of the textual transmission of Ovid in the Middle Ages. It records, first of all, the complex intertextual reception of the Ovidian corpus, as it variously supplements the *Metamorphoses* with readings from the *Heroides* and *Fasti* as well as with readings from other classical authors, notably Statius. It also carries over medieval classicism, not only in the form of mythographical commentary (Hyginus, Servius, Fulgentius, the Vatican Mythographers, John of Garland's *Integumenta Ovidii*, and Arnulf of Orléans), but also in the form of medieval reconstructions of Greek lore, such as the *Ilias latina* and Dares' *De excidio Trojae historia*. In taking over the works of commentators the author of the *Ovide moralisé* also appropriates exegetical structures and techniques, as his own prologue demonstrates. With this the poet also appropriates a set of discourses that medieval academics had used to define different aspects of what may be called, after Foucault, the "author-function."[65] Most broadly, as we have seen, the poet of the *Ovide moralisé* adopts the role of *expositor*. But through this vast project of translation as *exercitatio* in which he assimilates the work of many diverse predecessors, he also assumes the role of compiler, *compilator*.

The implications of *compilatio* in the *Ovide moralisé* extend beyond the activity of compiling or collecting *auctoritates*, which is the common understanding of the role of *compilator* in late medieval academic practice.[66] As noted earlier, the poet of the *Ovide moralisé* appeals to the conventional *utilitas* of *compilatio* in his prologue as a rationale for assembling Ovidian *fabulae* and moralizations. But under the role of *compilator* he has made the very enterprise of *translatio studii* the property of vernacular writing. His work is a *compilatio* of hermeneutical responses to pagan and Christian *auctoritates*, as he assumes variously the posture of moral expositor, biblical exegete, allegorist, and translator. The role of translator, in turn, involves the rhetorical principle of *exercitatio*, and here the power of the compiler assumes an added dimension. The poet of the *Ovide moralisé* incorporates existing vernacular versions of some Ovidian material: he uses a translation of the Philomela legend which has been associated with Chrétien de Troyes,[67] a Norman version of Pyramus and Thisbe which is really an amplified romance, and for Ovid's account of the Golden Age in *Metamorphoses* book 1 he introduces some material from the *Roman de la Rose* and from French versions of Boethius' Golden Age (*Consolatio* 2 m.5). Within his own project of *exercitatio* he has thus incorporated earlier *exercitationes*, directing his attention as a *compilator* to the vernacular tradition itself. In a sense his own translation project serves as an organizing structure for the transmission of a vernacular tradition of Ovid. Indeed, one might say that by assembling these existing vernacular texts he constitutes them as an authentic vernacular canon.

Thus his roles as vernacular *expositor* and translator intersect with his role as *compilator*, for within his own vast effort to substitute vernacular writing for *Latinitas* he includes earlier models of such substitution. His return to earlier French translations of Ovidian lore testifies to the way in which a native French literary language has already established its own cultural privilege, contesting the authoritative status of *Latinitas* even as it carries over classical texts for vernacular audiences. The use of these earlier French texts within the *Ovide moralisé* thus also constitutes a kind of vernacular subtradition of translation which mediates between the new translation and the "original" text.

In introducing the two French translations, the Norman Pyramus and Thisbe and the Philomela attributed to Chrétien, the poet of the *Ovide moralisé* adopts the posture of *compilator*. He offers the redaction of Pyramus and Thisbe with a conventional promise to respect the *ipsissima verba* of his source:

> Or vous raconterai le conte
> Et la fable sans ajouster,
> Sans muer et sans riens oster,
> Si comme uns autres l'a dité
> Puis i metrai le verité. (book 4, lines 224–8)

[Now I will recount for you the story and the fable without adding anything, without changing or removing anything, just as another has told it; then I will set forth the true meaning of it.]

His introduction to the Philomela even better exemplifies how the *compilator* can contrive his self-effacement:

Mes ja ne descrirai le conte
Fors si com Crestiens le conte,
Qui bien en translata la letre.
Sus lui ne m'en vueil entremetre.
Tout son dit vous raconterai,
Et l'alegorie en trairai. (book 6, lines 2211–16)

[But I will not recount the story other than as Chrétien told it, for he has translated the letter of the text very well. I do not wish to supersede his version. I will relate his whole poem to you, and then I will extract the allegory.]

The power of the *compilator* lies in the way that he can retreat behind the *ipsissima verba* of the texts and conceal the very control that he exerts as orchestrator of *auctoritates*. Here, by invoking the *compilator*'s conventional regard for the integrity of his materials, the poet of the *Ovide moralisé* claims for these vernacular texts a canonical privilege like that of Ovid's own text. Indeed, the introduction to the Philomela, "sus lui ne m'en vueil entremetre," carries the suggestion of interposing a (superfluous) new translation. This echoes the theme at the beginning of the *Ovide moralisé* of guarding against meddling with the *ipsissima verba* of Ovid's own text:

Aucun qui durent
L'autour espondre et declairier
S'entremistrent de l'empirier,
De l'auteur reprendre et desdire,
Disant que li autours dut dire:
"Les cors qui en formes noveles
Furent muez", mes teulz faveles
Ne doivent audience avoir. (book 1, lines 74–81)

[Certain persons who should have expounded and elucidated the author took it upon themselves to blame him, to accuse and confound the author, stating that he ought to have said: "the bodies which were changed into new forms"; but such falsehoods don't deserve an audience.]

In the passage from book 1 he insists upon the integrity of the Latin text which he is about to translate and expound; and in introducing the Pyramus and Thisbe and the Philomela he asserts the integrity of the vernacular texts that he is about to compile. In the first case it is the role of *expositor*, and the second case, the role of *compilator*, that requires his profession of fidelity. But in the latter case, his task of *compilatio* completed, he resumes the role of *expositor*, as he proceeds to supply a commentary for the translations he has just compiled. The fact that these vernacular versions are vastly different from Ovid's text and might themselves constitute a misrepresentation or betrayal of the Ovidian *ipsissima verba* does not pose a problem here. The vernacular translations he has compiled have so displaced the Latin, so supplanted it as a privileged *auctoritas*, that the expositor's loyalty to textual integrity can simply be transferred from original to translation. A vernacular tradition has quite literally interposed itself in the project of *translatio studii*.

Unlike Notker's expository translation, the *Ovide moralisé* achieves a complete linguistic synthesis of textual elements. It is as if a Latin manuscript containing a text of an *auctor* along with an accumulation of commentary and paraphrase has been rendered entirely into French. Thus the relationship between text and commentary that obtains in a Latin academic context can be replicated entirely in the vernacular. Whether the poet of the *Ovide moralisé* produces his own translation or borrows an extant one, his exegetical activity does not need to refer itself to the ulterior authority of the original Latin text.

Vernacular intermediaries have also to a degree supplanted Latin sources as the basis for expositions. This is strikingly exemplified by the rendering in book 1 of Ovid's *aetas aurea* (*Metamorphoses* 1, lines 87–112), where the *Ovide moralisé* draws supplementary material from Jean de Meun's *Roman de la Rose* and from Boethian analogues in Old French. The *Ovide moralisé* begins the *aetas aurea* by following Ovid's text relatively closely:

> Aurea prima sata est aetas, quae vindice nullo,
> sponte sua, sine lege fidem nectumque colebat.
> poena metusque aberant, nec verba minantia fixo
> aere legebantur, nec supplex turba timebat
> iudicis ora sui, sed erant sine vindice tuti. (book 1, lines 89–93)

[Golden was that first age, which, with no one to compel, without a law, of its own will, kept faith and did the right. There was no fear of punishment, no threatening words were to be read on brazen tablets; no suppliant throng gazed fearfully upon its judge's face; but without defenders lived secure.][68]

> Lors nasqui li dorez aäges.
> La gent de son gre, sans paour,
> Et sans crience de jugeour,
> Sans establissement de loy,
> Loiauté tenoient et foi;
> Sans paine et sans paour vivoient;
> Loiens ne chaënes n'avoient
> Pour loier les malfeseours . . . (book 1, lines 458–65)

[Then the golden age was born. The people, of their own will, without fear and without the pronouncement of a judge, without established law, maintained loyalty and faith; they lived without pain or fear. They had no bonds or chains to restrain criminals.]

Starting with line 463, the *Ovide moralisé* departs from Ovid's text by means of prolepsis, substituting a later effect for an earlier cause. Where Ovid writes of the absence of repressive laws ("nec verba minantia fixo / aere legebantur") and the freedom from legal authority ("iudicis ora sui," "sine vindice tuti"), suggesting an innocence of prohibitions in advance of crime, the *Ovide moralisé* reduces and simplifies this to describe the absence of harsh punishment ("Loiens ne chaëns n'avoient / Pour loier les malfesours"), which is of course the result of having prohibitions which can be violated. The *Ovide moralisé* then continues in this simplified proleptic vein, expanding the trope of effect (punitive measures) rather than Ovid's trope of cause (cruel proclamations of law):

N'ierent larrons ne robeours;
Sans doute de nulle joustise
Ierent simple et sans convoitise. (lines 466–8)

[There were no thieves or robbers. Truly, without punitive law, they were a simple people, without covetousness.]

The wording of these lines strongly echoes the wording in the *aetas aurea* section of Jean de Meun's *Roman de la Rose*:

Jadis, au tens des prumiers peres
et de noz prumereines meres,
si con la letre le tesmoigne,
par cui nous savons la besoigne,
furent amors leaus et fines,
sanz covoitise et sanz rapines,
et li siecles mout precieus.[69] (Lecoy ed., lines 8325–31)

[Of old, in the time of our first fathers and mothers, according to the testimony of the writings through which we know this field, loves were loyal and pure, without covetousness and rapine, and the world was a very precious place.][70]

This section of the *Roman de la Rose* (lines 8325–424) is a synthesis of Ovid's *aetas aurea*, Boethius' redaction of Ovid's account in *Consolatio* 2 m.5, and Jean's own elaborations. But as might be expected, Jean's treatment of the *aetas aurea* here in the *Roman de la Rose* bears a relationship to his reading of 2 m.5 in his own prose translation of Boethius' *Consolatio*, which he probably completed around the year 1300.[71] In the passage just quoted from the *Roman de la Rose*, the line "sanz covoitise et sanz rapines" is thematically indebted to the lines from *Consolatio* 2 m.5:

Sed saeuior ignibus Aetnae
feruens amor ardet habendi.[72]

[But the fervent desire for possessions burns more savagely than the fires of Etna.]

Boethius' own source for this is Ovid's line "vis et amor sceleratus habendi" (violence and the vicious love of possessions), *Metamorphoses* 1.131. For these Ovidian–Boethian lines Jean gave this translation in his version of the *Consolatio*:

Mais l'angoisseuse couvoitise de avoir art en nous plus cruesement que li feu de la montaigne Ethna qui touz jours art.[73]

[But the violent covetousness for wealth burns in us more harshly than the fire of Mount Etna, which burns constantly.]

The verbal correspondence between the *Roman de la Rose* and Jean's translation of Boethius is obvious. It seems also likely that Jean's use of the motif of avarice ("covoitise") in the *Roman* derived from his reading of the Boethius metrum, for Jean introduces it again, towards the end of the *aetas aurea* section in the *Roman*, in conjunction with another theme, the simple sleeping habits in the Golden Age, a theme which is only found in Boethius ("somnos dabat herba salubres," [the grass provided wholesome sleep], 2 m.5.10):

> et quant par nuit dormir voloient,
> en leu de coustes aportoient
> en leur caseaus monceaus ou gerbes
> de fuelles ou de mousse ou d'erbes . . .
> Seur tex couches con je devise,
> Sanz rapine et sanz covoitise,
> s'entracoloient et besoient
> cil cui li jeu d'amors plesoient. (lines 8369–72, 8401–4)

[and when they wanted to sleep at night, they did not use featherbeds, but, instead, carried piles or bundles of leaves or moss or grass into their huts . . . Upon such couches as I describe, those who were pleased by Love's games would embrace and kiss each other without rapine or covetousness.][74]

Thus Jean's rendering of the *aetas aurea* in the *Roman de la Rose*, indebted as it is to Ovid, is also inextricably bound up with his reading of Boethius' text, a reading which he also realized during his career in a full translation of Boethius.

If the *Ovide moralisé* is indebted to the Boethian readings in Jean's *Roman de la Rose* for its rendering of Ovid's *aurea aetas*, it may also be indebted to Jean's own Boethius translation. This debt may be direct or indirect. In the generation or so after Jean's translation of the *Consolatio* was submitted to public view, a number of new translations of the *Consolatio* in French appeared, and to varying degrees these later translations depend on Jean's. The particular problems surrounding the sequence of French translations of the *Consolatio* will be considered in some detail in the next chapter. For now it is sufficient to note that four of these versions use wording comparable to Jean's to translate "amor habendi." A prose and verse translation reads "couvoitise plus fort croit";[75] a revision of the prose–verse version reads "l'avarice des convoiteux";[76] and a version by an anonymous translator of Meun reads "Mais convoitise plus nous art."[77] From the 1330s, Renaut de Louhans' version of 2 m.5, which combines Ovid's structure of the four ages with Boethian elements as well as with some readings from the corresponding passages in the *Roman de la Rose*, applies Jean's wording several times: in his interpolations from Ovid about the third and fourth ages ("Car lors commença couvoitise," "Qui les cuers des hommes atise / Par avarice et couvoitise," "Tant ont du monde prins malice, / Couvoitise et avarice"), as well as to translate the end of Boethius' metrum ("Est bien couvoitise montee").[78] It should be noted that while "couvoitise" might seem an obvious lexical choice for rendering "amor habendi," it only comes into use after Jean's version. Earlier versions use "amour d'avoir." The dating of these various versions is uncertain; at least one, that of Renaut de Louhans, post-dates the *Ovide moralisé*, which de Boer places between 1316 and 1328.[79] The *aetas aurea* in the *Ovide moralisé* may be indebted to Jean's translation of the *Consolatio* through one of these later versions (the revised "mixed" version, for example, achieved enormous success, surviving in over sixty manuscripts). In this case the relationship between Ovid's *aetas aurea* and the *Ovide moralisé* would be mediated by multiple layers of a vernacular tradition deriving from Boethius and only indirectly from Ovid. But it is probably more likely that, like many French translators of Boethius, the poet of the *Ovide moralisé* borrowed directly from Jean's *Roman de la Rose* or from Jean's translation of the *Consolatio*. In this case, the *Ovide moralisé* joins a vernacular subtradition of Boethius translation in which Jean de Meun's renderings of Boethius and Ovid intervene in the later French reception of these Latin *auctores*. Indeed, Jean's account of the Golden Age in the *Roman de la Rose* is a direct source for much more of the corresponding account in the *Ovide moralisé* than the interpolation described above. Jean's text provides the *Ovide moralisé* with a number of suggestions for elaborating Ovid, so that Jean supplies the later translator with a kind of poetic gloss on the Latin original.[80] It seems that the poet of the *Ovide moralisé* uses Jean's French text as much as Ovid's Latin as the point of reference for his own *exercitatio*. This kind of intralingual *exercitatio* is no doubt inevitable in the later and well-developed stages of any vernacular literary tradition. We will see more extensive evidence of this shift in the value of *exercitatio* from interlingual to intralingual appropriation when we consider examples of the French and English traditions of Boethius translation.

The poet of the *Ovide moralisé* probably conceived his book as a work of mythography: as Paule Demats notes, his enlargements of the fables within the *Metamorphoses*, as well as his addition of fables from other sources, such as the *Heroides*, point to the mythographer's method.[81] Indeed, as we have seen, this author takes over, in some form, all the roles and practices of the exegete. To close this discussion of the *Ovide moralisé*, we can consider how these various practices are summed up and transformed in the treatment of the Tiresias legend from book 3 of the *Metamorphoses*.

The translation of the Tiresias episode (*Metamorphoses* book 3, lines 316–38; *Ovide moralisé* book 3, lines 999–1105) serves in the most basic capacity of *enarratio*: textual paraphrase. This is not unique to the treatment of the Tiresias legend, for all of the direct translations from Ovid in the *Ovide moralisé* serve the function of paraphrase, the starting point of *enarratio*. The *Ovide moralisé* exemplifies probably better than any other vernacular text how translation emerges out of and in conjunction with hermeneutical practice; and the particular complex of materials that develop out of and around the Tiresias passage provide a good paradigm for the way that *enarratio* generates and sponsors translation in this text as a whole. Here the rendering of Ovid's fable gives way to another exegetical procedure, the moral exposition of the fable according to the mythographer's method ("Or vous vueil espondre ces fables," line 1106).

The moral exposition of Tiresias is an integral part of the translative procedure of the whole poem, as it is itself translated from Fulgentius' exposition of the Tiresias myth in the *Mitologiae* 2.5.[82] Thus the translation of Ovid's Tiresias is contained by the framework of exegesis. But this exegesis, the allegoresis of the mythographer, carries forward in turn the activity of the translator, as Fulgentius becomes an *auctor*, like Ovid, to be rendered in the vernacular. On a greatly magnified scale this reproduces the format of translation that we have seen in Notker's practice, in which vernacular paraphrase breaks down the boundaries between text and commentary, between the object of understanding and the discourse of explication, which enters into the meaning of that which is to be understood. Here, as in Notker, the *Ovide moralisé* assimilates both these functions; it levels off the difference between the original text (Ovid) and supplement or ancillary text (Fulgentius' mythography) by making them both the objects of its understanding upon which it performs the explicative task of translation. The *Ovide moralisé* appropriates these sources into a new discursive system in which the difference between text and commentary has little actual meaning, and by conferring on them a new value within the system of vernacular paraphrase it effaces their originary force. In this way the vernacular translation supersedes its sources, co-opting them into a new system of values which it substitutes for those of its sources.

While the naturalistic exposition of Tiresias is borrowed from Fulgentius, it is obvious also that the poet of the *Ovide moralisé* associated the mythographer's method with more recent precedent, such as that of Carolingian writers, among whom Fulgentius was a strong and clear influence.[83] Other recent influences include the mythographic allegorists of the twelfth and thirteenth centuries, such as the Chartrians William of Conches and Bernardus Silvestris along with direct sources like the expositions of Arnulf of Orléans and John of Garland. But where the *Ovide moralisé* departs from these precedents is in introducing a second dimension to his exposition, a theological allegory of the pagan text.[84] This begins directly after the naturalistic explanation: "Or vous dirae l'alegorie / Que ceste fable signifie" (1189–90). The poet describes, (from Acts of the Apostles) how the Holy Spirit aided the disciples in their evangelizing which made his name known through the world. Through this many were converted from error. Those who were most sinful were most penitent and most fervently devoted to God. To exemplify this with respect to the Tiresias legend, the poet first recounts the conversion of Paul (Acts of the Apostles 90):

> C'est cil qui, par vertu devine,
> Perdi la corporel veüe,
> Qui au tiers jour li fu rendue,
> Mes, tant dis come il ne vit goute,
> L'enlumina Dieus si, sans doute,
> Qu'il vit touz les devins secrez . . . (book 3, lines 1256–61)

[It was he who, by force of divine will, lost his physical sight, which was restored to him on the third day. But for as long as he could see nothing, God enlumined him so much that, doubtless, he saw all the divine secrets.]

But the poet also introduces Mary Magdalene, whose penitence and devotion was even more intense and thus more pleasing to God (lines 1273–91). This shows that a woman's faith is more fervent than a man's, and presumably this corresponds with Tiresias' pronouncement that women take greater pleasure in love than men (for which Juno struck him blind).

This is characteristic of the theological explanations of the *Ovide moralisé*. There is no attempt here to tie this reading of meaning to an *intentio auctoris*. But on the other hand, the method of eliciting Christian significance from the pagan text is not that of analogy, such as we find in the work of the fourteenth-century English mythographer John Ridewall, who discovers in each myth a moral truth which can then be sanctioned by invoking a succession of theological authorities.[85] In contrast, the *Ovide moralisé* proposes a Christian theological significance that claims its origin, not unlike the allegory of the theologians, in the letter of the text itself.[86] It is this "Christianization" of Ovid, making him, in a peculiar way, the purveyor of Christian truths *avant la lettre*, that Paule Demats has called the "paradox of the *Ovide moralisé*."[87] The author makes no explicit attempt to "convert" Ovid, to attribute to him a prescience of Christian monotheism, in the manner of the *De vetula*, a thirteenth-century poem which the author of the *Ovide moralisé* seems to have known.[88]

This "paradox," however, is consistent with the terms of reading and the particular privilege of the exegete which the *Ovide moralisé* posits. A comparison with the theoretical pronouncements in the commentary on Virgil attributed to Bernardus Silvestris will be helpful here. The *accessus* to the "Bernardus" commentary describes a double intention for Virgil: he writes both as poet and as philosopher. As philosopher he writes *sub integumento*, and it is the task of the exegete to draw away the veil of fiction and expose the philosophical "plot" of the *Aeneid* as Virgil "intended" it to be read. The exegete, according to "Bernardus," thus carries out Virgil's own directives, reading according to a posited *intentio auctoris*. The poet of the *Ovide moralisé* has no comparable theory of the author's intention. In his prologue Ovid appears as a collector of fables, a very distant agent in their transmission:

Pour ce me plaist que je commans
Traire de latin en romans
Les fables de l'ancien temps . . .
Selonc ce qu'Ovides les baille. (book 1, lines 15–19)

[Thus I am pleased to commence my translation of the ancient stories from Latin into the vulgar tongue, just as Ovid presents them.]

But the poet of the *Ovide moralisé* does have a theory of *reading*, at and beyond the "letter" of the text. He articulates this very clearly towards the end of the poem:

Voirs est, qui Ovides prendroit
A la letre et n'i entendroit
Autre sen, autre entendement
Que tel com l'auctors grossement
I met en racontant la fable,
Tout seroit chose mençognable,
Poi profitable et trop obscure . . . (book 15, lines 2525–31)

[Certainly, whoever would take Ovid's texts at the literal level and not understand another sense, another meaning than what the author crudely presents in recounting the story, to this person everything would be a lie, of little profit and great obscurity.]

Ovid's function here is that of *raconteur* who is responsible for no more than the "letre" of the text, and whose intentional control of meaning stops there. This account of intentionality places all responsibility on the reader, whose task it is to invest the text with a meaning which is to be discovered somewhere beyond "la letre." This suggestion that intentionality for the meaning of a text can be located in the reader corresponds with the idea set forth in the prologue to the *Ovide moralisé*, where the poet places the exegete, rather than the author of the tales, in a kind of authorial partnership with God, that of the *duplex causa efficiens*. God makes those who are "sages" and "discrez" the repositories of his wisdom, and it is the responsibility of those in whom God has invested these powers of perception to disseminate their insights through expositions of texts (lines 1–14). On this view, then, the expositor assumes the highest authorial control, and Ovid is relegated to the subordinate role of *compilator* of the letter.

Omitting the kind of "intentional" step that we see in the Bernardus Silvestris commentary (where the ulterior philosophical scheme is attributed directly to Virgil's ingenuity) allows the poet of the *Ovide moralisé* to add a theological dimension to the writings of a pagan poet. If Ovid's intention applies only to the literal level of poetry, then the intentionality for the poem's ulterior meanings resides with the poet of the *Ovide moralisé* himself in his role as *causa efficiens*. In the Bernardus Silvestris commentary on Virgil, we have seen how the act of substituting the exegete's intention for the author's can be concealed under the formula of Virgil's double intention. But here in the *Ovide moralisé*, the exegete's claim to a priority over the text, the substitution of his intention for that of the author, is rendered overt, as part of the expressed theoretical apparatus that the exegete brings to his task. Thus the Christian (theological) explanation of the text is not problematic: it is openly the product of the power invested in the exegete. The theological readings can take precedence over all other levels of the text: the poet can claim, before producing a Christian interpretation of the Diana and Acteon myth, "Autre sense puet la fable avoir / Plus noble et de meillor sentence" (The fable can have another meaning, more noble and of greater import [book 3, lines 604–5]). His own theological reading is "plus noble." But since the fables have no veracity at the literal level (taken at this level they are simply "chose mençognable") the poet does not need to address, at least explicitly, the distinction between the allegory of the theologians and his own theological allegoresis of pagan texts. The allegory of the theologians, that is, interpretation of the various spiritual senses of Scripture, builds on the historical truth that the letter of Scripture is understood to contain (hence in the case of Scripture, the terms "historical" and "literal" are often interchangeable).[89] But the pagan fables of Ovid, which have no claim to veracity in their literal sense, only achieve their value through the offices of a good reader who recognizes them as integuments, and who, through the wisdom invested in him by God, can in turn disclose the divine wisdom concealed in them. As a good reader the poet of the *Ovide moralisé* assumes and fulfills the original task of rhetoric, to unite meaning with language, to integrate understanding with application.

The *Ovide moralisé* demonstrates how vernacular exegesis follows its Latin counterpart by taking causal control of the texts that it serves. Like traditional exegesis, vernacular *enarratio* substitutes the power of good reading for the power of good writing, and assumes a productive force that identifies it with the function of rhetoric. But the rhetorical character of vernacular *enarratio* is expressed more directly in its appropriation of certain authorial positions and strategies of traditional academic criticism; this appropriation is a form of *exercitatio*. In this way, moreover, vernacular translation-*enarratio* effects a rupture with the very tradition of the *antiqui* which it proposes to recuperate from the estrangement of historical distance: or perhaps it is more apt to say that it visibly embodies a rupture that was already, inevitably there in the tradition of *translatio studii*. If exegesis always carried a rhetorical motive of displacement, and always, like rhetoric, responded to the changing circumstances and demands of reception, then its project was always predicated on historicity or historical difference. Vernacular exegesis renders this historicity linguistically visible. Notker makes this rupture one of his explicit subjects when he points to the curious status of the vernacular as it tentatively inserts itself into an official domain. The poet of the *Ovide moralisé* manifests historical difference by extending the rhetorical motive of exegesis to a point where he has thoroughly substituted his own text for that of the *auctor*, where the product of his own disclosive readings takes explicit precedence over the *intentio auctoris*.

In the following chapter we will consider an even more powerful expression of historical difference in primary translation by examining how a series of vernacular versions of an *auctor* can constitute a nearly self-sufficient canon that creates its own textual legacy.

5

Translation and intralingual reception: French and English traditions of Boethius' *Consolatio*

Notker's work and the *Ovide moralisé* exemplify the two extremes of primary translation. These works also demonstrate how *exercitatio* defines itself through two models and two historical points of the interlingual transmission of texts. In both cases, the vernacular appropriation of academic discourse is part of the program of *exercitatio*. The *Ovide moralisé* takes this program to the furthest extent by using academic apparatuses to refer to itself, so that the translation being produced in the service of exposition has actually displaced the original text and its exegetical encrustations as the object of exposition. When we look between these two extremes of the continuum of primary translation, at texts that represent intermediate forms of primary translation, we see other ways for *exercitatio* to define itself. In this chapter I will consider how *exercitatio* can function in intralingual terms, within the same vernacular tradition or related vernacular cultures, where the translators not only contest the original text, but also build on and compete with earlier translations of the same text. This intralingual model of *exercitatio* anticipates the curious self-referentiality or self-sufficiency of the *Ovide moralisé*, where the vernacular translation becomes its own discursive subject.

To illustrate the intermediate range of primary translation in this chapter I have drawn from traditions of Boethius translation in French and Middle English. Medieval vernacular translations of the *Consolatio* have long been the subject of historical and critical investigation, and the last decade in particular has seen an efflorescence in the scholarly literature on these texts and their sources.[1] My interest here is to define the discursive contours of this tradition, the structures of the relationships between texts, structures that take shape as individual texts emerge into view. I have chosen this group of translations in French and Middle English precisely because we now know enough about them to see how they constitute a fairly integrated textual system. We can thus consider how they represent a kind of translation practice. These texts present another historical dimension of the twofold question of how translation defines itself through the intersection of rhetoric and hermeneutics and of how vernacular culture assimilates these critical discourses.

These vernacular versions of the *Consolatio* announce themselves as translations and operate under an exegetical directive of service to the original text. In this respect they can be grouped as primary translations. But while they have some formal alliance with the teaching methods of the medieval schools, they do not seem to be direct products of the kind of pedagogical context within which and for which Notker composed his exegetical translations. In most respects they are much more synthetic performances than Notker's translations. They are linguistically uniform; on the whole they incorporate commentaries for large conceptual units rather than for the restricted use of the lexical gloss (although Chaucer's *Boece* offers some exceptions to this); and some of these translations engage with the formal properties of the *Consolatio*, either reproducing its prosimetrum structure or producing an alternative from the repertoire of suitably illustrious native forms (e.g., rhyme royal stanzas). Such internal evidence, especially the concern with the "aesthetic" character of the text, suggests that these translations had a wider application than Notker's purpose of teaching *utriusque linguae*. But in the case of many of these translations, we cannot say with certainty what the intended audience would be. Notker's work can be historically contextualized by the fortunate survival of his letter to Bishop Hugo von Sitten and, more loosely, by the biographical information that we have about his long association with the monastic school at St. Gall. But many of these later Boethius translations come down to us without enough contextual information to allow us to judge whether they were intended to supplement Boethius' Latin text for bilingual teaching in monastic schools or even grammar schools, or whether they were intended for use by a more general lay audience. Some of the fourteenth-century French translations of Boethius were doubtless directed to the same aristocratic social milieu which encouraged the increasing production of other French translations from the classics, of philosophical, scientific, political, and historical texts.[2]

Because these translations of Boethius constitute vernacular subtraditions of Boethius, they raise a new set of theoretical problems about the nature of *exercitatio* and about the status of vernacular exegesis in the larger economy of medieval *translatio studii*. The implications of this intralingual *exercitatio* can be laid out here in brief. As vernacular translations which work also under the conditions of exegetical practice, these texts represent a twofold system of displacement, like the *Ovide moralisé* and Notker's school texts. As they vernacularize the Latin *auctores* and Latin commentaries they effect a linguistic rupture with the *antiqui*, substituting a potentially infinite linguistic multiplicity for the monolingual continuity of the Latin tradition; and as essentially exegetical productions, these texts carry over the contestative motives that already operate in medieval exegetical practice, reflecting the rhetorical and even agonistic character of medieval hermeneutics.

But these vernacular translations of Boethius also work, for the most part, as intralingual *exercitatio*: a later translator raises a challenge to one or more earlier translations in the same language, so that the new translation rivals its linguistic forebears. This introduces another dimension to the force of vernacular *exercitatio*. Here it also operates within a structure of lineality, of continuity within the same linguistic tradition, and hence within a structure of kinship or metonymy. Thus within the large system of substitutive relationships (vernacular to Latin and exegesis to original text) there is also a subsystem of organic linkage between generations, as later translators rival (or, in the classical sense, "emulate") the work of their predecessors by building upon those earlier efforts. This of course recalls the distinction in Roman theory between translation as an interlingual contest with aims to substitute Latin for Greek, and imitation as an intralingual contest which is based on ideas of kinship and genealogy within a linguistic community and which seeks to augment and renew rather than simply displace the work of earlier generations. In the case of medieval vernacular translations, this tension between metaphoric structure (difference, displacement, substitution) and metonymic structure (continuity and evolution within the same linguistic community) mirrors in reverse the structural pattern of the relationship of Latin commentary to Latin *auctores*. In the tradition of Latin commentary, the substitutive motive of exegesis is contained in a larger system of linguistic continuity which preserves a myth of kinship with the *antiqui*. But in the vernacular subtradition of multiple translations of the same text, the structure of lineality – between earlier and later translators – is contained within a dominant structure of rupture or difference with Latin culture. This vernacular subsystem of *translatio studii* thus also represents an undoing (or exposing) of the myth of historical continuity with the *antiqui* which Latin exegetical practice works to sustain. The intralingual character of this vernacular system of reception and translation offers a more powerful image of historical difference within the project of *translatio studii* than the work of Notker and of the poet of the *Ovide moralisé*: it derives its greater power from its near self-sufficiency as a vernacular system. These metonymic or lineal relationships that operate within a larger system predicated on linguistic difference suggest that the various vernacular traditions have already established themselves as authoritative literary languages. If there can be challenges to the prestige of preceding vernacular translations, then the vernaculars – and vernacular translations – have already inscribed their power within the system of *translatio studii*, as linguistic traditions that mediate between the ancient *auctores* and ever new receptions of those *auctores*. Intralingual *exercitatio* therefore affirms the capacity of native languages to appropriate and perform the function of *translatio studii* and to assimilate the discourses of academic culture.

The earliest complete French translation of Boethius' *Consolatio* which is known to us survives in a unique manuscript from the middle of the thirteenth century.[3] This prose text, written in a Burgundian dialect probably in the first part of the thirteenth century, stands outside the intralingual subtradition of Boethius in French. The Burgundian text has no apparent connections with earlier or later French translations. I have chosen to consider it here precisely because of its isolation from other French Boethius texts. For what reasons did this text fail to be incorporated into later French translations of Boethius? The Burgundian version represents an interesting intermediate stage between the kind of translation that we see in Notker and that which we see in the *Ovide moralisé*. It is closely dependent on the commentaries of Adalbold of Utrecht (early eleventh century) and William of Conches, as well as on the Vatican Mythographers. As such, it is an attempt to filter the specific intellectual interests of the cathedral schools into a vernacular environment. It shares a number of features with Notker's translations. Its alliance with a particular academic tradition is very clear, not only in its regular alternation of text and glosses or brief explications drawn mainly from William of Conches, but also in its attention to the larger argumentative scope of its exegetical sources. Thus, for example, it gives a close rendering of Adalbold's long commentary on 3 m.9 (which is all that remains of Adalbold's commentary).[4] Elsewhere, as in the passage on Orpheus (3 m.12), the Burgundian translator uses William of Conches for sustained interpolations. Like Notker's translations, the Burgundian text presents itself quite consciously as an academic product. The French translation supplies an *accessus ad auctorem*, much as Notker borrowed the Remigian *accessus* to Martianus Capella and to Boethius.[5] The Burgundian translation also announces its relationship to academic sources, as in the rubric that precedes the commentary taken from Adalbold: "Or avons dit les vers de cest metre e l'esposition briement; or dirons la grant glose de nos maistres de cest meesmes metre."[6]

But while, like Notker's texts, this translation is produced out of the schools, it is not as clear that it is directed back into the schools. It is not bilingual, alternating Latin and French, as Notker alternates Latin and German. As a monolingual production that deploys its exegetical sources towards a broad conceptual engagement with the text, it also seems to have some affinities with the *Ovide moralisé*, which similarly straddles academic traditions and the more recent emergence of lay reading. But it stops short of the self-referential and auto-exegetical character of the *Ovide moralisé*. Even as it takes over the authorial function of *expositor* from its Latin sources and adds to this a new authorial role of translator, it expresses its motive of appropriation in terms of service to the tradition that it proposes to carry over.

Yet in mediating the study of Boethius in the cathedral schools to a vernacular environment, the Burgundian translator replicates the contestative moves of his exegetical models. In taking over William of Conches' commentary on the Orpheus meter (3 m.12), the translator must also take over or reproduce the kind of prior intentional authority that allegoresis exercises over the text. We have already considered how this works in the commentary on the *Aeneid* attributed to Bernardus Silvestris. William of Conches also proposes a theory of the poetic allegory of philosophers, here in his Boethius commentary as well as in his commentary on the *Timaeus*. In the Boethius commentary, William enumerates *historia* and *integumentum* as modes of representation within philosophical discourse:

> [at 4 m.7] BELLA BIS QUINIS. Quia dixerat sapientes cum omni fortuna bellum conserere, ad illud prelium hortatur nos in istis versibus tribus modis: per historiam, per integumentum, deinde ponendo premia que sequuntur.[7]

[Because he has said that wise men wage war against every form of fortune, in these verses he exhorts us to battle in three ways: by means of the historical level, by means of the integument, and by setting out the rewards that are to follow.]

The Burgundian translator cites similar distinctions between fable, history, and integument or allegory, but seems to use the principles of *fabula* and *integumentum* as two poles around which to organize his own presentation of Boethius and William of Conches. His treatment of the meter begins with a fairly close rendering of all but the last seven lines, that is, the *fabula* as Boethius gives it.[8] But then the translator shifts into an expository mode, and offers a definition of *fabula*, *historia*, and *integumentum*, derived possibly from William of Conches, or from Bernardus Silvestris, or from some combination of ancient and contemporary sources:

La glose de cest metre: Nos devons saveir que li demonstremontz des auctors e des philosofes est feite par treis manieres: par fables, o par estoires, o par integument. Fable si est chose feinte semblant de veir, ausi come fait Ovides. Hystoire si est chose feite recontee issi come ele fu feite. Integumentz est quant om dit une chose e senefie autre, si come est ici de Orpheo. Ce apele hom en divinité allegorie. Ce est la fable de Orpheo.[9]

[The gloss of this meter. We must understand that exposition among authors and philosophers is handled in three ways: through fables, through historical narration, and through integument. A fable is something fictional that has the semblance of truth, such as the stories that Ovid wrote. History is an actual occurrence recounted just as it occurred. Integument is when one says one thing and signifies something else, as here in the case of Orpheus. This is what the theologian calls allegory. Such is the fable of Orpheus.]

The definition of integument here bears a confused resemblance to the distinction, set forth in the commentary on Martianus Capella attributed to Bernardus Silvestris, between allegory as a species of scriptural narrative (where the literal level is still historically true) and integument as a kind of fiction used in philosophical writing (where the literal level has no truth in itself). The Bernardus commentary restricts allegory to Scripture and integument to philosophical writing.[10] This distinction is echoed in the Burgundian translation. Nevertheless the translator's approach to interpretive method follows the lead of William of Conches and other exegetical allegorists. The translator supplies an authorial *intentio* for the work, an ulterior structure of meaning which can be revealed when the exegete reformulates the *dispositio* (or *modus agendi*) of the work in terms of two levels of narration, the integument and the philosophical argument to be disclosed through a good reading. The translator reorganizes Boethius' metrum around his own distinction between fable and integument. After having paraphrased Boethius' fable of Orpheus, he proceeds to paraphrase the fable as William of Conches tells it. William's version gives the background to Euridice's death and Orpheus' descent to the underworld by introducing Euridice's flight from her pursuer, a shepherd named Aristaeus.[11] Aristaeus is a detail that William derives from the Vatican Mythographers, or directly from Fulgentius, although he is careful to distinguish his own interpretation of it from that of Fulgentius.[12] The translator renders William's version of the fable, and also gives short redactions of William's exposition of Ixion, Tantalus, and Tityus. After this the translator returns to Boethius' version in order to translate the last lines of the meter. Then the translator moves to expound the meaning of the whole ("or diroms l'entegument de Orpheüs").[13] But as the subject of his exposition he substitutes William's philosophical integument for the "fable" that Boethius presents. His allegorical exposition is a simplified paraphrase of William's commentary on 3 m.12. The translator follows the major points of William's exposition. Orpheus represents wisdom and eloquence: to explain this the translator borrows a passage from William's commentary on 1 pr.1, where William cites Cicero on wisdom and eloquence (*De inventione* 1.1.1).[14] Aristaeus signifies virtue (which the translator rationalizes as "vertu de Deu"); Eurydice signifies natural concupiscence, and the descent into the underworld is the wise man's attempt to shake off his desire for temporal felicities.

Thus in the Burgundian translation, the fable of Boethius' text is displaced, first by the fable which William of Conches, Boethius' academic intermediary, had substituted for Boethius' version of the myth, and second, by the philosophical integument that William had supplied in expounding Boethius' meter. The translator shifts his own expository attention from Boethius' text to William's integument, that is, from the text of the ancient *auctor* to the textual intervention of a recent academic predecessor. He accords William's exposition a quasi-canonical status as a fixture in the textual tradition of Boethius. In this translation, then, the hermeneutical tradition becomes the very medium of a redisposition and appropriation of a Latin *auctor*.

This translation is almost a perfect model of how the rhetorical motive of *exercitatio* can be realized under the aegis of hermeneutical reception. But this text also seems to have borne no issue in later French translations. Perhaps a text like this would be read and used as an accompaniment or preparation to the grammatical study of classical *belles lettres* carried on in a school such as Orléans in the thirteenth century, in the wake of the Neo-Platonist scholars upon whom this translation so depends.[15] But if the Burgundian translation was used in this manner, it achieved little currency, as it survives in only one manuscript. The degree and nature of its dependence upon a particular school of academic exposition is unusual among vernacular translations of Boethius. It is more common for a translator to use a commentary or a combination of commentaries as a source of delimited explications rather than, as here, to draw on it at such reverent length for a kind of textual *Weltanschauung*. This kind of absorption in a particular school of exposition (the incipient Neo-Platonism of Adalbold of Utrecht and the full-blown form of this in William of Conches) is more what we would expect of a master preparing a redaction of his own masters for the benefit of his students. And perhaps it was as just such a *lectio* that this translation was undertaken. In so far as it does not reflect wider vernacular literary interests or precedents (in the way, for example, of the *Ovide moralisé*), it is never integrated into the French subtradition of Boethius. It is a form of vernacular *exercitatio*; but the structure of its imitative relationships is entirely interlingual.

Jean de Meun's translation of the *Consolatio*, known as the *Livres de Confort de Philosophie*, is also an academic exercise. Yet it was almost immediately integrated into a wide nexus of vernacular interests. On what grounds could Jean's academic orientation be accommodated, when that of a translator like the anonymous Burgundian found no later application? The explanation does not lie in the character of Jean's translation, which is, in its own way, no less academic than that of his Burgundian predecessor. The prologue that Jean uses for his translation is a close rendering of the prologue associated with William of Aragon's commentary on the *Consolatio* (after 1250), one of the earliest Aristotelian commentaries on Boethius.[16] Throughout his translation, Jean has recourse to a commentary on the *Consolatio*, most likely one in the tradition of William of Conches.[17]

But there is a context of vernacular readership and transmission that Jean establishes for his French Boethius. If it is the case that his translation is the product of an academic environment and represents a vernacular move to master the discourse of official culture, it is also the case that he directs the translation to a readership within a cosmopolitan court culture, as he dedicates it to Philippe IV (reigned 1285–1314). The beginning of his preface contains, along with much other information about the discursive context of the translation, his dedication to Philippe:

A ta royal majesté, tres noble prince, par la grace de Dieu roy des François, Phelippe le Quart, je Jehan de Meun qui jadis ou Rommant de la Rose, puis que Jalousie ot mis en prison Bel Acueil, enseignai la maniere du chastel prendre et de la rose cueillir et translatay de latin en françois le livre Vegece de Chevalerie et le livre des Merveilles de Hyrlande et la Vie et les Epistres Pierres Abaelart et Heloys sa fame et le livre Aered de Esperituelle Amitié, envoie ore Boece de Consolacion que j'ai translaté de latin en françois. Ja soit ce que tu entendes bien le latin, mais toutevois est de moult plus legiers a entendre le françois que le latin. Et por ce que tu me deis – lequel dit je tieng pour commandement – que je preisse plainement la sentence de l'aucteur sens trop ensuivre les paroles du latin, je l'ai fait a mon petit pooir si comme ta debonnaireté le me commanda. Or pri touz ceulz que cest livre verront, s'il leur semble en aucuns lieus que je me soie trop eslongniés des paroles de l'aucteur ou que je aie mis aucunes fois plus de paroles que li aucteur n'i met ou aucune fois mains, que il le me pardoingnent. Car se je eusse espons mot a mot le latin par le françois, li livres en fust trop occurs aus gens lais et li clers, neis moiennement letré, ne peussent pas legierement entendre le latin par le françois.[18]

[To Your Royal Majesty, most noble prince, by grace of God King of the French, Philippe IV, I, Jean de Meun, who previously, in the *Romance of the Rose*, after the point where Jealousy put Fair Welcome in prison, showed how to capture the castle and pluck the rose, and who translated from Latin into French Vegetius' *On Warfare*, the *Marvels of Ireland*, the life of Peter Abelard and the letters of Abelard and his wife Heloise, and Aelred's book *On Spiritual Friendship*, now present Boethius' *Consolation of Philosophy*, which I have translated from Latin into French. Although you understand Latin very well, it is nevertheless much easier to understand French than Latin. Since you told me – and I take your word as a commandment – that I should plainly render the sense of the author without the following the words of the Latin too closely, I have done this, as much as my meager skills permit, just as your graciousness has commanded. Now I beg all those who will see this book to pardon me if it seems to them that in any passages I have strayed too far from the words of the author, or if sometimes I have used more or fewer words than the author. For if I had sought to render the Latin word for word in French, the book would be too obscure for lay readers, and the clerks, who are no less lettered, would be unable to get a clear reading of the Latin from the French.]

The dedication uses certain *topoi* of translation theory that carry different thematic value depending on when and where they recur. Here the commonplace opposition between loose and literal translation, giving priority to translation according to sense ("que je preisse plainement la sentence de l'aucteur sens trop ensuivre les paroles du latin"), is framed by a larger structural opposition which classical and early medieval theorists could not have anticipated: Latin and European vernacular, clerks and laity. We encounter this particular cultural framework, the opposition between the academy and laity, in the theoretical discussions of other vernacular translators, as in John of Trevisa's preface to his translation of Ranulph Higden's *Polychronicon*, the "Dialogue between a Lord and a Clerk upon Translation," written in 1387, a century after Jean de Meun.[19] These are theoretical issues that also remain urgent for French translators of classical works in the century following Jean's translation of Boethius: in the works of Pierre Bersuire and Nicole Oresme, for example, we see how the *topoi* of translation theory serve to articulate a critical response to the liminal status of French as an emergent language of learning.[20]

In Jean de Meun's prologue, the translation from Latin to vernacular represents a translation of a certain intellectual property – Boethius' *Consolatio* – from clerical to lay culture. Jean had already defined the terms of such a transference in the *Roman de la Rose*, perhaps preparing for the appearance of his own translation, when he had Reason declare:

n'est pas vostre païs en terre,
ce peut l'en bien des clers enquerre,
qui Boece *De Confort* lisent
et les sentences qui la gisent,
donc granz biens aus gens lais feroit
qui bien le leur translateroit. (5005–10, Lecoy ed.)

[Your country is not on earth. One can readily learn this from clerks who study Boethius' *Consolatio* and the meanings that lie within it. Whoever would properly translate this for lay people would do something of great benefit for them.]

It is Jean himself, a product of that clerical culture, who will perform the service of mediating the wisdom of clerks (and the ancient wisdom of the *auctores*) to the vernacular laity. But in Jean's prologue to his French Boethius, this transference – or translation – of a kind of valuable intellectual property from the elite clerical sphere to the wider vernacular sphere of the laity is replicated in even more comprehensive terms by what the dedication itself accomplishes. To dedicate this translation to Philippe the Fair who, as the descendant of Philippe Augustus and St. Louis, embodies the accumulated historical prestige and power of the Capetian line, is to transfer possession of the wisdom of the ancients from the center of intellectual power, the university, to the center of French political power, the court of Philippe IV, "roy des François." Jean's use of this epithet is probably pointed: as "roy des François," Philippe represents the historical success of the Capetians in consolidating power within France as well as the more recent prestige of the French monarchy as a European power. In Jean's prologue, *translatio studii* becomes part of the enterprise of a *translatio imperii*.[21] But the identification between academic privilege and secular political power is one that already obtained in late thirteenth-century France, as Alexander Murray has suggested. The pre-eminence of French intellectual culture – specifically, the pre-eminence of the University of Paris – became a source of national pride and even arrogance, a way of defining the French character that could readily serve as a model for French claims to political precedence: the intellectual superiority of the French could translate into formidable political intelligence. In this way the ethos of an educated elite could exert an influence on a broader lay political consciousness.[22] In his dedication to Philippe the Fair, Jean dramatizes this association by quite literally turning possession of the *auctor* over to a secular Capetian monarch, emphatically identifying that monarch as a member of a vernacular reading public ("Ja soit ce que tu entendes bien le latin, mais toutevois est de moult plus legiers a entendre le françois que le latin"). Moreover, Jean's dedicatory gesture, the transfer of ancient learning from clergy to court, is itself a convention of vernacular culture. In France, the large-scale enterprise of learned translation from classical *auctores*, beginning with the reign of Philippe IV in the later thirteenth century, took its momentum from royal patronage and royal directives.[23] In the next century, the work of eight translators whose names are known (as well as of some anonymous translators) has been identified just with the reign of Charles V (1364–80); among these is Nicole Oresme, translator of Aristotle's *Ethics*, *Politics*, *De caelo et mundo*, and the pseudo-Aristotelian *Economics*.[24] The emergent power of the French language as a medium of *translatio studii* thus authorizes itself through a material identification with royal power. In these ways, then, we see that Jean de Meun can situate his *Livres de Confort de Philosophie* in a political culture that defines itself through vernacularity.

If Jean establishes a material vernacular context for his translation, he also situates his French Boethius in the intralingual nexus of his own considerable vernacular writing. In the dedicatory preface to the *Livres de Confort de Philosophie*, Jean cites his continuation of the *Roman de la Rose* and four other translations (Vegetius, the *De mirabilibus Hiberniae* attributed to Giraldus Cambrensis, Abelard's *Historia calamitatum* and letters, and the *De amicitia spirituali* of Aelred). As the *Roman de la Rose* had contained a kind of advertisement for Jean's forthcoming translation of Boethius ("donc granz biens aus gens lais feroit qui bien le leur translateroit"), so here, in the dedicatory preface to his translation, the *Roman* represents the authorizing ground of a vernacular tradition for the translation of Boethius. Jean's own writings comprise the network of vernacular interests within which the translation can situate itself. More narrowly, the Boethian material in the *Roman de la Rose* constitutes an intralingual tradition with which the *Livres de Confort de Philosophie* is allied and upon which it builds. Thus while the translation is a form of interlingual *exercitatio*, a vernacular appropriation of a Latin *auctor* and his intellectual legacy, its intralingual relationships are more immediate. The translation affirms the mastery of Boethian traditions that Jean had accomplished in the *Roman de la Rose*. Jean's translation is more a proof of this mastery than an exercise in it.

The Boethian elements of the *Roman de la Rose* are too well known to need much rehearsing here.[25] Since Jean's translation of the *Consolatio* lies behind some of the other Boethian translations that we will consider later, it will be most useful here to look at one example of the relationship between the *Roman de la Rose* and *Li Livres de Confort de Philosophie*. It is clear from the prologue to *Li Livres de Confort* that the *Roman* is the text which has defined his place among vernacular writers. In the same way, for Jean's public, the Boethian matter in the *Roman* defines or provides the intralingual precedent for Jean's actual translation of the *Consolatio*.

The discussions of Fortune from 2 pr.8 and the *Roman de la Rose* 4807–944 (Lecoy ed.) offer some very close parallels. This section of the *Roman* suggests that while writing the *Roman* Jean was working quite closely with Boethius' text, as in some places it corresponds directly with his very literal rendering of 2 pr.8 in *Li Livres de Confort*. One obvious correspondence occurs at the beginning of the *prosa*:[26]

Nondum forte quid loquar intellegis; mirum est quod dicere gestio, eoque sententiam uerbis explicare uix queo. Etenim plus hominibus reor aduersam quam prosperam prodesse fortunam. (2 pr. 8, 2–3).

[Perhaps you do not yet understand what I say. What I want to say is surprising, and so I can hardly explain its meaning in words. I think that bad fortune is of more use to men than good fortune.]

Et puis qu'a Fortune venons,
quant de s'amor sermon tenons,
dire t'en veill fiere merveille,
n'onc, ce croi, n'oïs sa pareille.
Ne sai se tu le porras croire,
toutevois est ce chose voire
et si la treuve l'en escrite:
que mieux vaut au genz et profite
Fortune perverse et contraire
que la mole et la debonaire. (*Roman*, 4807–16)

[And now that we come to Fortune when we hold a discourse about love, I should like to tell you a great marvel of which I don't believe you have ever heard the like. I don't know if you'll be able to credit it, but it is true nevertheless, and one may find it written, that perverse, contrary Fortune is worth more and profits men more than does pleasant and agreeable Fortune.][27]

Par aventure tu n'entens pas mes paroles. C'est merveille que je vueil dire et, pour ce, en puis je a paine desploier la sentence par paroles. Car je croi que fortune contraire, *felonnesse et pouvre*, profite plus aus hommes que fortune amiable, *debonnaire et riche*. (*Livres de Confort*, Dedeck-Héry, 203)

[Perhaps you do not understand my words. What I want to tell you is surprising, and so I can hardly explain my meaning in words. For I believe that adverse fortune, cruel and poor, is of greater profit to men than fortune that is kind, gracious and rich.]

It is clear that the *Roman* participates as directly in the process of exegetical translation as the full-scale translation does. The lexical choice in the two passages is comparable, even down to the word "debonnaire" as a gloss on Boethius' "prospera fortuna." The following lines in the *Roman* (4817–930) elaborate on Boethius' 2 pr.8 mainly by changing the structure of his argument against good and in favor of bad fortune, separating out Boethius' crisp antitheses ("illa . . . haec . . . illa . . . haec") with two long segments, one describing "la debonere et la mole," the other "la contraire et la perverse." At the close of this section, corresponding to the end of 2 pr.8, the *Roman* and *Li Livres de Confort* again offer parallel readings:

Quanti hoc integer et, ut uidebaris tibi, fortunatus emisses? (2 pr.8.7)

[How much would you have paid for this {the knowledge of who your true friends are} when you were unafflicted, and, as it seemed to you, fortunate?]

quant il iert riches a devise
que tuit a toujorz li offroient
queurs et cors et quant qu'il avoient,
que vosist il acheter lores
qu'il en seüst ce qu'il set ores?
Mains eüst esté deceüz
s'il s'en fust lors aperceüz. (*Roman* 4934–40)

[Wouldn't he, when he was as rich as he wished and everyone always offered him heart, body, and everything he owned, wouldn't he have wanted to buy then the knowledge that he now has? He would have been less deceived had he then understood.][28]

Quant tu estoies richez et aesiéz *et beneurez*, si comme il te estoit avis, combien vousissez tu lores ce avoir acheté, *ce est a savoir que tu les cogneussez lors si bien comme tu les cognois ores*. (*Livres de Confort*, Dedeck-Héry, 204)

[When you were rich and carefree and blessed, as it seemed to you, for how much would you have bought this knowledge then, that is, that you might then have discerned {who your true friends were} as well as you now discern them.]

Both the *Roman* and *Li Livres de Confort* incorporate a gloss explaining the temporal clause in the Latin, just as the standard exegetical sources anticipate the need for a gloss to open the syntax of this sentence.[29] These small details serve to illustrate an important principle: Jean's "academic" translation of Boethius participates in a wide vernacular literary orbit. This vernacular or intralingual nexus can, to varying degrees, displace the Latin legacy as the primary reference point for further experimentation or *exercitatio*. This vernacular displacement of the Latin tradition is simply an extension of the substitutive motive of academic exegesis. We see this substitutive motive at work in the Burgundian translation. But Jean's translation, unlike the earlier academic version by the Burgundian, locates its origins and establishes its legacy in vernacular culture, and so achieves the full force of the substitutive motive.

Jean's *Livres de Confort*, grounded in Jean's own vernacular productions, serves as a reference point or as an authorizing precedent for later French and English receptions of the *Consolatio*. Of the at least eleven separate versions (including revisions) of the *Consolatio*, seven appear to postdate Jean's translation, and several of these versions can be linked in different ways, either inherently or through manuscript tradition, with Jean's translation, or, by extension, with the *Roman de la Rose*. In discussing the *Ovide moralisé* I noted how four different French translations of the *Consolatio* incorporate some wording in 2 m.5 that can be traced either to the *Roman de la Rose* or to *Li Livres de Confort*. But there are other ways in which these later French versions of the *Consolatio* claim a certain connection with Jean's. In this they provide a particularly good paradigm of interlingual *exercitatio*, and of an evolutionary, organic relationship between texts in the same linguistic tradition.

Sometimes the association between Jean's work and that of later translators occurs through scribal *compilatio*. Here, scribal activity attests to the continual resituating of Jean's Boethian writings among later vernacular productions. One example of this comes from Renaut de Louhans' elaborate verse translation, composed some time during the 1330s. In the previous chapter I suggested that Renaut followed some of Jean's readings for 2 m.5, the *aetas aurea*. Given the Ovidian structure of Renaut's version of the *aetas aurea*, it may be that he took over the version of this in the *Roman de la Rose*, where Jean de Meun had combined Boethius and Ovid on this theme. Such an argument rests on internal textual evidence. But it has an analogue in the external evidence of scribal *compilatio*. One of the manuscripts of Renaut's translation, Paris Bibliothèque Nationale fr. 812, also contains a copy of the *Roman de la Rose*, written by the same scribe.[30] Renaut's translation contains a considerable number of narrative expansions, including one on Croesus, a myth that Boethius mentions in passing in 2 pr.2. Renaut's expansion of the Croesus legend is a composite from various mythographical traditions. In the *Roman de la Rose*, lines 6459–600, Jean's account of Croesus derives from the same tradition, possibly *via* William of Conches.[31]

In MS B.N. fr. 812, the scribe who copied both Renaut's translation and the *Roman de la Rose* made a connection between Renaut's version of the Croesus story and the version in the *Roman* by inserting into Renaut's account a short passage based on a theme that Jean had introduced into his version of the narrative, Croesus' rejection of what he considers to be his daughter's "false gloss" of his dream.[32] The scribe of B.N. fr. 812 thus exemplifies the process of cross-fertilizing within vernacular Boethian writings. These vernacular interests intersect at two levels of scribal *compilatio*: at one level, the placement of Renaut's French *Consolatio* together with the *Roman de la Rose* represents a comprehensive ordering of a vernacular canon, as Renaut's verse translation can assume a certain authority as poetic narrative by association with the *Roman de la Rose*. At the local level of intertextual interpolation, the Boethian matter of the *Roman de la Rose* pre-empts both Boethius and the Latin commentators as the source for Renaut's mythographical amplification.

Other forms of textual association contribute to the formation of this vernacular network. In the early fourteenth century a new translation of the *Consolatio* attempted to reproduce the formal character of Boethius' text by employing a prosimetrum scheme. This verse–prose translation contains a prologue which states its formal objectives (and which also defines its reading public):

Quar ceulx qui sont en grans tristeces
Conforte doucement Boece
C'on dit *De Consolacion*,
Propos ay et entencion
De lui translater en françois,
Si que chevaliers et bourgois
Y praingnent confort, et les dames,
S'ilz ont triboul de corps et d'ames.
Ou livre a vers et s'i a prose:
Si vueil si ordonner la chose
Que li vers soient mis en rime
Ou consonant ou leolime [sic];
La prose est mise plainnement.[33]

[For those who suffer great sorrow are sweetly comforted by Boethius in the book that is called *On Consolation*. I propose and intend to translate it into French, so that knights, burghers, and ladies may find comfort there, if they are troubled in body or spirit. The book is in verse and prose: I want to arrange the translation so that the verse sections are put into rhyme, either consonant rhymes or leonines; the prose is set forth plainly.]

Perhaps this prologue refers by implication to an absence of previous attempts to render the formal character of Boethius' text.[34] This verse–prose version marks one starting point of the kind of formal *exercitatio* among French translations of the *Consolatio* that will knit them together in a nearly self-contained system of textual genealogy. This textual system creates its own self-sustaining dynamic through continued *exercitatio*; each response to an existing text involves a new configuration of authorial functions which alters the status of the texts within the system. The prose–verse version did not achieve wide currency in its original state (which survives in only four manuscripts). But this version came into the hands of a reviser in the mid-fourteenth century. This revised "mixed" version exists in sixty-four manuscripts.[35] As formal *exercitatio*, in this case an attempt to establish a higher standard of the prosimetrum genre for the *Consolatio* in French, this revision is a response both to the first mixed-prose version and to the wider conditions and capacities of literary production in the contemporary vernacular milieu. In his role of reviser, the author of this second verse–prose translation confers a certain privileged status on the first "mixed" version, that of the originator of a formal program; but at the same time it rivals that first version by seeking to improve it, to rectify its perceived technical deficiencies, and to offer itself as the exemplary prosimetrum translation. The revised prosimetrum translation was certainly successful in its challenge to its French predecessor, so successful as to displace it almost completely. In seeking to improve the earlier prosimetrum, the revision also asserts the technical capacity of literary French to reproduce a form, the prosimetrum, long associated with an illustrious tradition of learned Latin writing from Boethius and Martianus Capella to Bernardus Silvestris' *De universitate mundi* and Alain de Lille's *De planctu Naturae*.

But it is the association with Jean de Meun's translation that most actively defines the vernacular status of this revised prosimetrum.[36] It achieves this association through various forms of *compilatio*. First and most important, in nearly all the manuscripts, this translation takes over Jean de Meun's prefatory material to the *Livres de Confort*: the dedicatory preface to Philippe IV and Jean's translation of the prologue to the commentary on the *Consolatio* by William of Aragon.[37] In so doing, of course, the translation appropriates the authorial prestige of Jean de Meun, and also lays claim to the academic foundations of Jean's translation. Most manuscripts of this version (forty-eight out of sixty-four manuscripts) offer another dimension of *compilatio*: they incorporate a system of exegetical interpolations, in French, derived largely from a compilation of the commentary by William of Conches. These were added to the text of the translation by a separate vernacular *expositor*. At least two manuscripts of this glossed prosimetrum translation also contain a version of the Latin commentary (known in some manuscripts as the *Commentum domini Linconiensis*) upon which the vernacular glosses have drawn, along with the Latin text of the *Consolatio*.[38] The glossed version represents the exegetical materials as an integral part of the textual tradition to be translated: it runs the exegetical interpolations together with the text, marking the difference between the two with the alternating rubrics "texte" and "glose."[39] The mechanics of these rubrics serve to announce the academic affinities of this translation. In some cases, such as the Orpheus meter and the *aetas aurea*, the dependence on the William of Conches commentary is especially noticeable.[40] The glossed version introduces yet another claim to academic status: to the prologue from William of Aragon translated by Jean de Meun it adds a continuation adapted from the prologue to the same compilation of William of Conches from which it takes its glosses.[41]

The application of William of Conches' commentary to the text strengthens the intralingual association with Jean de Meun and, more importantly, identifies the translation with the academic character of Jean's *Livres de Confort*. In other words, the translation is a product of multifold *compilatio* and of multiple authorial functions. It revises an earlier text, it uses the dedicatory preface and the prologue of the *Livres de Confort*, and possibly on the model of Jean de Meun, incorporates an exposition derived from William of Conches. But in applying the functions of *compilator* and *expositor* to a set of foregoing vernacular texts it effectively substitutes these texts for their Latin sources as the primary references in a French Boethius tradition. This process of *compilatio* is internal to the text of the revised prosimetrum. But in several manuscripts the scribes take the intralingual association with Jean de Meun much further. Two manuscripts, Bibliothèque Nationale fr. 809 and Bibliothèque de l'Arsenal 2669, combine Jean's prose translation of the meters with the translations of the proses from the revised "mixed" version.[42] In another manuscript, Dijon, Bibliothèque Publique 525, dated 1362, the scribe copied the revised "mixed" version up to 5 pr.3, and then substituted Jean's prose translation for the remainder of the text, with the rubric: "Up to this point suffices as much as pertains to the laity; what follows from here to the end has been taken from the translation that was made by Master Jean de Meun and which is very difficult to understand, except to those who are very learned."[43]

The second prosimetrum version identifies itself explicitly with academic practice, as does the earlier Burgundian prose translation. But unlike the Burgundian version, the revised prosimetrum was widely disseminated. The revised prosimetrum achieves its success through its positioning in an intralingual network, its identification with a vernacular textual lineage. The assimilation of academic practices helps to constitute this group of texts as a vernacular canon of the *Consolatio*. The vernacular appropriation of these academic functions, *compilatio* and *expositio*, is itself a form of *exercitatio*, a broadening of the scope of vernacular textual power. We have already seen similar appropriations of a whole discursive system in Notker and the *Ovide moralisé*. In the case of the network of French Boethius productions, the application of such academic functions to vernacular texts also changes the status of those texts. Certain translations assume a seminal or foundational value because they are imitated and augmented by new generations of vernacular translators. Jean de Meun's treatments of Boethius or of William of Conches become the standard by which Renaut de Louhans' translation, the two prosimetrum versions, and other versions are shaped, received, or judged. In the same way, the first prosimetrum version offers a stylistic standard against which the revised prosimetrum translation defines its position. So this intralingual tradition supplants its Latin models in two ways, as a focus of academic interest and as a focus of literary (stylistic, formal, narrative) interest.

In the French network of the *Consolatio*, the rhetorical motive of *exercitatio* is expressed, not only through adaptation of academic models, but also through formal (especially metrical) experimentation during the fourteenth century. In addition to the formal modifications that the first prosimetrum version undergoes in the hands of its reviser, there is Renaut de Louhans' verse translation which experiments with contemporary metrical forms, and which undergoes, in turn, three successive formal revisions.[44] This situation, in which translation becomes a filter for contemporary formal interests, has analogues in nearly all traditions of vernacular translation. An obvious parallel in English literary history is the relationship between Alfred's prose version of the *Consolatio* and the Alfredian *Meters of Boethius* which recasts the meters according to the terms of Anglo-Saxon alliterative verse.[45] At a more humble level this is exemplified in the successive Middle English recastings of a single Latin devotional text or a single hymn among different sermon handbooks (e.g. MS Advocates Lib. 18.7.21, John of Grimestone's commonplace book) and friars' miscellanies (e.g. MSS Trinity College, Cambridge 323 and Jesus College, Oxford 29).[46] This is the most common manifestation of intralingual *exercitatio* on any given text.

In all these cases, *exercitatio* is the mechanism through which translation becomes independent discursive production, through which translation as an exegetical performance asserts power over the text it officially serves. In *exercitatio*, the three meanings of *hermeneia*, exegesis, translation, and expression, come together. In this process the exegetical role of translation assumes the productive force of rhetoric. This is really the subject of the next two chapters, where I will trace the fortunes of rhetorical invention in medieval theories of discourse and in medieval translation. But to conclude this discussion of exegetical models of translation I would like to point towards these upcoming considerations with some examples that suggest the inventional force of *exercitatio*. These examples are drawn from the nexus formed with Chaucer's *Boece*.

The *Boece* is a response to two linguistic traditions, Latin and French.[47] It is an attempt to master and appropriate the academic discourse of Latin culture; but it also challenges the ascendency of French literary culture, represented by Jean de Meun's *Livres de Confort*. Like Jean's translation, the *Boece* participates in a wide orbit of vernacular interests: it builds upon vernacular foundations in French to become, in turn, the point of reference for other vernacular developments of the *Consolatio* in English. Its function for English writing is analogous with that of *Li Livres de Confort* for French: the *Boece* also serves as a model for intralingual *exercitatio*.

Like Jean's translation, Chaucer's *Boece* functions through its reception-history as a sign of the crossover of academic discourse from Latin to vernacular. Eight copies of *Li Livres de Confort* survive in bilingual manuscripts, that is, the French and Latin texts copied together, either facing page or in parallel columns, often with a marginal commentary (a version of the one by William of Conches) framing both.[48] Similarly, there are two known bilingual manuscripts of the *Boece*, one complete and one which survives only as a fragment.[49] In the complete copy, Cambridge University Library MS Ii.3.21, some marginal and interlinear glosses based on Nicholas Trevet accompany both the Latin text of Boethius and the English translation. This deployment of the gloss, as well as the bilingual format, confers a certain academic or critical authority on the English text, as if to insert the translation into the very mechanics of the *Consolatio* transmission rather than to present it as a subsidiary alternative positioned outside the official spheres of study. Thus in the case of the *Boece*, as in that of the French texts, a vernacular translation built out of exegetical systems carries over the rhetorical force of those systems to claim the same productive authority as the original text that it serves.[50] But in the case of the *Boece*, that productive authority is carried further into what, for the Middle Ages, is an explicitly rhetorical domain, poetic composition as a form of invention. Within the canon of Chaucer's writings, from the Boethian lyrics to *Troilus and Criseyde* and *The Knight's Tale*, the *Boece* serves as a link in the learned tradition from which these texts derive. In many instances it provides more than a link: it can occupy a foundational position, providing the actual source of further formulations rather than just an access to sources outside of English. In other words, in Chaucer's own career, the *Boece* performs the function of an academic reference in place of the *Consolatio*.

The *Boece* adds a new linguistic dimension to the network of Boethian writing that forms around Jean de Meun's translation. *Li Livres de Confort* is not simply a literary model for the *Boece*: more importantly, it is a model of a vernacular text empowered with the authority of the school tradition that it mediates for lay audiences. It is this kind of empowering that the *Boece* seeks to duplicate in English. The *Boece* is thus a double contestation: of the traditional ascendency of learned Latin writing, and of the comparatively recent empowering of French literary culture which lent such texts as the *Livres de Confort* a quasi-academic status. But there is a certain ambiguity in this picture of linguistic and cultural dependency and confrontation. On the one hand, the *Boece* is an unusual example of a double linguistic rupture, a displacement of two canonical models, one in French and one in Latin. But on the other hand, French is so deeply inscribed in Chaucer's own literary culture that the Boece can be seen as fully a part of the vernacular network and legacy of Jean's translation, so that it forms an alliance with its French model as part of the larger system of vernacular response to Latin culture. In this respect, it has a lineal, complementary relationship with Jean's text. It is part of a family of vernacular translations which, as a group, effect a rupture with the Latin tradition and which constitute a self-generating subtradition of Boethian writings.

We can illustrate these competing structures by considering the fortunes of one passage. Whereas Renaut de Louhans had used the commentaries of Nicholas Trevet largely for expanded narratives of myth and history, Chaucer relies on Trevet and on Jean de Meun more as Notker had relied on Remigius and as Jean had relied on William of Conches, for particular verbal and conceptual clarifications.[51] In 5 pr.3, for example, we can trace the genealogy of an exegetical interpolation.[52] A passage towards the beginning of the prosa reads:

quasi uero quae cuius rei causa sit, praescientiane futurorum necessitatis an futurorum necessitas prouidentiae, laboretur . . . (5 pr.3, 9)

Trevet's gloss on this reads:

QUOD VERO LABORETUR id est ista responsio procedit ac si laboretur querendo QUAE REI CAUSA SIT . . . (Silk, p. 698)

Jean de Meun translates the passage as follows:

– aussi comme se nous travaillons a enquerre la quelle chose soit cause de la quelle, c'est assavoir ou se la prescience est cause de la necessité des chosez a avenir, ou se la necessité des chosez a avenir est cause de la pourveance. (pp. 260–1)

[– just as if we labor to inquire what thing is the cause of what, that is, to know whether the foreknowledge is the cause of the necessity of things to come, or whether the necessity of things to come is the cause of the foreknowledge.]

In Chaucer's *Boece* the passage reads:

– but as it were Y travailed (*as who seith, that thilke answere procedith ryght as though men travaileden or weren besy*) to enqueren the whiche thing is cause of the whiche thing, as whethir the prescience is cause of the necessite of thinges to comen, or elles that the necessite of thinges to comen is cause of the purveaunce. (p. 459, lines 40–7)

The troublesome term for Chaucer is "laboretur," denoting, almost figuratively, the effort of placing a point at issue, perhaps in the sense of "belabor." Chaucer first tests out Jean's lexicon, giving an equivalent for Jean's "travaillons," "Y travailed." But, evidently dissatisfied, he explicates this term in a gloss drawn directly from Trevet's "ista responsio procedit," and tries two ways of rendering "laboretur," either by "travaileden," or "weren besy."[53] Yet the overall syntax of the passage in the *Boece* draws from Jean's economical formulation. But when this passage reappears in *Troilus and Criseyde* 4, in the context of Troilus' predestination speech, the presence of Boethius, Jean de Meun, and Trevet is nearly effaced. In *Troilus and Criseyde* 4, Chaucer seems to return to his own mediation of these sources in the *Boece*, which has become for him an intralingual point of reference and which takes on a kind of foundational role for the future text, the *Troilus*:

I mene as though I laboured me in this
To enqueren which thyng cause of which thyng be:
As wheither that the prescience of God is
The certeyn cause of the necessite
Of thynges that to comen ben, parde,
Or if necessite of thyng comynge
Be cause certeyn of the purveyinge. (1009–15)

The only direct echo of the sources is "laboured," which Chaucer does not use in the *Boece*, but which comes from the wording in Boethius' text ("laboretur"). The rest of the stanza takes us back to the mediating agency of the *Boece*, rather than directly to the sources that are filtered through the *Boece*. The stanza takes up at the point where those sources have been mediated, as if the *Boece* itself is a new beginning for the *Consolatio*. Within Chaucer's own canon of writings, the *Boece* effectively displaces its sources, to substitute itself for them as the point of departure for later Boethian efforts. This moment of substitution is the moment at which the hermeneutical function exerts its generative, heuristic power over textual production.

John Walton's verse translation of the *Consolatio* (1410) attests most eloquently to the changed status of the *Boece* from *exercitatio* to foundational text. It is well known that Walton makes extensive use of the *Boece*; we shall consider an example of this dependence here. In terms of intralingual *exercitatio*, the relationship of Walton's *Consolation* to Chaucer's *Boece* is, to some extent, comparable to the relationship between the first and the revised French prosimetrums, or between the revised prosimetrum and Jean de Meun's prose *Livres de Confort*. Walton's version is an attempt to make a better *Consolation* through a formal reworking of an earlier product. Because of its links with Chaucer's *Boece*, Walton's *Consolation* is also part of the network of vernacular engagement with the *Consolatio* that forms around Jean de Meun's translation.

In his prologue Walton draws on some commonplaces about translation that would seem to link his enterprise with the assumptions of certain early medieval theorists. But the epistemologies that carry these formulas have changed, so that the value of these commonplaces is not truly continuous with earlier assumptions.

> This subtile matere of boecius
> Heere in this book of consolacioun
> So hye it is, so hard and curious
> Ful fair abouen myn estimacioun,
> That it be noght be my translacioun
> Defouled ne corrupt to god I praye.
> So help me with hys inspiracioun
> That is of wisdom bothe lok and keye.[54] (stanza 2)

This stanza seems to echo the formulations of Boethius in his preface to the *Isagoge* of Porphyry, and of Eriugena in the preface to his translation of the *De caelisti hierarchia*, concerning the corruptibility of meaning through a false linguistic mediation. The stanza introduces this problem in much the same way that Boethius had set it forth, which suggests the durability of this post-patristic *topos*: the philosophical substance has an integrity beyond the accidents of language, and yet paradoxically is constituted by the force of the language that mediates it. Walton's next stanza takes this problem further:

As fro the text that I ne vary noght
But kepe the sentence in hys trewe entent,
And wordes eke als neigh as may be broght
Where lawe of metir is noght resistent.
This mater whiche that is so excellent
And passeth bothe my cunnyng and my myght
So saue it lord in thy gouernement
That kannest reformen alle thing to right. (stanza 3)

Thus to translate as far as possible according to the word is to secure the meaning from the kind of significative difference that a translation only *ad sensum* would introduce. Walton articulates this principle in terms that recall Eriugena's formulation in which he rejects the interpolative power of the *expositor*. For Walton, as for Eriugena, the text itself is the *locus* of "sentence," and the words themselves exert a directive power over the constitution of meaning.

But what is this "text" which Walton promises to deliver without variance? How is this "text" embodied? Walton reiterates the principles of Boethius and Eriugena, but the conditions that give those principles their value in a certain historical moment have changed. Walton is working in early fifteenth-century England; his project to translate Boethius in a vernacular high style (eight-line and rhyme royal stanzas) is itself a product of – or is enabled by – a long history of vernacular appropriation of Boethius, a history that for Walton's enterprise begins with Jean de Meun and his vernacular legacy. Chaucer's *Boece* is a response to Jean's *Livres de Confort* and establishes the familial network of Jean's legacy in England, through Chaucer's other writings which draw from the *Boece* and ultimately through Walton's verse revision of the *Boece*. Walton, like his earlier French counterparts, must work under the impress of the vernacular subtradition of the *Consolatio*. He makes the burden of this vernacular legacy clear in his own prologue: and here lies a clue to what the "text" of Boethius, to which he promises to play the *fidus interpres*, really means to him. After delivering the conventional oath of the *fidus interpres* (and committing the matter of the text to God – that is, beyond the accidents of human language – for correction) he says:

I haue herd speke and sumwhat haue i-seyne
Of diuerse men that wondir subtillye,
In metir sum and sum in prose pleyne,
This book translated haue suffyshauntlye
Into Englisshe tongue, word for word, wel neye;
Bot I most use the wittes that I haue;
Thogh I may noght do so, yit noght-for-thye,
With help of god the sentence schal I saue.

To Chaucer that is floure of rethoryk[55]
In Englisshe tong and excellent poete,
This wot I wel, no thing may I do like,
Thogh so that I of makyng entirmete;[56]
And Gower that so craftily doth trete

As in hys book[es] of morality;
Thogh I to theym in makyng am vnmete,
Yit must I schewe it forth that is in me. (stanzas 4–5)

Walton's invocation of a vernacular tradition of the *Consolatio*, and more specifically of Chaucer and Gower as linguistic forebears (although "bookes of moralite" may refer to Gower's Latin *Vox clamantis*), does not propose or claim a direct linkage between his project and earlier translations. Indeed, Walton's positioning of his project in relation to the intralingual tradition that he invokes here is curiously unclear. But these verses point beyond themselves – beyond their guarded indirectness – to the lineal history of Walton's enterprise, to its unacknowledged intralingual connections. As any careful reading of Walton's Boethius reveals, the "text" from which he promises "to vary noght / But kepe the sentence in hys trewe extent, / And wordes eke als neigh as may be broght," is as much Chaucer's *Boece* as Boethius' *Consolatio*.

It is not only in the *Boece*, however, that Walton finds his authoritative "text" of the *Consolatio*. Walton also draws on Trevet's commentary to elucidate the "sentence" of Boethius. As Ian Johnson has shown, Walton's reliance on Trevet's commentary is often greater and more marked than his debt to the *Boece*. Sometimes, in fact, the *Boece* serves as a "(generally reliable) short cut to Trevet."[57] In this, the *Boece* supplies a methodological precedent, as Walton "improves" Chaucer's text by advancing the vernacular mastery of a particular academic *expositor*. If Trevet's commentary is often a more important *auctoritas* for Walton than the *Boece*, then Walton's text is at two removes from Boethius' text: through the *Boece*, his immediate vernacular precedent, Walton discovers and exploits Trevet's exegetical mediation.

Walton's translation provides a perspective on the historical revaluation of traditional theories of translation. Like Eriugena, Walton assigns a privilege to the once debased aims of the *fidus interpres*. He deplores the possibility of corrupting "this subtile matere of boecius" through his translation, and proposes to keep the "sentence," and to conserve the words as much as the law of meter will allow. But within Walton's translation, Chaucer's *Boece* and Trevet's commentary figure as powerful interventionary forces, at almost every point controlling Walton's response to the *ipsissima verba* and "sentence" of Boethius. If Eriugena distinguished firmly between the roles of *interpres* (translator) and *expositor*, rejecting the expositor's license as a corruptive force, Walton assumes the mantle of the *fidus interpres* precisely through the role of expositor, using Trevet's commentary as access to the "sentence" of Boethius' text, just as Chaucer had done. In Walton's practice, translation and exposition are equivalent. Inasmuch as Walton seems to be a *fidus interpres*, he conceives this aim through the authorizing precedents supplied by his own late-medieval vernacular culture: the translation practice of that culture has defined the recuperation of antiquity in terms of vernacular control of the academic discourse that mediates the *auctores*. Thus for Walton the "text" of the *Consolatio* is also embodied in Trevet's commentary.

As an example of Walton's use of Chaucer and Trevet to mediate the text of Boethius, let us turn to another passage from 5 pr.3 on predestination and divine foreknowing.[58]

Nam si aliorsum quam prouisae sunt detorqueri ualent, non iam erit futuri firma praescientia, sed opinio potius incerta, quod de deo credere nefas iudico. Neque enim illam probo rationem qua se quidam credunt hunc quaestionis nodum posse dissoluere. (5 pr.3, 6–7)

Here is Jean de Meun's version of the passage:

Car se elles peuent estre destortes et autrement avenir que elles ne sont pourveues de dieu, ce ne sera ja pas ferme prescience des chosez a avenir, ainçois sera miex opinion et cuidance doubteuse sens certaineté; et ce croire de dieu, ce juge je a grant felonnie. Car ne celle raison neis ne loe je pas par quoy aucuns croient que il puissent soudre et deslier le neu de ceste question. (p. 260)

Chaucer's translation of this in the *Boece* reads:

For yif that thei myghten writhen awey in othere manere than thei ben purveyed, thanne ne sholde ther be no stedefast prescience of thing to comen, but rather an uncerteyn opynioun; the whiche thing to trowen of God, I deme it felonye and unleveful.

Ne I ne proeve nat thilke same resoun (as who seith, I ne allowe nat, or I ne preyse nat, thilke same resoun) by whiche that some men wenen that thei mowe assoilen and unknytten the knotte of this questioun. (p. 459, lines 19–29)

As always, Jean's text provides a syntactic model for Chaucer's. But Chaucer also has difficulty with one term, "proeve" as the equivalent of "probo," when the Latin in this context means not "demonstrate" or "prove" but "favor" or "agree with." In his gloss ("as who seith . . ."), to explicate his lexical choice, he tries Trevet's first gloss on this sentence: "NEQUE ENIM ILLAM excludit quandam responsionem que dari possit et circa hoc duo facit. Primo enim ponit responsionem. Secundo excludit eam ibi QUASI VERO" (Silk, p. 697). In this he finds the term "excludit," from which he derives the first alternative "ne allowe nat." The second alternative, "preyse," he derives either from Trevet's gloss of the word "probo" as "approbo," or from Jean's word "loe." "Preyse" is a problematic option because it must be taken here in its secondary meaning of "prize" or "value" (cf. Old French "precier"). Chaucer is no longer seeking an equivalent for "probo," but rather an equivalent for the glosses on that term, Trevet's "approbo" or Jean's "loe."[59] Chaucer also reproduces Jean's doublet "soudre et deslier," thus providing two metaphors, "assoilen and unknytten" for the Latin "dissolvere."

Here is Walton's rendering of this passage:

And if it may be-fallen other-wise,
It was noght seen before as I devise.
Than schall this be no verrey prescience,
But as an vncerteyn opynyoun.
But sikerly this were a foule offence
Of god to felen that conclusioun.

And som men wenen that this questioun
May ben assoiled thus as they beleue,
But thaire resones ne kan I noght appreue. (stanzas 849–50)

Walton's reading of the last two lines of stanza 849 does not correspond to Boethius' phrasing, nor to Chaucer's version of this passage. Chaucer, like Jean de Meun, attempts to reproduce Boethius' image of events being diverted or turned from their foreseen course ("aliorsum quam prouisae sunt detorqueri ualent"): Jean has "se elles peuent estre destortes," and Chaucer has "yif that thei myghten writhen awey" (cf. *Troilus* 4.986, "To writhen out fro Goddis purveyinge"). But Walton's reading, "And if it may be-fallen other-wise," is taken directly from Trevet's gloss, "NAM SI VALENT DETORQUERI ALIORSUM scilicet ut aliter eueniant QUAM PROVISE SUNT" (Silk, p. 697), which substitutes "literal" speech for Boethius' metaphor in the interests of philosophical clarity. In this instance, Walton's reliance on Chaucer's methodological precedent leads him past Chaucer to Trevet's simplified rendering of the "sentence." With the next stanza, we see that Chaucer's lexical deliberations have cleared the way for Walton. In the last line, it is as if Chaucer's struggles with "probo" have led Walton to the source of Chaucer's gloss in Trevet; here Walton solves Chaucer's dilemma by supplying "appreue" for "probo." Much of this passage is directly indebted to Chaucer's text for syntax and lexicon. This represents just a fraction of Walton's lexical and conceptual dependence on the *Boece*.[60] When Walton tells us in his prologue: "fro the text that I ne vary noght / But kepe the sentence in hys trewe entent / And wordes eke als neigh as may be broght / Where lawe of metir is noght resistent," we can see that those laws of meter often intervene between his text and the *Boece* rather than between his text and the *Consolatio*.

The relationship between Walton's translation and the *Boece*, and the relationships between the other Boethius translations that I have considered in this chapter, represent more than the elements of a particular reception history. These texts instantiate the combined power of *exercitatio* and of *enarratio* in defining the status of vernacular writing. These texts concretely illustrate the interplay of rhetoric and hermeneutics; as such, the Boethius tradition is only one configuration in the large economy of these disciplinary forces. In this and the previous chapter I have considered how these disciplinary structures and alliances govern the vernacular appropriation of academic culture. The practice of exegetical translation makes this cultural appropriation visible. We see this in the way that vernacular Boethius traditions establish their own canons of the text as well as of the commentaries; and we see this in the auto-exegetical character of the *Ovide moralisé*, where the exegetical translation displaces its Ovidian model.

In this and the previous chapter we have considered some texts that I have classified under the rubric of "primary translation": translations that identify themselves with exegetical service to an authoritative text. This form of vernacular translation carries the force of the disciplinary alliance of rhetoric and hermeneutics. Such translation emerges out of hermeneutical practice and carries the contestative, rhetorical motive of hermeneutics; it is for this reason that it works to displace the Latin academic traditions that it proposes to serve. By taking over the role of academic criticism vernacular translation embodies that privileged institutional discourse within itself. It is here that we see the greatest implications of rhetorical *exercitatio*, in both interlingual and intralingual contexts. Vernacular translation can transform academic modes of reading into modes of discursive production.

It remains now to extend these arguments to the problem of rhetorical invention itself, and to those translations which define themselves expressly in terms of rhetorical performance.

6

From antiquity to the Middle Ages II: rhetorical invention as hermeneutical performance

So far this book has emphasized the status and condition of exegesis, its relationship with rhetoric, and its role within vernacular translation. Now it is necessary to reverse that emphasis and to consider the fortunes of rhetoric, and specifically the role of rhetorical *inventio* in vernacular translation. The translations that I have discussed so far, Notker's translation of Martianus Capella, the *Ovide moralisé*, and the Old French and Middle English versions of the *Consolatio*, define themselves in terms of exegetical practice. In the final chapter I will consider translations that offer themselves as forms of rhetorical invention. In order to understand this latter form of translation we must first take account of how the value of invention changes from the context of classical oratory to that of medieval poetics. My interest in this chapter will be to retrace the history of the relationship between rhetoric and hermeneutics, but this time directing my focus to how this relationship defines the meaning of rhetorical *inventio* for the later Middle Ages.

INVENTION IN ANTIQUITY

In ancient rhetoric, invention is the discovery of a plausible and persuasive argument through a system of proofs. *Inventio* (Greek *heuresis*) literally means a "coming upon," a discovery of that which is there, or already there, to be discovered. The term has little to do with originality or with creation *ex nihilo*. In all of its theoretical avatars among the ancients, invention is what Roland Barthes has aptly termed an "extractive" operation.[1] No matter how the theoretical apparatus of invention changes from one ancient school of rhetoric to another, the function of invention remains the same: to formulate and establish proofs that are extracted methodically from existing signs and existing regions of argument, or topics.

From Aristotle onwards, invention, the task of finding something to say, is constituted mainly through a system of logical inquiry. Aristotle's discussion of invention in books 1 and 2 of the *Rhetoric* distinguishes two types of proof, artificial and inartificial. Inartificial proofs are all those means and materials that are not the products of the orator's art: the evidence supplied by laws, witnesses, contracts, tortures, and oaths. Such materials could be obtained in writing and read out in the court. But with these the orator relies as much on his own *techne* to manipulate the evidence as on the written document itself.

Aristotle's discussion of artificial proof establishes the conceptual framework for most subsequent systems of invention in ancient rhetoric. He divides artificial proof into three kinds, ethos, pathos, and logos. Logos is the proof achieved through probable arguments: rhetoric and dialectic both reason through probabilities, and they are both faculties for providing such arguments (book 1, chapter 2, 1358a34). The enthymeme is the characteristic form of deductive proof in rhetoric: Aristotle's discussion of the materials and forms of enthymematic proof gives rise to his outline of a system of topics, the *topoi* or "regions" of argument. Topics are of two kinds: those which are particular to a certain field of inquiry, such as physics or politics, and those which are "common," that is, applicable to all subjects. His treatment of enthymatic proof draws on the formal strategies of dialectical argumentation that he had previously outlined in the *Topics*. As Aristotle presents it, rhetoric, in its function and methods, is fully the counterpart of dialectic.[2]

As the needs and interests of rhetoric changed, this conceptual system of invention could be modified. But in antiquity this system always remained a conceptual one: the topics, whether they provide the substance or the form of the argument, remain abstract "regions" of argument, "places" that exist in precedent, in subject, and in method. While Hermagoras, and Cicero after him, fixed the emphasis of rhetoric onto the political question, the method of invention remained tied to systems of logical argumentation. The distinctions between rhetorical and dialectical argumentation are never exactly clear. Cicero's *Topica*, while purporting to be an explanation of Aristotle's *Topics*, is really a treatise on rhetorical invention through the assessment of issues which can supply topics for argument. Cicero's own work on the topics left some ambiguity about whether the topical system for rhetoric should be different from that of dialectic. While the system of the *De inventione* builds on the *circumstantiae* and goes back to Hermagoras, the *De oratore* and *Topica* present a system which he claims to have taken from Aristotle's dialectical method in the *Topics*. It was left to later commentators, among them Victorinus and especially Boethius, to work out and explain the relationship between dialectical and rhetorical systems. These disciplinary distinctions remained ambiguous even for medieval commentators such as Thierry of Chartres, Gundissalinus, and Petrus Helias, who carried forward and adapted the solutions posed by late classical commentators.[3]

What remains consistent about this theoretical tradition of topical invention from antiquity through the Middle Ages is that discussions of rhetorical invention must always be contained in some way by the question of dialectic. Rhetorical topics may rely on or differentiate themselves from those of dialectic, but dialectic is always the referent against which the scope of rhetoric is measured. What is true for dialectical invention thus also remains true for rhetorical invention: its concern is with a logical and discursive coherence configured in spatial terms (the notion of place or seat of argument). The forms and materials of invention are essentially logical constructs.

Rhetorical invention as hermeneutical performance

The hierarchical relationship between rhetoric and dialectic is perceived differently from one context or period to another. Aristotle regarded rhetoric as the counterpart of dialectic, classing them together because neither engages in a scientific study of a definite subject (book 1, chapter 2; 1358a30). Roman theorists placed rhetoric above philosophy, seeing it as a political science which could ground itself in the rigors of dialectical method, but whose practical application to civic affairs gave it a supremacy among all the arts. But in later antiquity Boethius could subordinate rhetoric to dialectic, as a species of the genus of dialectic. Its historical identification with dialectical method does not make rhetoric any the less a praxis: dialectic is also concerned with the practicality of discourse, with the furnishing of arguments in debate. But rhetoric is not the same as dialectic; it has different aims and applications, the discovery of the best means of persuasion and the actualization of those means in political oratory. This is why rhetoric is more than a method of inventing arguments, why it has four other functions – arrangement, style, delivery, and memory – that invest it with its particular kind of power to move minds and shape policy. As Quintilian reminds us, the art of rhetoric is realized in action (*Institutio oratoria* 2.17.26; 18.1–2).

But in late antiquity, the political and judicial structures that had given such momentum to the growth of public oratory began to decline, and the study of rhetoric had to be sustained under new conditions. The political conditions of the late Empire could no longer support the kind of forensic and deliberative oratory that had flourished during the Republic, and rhetoric gradually lost its special application to civic affairs. Rhetoric retained its importance as an academic discipline, but not its power as a praxis, an application of practical wisdom in public affairs. I have already considered how the study of rhetoric came increasingly under the aegis of dialectical study, and how invention attracted a disproportionate amount of attention in late classical compendia because it could be systematized along the same lines as dialectical invention. Or it is possible to say that interest in dialectic (as reflected, for example, in the work of such influential figures as Victorinus and Boethius) shaped interest in rhetoric. The compositional and affective aspects of rhetoric became either eclipsed by or cut off from inventional study, so that rhetoric ceased to deal with discourse in the way that it was originally equipped to deal with it, that is, as a total act of persuasion that embodied determinations of meaning (invention) in a coherent and regulated articulation (structure, style, delivery).

As such, rhetoric becomes the atrophied partner of dialectic. When it has no practical outlet it takes on the character of an autotelic textbook art. Because rhetoric, and especially rhetorical invention, was always underwritten by its strong disciplinary association with dialectic, it could readily be subsumed by dialectical study when it lost its own proper field of application. But despite its traditional association with dialectic it was never *identical* with dialectic, and here is the problem. While it may have been drawn into the orbit of dialectical study, it did not thereby assume the particular *arete* or practical value of dialectic, that is, to furnish and judge arguments. It did not automatically become an art of disputation just because it no longer actively functioned as an art of persuasion. Rhetorical invention is meaningless when it is studied as a foil to dialectic, when it is divorced from the other productive functions of rhetoric. It has no use if it is not applied to persuasion.

AUGUSTINE AND THE *MODUS INVENIENDI*

Where rhetoric does find a practical outlet is in preaching. The obvious function of rhetoric in preaching is to regulate affectivity, the style and form of the sermon. The presentational parts of rhetoric, arrangement, style, delivery, and memory, find a valuable application here. The fourth book of Augustine's *De doctrina christiana* is concerned with the mode of setting forth or communicating doctrine learned from Scripture, and to this end Augustine adapts Ciceronian dictates on style, thereby bringing some aspects of ancient rhetorical theory into a specific field of action.

But what of the role of invention in this program of sacred oratory? When rhetoric becomes a component of preaching, it also becomes tied inextricably with exegesis, which is the most basic element of any preaching system. In chapter 2 I discussed the privileged value of *enarratio* in this theological context, how it underlies all aspects of production in mediating sacred truth, and how *lectio* and *praedicatio* are dual forms of the same process. But the role of rhetoric in sacred oratory is not limited to prescriptions for structure, style, and delivery. Invention also finds an application in this system that reintegrates it with the other parts of rhetoric. The role of invention in this system is to provide the terms for the exegetical act itself. Here invention assumes the value and identity of hermeneutical action. In sacred and secular studies, the grammarian's art of *enarratio* takes over what had been rhetoric's function of discursive analysis and production. As a secular academic study rhetoric had ceased to perform this function in late antiquity. But if hermeneutics could take on the function and character of rhetoric, it is also the case that rhetoric, and specifically rhetorical invention, could be redefined as a hermeneutical procedure. The place to begin this inquiry into the transformation of *inventio* is Augustine's *De doctrina christiana*.

In *De doctrina christiana* Augustine explains the twofold purpose of his book and its two-part structure:

> Duae sunt res quibus nititur omnis tractatio scripturarum, modus inveniendi quae intellegenda sunt et modus proferendi quae intellectus sunt.[4]
>
> [There are two principles on which every treatment of Scriptures depends: the means of discovering {*modus inveniendi*} what is to be understood, and the means of setting forth {*modus proferendi*} that which has been understood.]

These two principles, *modus inveniendi* and *modus proferendi*, correspond, as Augustine's exposition reveals, to two divisions of rhetoric, *inventio* and *elocutio*. *Inventio* is defined here as a method of discovering those things that are to be understood, and *elocutio* (*modus proferendi*, statement) as the means of presenting what has been understood. In this single sentence Augustine manages to reorient *inventio* completely. In books 1–3 he explores the *modus inveniendi*. But these books set forth a theory and method of reading and interpreting Scripture. This method of *inventio* is predicated on the assumption that all truth to be known is contained in the scriptural text. The finding of things to say will be grounded on what has been learned here in this consummate textual framework.

While modern scholars have recognized the *De doctrina christiana* as a Christian rhetoric, few besides Richard McKeon have considered how its rhetorical scope extends beyond the obvious Ciceronian influence of book 4, where Augustine treats style and the *modus proferendi*.[5] The prescriptive rhetoric of books 1–3 is not visible as such, only because Augustine has so reconstituted the nature of *inventio* that the content of these books seems to have little in common with other rhetorical treatises. Actually the structure of the *De doctrina christiana* is quite similar to that of other late classical rhetorical compendia and treatises: it follows that contemporary pattern of giving most space and attention to *inventio*, and of relegating style and the other parts of oratory to comparatively little space.

But books 1–3 treat invention largely in terms of the work of the grammarian-exegete. These books treat of things and signs, of doctrine and how to understand its articulation in Scripture. In book 1 Augustine discusses things; in books 2 and 3 he considers signs. Book 2 concerns "unknown signs," both literal ("propria") and figurative ("translata"), and explains the remedies for these unknown signs in terms of study of languages and textual criticism, and knowledge of arts, sciences, and institutions. Book 3 treats the remedies against ambiguous signs, both *propria* and *translata*. Here Augustine's treatment of the *modus inveniendi*, the means of discovering what is to be understood in ambiguous signs, falls exactly within the traditional province of the grammarian: rectifying the text and analyzing figures and tropes. The definition of *inventio* as *textual* interpretation grounds it, not in the methods of dialectic, but in *enarratio*, strict exegetical procedure.

This wholesale reorientation of the materials, methods, and aims of invention does not mean that Augustine is speaking outside of rhetoric in books 1–3, or that he has somehow mistaken the principles of *enarratio* for those of *eloquentia*. In other words, we should not conclude that these books are not about rhetoric. Indeed, the prescriptive framework of these books draws directly on rhetorical tradition. Gerald Press, for example, makes a strong argument for reading the whole of *De doctrina christiana* as a rhetoric in terms of the technical language that it shares with Ciceronian rhetorics.[6] He finds the key to the disciplinary framework of the text in Augustine's use of the words *tracto* and *tractatio*, as in the first sentence of the prologue: "Sunt praecepta quaedam tractandarum scripturarum quae studiosis earum video non incommode posse tradi . . ." (there are certain precepts of treating the Scriptures which I think can be taught not improperly to students of them

. . .").[7] The terms *tracto* and *tractatio* are found widely in the *Ad Herennium*, in Cicero, and in Quintilian, and assume a technical meaning particular to these rhetorical contexts: the treatment, handling, or discussion of a subject. In these rhetorics, *tractatio* is used in the context of prescribing techniques of analysis, organization, and exposition. Most broadly, *tractatio* implies treating something mentally, orally, or in writing, and often overlaps with the term *inventio*.[8] Augustine's use of the term to designate the treatment of Scripture, "tractatio scripturarum" (1.1.1), is consistent with the use of the term in the ancient rhetorical tradition. Augustine also treates certain "topics": *res* and *signa*, *caritas* and *cupiditas*, the science of true and false reasoning; and he treats the same kinds of topics that come under *inventio* in the rhetorics, for example, documentary evidence, the *materia* of the controversy (i.e., the exposition of doctrine in book 1, *de rebus*), or the conventions of signification.[9]

One difference between Augustine and his Roman predecessors is that all of his uses of the terms *tracto* and *tractatio* apply to reading, comprehension, and exposition of a single group of texts, the Scriptures.[10] This returns us to one of the points that I raised earlier in this chapter, the materials out of which one invents. In classical antiquity, *inventio*, finding something to say, draws from a system of logic, a field of conceptual coherences in which written repositories of information have no particular primacy or necessary place. In Augustine, finding something to say can only be extracted from a field of textual coherences, for it is in Scripture that one discovers – invents or comes upon – the doctrine or *res* that one will expound in preaching. Augustine thus gives *inventio* a new application by changing the field of its operations to written discourse. In Augustine's program, the text itself has become the *topos* – the region of argument – from which what has to be said will be extracted.

The most important implication of this shift for later historical norms of invention is that Augustine transforms the *modus inveniendi* in to the *modus interpretandi*. The first three books of the *De doctrina christiana* are a hermeneutical treatise. Augustine presents a system in which finding something to say is achieved through – is identical with – textual hermeneutics. In this way, rhetoric, and especially rhetorical invention, is appropriated by and put to work in the privileged and powerful system of hermeneutics.

What is being invented in Augustine's program? He answers this at the beginning: "quae intellegenda sunt," those things which are to be understood in Scripture. The focus on textual interpretation is also a focus on a specific given text. Moreover, this single text offers up a unitary interpretation or meaning to be understood: this is the argument of book 1, which teaches *de rebus*, of things, and of the most important thing or truth of all, Christian *caritas*. This would seem to stabilize *inventio*: its object is to extract a single meaning from a single text. But in fact, Augustine's program opens or destabilizes *inventio* in a powerful new way. The problems, the questions, the "circumstances" of exegesis are infinite. In book 3, on reading ambiguous signs, Augustine introduces the *circumstantiae* into his explanation of reading figuratively:

Quid igitur locis et temporibus et personis conveniat diligenter adtendendum est, ne temere flagitia reprehendamus . . . Et quidquid ibi tale narratur, non solum historice ac proprie, sed etiam figurate ac prohetice acceptum interpretandum est usque in finem illum caritatis sive dei sive proximi sive utriusque.

[Careful attention is therefore to be paid to what is proper to places, times, and persons lest we condemn the shameful too hastily . . . And whatever is so narrated is to be taken not only historically and literally but also figuratively and prophetically, so that it is interpreted for the end of charity, either as it applies to God, to one's neighbor, or to both.][11]

The meaning itself may be unitary, but the signs which convey that meaning are subject to multiple interpretation, as their significance changes from age to age, from people to people:

In huiuscemodi moribus [i.e. bigamy] quidquid illorum temporum sancti non libidinose faciebant, quamvis ea facerent quae hoc tempore nisi per libidinem fieri non possunt, non culpat scriptura.

[With reference to customs of this kind, whatever the holy men of those days did without libidinousness, even though they did things that may not now be done in that way, is not blamed by the Scripture.][12]

To recall Gadamer here, a tradition can never be understood twice in the same way. If this is a program for *inventio*, then it returns rhetoric to its social importance and reconstitutes it as a praxis. This is not only because Christian truth has an application to social realities, to the determination of ethical value in the face of cultural difference. The ambiguity or multiple value of signs in Scripture also creates difference within the text itself, which it is the duty of the reader to resolve. For example, for ambiguous figurative signs Augustine prescribes comparison of usages in the text, and explains the principle of polyvalence:

Sed quoniam multis modis res similes rebus apparent, non putemus esse praescriptum utquod in aliquo loco res aliqua per similitudinem significaverit, hoc eam semper significare credamus. Nam et in vituperatione posuit fermentum dominus cum diceret: Cavete a fermento Pharisaeorum, et in laude diceret: Simile est regnum caelorum mulieri quae abscondit fermentum in tribus mensuris farinae donec totum fermentaretur . . . Sic et aliae res non singulae, sed unaquaeque earum non solum duo aliqua diversa, sed etiam nonnumquam multa significat pro loco sententiae, sicut posita reperitur.

[But since things are similar to other things in a great many ways, we must not think it to be prescribed that what a thing signifies by similitude in one place must always be signified by that thing. For the Lord used "leaven" in vituperation when he said, "Beware of the leaven of the Pharisees," and in praise when he said, "The kingdom of God . . . is like to leaven, which a woman took and hid in three measures of meal, till the whole was leavened." . . . In the same way other things signify not one thing but more, and not only two diverse things, but sometimes many different things in accordance with the meaning of passages in which they are found.][13]

This program gives the reader the power of invention. It gives reading and interpretation – the traditional province of the grammarian – a new status, as textual power shifts from authorial intention to "affective stylistics," to what the reader can do with the text. In practice it transfers responsibility for making meaning from the writer to the reader. Of course, meaning in Scripture is unitary, and is produced, not by the reader, but by God. But that meaning can be expressed ambiguously, so that it is up to the reader to judge carefully and to be equipped with the fundamentals of doctrine (signs and things, *caritas*) and with the *techne* of exposition. Classical rhetoric deals with ambiguities of meaning from the perspective of the orator, of the producer of the utterance. The facts of the case, the *res*, are ambiguous, and meaning is contingent upon the orator's effective use of language, of *signa*. It is up to the orator to argue the case from the most persuasive angle. Augustine's sacred rhetoric takes up ambiguities of meaning from the perspective of the reader. The "facts" of the "case," that is, the *res* or doctrine, are determinate and unitary, and what is ambiguous are the words, the signa. It is the responsibility of the reader to interpret these signs and to produce an account of their meaning. The whole responsibility of *inventio*, of discovery, is transferred to the reader, and the function of *inventio* is to make, not *res*, but *signa* meaningful.

My concern in the rest of this chapter will be to trace the implications of Augustine's sacred rhetoric as hermeneutical performance. I will consider its effect outside of the medieval scriptural tradition, in the transmission of rhetorical and grammatical lore in the arts tradition.

MODUS INVENIENDI AS *MODUS INTERPRETANDI*: THE *ARTES POETRIAE* IN THE MIDDLE AGES

Augustine's transformation of rhetorical invention had no bearing on the "academic" study of rhetoric from the Carolingian period onwards. The study of rhetoric as a trivium art in the monastic schools, and later the cathedral schools and universities (especially of northern Europe), was a conservative tradition. It carried forward the dialectical orientations of the late classical commentators on Cicero, Victorinus and Grillius.[14] This is a tradition of study that leaves its mark, not through the production of new treatises on rhetoric, but rather through the production of extensive commentaries, mainly on the *De inventione* and to a lesser degree on the *Ad Herennium*. The *De inventione* maintained enormous currency among medieval schoolmen because, with its own highly theoretical character, it lent itself readily to the philosophical interests of academicians; more specifically, its exclusive concern with invention, or discovery of proofs, complemented the standard curricular readings on dialectic.[15] The continuity of interests within this academic tradition is more notable than any continuity it might have achieved with the norms of classical rhetoric. From the Carolingian schools onward, the attention given over to *inventio* reflects a view of rhetoric as a mental discipline or intellectual system like dialectic. John Scotus Eriugena treats rhetoric as a division of probable argument, distinguishable from dialectic mainly for its circumstantial specificity.[16] This view extends into the efflorescence of rhetorical studies in the monastic and cathedral schools of the eleventh century. In northern Europe, and especially France, the study of rhetorical *inventio* was a by-product of dominant concerns with dialectical and terminological problems. In the northern cathedral schools of the twelfth century, the *De inventione* served as a substitute dialectical text for students working in a newly expanded curriculum in logic. Indeed, until the recovery of the text of Aristotle's *Topics* and of the *Organon* as a whole, the *De inventione* provided Western European scholars with a good dialectical and demonstrative method and a good system of topics.[17]

The influential commentaries of the late eleventh and twelfth centuries, notably that of Thierry of Chartres, reflect the continuing influence of Victorinus' treatment of the *De inventione*, although some also show a revived interest in the more practical framework of the *Ad Herennium* and of the *Institutio oratoria*.[18] One feature of these commentaries is their attempt to grasp the structural and theoretical elements of rhetoric as a system, to understand it in terms of its place in a comprehensive, hierarchical framework of knowledge. For example, the prologue to the commentary on the *De inventione* by Thierry of Chartres attempts to place rhetoric as a system among other disciplines or systems before tackling the elements of the art itself. The status of rhetoric was thus defined in terms of contemporary theoretical interests in classifying the sciences, and here rhetoric was typically classed with dialectic as a form of probable proof under logic.[19]

Thus the academic study of rhetoric as a discipline or science does not reflect Augustine's move to redefine invention as a textual hermeneutic. Nor, more broadly, do academic classifications of the science reflect Augustine's conflation of grammar and rhetoric. In terms of conceptual schemes for classifying the sciences, grammar and rhetoric retain their identities as distinct arts. From the ninth to the thirteenth centuries, grammar, rhetoric, and logic – the trivium as a whole – can be classed together in various ways. Eriugena, Martin of Laon, and Hugh of St. Victor class them together as parts of logic. Giles of Rome considers them instrumental arts (*scientiae adminiculantes*) and categorizes them under speculative science. One thirteenth-century commentator classes them together under *eloquentia*.[20] In these ways, rhetoric and grammar may be perceived as having some kind of related function (for example, along with dialectic they may be seen as *artes sermocinales*), but there is no recognition at this theoretical level of the overlapping or conflation of their functions in historical practice.

Where Augustine's transformation of invention and of the application of rhetoric does have a manifest effect is in two fields which are intimately related: hermeneutics and the *artes poetriae* or rhetorical poetics of the twelfth and thirteenth centuries. Augustine's definition of invention as an exegetical procedure is a prototype for one important conception of invention in late medieval rhetorical poetics. In the medieval *artes poetriae*, *inventio* is an extractive operation, as in its classical sense, a deliberation about a subject, about the potentials of "what to say" by drawing on a topical reserve. But in these rhetorical poetics, *inventio* can often assume the existence of a textual legacy, an inherited tradition of written authority which will provide a topical reserve. In this theoretical context, the place – the *topos* – out of which one invents is provided in palpable textual authority. This process of invention through textual reception is presented in the *artes poetriae* in ways that are nearly identical with the apparatus of hermeneutics, the tradition of *enarratio poetarum*. The apparatus for reading or analyzing texts in the manner of the grammarian-exegete (e.g., the attention to style or to authorial intention), which allowed medieval hermeneutics to appropriate ancient textual authority, is here, in the *artes poetriae*, applied to writing out of that body of textual authority. Here, as in Augustine's system, the *modus inveniendi* is achieved through – and is identical with – the *modus interpretandi*.

While the late medieval *artes poetriae* carry the imprint of Augustine's exegetical rhetoric, they are also – or even primarily – the products of classical preceptive traditions of rhetoric, that is, the legacy of Cicero, the *Ad Herennium*, and Quintilian, along with the poetic precept of Horace's *Ars poetica*. The academic conservatism of Ciceronian rhetoric in the Middle Ages produced one interesting side effect for poetic precept, in that continuing studies on the topics provided a stable reference for the *artes poetriae*. The poetics adapted established categories of topics to serve as tools for literary analysis. Matthew of Vendôme, Geoffrey of Vinsauf, and John of Garland all exploited these standardized topical systems.[21] One historical explanation of this is that the *artes poetriae* constituted poetry as an academic discipline, and promoted its participation in the methods of logic.[22] This historical view accords readily with the reclassification of the sciences in the wake of the introduction of Artistotle's *Organon* into the curriculum. After the mid-twelfth century, poetic, along with rhetoric, was sometimes classified as either a division or an instrument of logic. Dominicus Gundissalinus (fl. 1125–50), for example, classified Aristotle's *Rhetoric* and *Poetics* as parts of the Organon, and thus as pertaining to logical sciences; Aquinas classified poetry as a form of "inventive logic."[23]

These are necessary considerations, historically and conceptually: if rhetoric is the disciplinary or preceptive "container" for poetic, then poetic must, like rhetoric, locate itself under the method of logic. But such a historical construction of the *artes poetriae* also neglects the continuing force of grammar or hermeneutical analysis as a shaping force in their rhetorical programs.[24] Murphy has aptly termed these arts "preceptive grammars"; like rhetorics they offer precepts for the production of discourse, but their preceptive techniques derive to a great extent from the tradition of the *enarratio poetarum.*[25] They teach the art of composition through the art of formal literary analysis, and they are as much (if not more) the products of the tradition of Donatus, Priscian, and Servius as they are the products of Ciceronian rhetoric. But in the *artes poetriae* we also see the legacy of Augustine's synthesis of rhetoric and hermeneutics: as in Augustine's program, they define rhetorical *inventio* through exegetical procedure.

We can begin with one very visible instance of the confluence of hermeneutics and rhetoric in the *artes poetriae*: John of Garland's use of the inventional scheme of the *circumstantiae*. In chapter 3 we considered how the rhetorical system of the seven circumstances, traditionally used as a device for topical invention, came into use as a hermeneutical apparatus in the Remigian prologue. My treatment of the circumstantial *accessus* emphasized how hermeneutics appropriates the tools of rhetoric. I propose now to explore this relationship from the opposite angle. John of Garland's use of the *circumstantiae* as an inventional scheme illustrates how rhetoric – and specifically rhetorical *inventio* – can be defined through hermeneutical inquiry. As in Augustine's program, John of Garland's discussion identifies rhetoric with hermeneutics by diverting rhetorical invention away from dialectical method to textuality.

In standard rhetorical doctrine, such as that of Boethius, the seven circumstances – who, what, where, when, why, how, and by what means – provide comprehensive topics for invention. In the Remigian prologue, the circumstances lead us to a specific textual place – a *topos* – providing means for comprehensive interpretation. The Remigian prologue had a relatively short currency; by the twelfth century it was largely superseded by the "type C" prologue. But even when its popularity declined it was still recognized as a valid exegetical apparatus and, as I have argued, still exerted a certain force on later prologue structures (for example, the topic *cur* or *causa* corresponds to the topic of *intentio* in the later "type C" prologue).[26]

The question here is how and to what extent the use of the *circumstantiae* as an apparatus for textual interpretation might have colored later uses of this scheme outside of the strict Ciceronian rhetorical tradition, and especially in contexts associated with the *enarratio poetarum*. On the one hand, in purely academic rhetorical study, such as standard commentaries on Cicero, the *circumstantiae* as an inventional technique retained their "proper" value as a way of organizing information about the rhetorical hypothesis. But in such an eclectic text as John of Garland's *Parisiana poetria*, which is an example of the grammatical-rhetorical crossover of the *artes poetriae*, could the use of the *circumstantiae* as an inventional apparatus not also reflect a secondary grammatical heritage, that is, the use of the *circumstantiae* as a device for textual analysis?

John of Garland's *Parisiana poetria* (known also as *De arte prosayca, metrica, et rithmica*) was written and revised probably between 1220 and 1235.[27] It is thus among the later *artes poetriae*, which range in their dates of composition from about 1175 to the middle of the thirteenth century. John was himself a teacher of grammar and literature at the University of Paris, and was briefly a Master of Grammar at the University of Toulouse. His own prolific output places him solidly in the tradition of the grammarian-exegete. In addition to miscellaneous devotional and moral works, he composed several grammatical works and word books, and an allegorical exposition of Ovid's *Metamorphoses* (the *Integumenta Ovidii*).[28] The *Parisiana poetria* is a kind of *summa* of literary analysis and compositional precept. It covers not only poetry writing but also *dictamen*. Like the earlier *artes* by Matthew of Vendôme and Geoffrey of Vinsauf, John's *Parisiana poetria* combines Ciceronian precept on invention and arrangement, Horatian doctrine on decorum, and instructions on style (figures and tropes) derived from early and late medieval grammarians. The *Parisiana poetria*, then, synthesizes elements from the academic Ciceronian tradition and from grammatical teaching. The treatise is divided into seven books: invention, selection of material, beginning and arranging the chosen material, the parts of a letter (*dictamen*), vices peculiar to verse, poetic embellishment and word order in prose, and a final chapter exemplifying tragedy, forms of letters, and *rithmus*.

The synthesis of rhetoric and grammar is nowhere more visible than in John's curious treatment of the circumstantial system of invention in book 1. John's statement on invention promises a fairly conventional treatment of rhetorical doctrine:

> Inuenire est in ignote rei noticiam ductu proprie rationis uenire. Et sicut dicit Tullius in secunda Rethorica: "Inuencio est rerum uerarum et veri similium excogitatio que causam probabilem reddant. [*Rhetorica ad Herennium* 1.2.3] Sub inuencione species sunt quinque: vbi, quid, quale, qualiter, ad quid.
>
> [To invent is to come into knowledge of an unknown thing through the agency of one's own reason. Here is what Cicero says in the *Second Rhetoric*: "Invention is thinking up things that are true or at least realistic to make your case plausible." Under invention there are five species: where, what, what kind, how, and why {i.e., to what purpose}.][29]

The first part of this statement is Ciceronian. The second part is an abbreviated and modified version of the circumstances as found in Boethius. "Who," "when," and "whence" or "by what means" have been dropped from the list. The term *qualiter* (how) replaces the traditional term *quomodo*, and *ad quid* is used for *cur*. John also introduces a new term, *quale*, "what kind," which could have been suggested by the qualitative issue (*quale sit*) of *status* theory which concerns the nature, class, or quality of the act (cf. *De inventione* 1.8–11, and *Topica* 21).

While John's explanations of these topics contain certain elements of classical doctrine on the circumstances, his treatment of them is of a wholly different order. He gives nothing comparable to the classical circumstantial scheme, the attributes of the person and the act (e.g., who did it, what was done, where, and by what means). Under "where" he explains where to invent one's subject-matter: in character, examples, and etymologies and expositions of words. His explanation of invention out of the types of characters and persons may correspond loosely with Cicero's topics of the attributes of persons (*De inventione* 1.24.34ff.). Under *quid* John offers more resources and materials for invention, returning to persons, examples, and etymologies; under inventing from example he gives a long list of proverbs which is curiously reminiscent of Aristotle's list of maxims (*Rhetoric* 2.21), but which is probably John's original contribution to the subject of invention. Both of these topics, *ubi* and *quid*, function in the *Parisiana poetria* as resources of information about the *materia* to be discovered. But the difference between this treatment and Cicero's or Boethius' is striking: whereas the classical theorists use the circumstances to describe an action performed which is the *res* or the case to be argued (e.g., what was done, where was it done, and who did it), John uses the circumstances to describe the process of writing itself, to describe the text that comes into being through invention, so that "where" and "what" describe the author's own action, where he can look for a subject and what that subject will be. If the classical circumstances serve as topics to organize information about an action that exists or occurs outside the prospective text, John's use of them serves to organize the text itself. His treatment of these topics has more in common with their use in the circumstantial *accessus*, where the circumstances turn the text into a kind of action performed and the author into the performer of that action.

With his exposition of the remaining categories, *quale* (what kind), *qualiter* (how), and *ad quid* (why or to what end), John turns almost completely from the assumptions and methods of the classical doctrine of circumstances. He takes up the topic *quale*, the "nature" of the material to be invented, with a partial paraphrase from the *Ad Herennium* on instructions for the proem of a speech. Both the *Ad Herennium* and the *De inventione* give directions for constructing the proem or exordium based on an understanding of the "quality" of the case or cause to be argued: the *Ad Herennium* lists four *genera causarum*: honorable, dishonorable, doubtful (ambiguous), and petty (1.3.5; cf. *De inventione* 1.15.20). John of Garland takes up two of these *genera*: honorable and dishonorable. But he turns immediately from a discussion of the "quality" of the subject to a discussion of style appropriate to either kind of subject: an honorable subject calls for plain sentences and open language, whereas a disreputable subject requires subtle disguise through circumlocutions and figures of speech. At this point John paraphrases an example of metaphor from *Ad Herennium* book 4 (4.34.45), the book on style, figures, and tropes. In other words, his focus under this category of *inventio* shifts to stylistic precept governed by the categories of literary analysis, the business of the grammarian-exegete. A category of logic, *quale* or *genus*, becomes for John of Garland a directive for style or *elocutio*. The ground of *inventio* has shifted from dialectic to textuality.

What he does with *qualiter* (how) and *ad quid* (why) is even more telling. He explains *ad quid* briefly in the following way:

Qvia dicitur in premissis "ad quid," attendendum est quod per hoc denotatur finis inuentoris, scilicet vtilitas et honestas; et licet intendat accusare vel dampnare, secundum se finis bonus est.

[Since 'to what end" is mentioned above, let us notice . . . that this denotes the inventor's purpose, that is, of course, the utility and correctness {of what is invented}, and even though the author intends to accuse or condemn, that purpose is still good in itself.][30]

This explanation of "why" or "to what purpose" is nearly identical with discussions of *cur* in the Remigian prologue or with discussions of authorial *intentio* and textual *utilitas* in the "type C" prologue of the twelfth century. Indeed, the notion here of purpose is thoroughly informed by the *exegetical* concern of an author acting on a text. Any relation it bears to the topic *causa* in ancient rhetorical doctrine (where it is an attribute of the action) has already been mediated by exegetical transformations of the inventional system, which have made the text into an action performed by an author. John of Garland's treatment of this topic of *causa* (or *cur*, or, as he has it, *ad quid*) is so much indebted to its use in exegetical systems that he can combine this topic with other common prologue themes, such as the passing reference to the ethical utility of the author's purpose ("utilitas et honestas"). One of John's collocations, "intendat accusare vel dampnare" is reminiscent of ethical discussions of classical authors, as in a twelfth-century prologue to Ovid's *Heroides*, which claims: "intentio huius libri est commendare castum amorem . . . vel vituperare incestum amorem" (the intention of this book is to praise chaste love . . . or to condemn impure love).[31] The difference between John's treatment of the topic of *causa* and that to be found in prologues to the authors is that John, of course, assigns intention to the prospective author of a future text (the *finis inventoris*) rather than, as in prologues, to the given author of an existing text (cf. *intentio auctoris* or *intentio huius libri*). But the important fact remains that John derives his understanding and presentation of the topic "why" from the hermeneutical tradition, where it is defined as authorial intention and control over a text, not from the rhetorical tradition, where it is understood as an attribute of the action performed or the legal matter at hand. In other words, John, like the exegetes, identifies *causa* with the producer of the discourse, whereas the rhetoricians identify *causa* with the subject-matter of the discourse to be produced, and not with the intentions of the speaker himself.

Not surprisingly, the explanation of the topic *qualiter*, which corresponds to the circumstantial question *quomodo*, "in what way" or "how," has nothing to do with the performance of the action, as it would be understood in Cicero or Boethius. John treats it rather as the performance of a textual action, as it would be understood by the exegetes: it is a discussion of style, comparable to what we would find under *quomodo* in a Remigian prologue, for example, that the *modus* of Martianus Capella's *De nuptiis* is prose and verse. John lists and explains seven figures "by which subject-matter is embellished and amplified," and in the manner of a grammarian, provides examples from classical authors (Virgil, Statius, Ovid). The concern of invention thus shifts to the formal properties of textual production. The ancient rhetoricians would have relegated this to secondary consideration under *elocutio*. But form and style is a primary consideration of the grammatical tradition of *enarratio poetarum*. John conflates these two traditions, conferring a primary status on *elocutio* by treating it as a function of *inventio*.

The influence of academic prologues on John's inventional system thus manifests itself in a variety of ways. At the end of book 1, completing his treatment of invention, he makes brief reference to the Aristotelian paradigm of the four causes – efficient, material, formal, and final – as a device for investigating any subject. While this paradigm is familiar as a scholastic prologue form, it is more generally a conceptual apparatus for any kind of philosophical inquiry. It is therefore significant that John should associate it with its function in hermeneutical systems and through this adapt it as an inventional device:

De arte inueniendi materiam. Hoc artificio vtendum est in aliis orationibus, quod pueri uolentes ampliare et uariare materiam obseruent, non pretermittentes causas principales quattuor, scilicet causam efficientem, cuiuslibet rei sibi proposite. Ut, si tractet de libro suo, commendet eum uel uituperet per causam efficientem, idest per scriptorem; per causam materialem, idest per pergamenum et incaustum; per causam formalem, ut per libri disposicionem et litterarum protractionem; per causam finalem, considerando ad quid factus est liber, ad hoc uidelicet ut in eo et per eum nescientes scientes reddantur.

[*Concerning the art of inventing material.* Here is a device that is useful in certain kinds of writing, which students who want to amplify and vary their material may observe: they should not overlook the four principle causes, for example, the efficient cause, of any subject proposed to them. Thus, suppose one of them is treating of his book. He might praise or criticize it through the efficient cause, that is, through the writer; through the material cause, that is, through the parchment or the ink; through the formal cause, that is, through the arrangement of the book and the size of the letters; or through the final cause, by considering for what purpose the book was made, namely, that in it and through it the ignorant may be made more knowledgeable.][32]

The explanations of the causes, curious as they are in some instances, represent a system of textual analysis: the subject to be investigated is a book, the efficient cause (as in the scholastic *accessus*) is the author, and so on. Once again, John identifies invention with a form of textual hermeneutics. We have seen that medieval prologue traditions seem to color John's understanding of the *circumstantiae* as an inventional system, so that he represents rhetorical invention as hermeneutical performance. In similar fashion he understands the scholastic device of the four causes as a hermeneutical apparatus, and appropriates it in these terms as a device for rhetorical invention. If medieval hermeneutics borrows the tools of rhetoric and defines itself as rhetorical action, we now have an instance of rhetoric defining itself through hermeneutical maneuvers and systems.

Here we see the legacy of Augustine; rhetorical invention is constituted through the *modus interpretandi.* In John of Garland we have a situation in which the apparatus for invention is identical with the apparatus for the analysis and interpretation of literary authority. But this is only one instance of what we could call the "grammaticization" of rhetoric in the medieval *artes poetriae*. This has broad implications for our understanding of these arts, for the way that they redefine the function of rhetoric. Since poetics as a study and an art was historically associated with the domain of *grammatica*, late medieval attempts to approach poetics through rhetorical precept were nothing less than "projections" of grammar onto rhetoric. In Matthew of Vendôme, Geoffrey of Vinsauf, John of Garland, and Gervase of Melkley, invention itself becomes in large part a grammatical category: the burden of invention is shifted onto amplification and variation of *materia* that has previously been realized in some kind of linguistic form.[33] The traditional textual framework of late-medieval poetics may also account for the relative sketchiness of inventional theory in many of the *artes poetriae*, as all the important rhetorical work would be transferred to amplification, abbreviation, and ornamentation of the *materia* that tradition has selected.[34] This makes *inventio* virtually identical with *elocutio*, but also with the stylistic analysis of *enarratio poetarum*.

We can trace these questions in the inventional theory of two earlier poeticians, Matthew of Vendôme and Geoffrey of Vinsauf. They offer a more substantial and complex picture of the transformation of invention into an exegetical act. What is most important in these authors is first, the collocation of inventional theory with stylistic precept, especially directives for variation of given *materia*, and second, the reliance of both their inventional discussions on lines 119–33 from Horace's *Ars poetica* which deal with the reception and treatment of traditional material. The use of this passage from the *Ars poetica* in both Matthew and Geoffrey reflects the value that Horace's dictum had acquired in medieval commentaries where, among other things, Horace's lines are recognized as a commonplace of translation theory.

Matthew of Vendôme's *Ars versificatoria* (written before 1175) opens with a definition of verse as "metrica oratio," the purpose of which is to express the property and observed attributes of a subject.[35] This definition leads him into a brief explanation of substance and accident, terms which he has derived from the categories of dialectic, in order to introduce the way that a poem describes its subject. He continues with advice on how to begin a poem and on what stylistic errors should be avoided in such openings, and follows this with a long section on *descriptio*. In this, the longest section of the *Ars versificatoria*, he adapts the topical scheme of the attribute of the person and the act from the *De inventione* to provide commonplaces for *descriptio*.[36] But despite his application of Cicero's system of topical invention (which he also equates with the *circumstantiae*),[37] it is not clear that he identifies his exposition of this matter with a Ciceronian notion of the discovery of *materia*. First, he introduces this topical system without any reference to *inventio*, locating his exposition instead under precepts for *descriptio*.[38] Second, he views the various terms for this topical system of personal description, *proprietates*, *epitheta*, and *personae attributa* as synonymous with the term *colores operum*.[39] And finally, there is the way that he distinguishes the parts of his own treatise: the first part dealt with determining meaning through the attributes of the person and the act, the second part with verbal ornamentation, and the third part with schemes and tropes. Yet here he anticipates an objection, since all these parts of the treatise are concerned, as he puts it, with poetic ornamentation ("de ornatu metricae modulationis").[40] Thus he has identified all of his doctrinal coverage with *elocutio*. For this seeming confusion he offers an explanation:

> . . . quod in primo et in secundo et in tertio membro de ornatu metri quidem agitur, sed tripertito: quamvis enim in causa tractandi sit identitas, in modo tractatus varietas perpenditur; quia primo, de ornatu interioris sententiae agitur, secundo, de ornatu verborum, tertio, de qualitate dicendi. Unde non ulla ratio ordinis in illis tribus membris potest assignari. Etenim, sicut in praefata distinctione praecedunt sententiae, verba sequuntur, tertio qualitas dicendi subjungitur, similiter in poeticae facultatis exercitio praecedit imaginatio sensus, sequitur sermo interpres intellectus, deinde ordinatio in qualitate tractatus; prior est sententiae conceptio, sequitur verborum excogitatio, subjungitur qualitas scilicet materiae, sive tractatus dispositio.[41]
>
> [. . . indeed, the first, the second, and the third parts of the treatise deal with poetic ornamentation, but in a threefold way: while they are the same in terms of the cause of the treatment, they are different with respect to the method of the treatise. For the first part deals with ornament of the interior meaning {*sententia*}, the second part deals with verbal ornamentation, and the third part with style of discourse. Thus one cannot assign a random order to these three parts of the treatise. For just as, in the previous distinction, meaning comes first, and then words follow, and then comes character of expression, so in the exercise of the poetic faculty there is first a perception of meaning, then language follows as the interpreter {*interpres*, i.e. intermediary} of what has been perceived, and then finally the ordering in the nature of the treatise {*tractatus*}. First comes a conceptualization of meaning, then follows the invention {*excogitatio*} of words, and to this is added the character of the material, or the arrangement of the work.]

Here we have, on the one hand, an unmistakable definition of invention, a conceptualization of meaning (*conceptio sententiae*) to which language and structure give discursive form. But on the other hand, the part of Matthew's treatise that expounds this conceptual stage is the discussion of *descriptio*, the attributes of the person and the act. In other words, what he understands as invention and treats through the inventional system of topics is already understood and conflated with a device of *elocutio*, that is, description.[42]

Matthew's application of the classical topics of invention thus pertains not so much to invention or discovery of material (as in Cicero) as to the development of material that has already been discovered. Where he actually comes to an account of the resources of *materia*, that is, questions of invention, is towards the end of the treatise. Here he offers an important distinction between material that is already in literary form and material that has not been previously treated (or versified):

Amplius, materia de qua aliquis agere proponet, aut erit illibata, aut ab aliquo poeta primitus exsecuta.[43]

[Moreover, material which someone proposes to treat will be either fresh territory or previously treated by another poet.]

He follows with advice on how to rework *materia exsecuta* by amplifying and abbreviating the source. At the very end of the treatise, however, he takes up the question of *materia illibata*. Thus far, he says, his subject has been *materia pertractata*, material already treated by others, such as versified fables used in school exercises.[44] But in taking up *materia illibata* he recapitulates the precepts of his whole treatise, beginning with instructions for *descriptio* under attributes of the person and the action. At this point we realize that he has been speaking all along, from the beginning of the treatise up to this point, of *materia exsecuta*. He has borrowed the system of topical invention from Cicero in order to apply it to a *materia* that already exists in textual form. This system of invention has served, not to discover a pre-linguistic *res*, as in Cicero, but rather to discover the appropriate treatment of a given text.

Matthew's application of ancient inventional doctrine has a hermeneutical orientation and function. The discussion that really bears upon invention of material is his distinction between *materia exsecuta* and *materia illibata*.[45] This is prefaced with a reference to the exegetical practice of the schools:

Sequitur de exsecutione materiae, in qua quidam male disciplinati solent plerumque delirare et a semita doctrinali turpiter exorbitare, qui in scolastico exercitio fabulas circinantes poeticas verbum verbo sigillatim exprimunt, tanquam super auctores metrice proposuerunt commentare . . . Nec etiam aliquis verbo verbum proponat reddere fidus interpres.[46]

[We turn now to the treatment of material, in which certain ill-trained people habitually overstep the line and shamefully depart from preceptive guidelines. When paraphrasing poetic fables in school exercises, they render word for word, down to every figure of speech, as if they sought to produce a metrical commentary on the authors . . . One should not try to render word for word like a *fidus interpres*.]

Although this is cast in negative terms, proscribing excessive or mechanical dependence on a text, it also reveals the context in which discovery of *materia exsecuta* takes place, that is, the exegetical action of the *enarratio poetarum*. Horace's famous warning against the *fidus interpres* is marshalled here to discourage the appearance of a certain kind of exegetical performance – mechanical, reductive, unskilled. Matthew uses Horace's warning to distinguish, not between imitation and originality, but between *enarratio* and composition. In this context, to treat *materia exsecuta* effectively is to suppress the obvious mechanics and character of exegesis, and to turn the exegetical reception of textual authority into a rhetorical performance. In

Matthew's treatise, topical invention is undertaken as part of a large program of exegetical reception. Hermeneutics here uses the tools of rhetoric, and thus, as in Augustine, defines invention as a hermeneutical move.

Matthew's reference here to the *fidus interpres* passage from Horace's *Ars poetica* opens the question of what significance this theory of translation and literary reception takes on when medieval poeticians use it in their own inventional statements. Geoffrey of Vinsauf makes extensive use of these precepts from Horace in the *Documentum de modo et arte dictandi et versificandi* (written after 1213), in the only part of this treatise that he gives over to selection of material. In the *Documentum*, he begins immediately with *dispositio* (natural and artificial order) and proceeds to questions of amplification, abbreviation, and verbal ornamentation. Towards the end of the treatise he opens a new course of recommendations with the following statements:

Post praedicta est notandum quod difficile est materiam communem et usitatam convenienter et bene tractare. Et quanto difficilius, tanto laudabilius est bene tractare materiam talem, scilicet communem et usitatam, quam materiam aliam, scilicet novam et inusitatam. Hoc autem testatur Horatius in *Poetria* iis tribus versibus:

> Difficile est proprie communia dicere, tuque
> Rectius Yliacum carmen deducis in actus
> Quam si proferres ignota indictaque primus. [*Ars poetica* 128–30]

Sed, quamvis difficile, tamen est possible.[47]

[After the foregoing discussion, it should be noted that it is difficult to treat common and familiar material appropriately and well. And the more difficult it is, the more praiseworthy it is to treat such material well, that is, material that is common and familiar, than it is to treat the other kind of material, that is, what is new and unfamiliar. Horace testifies to this in the *Poetria* in these lines:

> It is difficult to treat common matter in a way that is particular to you; and you would do better to turn a song of Troy into dramatic acts than to bring forth for the first time something unknown and unsung.

But however difficult it is, it is nevertheless possible.]

Geoffrey then lists four ways of treating *communis materia* properly (or as one's own – *proprie*): not lingering where the source lingers, not using the same diction or vocabulary, not getting lost in overly complex transitions between divisions of the subject, and not beginning the poem with overly grand promises of scope (cf. *Ars poetica* 131–52). Then he supports this with more observations from the *Ars poetica*:

His igitur quatuor modis observatis, communem materiam egregrie diligens inspector poterit pertractare: quos modo Horatius commemorat in *Poetria*, ubi ait:

> Publica materies privati juris erit, si
> Non circa vilem patulumque moraberis orbem,
> Nec verbo verbum curabis reddere, fidus
> Interpres, nec desilies imitator in artum [Faral: arctum]
> Unde pedem proferre pudor vetet, aut operis lex.
> Nec sic incipies, ut scriptor cyclicus olim:
> "Fortunam Priami cantabo, et nobile bellum." [*Ars poetica* 131–7]

Vilis est locus qui omnibus patet. Et vile est in illo loco morari in quo omnes moram faciunt.[48]

[When these four methods are observed, the careful examiner will be able to handle common material in a distinctive way. So Horace recalls these observations in the *Poetria* where he says:

> Public material will be private property if you do not linger over the common and open way, and if you do not try to render word for word like a *fidus interpres*, and if, as an imitator, you do not throw yourself into narrow straights from which shame or poetic law will not let you escape. Nor should you begin, like the singer of the poetic cycles of long ago: "I sing of the fortunes of Priam and of the noble war."

The place that everyone passes through is of little value. And it is shameful to linger in the place where everyone lingers.]

Geoffrey's discussion of invention – that is, where and how to discover material – is thus a virtual commentary on lines 128–52 of the *Ars poetica*.[49] Why should Geoffrey's treatment of invention take the form of a commentary on this famous passage from the *Ars poetica*? If we look to Geoffrey's pronouncements here as a fair representation of inventional theory in late medieval poetics, then it is necessary for us to understand the assumptions that underlie all the ingredients of his theory. This passage also plays a part in Matthew of Vendôme's statement of invention in the *Ars versificatoria*. Are Geoffrey and Matthew simply incorporating an unproblematic, perfectly transparent *auctoritas* on literary imitation? What value and significance had this passage assumed in the Middle Ages, and how does its use by Geoffrey and Matthew reflect contemporary and earlier evaluations of Horace's dictum? Do they understand it as a dictum about translation, as Jerome, for example, used it, or is their understanding of it complicated by other considerations?

Since late antiquity, these lines from the *Ars poetica* had come to be understood in a number of ways. First, Horace's lines represented an ancient authority on translation theory, possibly a legacy of Jerome's use of the passage which became, as we have seen, a commonplace among early and later medieval translators. This is an important and complex aspect of the tradition of this passage, as Horace's words "nec verbo verbum curabis reddere fidus interpres" could serve different theoretical purposes according to historical or literary context.[50] But along with its traditional value for translation theory, this passage also received a great deal of attention in commentaries on the *Ars poetica* from late antiquity through the later Middle Ages (and into the Renaissance).

All commentaries from late antiquity onwards agree on one obvious point, that Horace proposes two choices for the poet: either to use traditional material or to form something new that is consistent in terms of characterization and plot. This agreement rests on the relatively uncontroversial statements at lines 119ff.: "Aut famam sequere aut sibi convenientia finge . . . si quid inexpertum scaenae committis et audes / personam formare novam

... "(Either follow traditional subjects or invent things that are self-consistent ... If you commit something untried to the stage, and dare to create a new character ...). The identification between "finge" in line 119 and "quid inexpertum" in line 125 was obvious and easy enough to make.

The problem for interpretation arose with the next passage, lines 128–35. For clarity in the following discussion I quote these lines again:

> Difficile est proprie communia dicere; tuque
> rectius Iliacum carmen deducis in actus,
> quam si proferres ignota indictaque primus.
> publica materies privati iuris erit, si
> non circa vilem patulumque moraberis orbem
> nec verbo verbum curabis reddere fidus
> interpres, nec desilies imitator in artum
> unde pedem proferre pudor vetet aut operis lex.

The first line, "difficile est proprie communia dicere," has proved one of the most controversial lines in Latin literature, even to modern commentators.[51] It is thus not surprising that ancient and medieval commentaries produced a variety of readings – often irreconcilable – of this line and the passage as whole.

The Pseudo-Acronian scholia, one of the standard commentaries on Horace from late antiquity that still had wide currency in the twelfth century, gloss the term *communia* as *intacta*, that is, "untouched," "untried," or even "pristine." The gloss gives a legalistic cast to *communia*: "in the same way that a house or a field without an owner is common (*communis*), and when occupied becomes personal property (*proprius*), so something that has not been given expression by anyone (*a nullo dicta*) is common."[52] In this legal sense of "common" as opposed to "owned," *communia* does not mean "owned by all," but rather "claimed by none." With this interpretation, *communia* cannot be equated with the *fama* of line 119, because traditional materials, by definition, have been treated by others. But this interpretation also does not equate *communia* with the *publica materies* of line 131. Rather, *publica materies* would be associated with *fama* of line 119: as "public material" it is the property of all, as traditional narratives and themes (*fama*) are public property and so open to all. Thus in this interpretation, *communia* means "new," not "common" or "communal."[53]

This interpretation of *communia* determines the way that the word *difficile* in the same line would be read, and how that line is read in relation to the rest of the passage. If *communia* means "new" or "untried," lines 128–30 would be understood in roughly the following way: it is hard to render new subjects properly; and you would do better (*rectius*) to put into acts a song of Troy than if you present for the first time familiar and untried subjects.[54] By placing *communia* in opposition to *Iliacum carmen*, that is, traditional narrative materials, this reading also places *difficile* in opposition to *rectius*: it is hard to use new subjects, so you would do better to treat traditional materials. In other words, *difficile* would have to carry a certain proscriptive force which would place "difficile est proprie communia dicere" in opposition to the advice proffered in the following lines. The sense is that it is more fitting or appropriate (*rectius*) to avoid the difficulty of *communia*.[55]

A sixth-century commentary, based on the Porphyrian scholia of late antiquity, takes a slightly different route in interpreting these lines:

difficile est communia dicere velut propria, sed si quis fecerit, rectius faciet, quam si quod alii ignorant, proferat et quod ante se nemo audierit.[56]

[It is difficult to treat *communia* as if they were *propria*; but if one were to do so he would do better than if he were to produce something that others know nothing about and that no one before him will have heard.]

The meaning of *communia* and *propria* becomes clear when we consider the context. If it is difficult to treat *communia* but better to do so than to set forth something that no one else has heard, then *communia* in this context must be equated with traditional material, the *fama* of line 119 or the *publica materies* of line 131. *Propria* as a substantive here (rather than the adverb *proprie* in Horace), and thus grammatically appositive to *communia*, assumes the force of "one's own material," as in *privati iuris*. The commentary then glosses *publica materies* as *materia vulgata*, which suggests, at least by collocation, that *communia* is taken in the sense of "common," "familiar," or even "popular." This commentary thus proposes a certain advantage to using *materia communis* or *vulgata*, but without specifying what that advantage is.

These readings are echoed, with some variations, in later medieval commentaries on this passage.[57] But these readings do not correspond with Geoffrey of Vinsauf's interpretation of this line:

. . . est notandum quod difficile est materiam communem et usitatam convenienter et bene tractare. Et quanto difficilius, tanto laudabilius est bene tractare materiam talem, scilicet communem et usitatam, quam materiam aliam, scilicet novam et inusitatam.

[. . . it should be noted that it is difficult to treat common and familiar material appropriately and well. And the more difficult it is, the more praiseworthy it is to treat such material well, that is, material that is common and familiar, than it is to treat the other kind of material, that is, what is new and unfamiliar.]

This not only identifies *communia* with *fama* or traditional narrative material, but also changes the terms of the earlier commentaries by reading "difficile communia dicere" as an invitation to poetic ingenuity rather than as a warning against the perils of taking up new subjects. Treating familiar materials (*communia*) is here a laudable challenge: the more difficult the pursuit the more admirable the achievement of it. Geoffrey's commentary urges the use of traditional materials, not as an alternative to the difficulty of new subjects, but rather for the very difficulty that traditional materials present. Here Geoffrey has thoroughly reversed the priorities that earlier commentaries had discerned in Horace's dictum.

Geoffrey's departure from the readings of the standard late classical and medieval scholia is significant in itself: it shows him accommodating the

Horatian text to a set of priorities that are particular to medieval theoretical concerns. He is not alone among medieval commentators in his departures from the standard authorities: his readings have some parallels in other roughly contemporary commentaries.[58] Trinity College, Cambridge MS 0.3.57 (late twelfth-century) contains a commentary on the *Ars poetica* which offers the following reading:

Nam DICERE COMMUNIA, idest communem materiam describere, et PROPRIE, idest ita ut videatur esse sua propria. Illud est difficile, sed est ibi maxima laus. Nam RECTIUS, idest cum maiori laude, DEDUCIS CARMEN ILIACUM, idest assumpta materia de troiae in actus tuos.[59]

[Now, "to handle *communia*," that is, to copy common material, and "*proprie*," that is so that it may seem to be your own. This is difficult, but there is greater glory here. Now "*rectius*," that is, with greater glory, "you will spin out a song of Ilium," that is, received material about the Trojan War in your own acts.]

Another twelfth-century commentary, which is found in a number of manuscripts, offers two ways of reading these lines, one which is in keeping with the tradition of the ancient scholia, and an alternative which is similar to Geoffrey of Vinsauf's version:

Nam DIFFICILE EST inaudita PROPRIE DICERE et hoc est DIFFICILE EST DICERE PROPRIE, id est competenter, COMMUNIA, id est inaudita. COMMUNIA dicit, quia omnibus in communi ad fingendum sunt posita. TUQUE RECTIUS. Quamvis illud sit difficile et ita laudabile, tamen sequi famam laudabilius . . . Vel totum legatur de famae exsecutione ita: Difficile est quod dixi vel famam sequendam vel fingendum convenienter. Laudabo inde famam sequi et COMMUNIA id est omnibus trita DICERE PROPRIE DIFFICILE EST.[60]

[Now "it is difficult to treat in a way that is *proprie*" subjects that have not been heard; which means "it is difficult to treat in a way that is *proprie*," that is, competently, "things that are *communia*," that is, subjects that have not been heard. He says *communia*, because these subjects are available for development to everyone in common. *Tuque rectius*. However difficult and thus praiseworthy it may be, it is nevertheless more praiseworthy to follow tradition . . . But this whole passage concerning the treatment of traditional material may be read in this way: There is difficulty, as he remarked, in using traditional matter or in making up something in a way that is consistent. On that basis I will praise following tradition; "it is difficult to treat competently that which is *communia*," that is, hackneyed material.]

These departures from the traditional scholia indicate that medieval schoolmen needed to develop new ways of making sense of the text, to bring it into accord with the priorities of later medieval poetics. That Geoffrey of Vinsauf, along with a number of contemporary commentators, should read these lines in the *Ars poetica* as an affirmation of the prestige of *materia exsecuta* over that which is *novam et inusitatam* suggests how much this passage could be accommodated to the theoretical interests of *enarratio poetarum*. In Geoffrey's context, the domain of the grammarian-exegete, the chief concern is recuperating the *auctores*, and hermeneutics is the master discourse. This interpretation of Horace's dictum as an invitation to the greater challenge of *materia exsecuta*, where difficulty and reward is to be found in traditional material, suggests how much exegesis has become the privileged term in this late medieval literary context: for as both Geoffrey of Vinsauf and Matthew of Vendôme demonstrate, exegesis provides the tools for handling *materia exsecuta*. To achieve difference with the given text is the test of the exegete's ingenuity, for his success depends on the skill with which he can suppress or conceal the very exegetical moves that govern his approach to the text. To amplify or abbreviate the source, to avoid delaying where others delay, are the techniques that underscore the mastery of exegetical procedure by disguising that procedure as a form of invention. These are the techniques of stylistic analysis that the grammarians of late antiquity and the exegetes of the Middle Ages took over from rhetorical theory and elevated to a role of primary importance, thereby blurring the boundaries between grammar and rhetoric; and these are the techniques that Matthew of Vendôme and Geoffrey of Vinsauf elevate to an even greater prominence by making them the very tools of rhetorical performance, of invention. It is not surprising that Matthew, and more explicitly Geoffrey, should so prize *materia exsecuta* above all else for the difficulty that they attribute to it; in transforming invention into a hermeneutical procedure they prize the ingenuity of the exegetical performance that can disguise its own moves through a consummate act of textual appropriation.[61]

It is interesting that Matthew of Vendôme associates Horace's warning against rendering word for word like a *fidus interpres* with exegesis as opposed to translation:

> We turn now to the treatment of material, in which certain ill-trained people habitually overstep the line and shamefully depart from preceptive guidelines. When paraphrasing poetic fables in school exercises, they render word for word, down to every figure of speech, as if they sought to produce a metrical commentary on the authors . . . One should not try to render word for word like a *fidus interpres*.

Both Matthew and Geoffrey use this passage from the *Ars poetica* in their pronouncements on invention, but the meaning they assign to it is not as transparent as it first may seem. If Matthew, for example, understands it as a central dictum of translation theory, then why does he identify rendering word for word like a *fidus interpres* with the awkward mechanics of an *enarratio poetarum* ("as if they sought to produce a metrical commentary on the authors") that cannot disguise its own moves to achieve difference with the text? Do he and Geoffrey of Vinsauf understand the term *fidus interpres* as "faithful translator" or as "faithful exegete"?

We have already seen in chapter 2 how Horace's phrase "nec verbo verbum curabis reddere fidus interpres" could become a ready formula for justifying whatever theoretical position on translation that a given cultural or historical context required. While Jerome popularized this formula, his understanding of it was only superficially similar to the value that it acquired in later discussions of translation, as we have seen in comparing his use of it with that of Boethius. While the Horatian commonplace remained a fixture in medieval discussions of translations, largely because of Jerome's authority, the patristic model of translation does not really account for the character of literary translation in the later Middle Ages, as we have also seen in chapters 4 and 5. What does account for the nature of medieval translation is a rhetorical motive of textual appropriation, akin to that of Roman translation, but which the Middle Ages finds in a newly empowered force and broadened scope of hermeneutical action.

The medieval *artes poetriae* represents one instance of this empowered and broadened hermeneutical action. They constitute a crossover of grammar and rhetoric: they are products of the grammatical tradition of *enarratio poetarum*, but they also transmit ancient rhetorical precepts for composition. They use the grammarian's methods of textual analysis, but they direct these methods towards discursive production. Their dominant discourse is that of hermeneutics: they lay out a system of interpretive control over textual authority, and they apply that control to contesting and appropriating textual traditions. If their privileged category of discourse is that of hermeneutics, is it not also possible that they would subsume the activity of translation under that of hermeneutics? To understand the options that were available to them for interpreting this commonplace about the *fidus interpres*, let us turn once again to some commentaries on these lines.

The scholia of late antiquity recognized the application of Horace's dictum to interlingual translation, and explained it in terms of the specific problems of Latin vocabulary. This is exemplified by the Pseudo-Acronian scholia:

NEC UERBUM UERBO CURABIS REDDERE. Idest noli curare singula uerba interpretari, ne facias poema tuum uile. Interdum enim inueniuntur, quae in Latinitatem conuerti non possunt.
UERBUM CURABIS. Ideo non debes persequi omnia, quia sunt, quae implere non possis aut quae conuersa in Latinum placere non possunt.[62]

[Do not try to render word for word. That is do not try to translate every single word, lest you make your poem worthless. Now and then you can coin words which can't be translated directly into Latin. Therefore you ought not to follow after every word because there are those words which you cannot use or which are unsatisfactory when they are translated into Latin.]

In the bilingual culture of late antiquity, it is natural to find this passage applied to translation from Greek into Latin. These scholia originally date from about the third century, and thus arise from a pedagogical context much like that of the fourth-century rhetorician Fortunatianus who regarded translation as a way of increasing Latin vocabulary. In the schools of late antiquity interlingual translation was a standard exercise. But these scholia were also being copied well into the fifteenth century so that they continued to exert an influence on the relatively monolingual culture of the medieval arts curriculum. It is evident even from commentaries that are not directly dependent on these early scholia that medieval schoolmen acknowledged this passage as having something to do with interlingual translation, even if they were not about to apply these dictates to the teaching of poetic composition. A gloss in a tenth-century manuscript expands "nec verbum verbo" to the fuller formula "sed sensum ex sensu."[63] In a twelfth-century manuscript, a marginal rubric next to line 128 reads "de lege translatoris."[64] And a gloss in a thirteenth-century manuscript explains "nec verbum verbo" with the advice: "in loco graeci verbi non ponas latinum."[65]

Thus there was every occasion for Matthew of Vendôme and Geoffrey of Vinsauf to encounter this dictum as a commonplace of the tradition of translation theory. But some medieval commentators read a somewhat different set of concerns in Horace's lines. A Carolingian commentary, attributed by its modern editor to Heiric of Auxerre (Remigius' predecessor at the monastic school), gives the following reading of "nec verbum verbo curabis reddere fidus interpres":

INTERPRES. Quasi haec faceres tunc non poeta sed interpres, idest glossator et singularum vocum expositor esses.[66]

[As if to say, if you were doing these things, you would not be a poet but an *interpres*, that is, a glossator and an expositor of individual words.]

This bypasses the meaning of *interpres* as "translator," and defines it instead as "exegete" or "glossator," which was, of course, one of the early meanings of the term. With the opposition that it sets up between *poeta* and *interpres*, this commentary draws a distinction between "literary" activity and exegesis. It does not acknowledge interlingual translation as the central issue in Horace's lines and shows no interest in the traditional debate over literal vs. loose translation. Instead it defines the question of literary imitation against the terms of *enarratio poetarum*. In this it is intriguingly similar to Matthew of Vendôme's application of Horace's phrase. The Carolingian reading is closely echoed in the commentary from Trinity College, Cambridge 0.3.57:

Nam dico nec curabis reddere verbum alicuis auctoris exponendo illud tuo verbo; quoniam sic non vocaberis poeta set tamen interpres, idest translator et expositor verborum. (fol. 22v.)

[Now I say that you should not render a word of some author by expounding it with your own word; because then you will not be called a poet but rather an *interpres*, that is, a "translator" and expositor of words.]

This reading identifies *translator* with *expositor*, equating both with *interpres*. This recalls Petrus Helias' definition of *interpretatio* as an interlingual gloss, as opposed to other forms of glossing, such as etymology, which do not involve translating a term from one language to another.[67] Like the Carolingian commentary, this commentary reads Horace's lines as pertaining to the difference between exegesis and composition; moreover the Trinity commentary makes an explicit association between translation and exposition. Both commentaries gloss *interpres* as *expositor*, exegete.

There are thus some analogues for the way that Matthew of Vendôme interprets this passage. It is unlikely that Matthew and Geoffrey of Vinsauf were unfamiliar with the more standard interpretation of this passage (that is, as a dictum about interlingual translation); indeed Geoffrey even cites and discusses Horace's remarks (*Ars poetica* 50–9) on coinage of words in interlingual translation.[68] Yet neither raises the question of translation when citing this passage. Given the dominance of the exegetical framework of their poetics, however, it seems that they have subsumed the question of translation under that larger, privileged category of hermeneutics. There is some medieval precedent for this move, as we see in the commentaries that read *interpres* as expositor, and especially in the Trinity manuscript that also reads *translator* as expositor. If Matthew and Geoffrey understand the passage in the traditional way as pertaining to interlingual translation, they apparently see no distinction between the processes of exegesis and translation: the problem of literal translation could be addressed under cover of a more general problem of exegetical reception that fails to suppress its identifiable mechanics and thereby fails to achieve difference with the source.

These differences within the commentary tradition and the ambiguities in Matthew and Geoffrey can serve to remind us how much medieval translation arises out of the context of *enarratio*, and how it resists efforts to reconcile the difference between *interpres* as translator and *interpres* as exegete. If Geoffrey and Matthew are asking for a form of writing that derives from traditional sources but at the same time suppresses the signs of its dependence on any source, the distinction that they are drawing is analogous to the distinction I have made between "primary" and "secondary" translation. Primary translations, as we have seen, operate according to the terms of exegesis: they give prominence to an exegetical motive by claiming to serve and supplement a textual authority, but they actually work to challenge and appropriate that textual authority. Secondary translations, on the other hand, give precedence to rhetorical motives, defining themselves as independent productive acts: characteristically they suppress any sign of exegetical service to a specific source, even though they produce themselves through such exegetical techniques.

Whether or not Geoffrey of Vinsauf and Matthew of Vendôme understand the *fidus interpres* as pertaining to interlingual translation is less important than the way that they show hermeneutical moves transforming themselves into rhetorical performances, that is, the way that they both locate invention within the operations of exegesis. What the poeticians offer is a precise paradigm for the way that translation works: for in the Middle Ages, translation is a form and product of an exegetical practice that has defined itself as a rhetorical practice. What matters for medieval translation is not the ancient polarity between literal and loose translation. Rather, what matters are the very terms in which Geoffrey and Matthew cast their readings of the *fidus interpres*: shall the text allow its exegetical character or rhetorical character to dominate? What the poeticians propose, a form of composition that suppresses the very exegetical moves that made it possible and that trades on the paradox of inventing *communis materia* (that which is *tractata*, already invented), is the defining characteristic of translation that represents itself as rhetorical invention, that claims for itself a kind of originary canonical status. I have designated this as "secondary" translation, and in the next chapter I will consider how it is exemplified in some of the work of Chaucer and Gower.

It is significant that Matthew and Geoffrey use the dicta about *communis materia* and the *fidus interpres* in the context of invention: it shows how grammar could give rhetoric a productive application to discourse. Rhetorical invention, which had become an atomized theoretical inquiry in the sphere of dialectical study, cut off from linguistic action as a practice, found a productive role as an exegetical operation. Augustine supplies a model for the transformation of invention, as he conflates the *modus inveniendi* with the *modus interpretandi*. We have seen how the implications of Augustine's transformation are played out in the *artes poetriae*. Most generally, we have seen how they develop techniques of invention out of the methods of stylistic analysis associated with *enarratio poetarum*. More particularly, we see how John of Garland formulates a theory of topical invention out of the traditions of the *accessus ad auctores*; and we see how Matthew of Vendôme and Geoffrey of Vinsauf revaluate the Horatian dicta about *communis materia* and *fidus interpres* in terms of an exegetical process that is, for them, identical with the inventional process. If it is a truth of historical practice that hermeneutics often borrows the tools of rhetoric, so we have seen how the obverse is also true: *grammatica*, in antiquity the debased term against which rhetoric defined its disciplinary superiority, can, in the Middle Ages, restore to rhetoric its proper identity as a praxis.

It remains now to consider how this transformation of rhetorical invention is played out in vernacular translation. The translations that I will consider in the next chapter define themselves as rhetorical inventions, at once suppressing and exploiting the exegetical foundations of their enterprise. This enables their claim, as English vernacular texts, to the prestige of canonical literary authority. But they achieve this authority by defining themselves through the very academic discourse that they seek to supplant. For these texts, *materia pertractata* or *exsecuta* to be appropriated is not so much the matter of traditional narrative subjects (mythology, epic, romance), but rather the *communis materia* of academic commentary. It is out of this exegetical tradition that they invent themselves and invent their claim to an originary canonical status by which they can supplant the cultural privilege of Latinity. For these texts, the *communis materia* out of which they invent themselves is the project of *translatio studii*. But their aim is not simply to insert the vernacular into that official discourse: it is rather to reinvent that official discourse within vernacular culture.

7

Translation as rhetorical invention: Chaucer and Gower

Augustine and his heirs, the "preceptive grammarians," restore rhetoric to a powerful discursive role by identifying invention with the activity of exegesis, the *modus inveniendi* with the *modus interpretandi*. Augustine achieves this by giving rhetorical control over to readers, empowering readers to make the text meaningful. Matthew of Vendôme and Geoffrey of Vinsauf take this further by locating the topics of rhetorical invention in textual *communis materia*. In this revaluation of rhetoric, hermeneutics is still the dominant force: rhetoric assumes an ascendent role only when it is defined in terms of the governing framework of hermeneutics, that is, when it is defined as hermeneutical performance.

This definition of rhetorical invention has important implications for vernacular translation, and ultimately for the status of translation as a form of academic discourse in the vernacular. If invention can be understood as a hermeneutical performance on a traditional textual source, this model of invention can also extend to certain forms of vernacular exegetical translation. For the tradition of academic translation that we have traced here, hermeneutics is also the dominant and defining force. But certain products of this tradition develop the contestative or rhetorical motive of exegesis to such an extent that their exegetical service becomes full-fledged rhetorical appropriation. Such texts constitute what I have called "secondary translation." In the following discussion I will examine the character of secondary translation by considering two English texts which redefine the terms of academic discourse in the vernacular: Chaucer's *Legend of Good Women* and Gower's *Confessio amantis*. These texts carry out the prescriptions of the *artes poetriae* by turning the techniques of exegesis into techniques of topical invention. In this way they also redefine the terms of vernacular translation itself: they use the techniques of exegetical translation to produce, not a supplement to the original, but a vernacular substitute for that original.

The ascendency of rhetoric, redefined as a hermeneutical act, also enables these translations to assert the priority of vernacularity itself. They appropriate the discourse of academic exegesis and apply it to their own texts, so that their translations advance their own claims to *auctoritas*. They take the rhetorical motive of difference and displacement one step further than primary translation: these secondary translations insert themselves into academic discourse, not by proposing to serve the interests of continuity with the *antiqui*, but rather by calling attention to their own status as vernacular productions and thus underscoring the fact of cultural and historical difference that vernacularity exposes. As we saw in Notker of St. Gall, the vernacular appropriation of academic discourse poses a threat to the traditional institutional privilege of academic criticism. We see the fulfillment of this threat in the translations of Chaucer and Gower, who authorize their own vernacular writings through a "genre of official discourse." But while they embody that discourse in their productions, they use it to the purpose of auto-exegesis, to address the implications of vernacular claims to *auctoritas*. In this way they exploit that discourse to foreground the very problem of linguistic and historical difference. In other words, they use that official tradition to construct a vernacular critical language about vernacular textuality. As we will see, these texts, unlike primary translations, define themselves expressly in terms of difference: they call attention to their own position in a historical rupture and in so doing advance their own claims to displace their sources.

In these translations we see a transference of academic institutional power to the vernacular. As I will show, the system that enables this shift of power is the rehabilitation of rhetoric through its identification with hermeneutics. But while the focus of the present chapter (and of this study as a whole) is how these problems become visible through the practice of translation, we must also recognize that these disciplinary configurations emerge in other fields of vernacular literary discourse and criticism. Dante's literary criticism in particular offers some important analogues with the kinds of questions that we will trace in the translations of Chaucer and Gower, because Dante directly addresses the question of how to define the status of the vernacular with respect to traditional academic systems.[1] In order to provide a broader context for the following discussion of secondary translation, and in order to "place" the attitudes expressed by Chaucer and Gower against a critical precedent, let us begin by considering how some very similar questions are worked out in Dante's *De vulgari eloquentia* and *Convivio*. In Dante's literary criticism we find concrete illustrations of vernacular claims to cultural authority through a redefinition of the terms of academic discourse.

DANTE'S VERNACULAR HERMENEUTICS AND THE REHABILITATION OF RHETORIC

De vulgari eloquentia is a "rhetoric" in the narrowly technical sense of the *Ars poetica* or the medieval *artes poetriae*, but also in the broader political sense of Cicero's *De oratore*, that is, as a far-reaching theory of communication and aesthetics. It grapples directly, if not always systematically, with the political or ideological issues at stake in its own project. In setting forth a rhetorical program for the vernacular, *De vulgari* acknowledges the *de facto* ascendency of vernacular culture. But in attempting to theorize a place for the vernacular in a hierarchy of languages, Dante seems to accept rather than challenge the given terms of that hierarchy. As Dante argues it here, Latinity defines the terms for a cultural and linguistic hegemony: *grammatica* or Latinity is a universal language, a stabilizing, unifying bulwark against decline and diversity (9.11). In asserting the force of the vernacular, Dante does not question the terms by which linguistic hegemony is traditionally defined, but rather claims those very terms for the vernacular. According to his argument, the vernacular is a universal language which can acquire an institutional apparatus: a grammar of literary production, a preceptive rhetoric, and a canonical poetic tradition which provides authoritative precedents. The major change here is that the idea of what constitutes universality is modified: the vernacular has its own nobility as a universal language, not because it resists historical and geographical difference, but because, in all of its diversity, it is enjoyed by all as a natural language (1.4). Thus Dante has not questioned the system of assumptions that values universality; he has simply changed the definition of universality itself, so as to insert the vernacular into the position that Latin traditionally occupies. Later in his argument, in establishing the terms for what he calls an "illustrious vernacular," he posits another version of the standard of universality: the "illustrious vernacular" is that which belongs at once to all and to none (16.6). This is a claim to something like the universal status of Latin, so that once again we see that the criterion of privilege has not been substantially revised or tested.

What we do find in *De vulgari eloquentia*, however, is a foreshadowing of Dante's more extended attempt, in the *Convivio*, to locate the vernacular in a system of rhetorical values. In *De vulgari*, poetry itself is ultimately elected as the "language" of the illustrious vernacular. Poetry can encompass all problems of ethics, politics, and religion: it can reform and teach.[2] This gives over to vernacular poetry the domain of pulpit oratory, a domain of ethically responsible discourse that Christian rhetoric had reclaimed from the decadent remains of ancient civic oratory. Dante inscribes the vernacular in this "official" discipline of rhetoric by investing the vernacular with the kind of social responsibility that rhetoric can carry. Thus in *De vulgari eloquentia* Dante authorizes the vernacular by giving it the moral weight of rhetoric. It is the moral value of rhetoric, rather than any claims to the universality of Latin, that underwrites Dante's arguments for the cultural privilege of the vernacular.

The *Convivio* enlarges the frame of reference for these arguments by locating its own project in a much larger landscape of discursive practice. The *Convivio* is conceived through rhetorical directives: it strives after communal benefit, to move men to wisdom and virtue.[3] In arguing for the alliance of rhetoric and moral philosophy and insisting on the power of speech to transform the behavior of an audience (4.2), the *Convivio* seems to embody a rebirth of the principles of Ciceronian rhetoric, where oratory is the focal point of civic life and public responsibility. The scheme of the sciences in book 2 affirms the power of rhetoric or eloquence to generate spiritual good:

rhetoric leads to knowledge through persuasion (2.6), it persuades through charm (2.11), and it is the mover of moral philosophy (2.14–15). The discussion of rhetoric in book 2 serves as an emblem for the aims of the *Convivio* as a whole, for the *Convivio* uses the delights of poetry and eloquence to expound the modes of wisdom and ethics so as to enlighten its readers and move them to understand and practice what is good. It seeks, in other words, to teach and persuade through delight.[4] It is for this reason that the third heaven, the realm of Venus or love poetry, is also the domain of rhetoric: the beauty of love poetry can persuade to knowledge.

But the *Convivio* also defines its rhetorical purpose specifically in terms of vernacularity. If the job of rhetoric is public communication for the public good, rhetoric cannot accomplish its office or achieve its end except through the medium that reaches the widest possible audience. The *Convivio* opens with an account of the forces that inhibit men from seeking or achieving knowledge: physical handicap, spiritual complacency, wordly cares, and finally the cultural conditions that impede access to the language and resources of learning (1.1). His concern with this last factor is a way of recognizing that the institutional privilege of academic discourse is a product of historical and material conditions rather than of some immanent value and mystified necessity. It is here that we also can see how vernacular literary criticism must take as one of its explicit subjects the ideological implications of opening academic discourse to linguistic and historical difference.[5] By introducing the possibility of extending academic discourse beyond the protective enclosure of the academy and its Latinity, the *Convivio* works as a critique of the ideological system that sustains the institutional power of the academic tradition. If it is only the material conditions or historical accidents of birth, station, language, and place that impede access to the fruits of intellectual culture, then the sovereign academic myth of diachronic continuity and synchronic universality is just that, a myth: academic culture is neither universal nor inevitable, but just the opposite, exclusive and contingent. Its mystifying apparatus, Latinity, does not overcome historical difference, but rather ignores and resists it. Moreover, academic Latinity is itself historically situated: to know Latin and to participate in the discourse of learning is as much a product of the historical accidents or material conditions of birth, station, place, and opportunity as not to know Latin. This is the kind of critique that can only come from outside the traditional structures of academic culture.[6] It is a critique that is presaged quite tentatively in Notker of St. Gall, and that Dante, several centuries later, can extend or complete; it is no accident that these two authors, Notker and Dante, straddle Latin and vernacular culture. As I will argue, Chaucer and Gower also integrate such a critique into their projects of vernacular translation.

If the enterprise of the *Convivio* is rhetorical, then rhetoric has become a lever to challenge the traditional hegemony of academic discourse. In the *Convivio*, the job of rhetoric is to break down the exclusiveness of academic culture and give the widest possible access to an enabling body of knowledge.

In this venture, the tool of rhetoric is the vernacular. But Dante, himself an accomplished Latinist, is not entirely willing to renounce the claims of Latin to a practiced and yet somehow also innate linguistic superiority. He thus offers the famous argument in 1.5 for the text as master and the commentary as servant. He promises to preserve this hierarchical decorum through linguistic decorum: the commentary on his vernacular *canzoni* will accordingly be in the vernacular rather than in Latin, lest the exegetical servant upstage its textual master through the greater nobility of its linguistic form. But in the next chapter (1.6) he consigns the linguistic master, Latin, to a kind of powerless privilege, having duly acknowledged its official sovereignty. Real power lies, not in status, but in effective, persuasive communication, and here the vernacular is clearly in charge. All servants must communicate well with their masters, in order to know their masters and facilitate the relations between the master and his friends. Here the servant, the critical commentary, must speak the language of its master, the poetic text, and of its master's friends, the audience of Dante's poems. Thus Dante transfers power to the vernacular by giving it the responsibility of effective communication, that is, the office of rhetoric.

But what is the form that this public office of rhetoric takes in the *Convivio*? It takes the form of exegesis. The *Convivio* is framed as an enormous exegetical project which aims to lead its audience to an appreciation of the highest good, knowledge, through an exposition of the ethical and philosophical content of Dante's own *canzoni*. Indeed, the *Convivio* is hermeneutics: it is commentary on Dante's own poems, and in the first Tractate, commentary on the nature of commentary itself. The argument of the *Convivio* is to lead to knowledge through persuasion (2.6). But this rhetorical directive is expressed as a powerful hermeneutics, as the text draws its real persuasive force from its ability to locate and expound the meaning of the *canzoni*. It is through a hermeneutical enterprise that the scope and power of rhetoric are defined and the office of rhetorical persuasion is performed. The *Convivio* exemplifies – probably better than any late medieval text – the implications of Augustine's legacy: it rehabilitates rhetoric as an inspired hermeneutical performance. Like Augustine, Dante extends or transfers rhetorical control to readers by locating the real power of ethical inquiry in the act of interpretation or reading and by offering his own exegetical performance as a kind of program for his readers. Moreover, the *Convivio* enjoins its audience to take on the responsibility of exegetical control by calling attention to its status as a vernacular academic text which makes the tools of informed reading broadly accessible.

In both its argument (what it says) and its structure (how it says it), the *Convivio* demonstrates the comprehensive role of hermeneutics in critical and cultural practices. Hermeneutics restores the discursive power of rhetoric, and rhetoric in turn empowers the vernacular as a voice of cultural authority. We might also sum up this chain of effects in reverse order. In the *Convivio*, the vernacular is the medium of public enlightenment, which is constructed as the highest good. The job of realizing this highest good is given over to rhetoric, as teaching is accomplished through the office of persuasive eloquence, embodied here in the charm or winning eloquence of Dante's own *canzoni* (so that, as in *De vulgari eloquentia*, rhetoric is equated to some extent with poetry). But the persuasive force of rhetoric and hence the communal benefit of its vernacular embodiment cannot be recognized for what it is and thus acted upon without the agency of interpretation, the apparatus of hermeneutics. Hence the *Convivio* can accomplish its rhetorical aims only through the enabling structure of hermeneutics. This actual structure of priorities, in which a vernacular hermeneutics is the true controlling force, upsets the very hierarchical relations of text–commentary, master–servant, and Latin–vernacular that Dante claims to preserve. The *Convivio* demonstrates how the servant, commentary, has become the master discourse, the locus of meaning and the agent of rhetorical control. And as the linguistic medium of an all-powerful exegesis, the vernacular is inscribed as the language of real cultural authority, for it is through a vernacular text and its vernacular commentary that the *Convivio* carries out the highest of all ethical imperatives.

This constellation of rhetoric, hermeneutics, and vernacularity in Dante's criticism provides an excellent frame of reference for understanding how vernacular culture redefines the value and status of traditional academic disciplines. When we turn to the translations of Chaucer and Gower, we find similar trajectories for such cultural and disciplinary formations. Like Dante, Chaucer and Gower insert the vernacular into academic traditions by making the question of vernacularity itself an explicit subject. Moreover, like Dante, Chaucer and Gower discover the cultural power of the vernacular in the disciplinary power of hermeneutics. We will consider here how Chaucer and Gower express this discovery through the question of translation. In Dante's *Convivio*, vernacular hermeneutics is represented as a momentous break with established exegetical practice. But for Chaucer and Gower as translators, the governing framework of vernacular hermeneutics is a product of a strong vernacular tradition in which translation develops as a powerful form of exegetical action. Finally, we can also say that like Dante, Chaucer and Gower show us a rhetoric rehabilitated as hermeneutical performance. But as translators, Chaucer and Gower manifest this rehabilitation of rhetoric in terms much closer to the theoretical precepts of the *artes poetriae*, where hermeneutical service is transformed into an expression of rhetorical difference from the source. This is to say that in the translations of Chaucer and Gower, hermeneutical practice becomes the point of departure for rhetorical invention.

At this point it may helpful to explain why I have chosen these two texts, the *Legend of Good Women* and *Confessio amantis*, to exemplify "secondary" translation. If "secondary" translation designates, among other things, the building of a native literary tradition through aggressive textual appropriation, then surely are there not many other examples of vernacular translation (English and continental) that could serve the discussion in this chapter? At one level, the choice of these two texts is a tactical one, consistent with the strategy of this book as a whole: to provide readings of representative texts which can stand for a variety of other possible examples. But at another level, the choice of the *Legend of Good Women* and *Confessio amantis* is determined by the particular focus of this study, the trajectory of vernacular translation through academic culture. There are many examples of late medieval translation which contribute to the formation of vernacular literary cultures, courtly and popular. Among these are a great number of Chaucer's writings which can be accommodated under the rubric of translation: *Romaunt of the Rose* (at least fragment A), *Knights's Tale*, *Troilus and Criseyde*, *Melibee*, *Clerk's Tale*, and even the *Book of the Duchess*. These texts, moreover, have received significant attention for their properties as translations.[7] But as important as these works – and others like them, for example, Hartmann von Aue's *Iwein*, or even Lydgate's massive output – are as translations, they exceed the necessary restrictions of the present study, which is devoted to a particular tradition of translation, vernacular receptions of classical authors through academic commentary. What I have called "primary" and "secondary" translation designates a specific set of historical relations to certain official modes of academic discourse; the terms "primary" and "secondary" are meant to help define the role of vernacular translation in the larger academic program of *translatio studii*, and, conversely, the status of that academic tradition in vernacular culture. Vernacular genres of translation such as romance (courtly or popular), and medieval receptions of other medieval texts (Chaucer's use of Boccaccio, Machaut, or even Petrarch, or Lydgate's near-epic amplifications of Guido delle Colonne and various French sources) have no proper place in the parameters of this discussion. It is hoped, however, that the arguments developed here will prompt further investigations of the role of academic discourse in other forms of vernacular literary production.

The intention here is to explore a basic paradox: that exegetical activity, which is ostensibly service to a foregoing, authoritative text, can be the agent of rhetorical invention, which for translation, as we have seen, historically implies effacement of and difference with foregoing *auctores*. One important way in which these translations at once produce and negotiate this paradox is through auto-exegesis. For Chaucer and Gower, auto-exegesis is a valuable mechanism for confronting the problematic status of vernacularity in relation to the traditional linguistic norms of academic culture. What do these moves imply for the status of the vernacular? I will argue that Chaucer and Gower affirm the ascendency of vernacularity by inserting their texts into the historical, official discourse of hermeneutics. What do these moves imply for academic discourse? In taking over academic discourse, these English translators also foreground the problem of difference or rupture that vernacularity represents, thereby redefining academic discourse itself within a framework of disjunction.

INTENTIO AUCTORIS AS INVENTIONAL TOPIC IN THE *LEGEND OF GOOD WOMEN*

In the *Legend of Good Women*, Chaucer authorizes his translations and receptions of classical *auctores* by taking over some terminology from the commentary tradition and assuming the authorial functions that come with this terminology: exegete, compiler, and ultimately *auctor*. Of course, this is achieved in a comic, fictive framework which playfully manipulates these authorizing postures through the device of a hesitant dreamer-persona, and which, in the individual tales, casts humorous doubt on Chaucer's narrative and interpretive competence.[8] But for purposes here, I bracket rhetorical consideration of this fictive dimension, the comic Chaucerian persona, his misapprehensions and misreadings, in order to concentrate on situating this text in a long history of discursive practice, the tradition of vernacular translation and the language of academic criticism. My concern is to show that this tradition manifests itself in the *Legend of Good Women*, not to show how the tradition is mediated and ironized by a comic fiction. The *Prologue* to the *Legend* certainly represents Chaucer's most sustained examination of vernacular authorship, and my purpose is to draw attention to the historical forces that inform the theoretical attitudes expressed in the poem.[9] It is also my implicit but working assumption throughout this discussion that the Chaucerian play on authoritative postures, both in the *Prologue* and in the individual legends, is a sign of the control that Chaucer, as a vernacular writer and translator, exerts over the academic tradition, a control that allows the free play of a self-reflexive comedy.

The *Prologue* to the *Legend of Good Women* functions as an *accessus* to Chaucer's English versions of the classical *materia*. It is here that Chaucer defines the terms of translation as an overt act of exegetical appropriation. Translation is always, in one way or another, an act of appropriation; so what is important here is that Chaucer defines this appropriation specifically through the use of academic criticism. The academic language of the *Prologue* serves two related purposes. First, it identifies vernacular writing with the language of official culture, thus conferring this cultural privilege on Chaucer's English texts. But in so inserting his vernacular writings into this academic critical discourse Chaucer also directs exegesis away from the *auctores* to his own texts. In applying these exegetical techniques to his own *Legend* he claims the status of *auctor*, thus constituting his translations as *auctoritates*.

I would like to offer here some specific evidence concerning the use of academic language in the *Prologue* and discuss some implications of such a vernacular reception of this language. In the light of this we can then consider some aspects of the legends as translations.

The crucial narrative scenario of the *Prologue* is the confrontation between the God of Love and the poet, and Alceste's intervention (F. 308ff.; G. 234ff.). The God of Love accuses "Chaucer" of having violated the order of Love with his previous writings, the translation of *Roman de la Rose* and *Troilus and Criseyde*. The God of Love condemns him, but Alceste intercedes on the poet's behalf (F. 339ff.; G. 315ff.). First she suggests that he may have written these transgressive texts without fully comprehending their "matere" (F. 365; G. 343). Or perhaps he wrote *Troilus* and the *Romaunt of the Rose* at someone else's bidding, "and durste yt nat withseye" (F. 367; cf. G. 347). In the F version she also suggests that he has repented of the criminal activity (F. 368). Besides, he has written a number of works in praise of love and of female virtue (F. 417–30; G. 404–20). At Alceste's request the God of Love forgives the poet, and lets Alceste devise a penalty. Alceste orders that as a penance he shall write a "glorious legende of goode wymmen" (F. 483–4; G. 473–4).

In sum, this narrative explains how the poet came to write the *Legend of Good Women*: he wrote it, under orders from a higher authority, to rectify the moral error of his earlier works. This explanation of the cause of the work corresponds to discussions of *intentio auctoris* in the *accessus ad auctores*: as we saw in chapter 3 above, the topic of *intentio auctoris* in the twelfth-century prologue form served the same function as the topic of *causa* in the Carolingian *accessus*, enabling the exegete to explain why the author came to write the work. But the particular explanation of *intentio* or *causa* in Chaucer's *Prologue* is also a familiar theme of the *accessus Ovidiani*, and identifies the *Prologue* with a specific exegetical tradition on the *Heroides*.

Of all the narrative sources for the *Legend of Good Women*, the *Heroides* exerts the strongest and most consistent influence for structure and design.[10] Like the *Heroides*, the *Legend* is an anthology of "women's tales." This structural correspondence between the *Legend* and the *Heroides* raises a particularly important question, that of critical responses to Ovid's work. How did medieval readers deal with anthologies like the *Heroides* that offer no obvious internal principles of organization? Exegetes found a solution to such structural heterogeneity through the critical mechanism of the *intentio auctoris*. We have already considered how arguments provided under this topic could often constitute a pronouncement of moral or thematic significance for the text as a whole: this discovery of significance through an exploration of cause or intention could serve to articulate an immanent principle of structure. In rhetorical terms, as we have seen, this can also represent a progression from *inventio*, determining the meaning of a text, to *dispositio*, ordering the structure of the text.[11]

In twelfth- and thirteenth-century *accessus* to the *Heroides*, the discussion of *intentio auctoris* allowed exegetes to discover a structural continuity or coherence in the significance of the work; the *accessus* could thus unite the disparate materials of such a collection under a single perceived *intentio*. One lengthy *accessus* to the *Heroides* offers a dizzying range of *intentiones auctoris*.[12] Each of these options provides a framework of perceived meaning to unify the materials of this otherwise heterogeneous anthology. Among the many alternatives given for *intentio auctoris* are two that bear an interesting resemblance to the *intentio* of Chaucer's *Prologue* to the *Legend of Good Women*:

Aliter, intentio sua est, cum in preceptis de arte amatoria non ostendit quo modo aliquis per epistolas sollicitaretur, illud hic exequitur. Aliter, intentio sua est in hoc libro hortari ad virtutes et redarguere vicia. Ipse accusatus fuit apud Cesarem, quia scripsis suis romanas matronas illicitos amores docuisset: unde librum scripsit eis, istum exemplum proponens, ut sciant amando quas debeant imitari, quas non.[13]

[Alternatively, his intention is to accomplish here what he neglected to do in the *Ars amatoria*, to show how one's emotions can be stirred up through letters. Or, his intention in this book is to exhort to virtue and to discourage vice. He was brought up on charges before Caesar, because in his writings he had taught Roman matrons about illicit love affairs: whence he composed his book for them, offering it as an exemplum, so that they should know which women they should imitate in the matter of love and which women they should not imitate.]

Here the *intentio auctoris* serves the same function as the older circumstantial topic of *causa*, or "why." The cause or intention of this anthology is discovered in its moral significance, and that significance lies in the intention of the work to compensate for earlier oversights. In the *Ars amatoria* he failed to show how love-letters can solicit affection, so in the *Heroides* he discharges this duty. Moreover, his purpose of exhorting to virtue and discouraging vice has a specific cause: he was charged before Caesar, the highest authority and guardian of law and morals, of having corrupted the morals of Roman matrons and his earlier writings on love. So on this view, the *Heroides* is a compensatory gesture, an opportunity to rectify his own moral standing by exemplifying the rules of chaste love. These two versions of the *intentio auctoris* (like any of the other options in this *accessus*) solve the problem of structural heterogeneity by proposing a unifying moral framework for the tales.

Chaucer's *Prologue* presents an *intentio auctoris* that is virtually identical in theme with the *intentio* of the *Heroides* prologue, differing from it only in circumstantial details. Chaucer's *Prologue* develops the theme of compensating for earlier moral oversights and answering charges before an absolute ruler who is the custodian of law and morality. Chaucer answers to the God of Love rather than to Caesar; the law that he has violated in his earlier writings is the law of Love, the codified "sensibility" of an elite literary culture, rather than the codified morality of conservative Roman patriarchy; the job of rectifying his earlier transgression is accomplished by exemplifying women who loved faithfully rather than by comparing chaste women with depraved women (as the *accessus Ovidiani* would see it). The point here is not to posit Chaucer's actual source for the *intentio auctoris* of the *Legend*, but rather to consider the implications of so close an analogue in the exegetical tradition of the *Heroides*. The *accessus Ovidiani* is so much a part of the medieval experience of reading Ovid that we do not need to look far to find a case for an analogue. We know that, in drawing extensively from the *Heroides* in the design and much of the material of the *Legend of Good Women*, Chaucer probably used a heavily annotated manuscript of Ovid's text, such as Bodleian MS Canon. Class. Lat. 1 (thirteenth century), or perhaps a manuscript containing introductions to classical authors, such as Munich Clm. 19475 (twelfth century), which contains the particular *accessus* that I have just quoted.[14] More important for our purposes, however, is to understand how that model of reading could become a model of writing: Chaucer's construction of *intentio auctoris* carries a rhetorical value similar to the construction of *intentio* in the *accessus* tradition. If Chaucer's *Legend of Good Women* is a vernacular response to the Ovidian anthology of "women's tales," then it is also a vernacular response to the medieval reading or exegetical reception of the *Heroides*. In the G version of the *Prologue* the God of Love even mentions the *Heroides* as a potential source of material on women who loved steadfastly (G. 305–6): this reference to the *Heroides* in the revised version of the *Prologue* further reinforces the idea of Ovid's anthology as an emblem for the framing of Chaucer's own *Legend* in a particular critical as well as literary tradition. In conception and design as an anthology, the *Legend of Good Women* would have posed for Chaucer the same structural problems that the *Heroides* posed for medieval readers. And in medieval exegetical solutions to the structural problem of the *Heroides* Chaucer would have found a solution to the problem of heterogeneity that the *Legend* presented.

Thus Chaucer turns to the exegetical concept of *intentio auctoris*, which discloses a principle of structure (*dispositio*) by discovering the meaning of the work in the cause or intention of the work (*inventio*). The *Prologue* to the *Legend of Good Women* does exactly what the *accessus Ovidiani* do: it gathers together disparate materials out of a single perceived *intentio*. But in Chaucer's *Prologue* that single, unifying *intentio* is not a retrospective perception of a later commentator on an earlier poet. Rather, it constitutes a *prospectus* to the *Legend*; it represents the *prospective* reasoning of the poet himself that brought the collection into being. But Chaucer's prospective stance is also curiously akin to the stance of the exegetes: in identifying Ovid's *intentio* from their own historically belated position, the exegetes arrogated to their perceptions a certain prospective power. The exegetes "reinvented" *their* Ovid, that is, a tractable, manageable Ovid, by supplying a putative textual foreknowledge in the form of *intentio auctoris*. They themselves enacted the process of rhetorical invention and co-opted the role of rhetorical producers of the text by discovering its ulterior meaning, and realizing that meaning in their exposition of the text. Similarly, in positing an *intentio auctoris* for his text, Chaucer describes the *invention* of the *Legend of*

Good Women, the process of discovery that generated the text. The idea of rectifying earlier moral oversights is the *topos* out of which he invents the text. Through this we can see how rhetorical invention has come to be understood in terms of hermeneutical procedure: Chaucer maps out the invention of his text in terms of the mechanisms or techniques of hermeneutics. He has appropriated an exegetical method, that of projecting a unifying significance through positing an *intentio* for the work, as the point of invention for his own text. In other words, he invents the *Legend of Good Women* out of hermeneutical discourse, by assuming the conventional exegetical stance that comes with the materials of the *accessus Ovidiani*. In the *Prologue*, Chaucer defines the *modus inveniendi* in terms of the *modus interpretandi*.

These observations allow us to draw a distinction between the explicit theme of "old books" in the *Prologue*, that is, the veneration of classical authority that modern criticism has justly recognized as crucial to the *Legend*,[15] and the discourse of academic exegesis that mediates that tradition, and that represents the real source of Chaucer's own claims to *auctoritas*. The famous lines about the wisdom and lore preserved in old books introduce the problem of historical difference and the hermeneutics of recovery that both versions of the *Prologue* explore:

> Thanne mote we to bokes that we fynde,
> Thourgh whiche that olde thynges ben in mynde,
> And to the doctryne of these olde wyse
> Yeven credence, in every skylful wyse,
> And trowen on these olde aproved storyes
> Of holynesse, of regnes, of victoryes,
> Of love, of hate, of othere sondry thynges,
> Of which I may not make rehersynges.
> And if that olde bokes weren aweye,
> Yloren were of remembraunce the keye.
> Wel oughte us thanne on olde bokes leve,
> There as there is non other assay by preve. (G. 17–28)

While these lines are the same in both versions of the *Prologue*, the context of G changes the value of these lines by articulating more forcefully the academic themes that are immanent in them. In the context of G as a whole, the "key of remembrance" is not just the old books themselves: G defines the key of remembrance with greater specificity in terms of the system of retrieving ancient lore, a tradition of exegetical reception. While F, the earlier version, broaches these problems suggestively, G, the later version, develops these possibilities further. As I will show, the G *Prologue* foregrounds the identification with exegetical practice by emphasizing the presence of technical academic language and by adding new references to the *auctores* of the arts curriculum.

Both versions of the *Prologue* use terminology commonly associated with literary *accessus* of the twelfth century, especially the terms *intentio* ("entente") and *materia* ("matere"). But compared to G, F uses the terms infrequently and only incidentally; for it is the revised version, G, that develops a genuine semantic field for these words. Each text opens the narrative sequence with a passage in praise of daisies, an obvious nod in the direction of French Marguerite poetry.[16] But F elaborates this theme further (F. 50ff.), sharpening the association with French love poetry. Thus the following lines in F, which have no parallel in G, develop the literary references to the tradition of the French love poets:

> Allas, that I ne had Englyssh, ryme or prose,
> Suffisant this flour to preyse aryght!
> But helpeth, ye that han konnyng and myght,
> Ye lovers that kan make of sentement;
> In this cas oghte ye be diligent
> To forthren me somwhat in my labour,
> Whether ye ben with the leef or with the flour. (F. 66–72)

These lines locate themselves immediately in an intravernacular frame of reference (that is, from one vernacular to another). They emphasize one historical strain in Chaucer's own literary career, his imitative relationship with French love poetry. The first two lines, deploring the insufficiency of English meter and prose, also seem to echo the lines in the envoy of "The Complaint of Venus":

> Princes, receyveth this compleynt in gre,
> Unto your excelent benignite
> Direct after my litel suffisaunce . . .
> And eke to me it ys a gret penaunce,
> Syth rym in Englissh hath such skarsete,
> To folwe word by word the curiosite
> Of Graunson, flour of hem that make in Fraunce.

It is not just accident that we should hear the echoes between these two texts. The "Complaint of Venus," a translation of a triple ballade by Oton de Graunson, exemplifies the kind of reliance upon prestigious French models that the F version of the *Prologue* also tries to foreground. In the F version, the old books of the *auctores* (the "key of remembrance") have given way – at least for the moment – to the more contemporary attractions of the daisy, that is, French love poetry. An illustrious vernacular tradition, the Marguerite poetry of Machaut, Froissart, and Deschamps, pre-empts the force of the classical *auctores*, and in this spirit of intravernacular reception, the narrator invokes the French poets, "Ye lovers that can make of sentement," as tutelary authorities. In one sense it is possible to say that at this point in the F *Prologue*, the narrator inscribes himself in one of the authorial roles of academic exegesis, perhaps that of supplementary commentator to acknowledged *auctores*, one who can only follow in the wake of his predecessors. But on the other hand, the emphatically vernacular (French–English) literary context of the F *Prologue* directs us away from this kind of association with academic writing, or at best leaves this possibility undeveloped.

The G *Prologue* omits the lines of F quoted above, thus omitting, along with the denser detail of Marguerite poetry, the invocation to vernacular masters. G joins up with F to repeat the passage about the poet-narrator coming after those who have reaped and led away the fruits of writing (F. 73–83; G. 61–70). G then inserts a passage that occurs later in F (G. 71–80; F. 188–96), but changes the character of the passage with a few strategic additions (emphasis mine):

> That nys nothyng the *entent* of my labour.
> For this *werk* is al of another tonne,
> Of olde story, er swich strif was begonne. (G. 78–80)

This is the first of a number of occasions where Chaucer introduces the terminology of the *accessus* into the revision. On their own, these words, "entente" and "werk," do not necessarily carry the semantic value of academic terminology, that is, *intentio* and *opus*. But along with other revisions these terms signal the redirection in G away from the recent traditions of vernacular love poetry to the distant history of "olde story" and its exegetical traditions. The lines that immediately follow are also revisions of F:

> But wherfore that I spak, to yeve credence
> To bokes olde and don hem reverence,
> Is for men shulde *autoritees* beleve,
> *There as there lyth non other assay by preve.*
> *For myn entent is, or I fro yow fare,*
> *The naked text in English to declare*
> *Of many a story, or elles of many a geste*
> *As autours seyn; leveth hem if yow leste.* (G. 81–8)

I have added emphasis to the words and lines that have no counterpart in F. The theme of old books, already present in F, is here seized and brought into sharp focus in G, foregrounded in a new environment of now unmistakable academic language. We are now in the world of *auctoritates* and of the poet's own *intentio* in relation to those *auctores*. The lines "for myn entent is, or I fro yow fare / The naked text in English to declare," are possibly the revisionist response of the G version to the lines in F, "Allas, that I ne had Englyssh, ryme or prose / Suffisant this flour to preyse aryght"; in the G version, the business of "Englishing" is directed away from intravernacular traditions (English against illustrious French models) to a larger historical arena, the vernacular and its relationship to Latin culture (English and the *auctores*).[17]

At this point the G version also brings to the foreground a certain ambiguity in the authorial stance of the speaker. He promises to "declare" in English the "naked text" of the stories of the *auctores* ("as autours seyn"). *Declare* can mean "to tell," but it can also mean "to explain," "to interpret." In its immediate context here, "to declare in English the naked text of stories *as autours seyn*," "declare" seems to lean towards the former meaning, to recite or tell.[18] In this respect, then, these lines suggest the conventional posture of the translator or even vernacular compiler who disclaims responsibility for the *sententia* of his text.[19] Certainly the *Prologue* to the *Legend of Good Women* offers itself, among other things, as a translator's prologue: there are references throughout, in both versions, to the "Englishing" of sources (*Roman de la Rose* and *Troilus*) and to "translating" the writings of "olde clerkes" (F. 370, G. 350). But on the other hand, the term *entent* ("myn entent is") signals an ambivalence, a pull in the opposite direction, as Chaucer's narrator invokes the topic *intentio auctoris*, not to explain the intention of the *auctores* whose works he is about to "declare," but rather to explain his own intention in declaring those works. Given that the *Prologue* as a whole appropriates the program of *intentio auctoris* from the *accessus Ovidiani* and applies it to Chaucer's own redaction of the Ovidian legends, the term *entent* here would suggest a certain incongruity or conflict with the traditionally self-effacing stance of the translator. In this way the word "declare" would also suggest its other meaning, "to interpet," for it is through exegetical interaction with the text that the translator can insert his own authorial power. We have already seen some example of a slippage from *accessus ad auctorem* to *accessus ad commentatorem* in the commentary tradition itself, notably in the prologue to the commentary on the *Aeneid* attributed to Bernardus Silvestris. We have also seen how the *Ovid moralisé* extends the implications of this auto-referentiality to the sphere of vernacular translation-commentary. Through the appropriation of certain authorial functions of academic criticism, the poet of the *Ovide moralisé* substitutes his own disclosive readings for the text of the *auctor*. I suggest that the *Legend of Good Women*, as an example of secondary translation, builds on such slippage, to take it one step further: through auto-exegesis it confers full authorial status on the vernacular translator.

This process is already at work in F, but the revisions of G throw it into sharper focus, making it more visible. F and G present slightly different accounts of how the poet went out to enjoy the flowers, fell asleep, and dreamed of the meeting with the God of Love and Alceste, the confrontation that caused him to write the present text. The dream narrative is obviously modeled on the conventions of French love poetry. But given the way that the *Prologue*, especially the G version, builds on the conventions of the *accessus ad auctores*, this narrative can also take on something of the character of a *vita auctoris*, describing something that happened in the author's life that "caused," or at least bears upon, the text in question. The relationship between *vita auctoris* and textual *causa* or even *intentio* is exemplified most dramatically in twelfth- and thirteenth-century *accessus* to Boethius' *Consolatio*, where the narrative of Boethius' misfortunes and sufferings is tied directly to his philosophical exploration of Fortune and her inconstancy.[20] We find a similar link between life and literary work in some *vitae* of Lucan.[21] In Chaucer's *Prologue*, with its strong overtones of the academic *accessus*, the literary convention of the poet-narrator's walk through the meadow and his dream can also constitute a kind of *vita auctoris*, if not in form, then at least in function. This also gives us a way of measuring the difference between the *Ovide moralisé* (which represents an extreme of primary translation, bordering on secondary translation) and the *Legend of Good Women*. As I have argued (in chapter 4), the *Ovide moralisé* omits the conventional *accessus* element of *vita auctoris* because this translator's exegetical prologue is auto-referential, and Ovid as historical *auctor* has little sovereignty in this sphere where the translator-exegete shows little interest in Ovid's intentions. But the *Ovide moralisé* does not go so far in its effacement of Ovid as to produce a *vita* or any personal narrative of the translator himself. In relative terms, the vernacular exegete has not emerged from behind the self-effacing shadows of an instrumental or supplementary role. But in Chaucer's *Prologue* to his exegetical translations of Ovidian and other classical texts, the focus is plainly directed to the translator as *auctor* whose own personal experience (the comic fiction of his love of daisies, his dream, the accusation of moral transgression in his earlier literary career) is the direct cause of the present text. Here we have a concrete measure of the difference between primary and secondary translation.

What may really confirm the assumption that this narrative works as a kind of authorial *vita* is the actual content of the dream. From the God of Love's accusation and Alceste's defense of the poet emerges a virtual catalogue of Chaucer's own works: *Troilus*, *Romaunt of the Rose*, the early dream poems, the lyrics, and other texts (F. 329–32, 416–330; G. 255–65, 405–20). It is not uncommon to find such lists of an author's works in *accessus ad auctores*, especially in fuller or more extensive introductions. Such catalogues can be attached to the *vita auctoris* (or sometimes the *nomen auctoris*). In the absence of a specific medieval term for such catalogues we can call this convention "*opera auctoris*" and designate it loosely as a subgenre of the *vita auctoris*. Conrad of Hirsau's *Dialogus super auctores* often integrates an "*opera auctoris*" into the discussion of an author or an author's *vita*.[22] Giovanni del Virgilio's *accessus* to his exposition of the *Metamorphoses* (early 1320s) provides a striking example of this. Giovanni uses the fourfold scholastic scheme of efficient, material, formal, and final cause. Under efficient cause, which defines the author's role in producing the text, he provides brief accounts of the life and name of the author, and proceeds with an extended catalogue and discussion of Ovid's various *opera*.[23] The conventional association between *vita auctoris* and "*opera auctoris*" – especially in prologues to Ovid – gives us some insight into the way that Chaucer has constructed the *Prologue* to his own Ovidian collection, the *Legend of Good Women*. The catalogue of his works, the "*opera auctoris*," is a generic signal of a *vita auctoris*, which the author himself supplies in the manner of a conventional *accessus* to the curricular authors. The *Prologue* to the *Legend of Good Women* appropriates academic theory, not just to claim that discursive field for vernacular writing (as, for example, in Notker of St. Gall or some of the French translations of Boethius), but to claim the powerful role of *auctor* for the vernacular translator. In this way Chaucer's "*opera auctoris*," like Jean de Meun's list of his own works in his preface to *Li Livres de Confort*, also establishes an authorizing context of vernacular writing for the present work. Like Jean de Meun, Chaucer can exploit his *de facto* reputation as a vernacular poet to situate his translation in a framework of intralingual interests, so that his translation is perceived as a product of an ongoing vernacular tradition rather than as a lone intervention in a dominant Latin tradition. But it is important to recognize that the self-authorizing devices in the *Prologue* to the *Legend of Good Women* are not simply functions of Chaucer's particular renown or even of his own innovative powers (in which case any comparisons with the poet of the *Ovid moralisé* or with Notker of St. Gall would be moot points). In the *Prologue* Chaucer associates his present work with a tradition of vernacular translation (as the *Prologue* repeatedly addresses the problem of "Englishing" sources from other literary traditions), and it is important to see how the *Legend* is produced and enabled by that historical system of translation. For Chaucer to use the critical vocabulary normally applied to Ovid and to apply it to himself in his translations of Ovid and other *auctores* is to carry through on the motive of displacement always at work in exegesis and in exegetical translation: in the *Legend of Good Women* Chaucer invents his own authorship out of the conventional *topoi* of Ovidian exegesis.

The God of Love's accusation rests on Chaucer's earlier choice of the *Roman de la Rose* and the story of Criseyde as sources. But the G version of the *Prologue* takes the accusation further (G. 270–312), beginning with the lines:

> Was there no good matere in thy mynde,
> Ne in alle thy bokes ne coudest thow nat fynde
> Som story of wemen that were good and trewe? (G. 270–2)

The term "matere" appears three times in this amplified version of the God of Love's accusation (lines 270, 279, 309), punctuating the list of *auctores* (or "clerkes"), both ancient and modern (i.e., "Vincent in his Estoryal Myrour") from which Chaucer might have drawn some information about good women. In the same way that the topics of *intentio auctoris*, *vita auctoris*, and the subgenre of "*opera auctoris*" have been redirected to refer to the translator exegete, so here in G the accessus topic *materia* also refers to Chaucer, to the resources of the vernacular translator-exegete-*auctor*. This list of authors – Valerius, Livy, Claudian, Jerome, Ovid, Vincent of Beauvais – is not just hypothetically prescriptive: it is also descriptive, like the topic of *materia* in the traditional *accessus*. It designates the actual matter, the sources, themes, and narratives, that Chaucer drew upon for the *Legend*.

Curiously, in both versions of the *Prologue* the defense (and self-defense) of the poet-narrator rests on disclaimers of his authorial control which inscribe him in the supplementary role of the translator, a role that is clearly related to the self-effacing posture of the exegete or compiler:

He may translate a thyng in no malyce,
But for he useth bokes for to make,[24]
And taketh non hed of what matere he take,
Therfore he wrot the Rose and ek Crisseyde
Of innocence, and nyste what he seyde . . .
He ne hath not don so grevously amys
To translate that olde clerkes wryte,
As thogh that he of maleys wolde endyte
Despit of love, and hadde hymself ywrought.
(G. 341–52; cf. F. 363–72)

Similarly the narrator's self-defense stands on a disclaimer of authorial responsibility for a controversial text and takes cover under exegetical justifications for the ultimate moral *utilitas* of a text:

What so myn auctour mente,
Algate, God wot, it was myn entente
To forthere trouthe in love and it cheryce,
And to be war fro falsnesse and fro vice
By swich ensaumple; this was my menynge.
(G. 460–4; cf. F. 470–4)

As Minnis has pointed out, this is precisely the kind of *utilitas* through which the writers of the *accessus Ovidiani* justify their attention to Ovid's scurrilous works.[25] While these crucial passages secure the *Prologue*'s identification with a tradition of academic exegesis, they also return Chaucer to the role of expositor rather than *auctor* in his own prologue. But it is also here, with this ambivalent pull between the disclaimers of the exegete and the claims of *auctor*, that F and G definitively part ways. At the end of the F version, the God of Love commands Chaucer to make the *Legend* from the *materia* he will find in his books (F. 556), and continues with this bidding:

Suffiseth me thou make in this manere:
That thou *reherce* of al hir lyf the grete,
After thise olde auctours lysten for to trete. (F. 573–5)

The God of Love exhorts Chaucer to *reherce* the matter according to the treatments of the "olde auctours." The use of the word *reherce* is interesting here. It means "repeat," "recount," or "recite"; Trevisa used the term as an English equivalent of the Latin term *recitare*, meaning "to repeat," as in repeating the opinions of others, as opposed to asserting one's own opinion. To repeat or rehearse (*recitare*) was recognized as the job of the *compilator* who gathers together the opinions of others rather than setting forth his own.[26] In the F version this final command of the God of Love to "reherce" the treatments of the "olde auctours" casts the translator in the subordinate role of a compiler or gatherer of others' material. But these lines are entirely omitted in the G version. Here the God of Love exhorts him to "let be the chaf, and writ wel of the corn" (G. 529), to include the exemplary Alceste, and to begin with Cleopatra. The changes in the final couplet of the

Prologue from F to G witness this significant difference in authorial stance. F reads:

> And with that word *my bokes gan I take*,
> And ryght thus on my Legende gan I make.
> (F. 578–9, emphasis added)

This makes sense: the God of Love has just sent him off to rehearse the "olde auctours." But in G these lines read:

> And with that word, of slep I gan awake,
> And ryght thus on my Legende gan I make. (G. 544–5)

"That word" here is simply the God's command to begin with Cleopatra, not, as in F, to "reherce" the "old auctours." With the revisions and significant omissions of G it is clear that Chaucer as translator affirms his claim to *auctoritas* and underscores the auto-exegetical force of his *Prologue*.

In emphasizing the language of academic hermeneutics the G *Prologue* inserts the vernacular translator into that privileged tradition, to the point where the translator himself becomes the subject or focus of that academic language. Thus in the final section the G *Prologue* omits this academic terminology in order to propose a new definition of the translator's status. In mastering that academic discourse the vernacular translator has become the subject of that discourse: no longer just an exegete, a transmitter or "rehearser" of lore about the *auctores*, he is himself an *auctor*. In moving from the F to the G version of the *Prologue* we really move from primary to secondary translation. G is not just a revision of textual details, but of an entire discursive attitude. Whereas primary translation empowers the vernacular by inscribing it in the official discourse of exegesis, secondary translation makes the vernacular text the *subject* of that official discourse. It is through the disciplinary force of hermeneutics that the translator can discover – literally "invent" – the ascendency of the vernacular.

Whether we read the F or the G *Prologue*, the legends themselves remain the same. But the point of the foregoing observations is to show that the G version, better than the F version, articulates what is discursively at stake in the *Legend of Good Women*. The *Legend* is caught in – and we might say also dramatizes and even plays on – the paradoxes produced by a long tradition of vernacular translation of curricular *auctores*, a tradition which expresses the competing claims of exegesis and rhetoric. The *Legend of Good Women* constucts its relationship to the *auctores* out of the conventional postures of exegesis, service to and conservation of the authoritative text; but it also finds a way of stressing or insisting upon its difference from its sources, making that very difference the explicit subject of rhetorical invention.

In the legends themselves, the most obvious expression of this paradox is through the rhetorical devices of *occupatio* and *abbreviatio*. As Robert Frank and others have pointed out, the use of *occupatio*, a way of saying something in the very act of promising not to say it, serves as a mechanism for announcing the particular narrative constraints of the text and thus often for showcasing the narrator's desire to condense or abbreviate his sources.[27] There are various ways in which *occupatio* and *abbreviatio* can be used locally in the individual tales of the *Legend of Good Women*, among them, of course, to play up the comic reluctance of the narrator-persona to conform to the strictures imposed upon him. But the net effect of the devices is to raise and negotiate a paradox: these devices point to the immanent authority and controlling presence of sources, but also point to the way that the vernacular text can refuse and resist the authority of the sources in favor of a new *intentio auctoris*, that which is described in the *Prologue*. Moreover, while *occupatio* or *abbreviatio* announce the authority of Chaucer's classical sources over his translations, Chaucer's text constantly displaces those sources with medieval exegetical receptions (manuscript scholia, the *Ovide moralisé* and other vernacular sources), thus underscoring the vernacular control of this privileged academic tradition.

One common form that *abbreviatio* takes in the *Legend* is referring the reader to the *auctor*: Ovid, Virgil, or others. In the "Legend of Hypsipyle" the narrator refers us to the *Argonautica*, to Guido delle Colonne, to *Heroides* 6, and to "th'origynal, that telleth al the cas" (1558). Similarly, the legends of Medea and of Ariadne close with a reference to the higher authority of Ovid's original, which is represented as the source of more extended and precise detail. But the "Legend of Dido" offers a more complete paradigm of the function of *abbreviatio*. The invocation of Virgil and Ovid in the opening lines of the "Legend of Dido" work as a diminutive *accessus*:

> Glorye and honour, Virgil Mantoan,
> Be to thy name! and I shal, as I can,
> Folwe thy lanterne, as thow gost byforn,
> How Eneas to Dido was forsworn.
> In thyn Eneyde and Naso wol I take
> The tenor, and the grete effectes make. (924–9)

The opening apostrophe is immediately undercut by the way that the translator-narrator makes his own intervention. The momentous invocation of Virgil's name finds its effect in the narrator's own *intentio*: to follow, "as I can," Virgil's story of the betrayal of Dido. But the shift of attention to the translator's own purpose also produces an awkward uncertainty, suggesting in the phrase "as I can" another kind of betrayal, that of a translator whose inadequacy or tentativeness will betray his source (and here we should recall a similar hesitance in the echo of Virgil in the *House of Fame*, lines 143–4: "I wol now synge, *yif I kan*, / The armes and also the man").[28] But this hint of textual betrayal also becomes the bridge into the narrator-translator's statement of his *materia* and *modus agendi*: out of the "tenor" of the *Aeneid* and Ovid's *Heroides* he will "make" the "effectes." How to define and differentiate the value of the words "tenor" and "effect" is not easy. Their meanings can overlap, both suggesting "substance" or "significance." Perhaps the legal force of the Latin term *tenor*, as in the "contents," "sense," or "tenor" of a law, makes best sense in this context, suggesting the literal or actual contents of the Virgilian or Ovidian narrative.[29] In this way we can differentiate "tenor" from "effect," letting the latter term carry the semantic value of "meaning" or "purport," or even "significance." If these semantic distinctions are correct then the sense of these lines is something like: "I will take the matter from Virgil and Ovid and I will make (or forge) their significance." In any case, we can see that these lines distinguish between two domains, the textual authority of Virgil and Ovid and the significative control that the translator exerts over the received *materia*. Through this the translator's tentative intervention builds into an affirmation of his own powerful role in this process of reception.

The translator-narrator identifies his power with what he does with his *materia*; and here he brings the device of *abbreviatio* into play:

> But of his aventures in the se
> Nis nat to *purpos* for to speke of here,
> For it acordeth nat to my *matere*.
> But, as I seyde, of hym and of Dido
> Shal be my tale, til that I have do. (953–5; emphasis added)

Along with *amplificatio*, *abbreviatio* is the major device that the *artes poetriae* recommended as a means of achieving difference with the source. But here that rhetorical device and the difference that it enables is brought to the foreground through the use of exegetical language and postures. The opening invocation of Virgil and Ovid locates the narrator in a complex relationship to the *auctores*: in the manner of an exegete he speaks of them as founts of textual authority, but he also twists that exegetical relationship into auto-exegesis, by shifting the focus to his own intentional control over the matter they supply. So also in the passage just quoted, his concern is with the difference between the *materia* of the *auctores* and his own *materia*, that is, with his own "purpos" (*intentio* or *utilitas*) in treating what has become "*my* matere." His treatment of that "matere" is of course governed by the particular *intentio auctoris* stated in the *Prologue*: to provide a palinode for his earlier works by writing here "of women trewe in lovynge al here lyve" (G. 427).

As we have seen, Chaucer's prospective statement of an *intentio auctoris* is a variation on the exegetical perceptions of the traditional *accessus*, where the commentator retrospectively posits an *intentio auctoris*. But these retrospective perceptions of the commentator also have a *prospective* value, for they determine the way that the commentator will treat (or will have treated) the text in his commentary. Indeed, what the commentators do is to posit an *intentio* and then in their commentaries suppress some material and amplify other matter in order to make the authorial text conform to the intentional scheme they have supplied. This is a kind of rhetorical control that they exert over the authoritative text. We have seen this, for example, in Remigius' commentary on Martianus Capella (see chapter 3 above). Remigius' own immediate academic heritage in Eriugena and Martin of Laon shapes his interest in Martianus' text, which he sees in terms of contemporary debates about new schematic classifications of the sciences. He constructs the *intentio* (or *causa*) and the *materies* of Martianus' text in terms of such metadisciplinary interests, and in the body of his commentary proceeds to draw out and emphasize those elements of the text that most invite theoretical discussion about reclassifying the sciences. Here he amplifies his commentary, introducing matter from Eriugena and Martin of Laon, while he gives comparatively short shrift to other parts of the text that do not lend themselves to such metadisciplinary concerns. In sum, the exegete treats the text in terms of its relevance to a governing exegetical scheme which is stated prospectively in the *accessus* under *intentio auctoris*.

In the "Legend of Dido," the narrator's statement of what is relevant to his "matere" serves the same purpose: it calls attention to the way his treatment is governed by the intentional scheme established in the *Prologue*. The irony of this cuts two ways: it foregrounds the fact that the Virgilian *materia* has become the translator's "matere," to be shaped by the translator's interests, which center on Dido rather than on Aeneas' adventures; but it also dramatizes how the translator has achieved the intentional control of an *auctor* by exploiting the rhetorical possibilities of exegetical discourse, locating himself in the powerful position of the commentator who supplies the text with an *intentio auctoris* to which he makes the text conform in his exegetical treatment. Whereas in exegesis these rhetorical possibilities remain implicit to the practice, never actually acknowledged, Chaucer as translator draws them out and makes them an explicit part of his treatment. Thus the translator calls our attention to his rhetorical control over the material precisely by reminding us of how he is cutting or abbreviating the authorial text. For these reasons the conventional apology of the translator with regard to how closely he will follow his source –

> I coude folwe, word for word, Virgile,
> But it wolde lasten al to longe while (1002–3)

– becomes instead a statement of liberation from the constraints of that source. He finds the possibilities for this liberation through the conventional exegetical structure of *intentio auctoris*, which he applies auto-exegetically; and he achieves this liberation through the rhetorical device of *abbreviatio*. This demonstrates, in miniature as it were, how the governing framework of hermeneutics can restore rhetoric to its former discursive power: the rhetorical device of *abbreviatio* has its value here only through the larger context of the exegetical *intentio auctoris*. Within these terms we can also see the irony of the frequent invocations of the "author" or the "book" in the "Legend of Dido" ("Thus seyth the bok, withouten any les," 1022; "The autour maketh of it no mencioun," 1228; "But as myn auctour seith, yit thus she seyde," 1352). While these suggest themselves as translator's disclaimers by referring us to the immanent authority of the sources, they also point up the very difference between this text and its sources precisely by protesting the translator's fidelity. Perhaps this is why the "Legend of Dido" can end itself effectively on so obvious and open-ended an *abbreviatio*:

> But who wol al this letter have in mynde,
> Rede Ovyde, and in hym he shal it fynde. (1366–7)

We encounter this paradigm, with some variation and in less developed forms, in some of the other legends: Hypsipyle, Medea, Ariadne, Philomela, and Phyllis. In "The Legend of Ariadne," the narrator invokes his "matere" to recall himself from a digression (1959), and refers us, by way of *abbreviatio*, to *Heroides* 10 (2218–21). In "The Legend of Phyllis," the line "Now to the effect turne I of my matere" (2403) serves as a bridge between a general denunciation of false men in the proem and the proof of this generalization in the tale. In this tale also the narrator exposes the double nature of his relationship to his source by at once promising to "rehearse" it in part and refusing to expend energy on information that is not to his purpose:

> Allas! – that, as the storyes us recorde,
> She was hire owene deth ryght with a corde,
> Whan that she saw that Demophon hire trayed.
> But to hym first she wrot, and faste him prayed
> He wolde come and hire delyvere of peyne,
> As I reherce shal a word or tweyne.
> Me lyste nat vouche-sauf on hym to swynke,
> Ne spende on hym a penne ful of ynke,
> For fals in love was he, ryght as his syre. (2484–92)

At the very moment that he promises to rehearse his source in the manner of a translator or compiler he interposes his own intentional and moral control over the narrative with a brief *occupatio* about how Demophoön does not deserve his attention. It is also worth noting that how Phyllis died is not clear from *Heroides* 2: if, "as the storyes us recorde," Phyllis committed suicide by hanging herself, those "storyes" are not Ovid's text, but either the *Roman de la Rose* (13181–4, Lecoy ed.) or a gloss in a manuscript of Ovid (which may also account for Jean de Meun's information).[30] Thus even the immanent authority of Ovid's original text is contested. We see something similar to this in the "Legend of Philomela," where the very purpose (the "effect") of Ovid's story, the revenge of Procne and Philomela on Tereus and the metamorphosis of the characters into birds, is pointedly suppressed ("The remenaunt is no charge for to telle," 2383) in favor of a moralization about wicked men that refashions the tale according to the constraints of the narrator's purpose or *intentio*.

Such flattening out of the difference between various tales in favor of a comprehensive moral purpose, that is, the narrator's intention to show the suffering of faithful women, also has its analogue in medieval commentaries on the *Heroides*. The commentaries on the *Heroides* tend to streamline the significance of the Ovidian text into the moral categories established by the *intentio auctoris*, most commonly the intention of condemning foolish or scandalous love. Such a notion of the *intentio auctoris* carries from the general *accessus* to the various prologues to the individual epistles: if an *accessus* to the entire *Heroides* states that the *intentio* is "to condemn men and women caught up in foolish and illicit love," the prologues to the individual epistles will often give this reasoning a specific application, for example, with regard to Medea: "the author rebukes foolish love through the example of this woman who, through her love for a stranger, betrayed her father, abandoned her country, and tore her brother to pieces."[31] In the same way, the narrator of the *Legend of Good Women* streamlines or abbreviates his *materia* in order to emphasize its function within the master plan of the collection, the moral purport of the narrator's own *intentio auctoris* as set forth in his *Prologue*. Thus for the constraints of the original text or texts the translator-narrator has substituted the constraints of his own moral purpose, in this way co-opting and exploiting the conventions of Ovidian exegesis. While he finds his *materia* in classical texts, he "reinvents" that *materia* through the apparatus of hermeneutical tradition, giving that classical matter a new, self-generated *intentio auctoris*.

The *Legend of Good Women* exemplifies how the Middle Ages could recover the Roman model of translation as displacement. The text cannot be read as a translation in the sense of a supplement to an authoritative source. This is precisely what Cicero intended with his rhetorical model of translation as a form of displacement: the translation should substitute itself for its source and efface the presence of that source. The Middle Ages recovers the Roman model of translation by recovering rhetoric; but ironically, the force of rhetoric is now defined through exegetical performance. Where Cicero excluded grammar or exegesis as incompatible with the aims of rhetoric and rhetorical translation, the Middle Ages restores rhetoric to its ascendent role in translation by inscribing it in an empowered hermeneutics.

TRANSLATION, DIFFERENCE, AND ETHICAL ACTION IN *CONFESSIO AMANTIS*

Gower's *Confessio amantis* represents the furthest extreme of secondary translation. The individual tales are best defined by their differences from the sources, and in fact can scarcely be read as translations. It marks the point on our continuum at which translation, working within the structures of exegetical service, becomes full-fledged rhetorical appropriation, and thereby asserts its own canonical authority. *Confessio amantis* is not typically studied as a translation, precisely because it has so convincingly differentiated itself from its sources. Yet this text is very much a product of the tradition of academic translation, and its relationship to that tradition needs to be explored. As a collection of tales (mainly Ovidian) held together by an exegetical structure, it has an obvious antecedent in the formal and conceptual design of the *Ovide moralisé*. It is comparable as well to earlier kinds of exegetical translation that engage the source *materia* according to fixed interpretive concerns or paradigms, for example, the Burgundian translation of the *Consolatio* that subordinates Boethius' text to William of Conches' allegorical commentary. Its use of narrative sources also links it materially with a foregoing tradition of vernacular translation, for it relies considerably on earlier vernacular renderings of classical *auctores*, notably the *Ovide moralisé* and the *Roman de Troie* of Benoit de Sainte-Maure.[32] In forming itself so much out of other translations, it locates itself in an intravernacular tradition of classical material and contains the products of that tradition within its own vast compilative enterprise.

In *Confessio amantis* we see the extent to which vernacular translation can exploit academic discourse. Here the exegetical structure has become so dominant that its primary function is to accentuate the *difference* between Gower's text and its sources. The exegetical system dominates at all levels and junctures of this text. Prologues frame the text, marginal commentary interpolates the text, and the conventions of *ordinatio* give the text its structural underpinnings. The text also embodies an exegetical system in the form of the interpretive ministrations of Genius (which serve the same function as the translator's moral expositions in the *Ovide moralisé*). These interpretive systems, which operate both internally and externally to the text, position the work within a larger discourse on wisdom and ethics, and it is through this interpretive framework that the various tales of *Confessio amantis* take shape. The individual tales of *Confessio amantis* do not stand as serial redactions of classical or other traditional matter, in the way, say, of the Vatican Mythographies, in which the summaries of classical myth are organized together as topical entries in an encyclopaedic guide. Rather, the tales of *Confessio amantis* are subordinated to a thematic principle, wisdom and ethics, which is controlled by and articulated through the governing exegetical structures of the text: the prologues, headnotes, sidenotes, the elaborated structure of *compilatio*, and the interpretive directives of Genius.

As the dominant force of the text, the exegetical structure of *Confessio amantis* becomes the primary vehicle of rhetorical invention. It is through this structure that Gower articulates the specific "arguments" that render the "cause" of his text plausible, the argumentative purposes to which he subordinates the *materia* drawn from classical and modern *auctores*. The tales serve in the exposition of this argument in the way that the *exemplum* serves as a form of extrinsic proof in the classical oration (see e.g., Quintilian, *Institutio oratoria* 5.11.1ff.), or in the way that *exempla* serve in medieval Christian rhetoric and related traditions.[33] It is through the exegetical structure that the text can express its difference from its sources, through this structure that Gower reinvents the *materia* of literary tradition. *Confessio amantis* thus turns hermeneutical convention into a source of topical invention, and in this way successfully carries out the program of invention prescribed in the *artes poetriae*. Indeed, we might say that *Confessio amantis* finds its most valuable sources of topical invention, not in traditional narrative materials, but in the *communis materia* of academic discourse itself. The following analysis will focus on Gower's transformation of traditional disciplinary systems rather than on his transformations of individual literary sources: the general paradigm for his treatment of narrative sources proceeds from the governing hermeneutical structure.

The most basic function of the two prologues (the *Prologus* and the prologue to book 1) is to recontextualize the traditional *materia* upon which Gower draws, to make that material part of a new system of *intentio* and *utilitas*. Minnis has shown that the *Prologus* is actually an "extrinsic" prologue which explains the art or "part of philosophy" to which the text belongs, here that of ethics and wisdom, and that the introduction to book 1 serves as an "intrinsic" prologue which identifies the workings of the text itself, the *Confessio amantis*.[34] The *Prologus* open with a promise of new purpose applied to old matter:

> Of hem that writen ous tofore
> The bokes duelle, and we therfore
> Ben tawht of that was write tho:
> Forthi good is that we also
> In oure tyme among ous hiere
> Do wryte of newe som matiere,
> Essampled of these olde wyse
> So that it myhte in such a wyse,
> Whan we ben dede and elleswhere,
> Beleve to the worldes eere
> In tyme comende after this.[35] (Pr. 1–11)

The purpose is to write a book that mediates between the questions of love and wisdom (*Prologus*, 17–21), but that locates these questions in a large context of historical commentary (53–60) and thus also provides moral example to powerful men:

> And in this wyse I thenke trete
> Towardes hem that now be grete,
> Betwen the vertu and the vice
> Which longeth unto this office. (Pr. 77–80)

The prologue to book 1 establishes the particular grounds of the text through the technical apparatus of *modus agendi* ("the Stile of my writinges," 1.8–14), *materia* ("And that is love, of which I mene / To trete," 15–16) and *intentio* ("To hem that ben lovers aboute / Fro point to point I wol declare / And wryten of my woful care . . . That men mowe take remembrance / Of that thei schall hierafter rede," 72–7). Even Genius complies with the author's intentions: he promises to apply ("remene") his sermons on the vices to "thi matiere / Of love" (278–9). The theme of discovering a moral purpose in writings about love is an echo of the *accessus Ovidiani*, and through such thematic echoes Gower's prologues retrace the paths of traditional *accessus* to

Ovid's works. But more importantly, it is through these conventional routes that he directs us to the moral *intentio* of his own anthology of *auctores*.

Confessio amantis takes the mechanics of auto-exegesis much further than Chaucer does in the *Legend of Good Women*. Like the *Legend of Good Women*, *Confessio amantis* invents its own textual argument out of the conventions of exegesis, notably out of the terminology of the *accessus* and, as we will see, the structures of *compilatio*. But more than this, *Confessio amantis* implants certain sets of hermeneutical instructions in the text. The most obvious of these is the figure of Genius as the confessor-commentator. Genius serves the same function as the translator's moralizing commentary in the *Ovide moralisé*. But Genius does not simply provide a running commentary on the material derived from Ovid and other authors. First, as a figure of the frame fiction, participating in and constructed by that fictional narrative, Genius allows the text, in a sense, to interpret itself: while his function is the same as that of a gloss interposed between blocks of text, such as we see in the revised "mixed" French version of the *Consolatio*, Genius as interpreter is also part of the fictive narration that contains and governs the presentation of the tales. He is as "textual" as the tales that he narrates. Second, and more important, however, is that Genius' words direct interpretation, not only to the text, but also back to the author and authorial purpose. One of the first sidenotes in book I declares:

Hic quasi in persona aliorum, quos amor alligat, fingens se auctor esse Amantem, varias eorum passiones variis huius libri distinccionibus per singula scribere proponit.

[Here, as if in the *persona* of others whom love has fettered, the author, pretending to be Amans, proposes to write of their various sufferings in each individual section of his book.][36]

The author impersonates Amans and so becomes Genius' interlocutor. Genius, in turn, directs his commentary on each tale to the particular circumstances of Amans' moral condition, thus organizing the tales and their commentary around a scheme appropriate to the Lover's state, the confessional system of the Seven Deadly Sins. In so accommodating the moral interests of Amans, Genius also functions as a projection of the "author," or as a voice of the *intentio auctoris* which monitors the purveying of meaning throughout the text, proposing to keep it in line with the *intentio* as announced in the two prologues. Genius' role is to act as guardian of Gower's argument, to keep Gower's reinvention of his *materia* on its course.[37]

But even while he is a projection of *intentio auctoris*, Genius is also an actor in the narrative. He serves therefore as a rhetorical sleight of hand, as a disguise for the author's auto-exegesis: as a "character" in the "plot" Genius masks the author's self-referentiality to make it appear a necessary element of the narrative action. This allows the author to co-opt the role of exegete for his own text, but to carry it out under cover of certain rhetorical tropes, personification, allegory, and irony. In some ways this resembles the narrative and auto-exegetical configuration of Dante's *Inferno* and *Purgato-*

rio, where Virgil as a personification is both actor in and expositor of the narration. In Gower's text, when Genius explains the application of a tale such as what "Ovide telleth in his bok" (1.334), or adduces the evidence of "a tale which to this matiere acordeth" (1.387–8), he expounds, not Ovid's *intentio*, but Gower's purpose in transforming and abbreviating Ovid's text, in making Ovid's text different. Genius serves to explain the grounds for Gower's particular reception of his sources; but as a personification Genius makes his exegesis look like narrative action. Thus Gower's own hermeneutical action on his sources is disguised as part of the invention of his own narrative. In this way we can see how certain rhetorical processes – Genius as a preacher, as monitor of an argument, and as a poetic trope – are generated out of a hermeneutical function, the author's exegetical control over received *materia*.

The exegetical structure that dominates in *Confessio amantis*, that truly holds the text together, is *compilatio*.[38] The whole work is an anthology of classical and much other material. As a side note to the first recension of the *Prologus* declares:

> . . . tanquam fauum ex variis floribus recollectum, presentem libellum ex variis cronicis, historiis, poetarum philosophorumque dictis, quatenus sibi infirmitas permisit, studiosissime compilauit.[39]

> [{the author}, in so far as his illness has permitted, has studiously compiled the present book, like a honeycomb gathered from various flowers, from various chronicles, histories, and the words of philosophers and poets.]

The various elements of the anthology are subordinated to a controlling structure which works through *divisio textus*, division of the text into coherent sections, and *ordinatio*, a hierarchical arrangement of information.[40] The development of the procedures of *ordinatio* and *compilatio* in the thirteenth century enabled scholars to make what were, in effect, new books out of inherited materials, whether by applying new headings and divisions to old texts, or by gathering multiple *auctoritates* from many sources and arranging them under a new classificatory scheme, as in Vincent of Beauvais' *Speculum maius*.[41] But these scholastic principles of the order and division of texts and knowledge were such powerful directives for late medieval epistemology that the very classificatory structure itself could be regarded as the primary vehicle of meaning.[42] In the first part of the thirteenth century, Alexander of Hales expressed this scholastic conflation of meaning and structure in terms of the logical procedure of the human sciences:

> Primus modus definitivus debet esse, divisivus, collectivus, et talis modus debet esse in humanis scientiis, quia apprehensio veritatis secundum humanam rationem explicatur per divisiones, definitiones, et ratiocinationes.[43]

> [The first mode {the human sciences} must be definitive, divisive, and collective; and such must be the mode in the human sciences, because the apprehension of truth, according to the terms of human reason, is explained through divisions, definitions, and ratiocinations.]

This scholastic idea of human knowledge as a formal "mode" is reflected in the importance that Gower accords to textual *dispositio* in *Confessio amantis*. In *Confessio amantis* it is the structure of the text, its organization as a compilation, that is the principal expression of meaning in the work, that articulates the thematic directives of the *intentio auctoris*. The structure that Gower imposes on his inherited *materia*, the division of the tales according to the penitential scheme of the Seven Deadly Sins, and the incorporation of these *auctoritates* into a governing scheme of instruction on wisdom, ethics, and politics (as set forth in the *Prologus* and book 7), speaks, more eloquently than the actual "content" of the work, to the inventional control that he exerts over his *materia*. As a compiler, Gower quite literally makes a new book out of inherited materials: the structure of his text confers new meanings on his sources, which are now organized to pertain to different stages of sin and to exemplify the laws of human and divine love. It is for this reason as well that the classical tales are transformed in the retelling, abbreviated, amplified, and refigured so as to comply with their new textual purpose. At this most fundamental level, Gower as a vernacular transmitter and transformer of the classics carries out the inventional precepts of the *artes poetriae*: out of the procedures of exegetical service, *enarratio poetarum*, he discovers and asserts rhetorical difference with his sources. It is through the elaborate system of *compilatio* that Gower accomplishes his thematic purpose: the exegetical procedure of *compilatio* allows him to reorganize his inherited material in accordance with his own *intentio*.

The most basic principle of *compilatio* is *divisio*: division of the text and the ordering of its parts. Under the impress of Aristotelian science, *divisio* is, moreover, an epistemological principle, an understanding of the categories of knowledge in terms of relation and subordination. As a general way of knowing (*divisio scientiae*) mirrored in standards of textual procedure (*divisio textus*), *divisio* in Gower's *Confessio amantis* is the source of the most powerful hermeneutical directives in the poem. It is through *divisio* that Gower takes auto-exegesis to its fullest implications: *divisio* serves both as a device of textual organization and as a vehicle of ideological critique.

In tracing out the ramifications of *divisio* in *Confessio amantis*, we must begin with book 7. This book is inserted into the structural *divisio* of the Seven Deadly Sins, as a hiatus between the treatment of Gluttony (book 6) and of Incest (book 8). Book 7, however, represents *divisio* in both its technical and epistemological sense. It is a discourse on the division of the sciences, a *divisio* of virtue and ethics in terms of Aristotelian distinctions between theoretical and practical sciences. As an exposition of the sciences, book 7 is itself divided and ordered to mirror the conceptual structure of this system of knowledge. Within the narrative framework of the education of Alexander (which had become a conventional motif in late medieval narrative fiction),[44] Genius sets forth three principal parts of Philosophy, "Theorique," "Rethorique," and "Practique." Each of these has its own parts and subdivisions or properties to be expounded in order. Gower's division of the sciences is based on the Aristotelian division into theoretical, practical, and productive. But in making rhetoric one of the principal divisions, Gower has elevated it from its usual position as a subdivision of one of the categories, either of practical sciences, as in Gundissalinus, or of theoretical sciences, as in Giles of Rome.[45] This is an unusual configuration of *divisio scientiae*. In order to understand the implications of Gower's revision of the standard categories of knowledge, we must first investigate how Gower derived his particular version of this system, and especially how he came to assign rhetoric so important a role. Gower derived his scheme of the sciences, not just from Aristotelian epistemology, but also from the particular *divisio textus* of one of his major sources for book 7, Brunetto Latini's compendium, *Li Livres dou Trésor* (written between 1260 and 1266). It is to the influence of Brunetto's compilation that we must look for an explanation of Gower's division of the sciences into "Theorique," "Rethorique," and "Practique."

In book 1 of the *Trésor*, Brunetto offers a threefold division of the sciences into theoretical, practical, and logical (1.2–5).[46] This scheme is obviously a conflation of the Aristotelian division into theoretical, practical, and productive sciences and the Hellenistic division into logic, ethics, and physics. More important, however, is that this hybrid scheme is mainly a heuristic device for Brunetto, a kind of superstructure which is only loosely related to the actual exposition of his subject in the *Trésor*. Thus we see that Brunetto has rather little to say about logic, confining the bulk of his remarks on this subject to one brief section of his prologue (1.5), where he offers a schematic account of logic and its parts. Otherwise, logic as a category of human knowledge plays little or no role in the material ordering, the *divisio textus*, of the *Trésor*. Brunetto's prologue proposes the epistemological categories of theoretical, practical, and logical sciences as the guiding principles of his *divisio textus*. The first part of the treatise will expound the parts of knowledge that come within the purview of theoretical science, theology, history of the world, and natural history; the second section, a discussion of virtues and vices translated in part from Aristotle's *Ethics*, will correspond to the second and third parts of philosophy, the practical and logical; and the third part of the treatise will continue the treatment of practical science by discussing rhetoric and politics.[47] But the actual division of the text is not congruent with the principles of *divisio scientiae* as set forth in the prologue. Book 2, on ethics, offers no technical exposition of logic as a science: the only justification for invoking the category of logic here is that the practical and logical sciences "ensegne a home çou k'il doit faire et quex non, et la raison pour quoi on doit les une faire et les autres laissier" ("teach man what he should and should not do, and the reason for which he ought to do certain things and avoid others").[48]

It soon becomes apparent that Brunetto's *divisio textus* corresponds to a much more simple *divisio scientiae*, a twofold division of *theoretica* and *practica*, a version of the Aristotelian scheme which was current in the earlier Middle Ages.[49] Brunetto's *divisio textus* articulates this scheme quite clearly:

book 1 treats the theoretical sciences, and books 2 and 3 represent traditional subdivisions of *practica*, ethics and politics. Brunetto's own construction of *practica* corresponds to this: the practical sciences are ethics, economics, and politics, and politics in turn is divided into the mechanical sciences and the *artes sermocinales*, grammar, dialectic, and rhetoric.[50] In his introductory remarks on the relationship between politics and the *artes sermocinales*, Brunetto gives fairly short notice to grammar and dialectic (one sentence apiece), but devotes relatively greater space to a discussion of rhetoric, its relationship to politics and to human and divine law. Rhetoric, "cele noble science," facilitates healthy political activity among humans. It is significant that Brunetto devotes so much attention to rhetoric in the context of ethics and politics, for it is this set of relations that constitutes the real *materia* of books 2 and 3 of the *Trésor*. In these prefatory remarks he establishes the connection between the *materia libri* and the *ordinatio partium* or *divisio textus*. Book 1 deals with the matter of *theoretica*, book 2 treats of *practica* by considering ethics, and book 3 extends the treatment of *practica* to politics, with a long introductory section on rhetoric.

The structure or *forma tractatus* of book 3 of the *Trésor* is very important here. The treatment of rhetoric occupies nearly seventy per cent of book 3, because rhetoric is not simply an art of speech: Brunetto elevates it from a subdivision of *civilis racio* to the premiere science of politics:

Et Tuilles dist que la plus haute science de cité governer si est rectorique, c'est a dire la science du parler; car se parleure ne fust cités ne seroit, ne nus establissemens de justice ne de humaine compaignie.[51]

(And Tully says that the highest science of civic government is rhetoric, that is, the art of speaking; for if there were no speech there would be no cities, nor any establishment of justice or of human communities.]

The *divisio textus* of the *Trésor* elevates rhetoric, along with politics, virtually to the status of an epistemological category, making rhetoric and politics together almost a division of knowledge, rather than subordinate elements of one of those divisions. In other words, the scheme of knowledge or scheme of the sciences that emerges from Brunetto's *divisio textus* is this: *theoretica*, *practica*, *rhetorica-politica*. This is never formally articulated as a *divisio scientiae*, but it is implicit in the structure of the work, which expresses – more forcefully than any formal statement of the classification of knowledge – Brunetto's overriding concern with political thought. For Brunetto, all the sciences pertain to and hinge on politics.[52]

From this it is clear how Gower arrived at his epistemological scheme of "Theorique," "Rethorique," and "Practique." Like Brunetto's *Trésor*, Gower's *Confessio amantis* is overwhelmingly a political text, tracing a thematic move from the "singular profit" of *fin'amor* to the "common profit" of political *caritas*.[53] The concerns of book 7 announce this thematic shift. Book 7 is largely indebted to Brunetto's *Trésor* for material and structure; and in the implicit *divisio scientiae* contained in Brunetto's *divisio textus*, Gower found a congenial model for a scheme of knowledge. It is as if he looked at the *divisio textus* of the *Trésor* and saw a tripartite division into theoretical sciences, practical sciences, and rhetorical-political sciences, and transposed this implicit scheme into his own system: *theoretica* (theology and natural history), *rhetorica*, and *practica* (political ethics and governance). Under *practica* he condenses and combines the matter that Brunetto treats in book 2 and the second part of book 3 of the *Trésor*. For Gower as a reader and redactor of Brunetto's *compilatio*, the *divisio textus* of the *Trésor* assumes the force of an epistemological system.

In Gower's treatment of rhetoric we see the influence of Brunetto's particularly political vision of the sciences. For Gower, rhetoric is defined in almost entirely political terms. His short treatment of rhetoric (7.1507–1640) is chiefly a distillation of Brunetto's treatment of rhetoric as a civil science.[54] Gower's Latin heading to the section on rhetoric locates eloquence firmly in the sphere of practical wisdom:

> Compositi pulcra sermonis verba placere
> Principio poterunt, veraque fine placent.
> Herba, lapis, sermo, tria sunt virtute repleta,
> Vis tamen ex verbi pondere plura facit.[55]

[Beautiful words will please at the start of an orderly speech; at the end, it is true words that please. Herb, stone, word: these three things are imbued with strength; but the greatest strength, however, comes from the weighty word.]

Along these lines, Gower gives a near-Ciceronian account of the place of rhetoric among the arts, representing it as the queen of the arts of the medieval trivium, served by grammar and logic:

> Whereof touchende this partie,
> Is Rethorique the science
> Appropred to the reverence
> Of wordes that ben resonable:
> And for this art schal be vailable
> With goodli words forto like
> It hath Gramaire, it hath Logiqe,
> That serven bothe unto the speche. (7.1522–9)

Gower's use of the *Trésor* suggests the force and importance of *divisio* as a technical apparatus derived from exegetical practice. Brunetto's *divisio* of his book becomes Gower's *divisio* of knowledge in book 7 of *Confessio amantis*. But Gower's *divisio* of knowledge – his epistemological system – serves, in turn, as the guiding principle of the structural *divisio* of book 7. This book works as a comprehensive account of the disciplines, an ordered arrangement and explanation of available knowledge. In his book, Gower is also a compiler, both of previous compilations, that is, Brunetto's *Trésor*, Vincent of Beauvais' *Speculum maius*, Giles of Rome's *De regimine principum*, and the *Secretum secretorum*, and of many other literary and historical sources from which he derives the exempla used to illustrate the principles of governance and political ethics under the discussion of *practica*.

But book 7, as a *divisio* of knowledge and as an example of *divisio textus*, also serves a metacritical purpose. It is a hermeneutical key to the *divisio textus* of the entire *Confessio amantis*. Book 7 is an index to reading *Confessio amantis*. The poem is about wisdom and ethics, and book 7, as a *divisio* of knowledge with special reference to the place of ethics in that system, is a guide to the structure of *Confessio amantis* as a whole, which is also divided according to the principal parts of ethics. While Genius serves as the author's exegetical voice, book 7 serves as an interpretive model for the structure of the whole poem. In this way the poem contains its own hermeneutical key: it implants within itself a guide to its own structural system.

Books 1–6 and book 8 represent the divisions of sin according to its parts. Book 7 provides a broader perspective on the *divisiones* of sin in the other seven books: it takes the problem of sin beyond the sphere of private morality, the one-on-one relationship between Amans and his Confessor, and locates it in the larger domain of public ethics, the education of Alexander, a mirror for princes.[56] In this way book 7 refers the narrative elements of the rest of the poem (books 1–6 and 8) back to the first prologue, with its discourse on wisdom, its critique of the three social estates, and its exposition of human history (Nebuchadnezzar's dream). Similarly, book 7 projects forward thematically to the epiloque, which recapitulates the social critique of the prologue and urges the turn from singular to common profit. Together, the prologue, book 7, and the epilogue form a tripartite structure that integrates the various concerns of the poem under an ultimate concern of public and political morality. Book 7 also forms part of another tripartite structure, a theoretical analysis of the three estates: book 4, on Sloth, contains an exposition of the origins and nature of labor (4.2363–700); book 5, on Avarice, offers advice to the clergy, in the form of a history of religion (5.729–1970); and book 7 takes up the problem of rulership, with its long examination of the virtues of polity.[57] These integrating structures become visible through the agency of book 7, with its explicit application of ethics or virtue to the divisions of knowledge and the nature of polity.

As both *divisio scientiae* and *divisio textus*, book 7 serves also as an interpretive guide to the principles of translation and selection of inherited materials throughout the poem. As a *divisio* of the principal parts of wisdom and ethics, it provides an interpretive structure that can explain Gower's use of *abbreviatio* or *amplificatio* on his sources. The individual books of *Confessio amantis* already represent the *divisiones* of private morality according to the confessional structure of the Seven Deadly Sins, and the tales within these books are obviously selected and revised to fit their immediate setting: for example, Ovid's tale of Acteon and Diana is considerably condensed and modified to conform to the scheme of pride in book 1; and the tale of Dido and Aeneas in book 4 takes its point of departure from *Heroides* 7, but reduces Ovid's text to bring the tale under the specific aegis of the sin of sloth or reticence in love. But book 7 explains the larger context in which Gower reinvents his *materia* by articulating the relationship of the parts of the work to the *intentio* and *utilitas* of the whole work. The value of the individual tales as *exempla* of private sin is explained by their function within the general framework of an analysis of public virtue.[58] Giles of Rome, setting out the *modus agendi* of his *De regimine principum*, argues that any analysis of ethics must proceed by means of particular, concrete examples, since ethics, as a practical science, works through individual circumstances rather than universals:

in toto morali negotio modus procedendi secundum Philosophum est figuralis et grossus: oportet enim in talibus typo et figuraliter pertransire, quia gesta moralia complete sub narratione non cadunt . . . Quia ergo sic est, ipsa acta singularia, quae sunt materia huius operis, ostendunt incedendum esse figuraliter et typo.[59]

(According to the Philosopher, the mode of procedure in every moral question is through concrete images; it is thus necessary to penetrate such questions by the use of image and figurative representation, because the subject of moral action is not completely suitable to abstract exposition . . . Thus because this is so, particular actions, which are themselves the matter of this work, show what has to happen through the use of figure and type.]

This also illuminates Gower's *modus agendi* as translator: the narrative materials inherited from classical authority become the inventional *topoi* for *gesta moralia*, and achieve profound difference from their sources precisely through their new illustrative function within a *divisio* of ethics that leads from private to public virtue. It is the device of *divisio*, borrowed from exegetical tradition, that enables book 7 to bring the whole structure of *Confessio amantis* into focus and thus to contextualize the rhetorical principles of *inventio*, *abbreviatio*, and *amplificatio* that inform Gower's renderings of his narrative sources. It is because his vernacular versions find their place within this new system of *divisio* that they can achieve such difference with their sources. The system of *divisio* enables these vernacular tales to assume a discursive authority independent of their sources.

But the question of *divisio* goes beyond that of hermeneutical procedure (*divisio textus*) and of epistemological system (*divisio scientiae*). These models of *divisio* in *Confessio amantis* emerge in the context of another kind of division: the *divisioun* of the state, of history, of society, and of language. *Divisioun*, or discord and fragmentation, is the major theme (as well as verbal motif) of the extrinsic prologue, with its critique of the three estates and exposition of human history through Nebuchadnezzar's dream. Indeed, the exposition of historical decline is presented as a kind of iconographic *divisio* of *divisioun*: each segment of the statue, from head to foot, from gold to silver to brass to steel and clay, represents a discreet stage of history:

Bot in this wise a man mai lere
Hou that the world is gon aboute,
The which welnyh is wered oute,
After the forme of that figure

Which Daniel in his scripture
Expondeth, as tofore is told.
Of Bras, of Selver, and of Gold
The world is passed and agon,
And now upon his olde ton
It stant of brutel Erthe and Stiel,
The whiche acorden nevere a diel;
So mot it nedes swerve aside
As thing the which men sen divide . . .
    So may we knowe,
This ymage is nyh overthrowe,
Be which this world was signified . . .
And stant divided ek also
Lich to the feet that were so,
As I tolde of the Statue above.
And this men sen, thurgh lacke of love
Where as the lond divided is,
It mot algate fare amis:
And now to loke on every side,
A man may se the world divide . . . (Pr. 868–96)

The analysis of historical *divisioun* forms, in its turn, an introduction to an exposition of the present state of cosmic and spiritual *divisioun* or disorder, of which man is the cause for his violations of divine order and charity (lines 905–1088).[60]

It is significant that one of Gower's emblems for social fragmentation or *divisioun* is the myth of Babel:

And over that thurgh Senne it com
That Nembrot such emprise nom
Whan he the Tour Babel on heihte
Let make, as he that wolde feihte
Ayein the hihe goddes myht,
Whereof divided anon ryht
Was the langage in such entente,
Ther wiste non what other mente,
So that thei myhten noght procede.
And thus it stant of every dede,
Wher Senne takth the cause on honde,
It may upriht noght longe stonde;
For Senne of his condicioun
Is moder of divisioun
And tokne whan the world schal faile. (Pr. 1017–30)

The myth of Babel is a medieval commonplace for the diversity of human languages. Gower uses it in the context of *divisioun* to signify the disorder and confusion that results from sin (compare, for example, Dante's use of Babel in *De vulgari eloquentia*, 1.7.4–8). But there is another context for this emblem of the multiplicity of languages, one which is suggested in Gower's words "divided . . . was the langage." In the Vulgate, the multiplication of languages as punishment for the tower is described as a "confusion": "confundamus ibi linguam eorum," and "ibi confusum est labium universae terrae"; "division" is only applied to the peoples of the earth, "divisit eos Dominus ex illo loco in universas terras" (Gen. 11.7–9).[61] But in medieval exegesis, the distinction between the "confusion" of languages and the "division" of people was not always preserved. In particular, thirteenth-century exegetes began to speak of a *divisio linguarum*, thus conflating the idea of division with that of confusion. *Divisio linguarum* thus suggested the confused fragmentation of human speech through the presumption of Nimrod. But in thirteenth-century scholastic contexts, *divisio linguarum* also came to connote the classification of different human languages into discrete divisions.[62] Under the force of scholastic systems of *divisio scientiae*, the notion of *divisio linguarum* became associated with the academic activity of classification itself; the myth of Babel became a "conceptual tool for classifying languages and analyzing the relationships between them."[63] We see Dante using the myth of Babel in this way, as a heuristic device for his extended classification of languages in *De vulgari eloquentia*. Arno Borst has detailed the value of the Babel myth in the thirteenth and fourteenth centuries for inventories and taxonomies of languages, both ancient tongues and contemporary vernaculars.[64]

Gower's use of the term "divided" ("whereof divided anon ryht / Was the langage in such entente") shows the influence of the scholastic preference for the notion of a *divisio linguarum* over that of a *confusio linguarum* as the outcome of the building of the tower of Babel. To understand the origin of linguistic multiplicity as the origin of *divisio* rather than simply of a disordered *confusio* enabled scholastic exegetes to accommodate that sacred myth within the terms of their own classificatory and world-ordering instincts. For Gower, the Babel myth of linguistic fragmentation is similarly a heuristic device within his own complex ordering or *divisio* of sin and its remedies, ethics and wisdom. Indeed, the function of *divisio* as theme and as technical device in *Confessio amantis* is equivocal. The first prologue, for example, orders itself and its relationship to the book as a whole according to the principle of *divisio textus*:

For this prologue is so assised
That it to wisdom al belongeth:
What wysman that it underfongeth,
he schal draw into remembrance
The fortune of this worldes chance,
The which noman in his persone
Mai knowe, bot the god al one.
Whan the prologue is so despended,
This bok schal afterward ben ended
Of love, which doth many a wonder
And many a wys man hath put under.
And in this wyse I thenke trete
Towardes hem that now be grete,

Betwen the vertu and the vice
Which longeth unto this office. (Pr. 66–80)

Here the prologue defines its own role within a *divisio textus*. First, it is arranged ("assised") in such a manner that all of it pertains to wisdom (as if to answer the question "qui parte philosophiae supponitur?") Then it prescribes the manner in which it should be read as a prologue and establishes the boundaries between itself as a prologue and the "book" proper, which is about love. Finally the prologue sums up the various parts of the work under a general statement of *intentio* ("And in this wyse I thenke trete"). But this orderly example as well as pronouncement of *divisio textus* is also the introduction to a long exposition of *divisioun* or disorder. The concept of *divisio* is itself divided: when it constitutes a principle of textual and epistemological order it is a good thing; when it signifies the *divisioun* of society, of history, and of language, it is deplorable. In this latter meaning, *divisio* is equivalent to the biblical notion, in the story of Babel, of the *confusio linguarum* that resulted from human sin. Yet that *divisioun* or disorder can also be expounded in an orderly fashion, according to the terms of *divisio textus*, as we see in the first prologue as a whole.

This "division" of *divisio* brings us to the ideological questions which *Confessio amantis* poses, questions about its own vernacular status in relation to the tradition of academic discourse. The myth of Babel in Gower's prologue is an emblem of the *divisioun* or fragmentation of languages. As such it must also and inevitably call attention to the fact of vernacularity. As a symbol of the historical division of languages, the myth of Babel makes the vernacular visible as a cultural and historical reality. As we have noted, the Babel myth served this purpose for medieval scientific inventories of linguistic changes and differences. But in Gower's prologue, the Babel myth assumes a particular emblematic value for Gower's own text: in calling attention to the division of languages and thus, by association, to the cultural fact of vernacularity, the Babel myth implicates Gower's own *Confessio amantis* in this *divisioun* of languages. It refers us back to the opening of the prologue, where Gower announces the making of his own vernacular product:

And for that fewe men endite
In oure englissh, I thenke make
A bok for Engelondes sake. (Pr. 22–4)

This theme of a vernacular product is echoed in the epilogue:

And now to speke as in final,
Touchende that y undirtok
In englesch forto make a book
Which stant betwene ernest and game,
I have it maad as thilke same
Which axe forto ben excusid,
And that my bok be nought refusid
Of lered men, whan thei it se,
For lak of curiosite. (8.3106–14)

Here in the epilogue, the *apologia* for the book before "lered men" is conventional; but given that the humility *topos* is invoked here in the immediate context of a declaration of the "Englishness" of the book, this *apologia* also bears the faint traces of earlier medieval protestations of the inadequacy of the vernacular within the domain of learned culture.

By underscoring such references to the "Englishness" of the text, the Babel myth helps to make the vernacular status of *Confessio amantis* not only visible, but one of the salient properties of the text. Like *Legend of Good Women*, *Confessio amantis* calls attention to its own vernacular status as one way of expressing its rhetorical difference from its sources. But *Confessio amantis* exploits the issue of vernacularity in much more complex ways. Here, the emblem of linguistic difference is the story of Babel, which signifies not just linguistic heterogeneity, but the fragmentation of languages which, like the *divisioun* of society and history, results from human sin. Babel mirrors on the vast scale of sacred history the contemporary fact of linguistic difference between Latin, with its mythic claim to grammatical stability and unity, and the vernaculars, which in their very natures represent mutability and division. Of course, all human speech, including Latin, is implicated in the Babel myth; but Gower's text acknowledges the fragmentation of Babel from within the perspective of a more immediate sense of fragmentation, that of vernacular writing as different from Latinity. Gower's book, which announces its own vernacularity, devolves from that latter-day *confusio linguarum* that academic culture seeks to contain and order. The book is a product, in a sense, of two linguistic divisions: the sinful division that originally fragmented all languages; and a latter-day, secondary division, the difference between Latin, whose ideological project is to contain disorder as far as possible within a fallen world, and vernacular speech, which is the living witness to the breakdown of cultural unity since the fall of the Roman *imperium*. If the myth of Babel implicates *Confessio amantis* itself as vernacular writing, then in this context Gower's vernacular book is a product of that sinful *divisioun*, a text whose own vernacularity is a sign of the condition of sin that produced linguistic *divisioun* or difference. *Confessio amantis* not only speaks about *divisioun*, but as a vernacular text, speaks through and from the most visible sign of that historical condition of *divisioun*. In this way the myth of Babel is not just an emblem for linguistic difference, but also for Gower's present enterprise of vernacular *translatio studii*.

It is thus from within the *divisioun* of language and of history that *Confessio amantis* sets forth its critique of *divisioun*, of the social, political, and moral disorder that results from human sin. The very site of Gower's critique is a vernacular text, and thus a living, material sign of cultural and historical disjunction. Indeed, this disjunction is witnessed in Gower's text through the palpable difference between the language of the poem and that of the scholastic apparatus that Gower provides to explain the poem. Even the first Latin heading of the poem announces the "Englishness" of the text, so that at the very outset the force of the vernacular is registered through its non-identity with Latin: "Qua tamen Engisti lingua canit Insula Bruti / Anglica Carmente metra iuuante loquar" (Yet in the tongue of Hengist in which the island of Brutus sings, I will set forth English metres with the help of Carmentis).[65] The visual difference between the vernacular poetry and the Latin headings which point up the academic affiliations of the poem expresses a kind of tension within the work, as the Latin apparatus can be seen as a mechanism for controlling the potential subversiveness of the poetic fiction.[66] But at another level, this visible tension between Latinity and vernacularity within the text also brings to the foreground the very condition of fragmentation within which all human language, after the fall of Babel, must operate. In Gower's poem, the vernacular is an insistent reminder of the limits of the power of Latinity to contain difference through an idealized linguistic order transcending time and place.

As a linguistically heterogeneous text, *Confessio amantis* acknowledges the reality of fragmentation represented by the vernacular, and thereby defines its own function: to call into memory that wisdom of the ancients that can be too easily lost through historical and cultural rupture:

> What schal befalle hierafterward
> God wot, for now upon this tyde
> Man se the world on every syde
> In sondry wyse so diversed
> That it welnyh stant al reversed,
> As forto speke of tyme ago . . .
> And natheles be daies olde,
> Whan that the bokes weren levere,
> Wrytinge was beloved evere
> Of hem that weren vertuous;
> For hier in erthe amonges ous,
> If noman write hou that it stode,
> The pris of hem that weren goode
> Scholde, as who seith, a gret partie
> Be lost . . .
> Thus I, which am a burel clerk,
> Purpose forto wryte a bok
> After the world that whilom tok
> Long tyme in olde daies passed:
> Bot for men sein it is now lassed,
> In worse plit than it was tho,
> I thenke forto touche also
> The world which neweth every dai,
> So as I can, so as I may. (Pr. 26–60)

This statement of *intentio* locates the present enterprise within that state of progressive rupture ("in sondry wyse so diversed . . . In worse plit than it was tho"). At the same time it insists on the contemporary rewriting of ancient books as the surest key to social and ethical rehabilitation and thus to some reintegration with "hem that weren vertuous." In this image of historical and cultural recuperation lies one of the most powerful contradictions of Gower's vernacular project. The idea of conserving the past as a bulwark against the mutability of the present ("the world which neweth every dai") invokes the very ideological assumptions of medieval academic culture: to preserve a lineal continuity with the *antiqui*, a myth of continuity which is most forcefully expressed in the linguistic practice of *Latinitas*. But even as Gower's text invokes this ideal of continuity and undertakes the project of cultural recuperation, it embodies the very process of rupture and mutability that it decries: its own vernacularity is an image of the outcome of Babel, of the very rupture of memory and of history that the text proposes to heal.

How then does this vernacular text, speaking through the condition of *divisioun*, propose to critique and heal that *divisioun*? It turns, for its model of critique, to the other kind of "division": the exegetical model of order and integration, *divisio textus*. It achieves its critique by exploiting the equivocal value of *divisio*: through *divisio textus*, which illuminates truth through ordered analysis, it offers a remedy for *divisioun*, social and moral disorder. The structure of the poem suggests that the *divisioun* or disorder of human sin can be somehow rectified through the ordering apparatus of *divisio textus*. In the same way that scholastic exegesis could substitute the notion of *divisio linguarum* for that of *confusio linguarum*, and thus discover a principle of order in what began as a state of disorder, so Gower proposes to rectify the *divisioun* of history through the tool of scholastic academic discourse, *divisio*. The purpose of this book in English, midway between earnest and game, is to lead to an understanding of the principles of ethics. The purpose is served precisely by the hermeneutical structure of *divisio* and *ordinatio*: the whole text divided according to the confessional scheme of the Seven Deadly Sins, representing personal governance, and the interpretive key of book 7, ordered according to the system of *divisio scientiae*, representing the application of epistemological systems to the teaching of ethics.[67] Gower's text thus uses the academic system of *divisio* to achieve its directive of ethical rehabilitation. But the use of the system of *divisio* in this way also turns the textual activity of *divisio* into a form of ethical action. By using the principles of *divisio* to expound the parts of sin and its remedies and to situate these parts within a governing analytical scheme of wisdom, *Confessio amantis* proposes to lead its readers, along with Amans, from singular to common profit, and from a discourse of self-governance to a discourse of public morality. As a means of achieving these ethical objectives, the hermeneutical tool of *divisio* becomes a kind of action upon the inherited materials that form the text: it delineates the various components of ethical teaching and makes those components accessible and understandable as parts of a large system of practical wisdom.

For Gower to turn the hermeneutical apparatus of *divisio* into a form of ethical action vastly increases the stakes in the opposition between the vernacular and Latin academic culture. It augments the value of the vernacular as the site of difference in translation. Gower's central concern is the question of difference, not just as a textual and linguistic phenomenon, but as a historical, political, and moral force. This pervasive thematic concern brings together the discursive and ideological questions of difference that emerge throughout the tradition of vernacular translation. Gower uses academic discourse for the explicit task of political rehabilitation, and it is of necessity a *vernacular* academic discourse that he deploys for this purpose. He takes over the hermeneutical techniques of *compilatio*, and constructs an exegetical voice for the text in the figure of Genius, and in making this exegetical apparatus refer to his own text he establishes his own claims, in this vernacular context, to the powerful role of *auctor*. In this role he also becomes the guardian of memory, for he controls the tools of cultural conservation, that is, academic discourse. But he redefines that privileged discourse of conservation by using it in an openly political way: to assess and critique the reality of rupture and disorder that academic culture, by its very nature, refuses to acknowledge.

By using *divisio* – in both its textual and epistemological applications – as the key mechanisms of this critique, *Confessio amantis* uses a discourse of order, a discourse that seeks to impose unity and coherence upon texts and upon the world, to acknowledge a discontinuity and fragmentation of textual and historical culture signified by vernacularity itself. It is thus the vernacular that puts academic discourse into social practice as a vehicle of moral and political rehabilitation. The vernacular cannot suppress or conceal the inevitability of historical difference under a myth of linguistic and cultural continuity. Vernacular translation, and through this vernacular academic discourse, exposes and enacts that process of difference at many levels: the displacement of sources through exegetical reworking; the use of an exegetical apparatus as a tool of rhetorical invention, which gives prominence to textual difference; auto-exegesis, which also manifests the appropriation of authoritative sources; and vernacularity itself as a sign of difference from Latin culture. But *Confessio amantis* uses all these enactments of difference to reconceive the function of academic discourse: to work for the common profit from within the site of that communal enterprise, vernacular culture. *Confessio amantis* uses its own status as a vernacular text to acknowledge rupture, and by locating academic discourse in the vernacular it must also acknowledge the impossibility of the myth of unity and coherence that that discourse traditionally sustains. It uses academic discourse, not to evade the problem of difference, but to engage that problem. Vernacular culture becomes the site for an ethical application of academic discourse, ethical because the vernacular makes it a discourse of inclusion rather than of privileged exclusion. Throughout this study we have seen how academic discourse defines the status of vernacularity; here in *Confessio amantis*, we see how the vernacular can redefine the status and function of academic discourse. Gower makes the project of vernacular translation – and vernacular *translatio studii* – the vehicle of this ethical revaluation of academic culture.

In this way *Confessio amantis* recalls Dante's project in the *Convivio*: to open the institution of learning to the widest possible audience and thereby empower it as a persuasive tool, leading to knowledge of the good. It is also along the lines of Dante's *Convivio* that we may understand Gower's framing of his ethical instruction within the conventions of romance or love poetry: the realm of Venus is the stronghold of rhetoric, for eloquence achieves its persuasive aims through delight, which teaches and moves even as it charms. Moreover, like the *Convivio*, *Confessio amantis* shows us a rhetoric rehabilitated as hermeneutical performance. It represents the office of persuasion in terms of leading its readers to the apprehension of the good, and in the "conversion" of Amans the text offers a paradigm of its persuasive success. But it undertakes and accomplishes this persuasive end through the techniques of hermeneutics. Genius as exegete performs the office of rhetorical persuasion, leading his charge "to reule with [his] conscience" (1.248) by providing good readings of exemplary texts. Indeed, in the figure of Genius we see the synthesis of rhetoric and hermeneutics that Augustine's precepts established for Christian oratory. More generally, *Confessio amantis* uses the hermeneutical technique of *divisio textus* to transform traditional materials into a sustained ethical argument. It is in this that we see how rhetoric can be elevated to such importance in the scheme of the sciences in book 7, where it represents a whole category or division of knowledge. For Gower, it seems, all forms of knowledge are tools of ethics or practical wisdom; the various divisions of knowledge, along with their subdivisions into various arts and specific fields, are classifiable according to the way that they pertain to or lead to ethics. If, as Gower says (7.1545–9), there is more power in human language than in all other earthly things, that power must be harnessed for its greatest usefulness; and rhetoric, as public eloquence, is the instrument that can best direct this verbal power to serve an ethical cause. As the instrument of ethical communication, rhetoric represents the science of language and becomes, in turn, one of the primary divisions of knowledge. But in the text of *Confessio amantis*, this is a rhetoric that operates within a structure established and defined by the ordering system of hermeneutics, the ethical application of *divisio*.

Afterword

Gower's critique of academic discourse would not be possible without the tradition of vernacular translation which emerges from the interpretive practice of the medieval schools. We have seen how translation redirects and assimilates those practices into a vernacular hermeneutics. The tradition that I have examined here, translation of *auctores* from the arts curriculum, articulates some of the most important critical structures that govern the relationship between Latin and vernacular in the Middle Ages. Constructing such a history of translation invites us to study medieval critical practices themselves more critically, to analyze criticism the way we have come to interrogate literary texts, making visible the competing forces of signification within seemingly unified theoretical systems. Thus we see that when rhetoric in antiquity most boldly proclaims its difference from grammar is when it is most grammatical in its orientation; and when medieval exegesis professes its subservient and supplementary relation to master texts is when it most threatens to overtake and displace those texts.

A critical reading of the history of criticism yields more, however, than the intellectual satisfaction of showing how theoretical systems subverted their own claims to coherence. It also helps us to discern what was ideologically at stake in academic representations of textual culture. Latin exegesis of the *auctores* must profess its own supplementarity (and the exegetes must believe this) because the *raison d'être* of Latin clerical culture is to function as a sign of continuity between the pagan and the Christian intellectual *imperia*: in the interests of such continuity, medieval criticism cannot propose to outdo and supplant the revered *auctores*. Medieval criticism represents its relationship to the past in metonymic terms, and the whole system of textual interpretation is organized to sustain this representation along with belief in its validity.

Medieval translation is part of the larger history of critical theory and interpretive practice. Seen from this perspective, the picture of medieval translation is enormously complex, so much so that it almost defies summary here. But from the vantage point of a conclusion, we can indicate the most important lines of argument along which this study has developed. We began with Roman antiquity, where translation was a vehicle of the conflict between the disciplines of rhetoric and grammar, and of the cultural contest between Rome and Greece. Defined through the aims of rhetoric, translation was an aggressive project through which Roman literary culture could both assimilate and displace the textual tradition of Greece. In the Middle Ages, translation was also a product of the tension between rhetoric and the grammarian's art of exegesis. Moreover, in the Middle Ages, as in Roman antiquity, translation was a vehicle for expressing or playing out large questions of cultural difference.

These similarities, however, are deceptive. In fact, the role of translation in ancient Rome is comparatively easy to define when we consider the heterogeneity and theoretical complexity of the medieval tradition. In the first place, medieval translation theory often borrows the critical formulations of Cicero and Horace about translating "sense-for-sense"; but those commonplaces have been mediated through Jerome's system, which reverses Cicero's priorities and makes translation according to "sense" an ideal of access and conservation rather than a model of rhetorical displacement. Thus the appearance of those commonplaces in medieval translations does not mean that they carry the same value that they did in antiquity. Second, while medieval vernacular translation is motivated by the aim of displacement, that motive is often obscured, because so much vernacular translation was produced within the economy of exegesis, and represented itself as a form of exegetical service to an authoritative text. This brings us to the crucial difference between classical and medieval models of translation. In ancient Rome the dominant critical discourse was rhetoric, and the ideal of translation carried an explicit agenda of rivalry with the source through the force of rhetorical invention. But in the Middle Ages, the dominant discourse has become hermeneutics, which – in the absence of a strong rhetorical practice – has assumed the rhetorical function of a productive application to discourse. It is also hermeneutics that gives rhetoric new life, that restores the power of rhetoric by redefining *inventio* as hermeneutical inquiry, as the discovery of the meaning of inherited textual matter. Rhetorical production represents the elucidation of that discovered meaning. The tradition of vernacular translation that emerges from academic hermeneutical practice achieves the same effects that Cicero's ideal of translation proposed, but it achieves these aims under a very different aegis, a strong exegetical directive.

This big picture of disciplinary relationships can provide some new answers about old problems in translation theory. No discussion of the Western tradition of translation can avoid the commonplace polarity of "literal" versus "loose" translation, one of the legacies of ancient criticism. This polarity may be expressed along the lines of translating word-for-word as opposed to sense-for-sense, or even as the difference between "slavish translation" (as in Horace's *fidus interpres*) and "re-creation." While it is not entirely possible (or even useful) to break the habitual hold that this model has on our conception of translation, I have tried to specify its value in different historical contexts. It does not have an absolute, trans-historical meaning. In antiquity, the difference between literal and loose translation really signifies a difference between grammar and rhetoric, between grammatical exegesis, which glosses word for word, and rhetorical invention, which is concerned with producing new arguments. In this context literal translation is the debased form of the practice, because it is associated with the restricted competence of grammatical teaching (here we should recall what Cicero says, that he translated, not as an *interpres*, or glossator, but as an *orator*). But in medieval vernacular practice, "loose" or sense-for-sense translation is achieved precisely through the force of exegesis, and we see this in both primary and secondary translation. Indeed, primary translation, which identifies itself with exegetical claims of service to the source, can be just as "loose" or "re-creative" as anything that Cicero could have desired in a rhetorical translation. And, as we have seen, secondary translation achieves difference with the source by exploiting the inventional or productive powers of exegesis.

In defining the trajectory of vernacular translation through academic culture, I have not tried to give an internal history of translation. My purpose has been to locate translation within other discursive fields. If the tradition of translation that I have considered here can be understood through its historical placement in the academic systems of rhetoric and hermeneutics, it also carries the ideological import of those systems, and it transfers their ideological tensions to another plane, the confrontation between Latinity and vernacularity. Here translation is a lens through which we can see the relationship between vernacular and academic cultures. But translation is not only a lens: it is also an active force, because it redefines the character of academic discourse. Academic exegesis of the *artes* authors carries a guarantee of historical and cultural continuity between the ancients and the moderns, a guarantee expressed in two ways: at the level of the language, as the medieval exposition participates in the conservation of *Latinitas*; and at the level of exegetical practice itself, which claims subservience to the primary authority of the curricular text. The vernacular translation that develops out of exegesis calls these guarantees into question, also at the levels of language and of practice. It introduces interlingual transfer, thereby opening the project of *translatio studii* to linguistic diversity and exposing the unifying claims of *Latinitas* as a myth serving the interests of cultural privilege. By introducing linguistic disjunction translation undermines a more fundamental claim of exegetical practice, its construction as self-effacing service to an authoritative text. Within exegesis, there was always an effect of displacement, even if that effect was innocently perceived as mere supplementation. But vernacular translation makes difference so visible that it cannot sustain the illusion of exegetical supplementation: it foregrounds the real nature of exegetical practice, which is to appropriate the text and sometimes to eclipse it. In reproducing the strategies of exegesis, the vernacular also reproduces the very system of exegesis. Vernacular writing thus lays claim to the official discourses of academic culture. This is the most profound effect of translation as displacement: the transference of intellectual methodology from Latin to vernacular.

While vernacular translation works to expose the ideological contradictions of Latin academic discourse, it is not without its own internal contradictions. For example, Notker's anxiety about using the vernacular to present the *auctores* shows him to be complicit with the ideological system of *Latinitas* even as his writings undermine the assumptions of the system. At the other end of the spectrum, we see how Gower's *Confessio amantis* proposes something like a resolution to the internal contradictions of translation by using academic discourse as a tool of social and ideological critique. All the texts considered in this study pose the same question: to what extent can vernacular translation provide access to academic culture? Each text poses – and answers – the question in its own way, denying us the comfort of ready generalizations. I would like, however, to offer some further reflections on this question.

In surveying the work of English translators in the late Middle Ages, Richard Firth Green notes that a major force behind the enormous industry of translation, especially of didactic texts, from the late fourteenth through the fifteenth century is aristocratic interest and patronage. The broad historical pattern of legitimizing vernacular writings through translation of moral, didactic, and sometimes classical texts is not be be attributed to the "social pretensions of a new, middle-class reading public," but rather to the mutual interests of aristocratic readers and the writers who sought the continued support of these powerful and wealthy patrons.[1] This is a sobering insight to bring to Gower's ideological critique of the exclusiveness of academic discourse. As a mirror of princes, the *Confessio amantis* can be seen as part of this pattern of transferring learning from academy to court. While, as I have argued, Gower uses the vernacularity of his *Confessio amantis* to acknowledge temporal and linguistic difference, proposing to heal social *divisioun* by speaking from the very site of cultural difference, we should not forget that the vernacular audience addressed in the mirror of princes is little more socially inclusive than the projected clerkly readership of an academic text. On the one hand Gower exploits the vernacular as a witness of loss and fragmentation, implicating all of his readers in the process of historical division, and urging all readers to an understanding of ethics. But on the other hand, who are "all" his readers? In a sense then, it is possible to see Gower as simply substituting the privileged stratum of the aristocracy for that of clerks. Under the historical conditions of audience and patronage, the transference of academic discourse from Latin to vernacular does not necessarily imply a broad participation in learned culture: learning can also be appropriated as a status symbol by a lay aristocracy, used to signify the strength of secular political power.

Viewed from this perspective, *Confessio amantis* offers a cautionary message: we should not always equate appropriation with access. Vernacular translation may appropriate the discourse of academic culture and in so doing may enable a valid critique of the insularity of that culture, as in the case of *Confessio amantis*. But the vernacular appropriation of a certain cultural privilege is not necessarily a dismantling of that privilege: in many respects it is only a transfer (literally a "translation") of cultural authority from one sphere to another. To what extent *can* vernacular translation actually open academic discourse to non-hierarchical use? I wish to consider some of the implications of this question for the present study, and in this way to suggest some possibilities for future exploration.

First, it is worth noting that when translation is theorized strictly as access to a textual legacy, it is not theorized as appropriation. Indeed, the two aims are incompatible with each other. The Prologue to the Wycliffite Bible defines translation expressly in terms of a hermeneutics of access. Here accessibility is a property both of the text, which must be "open" or lucid, and of social reception, for the text will be available to all audiences, and translation becomes a socially inclusive gesture:

> First it is to knowe that the beste translating is, out of Latyn into English, to translate aftir the sentence and not oneli aftir the wordis, so that the sentence be as opin either openere in English as in Latyn . . . [L]et the sentence euere be hool and open . . . Therfore Grosted seith that it was Goddis wille that diuerse men translatiden, and that diuerse translacions be in the chirche, for where oon seid e derkli, oon either mo seiden openli. Lord God, sithen at the bigynnyng of feith so manie men translatiden into Latyn and to greet profyt of Latyn men, lat oo symple creature of God translate into English for profyt of English men! For if wordli clerkis loken wel here croniclis and bookis, thei shulden fynde that Bede translatide the Bible and expounide myche in Saxon, that was English either comoun langage of this lond in his tyme . . . Also Frenshe men, Beemers and Britons han the Bible and othere bokis of deuocioun and of exposicioun translatid in here modir langage. Whi shulden not English men haue the same in here modir langage?[2]

In this model there is room for multiple translations, for as many translations as there are languages and people. There is also room for retranslation: "where oon seid e derkli, oon either mo seiden openli." There is no aggressive rivalry implied here: translation is a collective work of correction in order to achieve an open text. The Lollard definition of translation as a hermeneutic of access really traces its descent from the patristic-Hieronymian position, which is counter-rhetorical and which locates meaning in a supra-linguistic reality. According to this principle, the act of translation points beyond itself to an originary authority that cannot be overtaken or displaced. The application of Jerome's teleological principle to vernacular translation of the Bible is as logical as it was historically opportune. Translation as appropriation has no place in this system: the point of translation here is not to resignify (or even to elaborate), but to manifest a truth that lies beyond the accidents of translation, a truth to which there should be a communality of access.

John of Trevisa also articulates a position that is related to the Hieronymian model and that has something in common with the Lollard model. In the "Dialogue between a Lord and a Clerk upon Translation" (*c.* 1387), Trevisa has the Lord recommend multiple translation for the purpose of correcting imperfect versions:

Clerks know well enough that no sinful man doth so well that it ne might do better, ne make so good a translation that he ne might be better. Therefore Origines made two translations, and Jerome translated thrice the Psalter. I desire not translation of these the best that might be, for that were an idle desire for any man that is now alive, but I would have a skilful translation, that might be known and understood.[3]

These remarks are from a preface to Trevisa's translation of Ranulf Higden's *Polychronicon*, and like Trevisa's translation itself, can be identified with the aims of the tradition of learned and philosophical translation from Greek into Latin. This medieval tradition derives its assumptions from Jerome's precepts about translation of non-scriptural texts, and takes a utilitarian view of translation, seeing it as a form of transparent access to a stable and transmissable set of ideas.[4] Corrective retranslation is encouraged because, as Trevisa says, no product of human language is perfect. But translation does not seek to displace the original under what Bruns has called a "sanction of embellishment." Trevisa's formula of "skilful translation, that might be known and understood" is a direct, if distant, descendant of Jerome's counter-rhetorical theory of translation in which a spirit of transgressive appropriation has no place.

But vernacular translation that works under the directive of grammatical exegesis does not propose such transparent access to the text. It is informed, rather, by the same rhetorical principle of appropriation that defines the Ciceronian model of translation, which the Middle Ages recovered through exegetical practice. Moreover, exegetical translations of the classical *auctores* do not necessarily promise open access of official systems of academic discourse in the same way that Lollard principles of translation offer unambiguous access to the tradition of biblical hermeneutics. To what extent does vernacular intervention into the regulated system of *translatio studii* propose to open that system to what Ralph Hanna has called a cultural "polyvalence," in which both texts and the discourses of interpretation "might get used in ways which were foreign to their controlled use in clerical culture"?[5] Let us return, with this question, to some other representative texts.

Notker of St. Gall certainly attempts to provide vernacular access to the curricular texts and to the authorized systems of interpretation that mediate those texts in the schools. But this is not an unqualified access. Notker's audience is the classroom, the students of the monastic school who are being trained as academic readers to carry on the regulatory work of *translatio studii*. Notker introduces vernacular translation and exegesis with some misgivings, as if the vernacular threatens to destabilize the unified and culturally self-contained system of *Latinitas*. But even while his translations do fulfill this threat by taking exegetical possession of the Latin texts, Notker's purpose is to lead his students through this vernacular access back to *Latinitas*. As he says in his letter to the Bishop, it is easier to make sense of the curricular texts in one's native language before tackling them in their proper linguistic form, Latin. In other words, Notker's professed intention is to open the system of reading – the *auctores* and the discursive tools of interpretation – into the vernacular in order to return it to the secure confines of official Latinity. Thus as much as the vernacular displaces its Latin sources, it can also be used in a way that is consistent with the ideology of Latin culture.

We find another kind of ambiguity in Jean de Meun's stance as a translator. In the *Roman de la rose*, Reason declares that the *Consolatio* should be translated for the benefit of lay people. Jean de Meun's own translation certainly fulfills this purpose, even in ways that Jean could not have foreseen: in its reception by later generations, Jean's translation inspired what could almost be called an industry of turning the *Consolatio* and its commentaries into French. Jean's preface to his translation similarly proposes to provide a lucid text for lay readers. But Jean's dedication of the translation to the King of France also specifies at least one intended audience for the work. The *Consolatio* is transferred from university to court, and while the readership of Jean's work is not necessarily limited to royalty, its symbolic function is that of royal possession. Just as the Latin tradition of the *Consolatio* is appropriated by vernacular literary culture, the clerical tradition of the text can be appropriated by the royal court, which augments its own prestige by possessing this intellectual property. As a cultural symbol, the text and the interpretive systems that support it are transferred from one sphere of privilege to another. Thus even as the *Consolatio* is opened to vernacular readership, it becomes a sign of another kind of exclusionary authority, the power of a secular monarch.

Chaucer's *Legend of Good Women* takes these problems further. Here the vernacular text takes over academic discourse, not simply to appropriate cultural privilege, but to assume the function of guarding history and memory, to provide a "key of remembrance" to the classical past. In the *Prologue* (especially the G version), Chaucer suggests that the condition of vernacular writing is difference or rupture with the tradition of the *auctores*, and hence a kind of loss. The function of the key of remembrance is to keep memory alive in the face of historical loss and cultural fragmentation. But for Chaucer, the key of remembrance is not just the books of the ancient *auctores*: it is also the tradition of academic discourse out of which his own vernacular translation emerges. This is the discourse that conserves and controls memory of the past within certain official interpretive lines. But how can the *Legend of Good Women* acknowledge that the condition of writing in the vernacular is a measure of historical loss, and at the same time claim to guard the continuity of memory, unless by struggling against its own vernacularity? This is the paradox of the *Legend of Good Women*. To guard against the loss of history and memory is to guard against the vernacular itself; and to try to conserve a unified tradition of authoritative interpretation is to identify with the ideology of Latin academic discourse. Thus even in the vernacular, academic discourse can assume a regulatory function, replicating the conservative role it performs in Latin culture.

Thus we see that the vernacular can have an ambiguous value: vernacular translation may promise access to Latin culture, but it may also reproduce the systems of containment and control that sustain the Latin academic tradition. This inference, however, is based on texts from the eleventh to the late fourteenth centuries; and in this book as a whole the latest text considered has been John Walton's translation of the *Consolatio*, from the first decade of the fifteenth century. Further study would reveal just how much chronology is a factor in redefining the relationship between vernacular and Latin. To suggest how this might be the case, I would like to end by looking at one example of a classical translation from the second half of the fifteenth century. In Robert Henryson's *Orpheus and Eurydice*, the relationship between vernacular and Latin is configured in terms somewhat different from what we have found in earlier translations.

Orpheus and Eurydice is a narrative elaboration of Boethius' *Consolatio* 3 m.12. Henryson builds upon the suggestions of Boethius' meter to construct an account of the Orpheus story that is rich in learned mythographical detail. His sources include the *Graecismus* of Eberhard of Béthune for the list of the Muses (lines 36–60), Fulgentius' *Mythologiae*, Macrobius' commentary on the *Somnium Scipionis*, Trevet's commentary, and various compendia of mythographical lore.[6] The narrative is thus a poetic compendium of sorts, a tissue of familiar materials which stands in a densely mediated relationship to the text of the classical *auctor*, Boethius. In fact, its actual dependence on Boethius' meter is so loose that it might as well be associated with Ovid's version.

The identification with Boethius' meter really comes from Henryson's application of Trevet's commentary on 3 m.12, which is translated in reduced form and affixed to the end of the poem as a *moralitas*. At the opening of the *moralitas*, Henryson provides a little introduction:

> Lo worthy folk, Boece, that senature,
> To wryte this feynit fable tuke in cure,
> In his gay buke of consolacion,
> For oure doctryne and gude instruction;
> Quhilk in the self suppose it fenyeit be,
> Yit maistre Trewit, doctour Nicholas,
> Quhilk in his tyme a noble theolog was,
> Applyis it to gude moralitee,
> Rycht full of frute and seriositee. (415–24)

Here Henryson cites Boethius' meter, not as his own source, but as a point of reference for Trevet's commentary. The place of Trevet's allegorical exposition is interesting. It is used to supplement Henryson's fable, which itself is at quite a remove from Boethius' meter. In terms of its place in the structure of the poem as a whole, the adaptation of Trevet's commentary stands in a dependent relation to Henryson's fable. In fact, *Orpheus and Eurydice* has the same structure as Henryson's *Moral Fables*, narrative with accompanying *moralitas*.

On the one hand, Henryson's poem announces its dependence on the authoritative school tradition; on the other hand it subordinates that tradition to the vernacular narrative, making Trevet's commentary a supplement to the poetic fable. The deployment of the commentary here is different from the use earlier translators make of academic commentaries. In earlier translations, for example, the thirteenth- and fourteenth-century French versions of the *Consolatio*, the commentary may be incorporated in the text and may be used in such a way that it displaces the original text (as in the anonymous Burgundian version of the *Consolatio* which is structured around the commentary by William of Conches). In the *Ovide moralisé*, the translator uses the systems of exegesis to expound his own intentions. Chaucer and Gower also use exegetical techniques auto-referentially and, moreover, turn exegetical materials into the sources of topical invention.

But Henryson's use of commentary is much less complex, much more direct. He appropriates Trevet's allegorical exposition, translates it more or less as a whole, and appends it to his own reworking of the Orpheus myth. Its application to Boethius' meter is openly stated. The boundaries between Henryson's tale and Trevet's exposition are clearly marked, and the commentary is easily incorporated into a structural system that Henryson uses elsewhere, narrative and *moralitas*. The structural transparency of the layout of text and commentary here may tell us something about the status of the vernacular in mid-fifteenth-century literary culture. The vernacular seems to be so self-sufficient that Henryson can invoke the authority of the schools as if by convention, and at the same time smoothly incorporate academic discourse into his own textual system. The text does not struggle to authorize itself against Latin academic writing; rather, it assimilates the Latin commentary into its own dominant system. The force of appropriation is so complete that the Latin text simply becomes part of the vernacular text. To a large degree, the hierarchical difference between Latin and vernacular has been levelled off, and the presence of a useful commentary can be taken for granted. Henryson's poem is not representative of all fifteenth-century translation. But it does suggest that the idea of access to academic discourse, which was so conflicted and difficult a question for earlier translators, no longer poses a challenge for a later generation in which vernacular translation has become a norm of textual culture.

Notes

INTRODUCTION

1 For a description of the manuscript see Birger Munk Olsen, *L'Etude des auteurs classiques latins aux XIe et XIIe siècles*, 2 vols. (Paris: Editions du Centre National de la Recherche Scientifique, 1982–5), 1:443. This elaborate pictorial presentation of a commentary is unusual, although the technique of word painting, or making images out of a text, has some analogues in other manuscript traditions, notably in the practice of micography (drawing with microscopic writing) in Hebrew manuscripts of the later Middle Ages; see Thérèse and Mendel Metzger, *Jewish Life in the Middle Ages: Illuminated Hebrew Manuscripts of the Thirteenth to Sixteenth Centuries*, trans. Rowan Watson (New York: Alpine Fine Arts, 1982), pp. 189–95.

2 The term "originary" is used here and throughout in the sense that it has acquired in modern philosophical and critical discourse in association with the writings of Heidegger and Derrida, where it is not a synonym for "original" or "originating," but rather is construed in the sense of claiming the value (or attributing to something the value) of a fixed origin or foundational force. See, for example, the "Translator's preface" to Jacques Derrida, *Of Grammatology*, trans. Gayatri Chakravorty Spivak (Baltimore: Johns Hopkins University Press, 1976).

3 I refer here in particular to the work of Judson B. Allen, Paule Demats, Peter Dronke, A. J. Minnis, Glending Olson, Brian Stock, and Winthrop Wetherbee. See bibliography for full references.

4 See, for example, Michael Cahn, "Reading Rhetoric Rhetorically: Isocrates and the Marketing of Insight," *Rhetorica* 7 (1989): 121–44.

5 In this study, the term "discipline" (generally synonymous in the Middle Ages with science or art) is reserved for rhetoric, which does constitute an identifiable discipline. But hermeneutics, as a science of interpretation, that is, as a regulated system or method, might well be comprehended under ancient and early medieval notions of *disciplina* in its largest sense as a formal intellectual inquiry. See H[enri]-I. Marrou, "'Doctrina' et 'disciplina' dans la langue des Pères de l'Eglise," *Bulletin du Cange* 9 (1934): 5–25.

1. ROMAN THEORIES OF TRANSLATION: THE FUSION OF GRAMMAR AND RHETORIC

1 See, for example, the survey of such statements by medieval English translators in Flora Ross Amos, *Early Theories of Translation* (New York: Columbia University Press, 1920; rpt. New York: Octagon Books, 1973).

2 Henri Marrou, *A History of Education in Antiquity*, trans. George Lamb (New York: Sheed and Ward, 1956), p. 262.

3 Marrou, *A History of Education in Antiquity*, pp. 255–63.

4 For the idea of "vertical" as opposed to "horizontal" translation (that is, between languages of unequal prestige as opposed to languages of equal prestige), see Gianfranco Folena, "'Volgarizzare' e 'tradurre': idea e terminologia della traduzione dal medio evo italiano e romanzo all'umanesimo europeo," in *La traduzione: saggi e studi* (Trieste: Lint, 1973), pp. 57–120. Folena uses these terms to describe the differences in prestige between various medieval languages; but his terms are also applicable to the perceived difference in prestige between Greek and Latin in antiquity.

5 Marrou, *A History of Education in Antiquity*, p. 255.

6 *De finibus bonorum et malorum*, ed. and trans. H. Rackham, Loeb Classical Library (Cambridge, Mass.: Harvard University Press, 1914), 1.2.4–6, 1.3.10, 1.4.11. Unless otherwise noted, all English translations from Latin and Greek are those provided in the edition or source cited.

7 Stanley F. Bonner, *Education in Ancient Rome: From the Elder Cato to the Younger Pliny* (Berkeley and Los Angeles: University of California Press, 1977), pp. 47–51.

8 Wilhelm Dilthey, "The Rise of Hermeneutics," trans. Fredric Jameson, *New Literary History* 3 (1972): 229–44.

9 See Kathy Eden, *Poetic and Legal Fiction in the Aristotelian Tradition* (Princeton: Princeton University Press, 1986), pp. 54–75.

10 Bonner, *Education in Ancient Rome*, pp. 52–5.

11 See Nancy Struever, *The Language of History in the Renaissance: Rhetoric and Historical Consciousness in Florentine Humanism* (Princeton: Princeton University Press, 1970), pp. 16 and 29. On Stoic theories of language and their influence on Latin rhetoric, see Karl Barwick, *Probleme der stoischen Sprachlehre und Rhetorik*, Abh. der Sächsischen Akademie der Wissenschaften zu Leipzig, Philologisch-historische Klasse 49. 3 (Berlin: Akademie, 1957), pp. 80–111.

12 *De oratore*, ed. and trans. E. W. Sutton and H. Rackham, Loeb Classical Library, 2 vols. (Cambridge, Mass.: Harvard University Press, 1942, rpt. 1976).

13 *Institutio oratoria*, ed. and trans. H. E. Butler, 4 vols., Loeb Classical Library (Cambridge, Mass.: Harvard University Press, 1920). Cf. *Orator* 2.14–17, and *De inventione*, 1.2.3 ("mute and voiceless wisdom").

14 Text in *Grammatici graeci*, vol. 1 part 3, ed. A. Hilgard (Leipzig: Teubner, 1901), p. 10.8; cited in Marrou, *A History of Education in Antiquity*, p. 165.

15 Marrou, *A History of Education in Antiquity*, p. 169.

16 *Ad Lucilium epistulae morales* 2, ed. and trans. Richard M. Gummere, Loeb Classical Library (London: Heinemann, 1920).

17 See R. H. Robins, *Ancient and Medieval Grammatical Theory in Europe* (London: Bell, 1951) p. 38.

18 Tzvetan Todorov, *Theories of the Symbol*, trans. Catherine Porter (Ithaca: Cornell University Press, 1982), p. 61.

19 See Struever, *The Language of History in the Renaissance*, p. 15.

20 For this Aristotelian scheme of the sciences, see *Metaphysics* 6.2, *Topics* 7.1, and *Topics* 8.1.

21 All quotations from *Nicomachean Ethics* are from the translation by W. D. Ross, revised by J. O. Urmson, in Jonathan Barnes, ed., *The Complete Works of Aristotle: The Revised Oxford Translation*, Bollingen Series 71 (Princeton: Princeton University Press, 1984) 2.

22 See *Metaphysics* 6.1, 1026a1. On the speculative sciences in Aristotle, see Joseph Mariétan, *Problème de la classification des sciences d'Aristote à St-Thomas* (Paris: Alcan, 1901), pp. 25–37.

23 On the difference between theoretical and practical sciences, see Wesley Trimpi,

Muses of One Mind: The Literary Analysis of Experience and its Continuity (Princeton: Princeton University Press, 1983), pp. 97–129, esp. pp. 118–19.

24 Translated W. Rhys Roberts, in Barnes, ed., *The Complete Works of Aristotle* 2.

25 On the instrumentality of dialectic, see Mariétan, *Problème de la classification des sciences* pp. 22–5.

26 See Lois S. Self, "Rhetoric and *Phronesis*: The Aristotelian Ideal," *Philosophy and Rhetoric* 12 (1979): 130–45. See also the discussion by Victoria Kahn, *Rhetoric, Prudence, and Skepticism in the Renaissance* (Ithaca: Cornell University Press, 1985), pp. 30–6.

27 On Quintilian's treatment of the sciences in *Institutio oratoria* 2.18.1–5, and its relationship with the system in Aristotle's *Nicomachean Ethics*, see Jean Cousin, *Etudes sur Quintilien* (Paris: Boivin, 1935–6; rpt. Amsterdam: Schippers, 1967), 1:152–3.

28 *De officiis*, ed. and trans. Walter Miller, Loeb Classical Library (Cambridge, Mass.: Harvard University Press, 1938). I have modified the Loeb translation slightly. It has been noted of this passage that where Cicero speaks of wisdom (*sophia*), he actually means, according to his own definition, practical wisdom (*phronesis*), even though he tries to separate the two by claiming that his definition of wisdom is other than what the Greeks call "practical wisdom." On this confusion in Cicero's terminology, see the note in the Loeb ed., pp. 156–7; and Kahn, *Rhetoric, Prudence, and Skepticism in the Renaissance*, p. 201, note 19.

29 On this passage see Michael Frede, "Principles of Stoic Grammar," in J. M. Rist, ed., *The Stoics* (Berkeley and Los Angeles: University of California Press, 1978), p. 30.

30 James J. Murphy, *Rhetoric in the Middle Ages: A History of Rhetorical Theory from St. Augustine to the Renaissance* (Berkeley and Los Angeles: University of California Press, 1974), p. 26, n. 55.

31 George Kennedy, *The Art of Rhetoric in the Roman World: 300 B.C.–A.D. 300* (Princeton: Princeton University Press, 1972), p. 93.

32 Cf. Paul Ricoeur, "What is a Text? Explanation and Understanding," in Paul Ricoeur, *Hermeneutics and the Human Sciences*, ed. and trans. John B. Thompson (Cambridge: Cambridge University Press, 1981, rpt. 1984), p. 162.

33 On Gadamer's use of *Nicomachean Ethics*, see Richard J. Bernstein, "From Hermeneutics to Praxis," in Robert Hollinger, ed., *Hermeneutics and Praxis* (Notre Dame: University of Notre Dame Press, 1985), pp. 272–96.

34 Hans-Georg Gadamer, *Truth and Method*, trans. Garrett Barden and John Cumming (New York: Crossroad, 1975), p. 258.

35 Gadamer, *Truth and Method*, pp. 274–5. Cf. David Couzens Hoy, *The Critical Circle: Literature, History, and Philosophical Hermeneutics* (Berkeley and Los Angeles: University of California Press, 1978, rpt. 1982), pp. 14–15, 51–3, on E. D. Hirsch's critique of Gadamer's dialectical integration of these faculties. Cf. also Gadamer's critique of the historical backgrounds of hermeneutical theory, esp. objective historical consciousness of Dilthey and Schleiermacher, in *Truth and Method* Part 1.1 and Part 2.1.

36 Gadamer, *Truth and Method* p. 280.

37 Hoy, *The Critical Circle*, pp. 55–61.

38 On the sophistic principle of *kairos*, see Mario Untersteiner, *The Sophists*, trans. Kathleen Freeman (Oxford: Blackwell, 1954), pp. 108–31, 195–8. See also James L. Kinneavy, "*Kairos*: A Neglected Concept in Classical Rhetoric," in Jean Dietz Moss, ed., *Rhetoric and Praxis: The Contribution of Classical Rhetoric to Practical Reasoning* (Washington, D.C.: The Catholic University of America Press, 1986), pp. 79–105.

39 Cf. Gadamer, *Truth and Method* p. 288: "Understanding is a modification of the virtue of moral knowledge . . . Thus it is a mode of moral judgment."
40 *Truth and Method*, p. 264.
41 "On the Scope and Function of Hermeneutical Reflection," in Hans-Georg Gadamer, *Philosophical Hermeneutics*, trans. and ed. David E. Linge (Berkeley and Los Angeles: University of California Press), p. 24.
42 See James Zetzel, *Latin Textual Criticism in Antiquity* (diss. Harvard, 1972, rpt. Salem, New Hampshire: Ayer Company, 1981).
43 Tiberius Claudius Donatus, *Interpretationes Vergilianae*, ed. Heinrich Georges, 2 vols. (Leipzig: Teubner, 1905–12; rpt. Stuttgart: Teubner, 1969), 1:1–5.
44 See Kathy Eden, "Hermeneutics and the Ancient Rhetorical Tradition," *Rhetorica* 5 (1987): 59–86.
45 Marrou, *A History of Education in Antiquity*, pp. 255–64.
46 On these manuals see Marrou, *A History of Education in Antiquity*, pp. 263–4, and p. 428, n. 18. Texts in G. Goetz, *Corpus glossariorum latinorum* 3 (Leipzig: Teubner, 1892).
47 See my discussion of exegetical paraphrase in chapter 3, pp. 83–6.
48 Bonner, *Education in Ancient Rome*, pp. 218–49.
49 William G. Rutherford, *A Chapter in the History of Annotation, being Scholia Aristophanica; vol. III* (London: Macmillan, 1905), pp. 336–50.
50 See Murphy, *Rhetoric in the Middle Ages*, p. 25; on the question of the boundary between the two disciplines see also Ernst Robert Curtius, *European Literature and the Latin Middle Ages*, trans. Willard R. Trask (Princeton: Princeton University Press, 1953, Bollingen edition, 1973), p. 42.
51 Suetonius, *De grammaticis et rhetoribus*, ed. Giorgio Brugnoli (Leipzig: Teubner, 1963), 25.8, p. 29.
52 On Dionysius of Halicarnassus, see J. W. H. Atkins, *Literary Criticism in Antiquity*, 2 (Cambridge: Cambridge University Press, 1934), pp. 104–36; E. H. Gombrich, "The Debate on Primitivism in Ancient Rhetoric," *Journal of the Warburg and Courtauld Institutes* 29 (1966): 24–38; Richard McKeon, "Literary Criticism and the Concept of Imitation in Antiquity," *Modern Philology* 34 (1936–37): 1–35, rpt. in R. S. Crane, ed., *Critics and Criticism* (Chicago: University of Chicago Press, 1952), pp. 117–45; A. Guillemin, "L'Imitation dans les littératures antiques et en particulier dans la littérature latine," *Revue des études latines* 2 (1924): 35–57.
53 *Epistle to Pompeius* in W. Rhys Roberts, ed. and trans., *Dionysius of Halicarnassus: The Three Literary Letters* (Cambridge: Cambridge University Press, 1901), pp. 88–127. For the studies on Attic orators, see Stanley F. Bonner, *The Literary Treatises of Dionysius of Halicarnassus: A Study in the Development of Critical Method* (Cambridge: Cambridge University Press, 1939). See also Kennedy, *The Art of Rhetoric in the Roman World*, pp. 342–63.
54 G. M. A. Grube, *The Greek and Roman Critics* (London: Methuen, 1965), p. 212.
55 "Longinus," *On Sublimity*, trans. D. A. Russell, in D. A. Russell and M. Winterbottom, eds., *Ancient Literary Criticism: The Principal Texts in New Translations* (Oxford: Clarendon, 1972), pp. 460–503; see especially pp. 501–3.
56 *On Sublimity*, in Russell and Winterbottom, *Ancient Literary Criticism*, p. 475.
57 *On Sublimity*, in Russell and Winterbottom, *Ancient Literary Criticism*, pp. 475–6.
58 Elaine Fantham, "Imitation and Evolution: The Discussion of Rhetorical Imitation in Cicero's *De oratore* 2.87–97 and Some Related Problems of Ciceronian Theory," *Classical Philology* 73 (1978): 1–2.
59 See Fantham, "Imitation and Evolution," 2.

60 See Fantham, "Imitation and Evolution," and Elaine Fantham, "Imitation and Decline: Rhetorical Theory and Practice in the First Century after Christ," *Classical Philology* 73 (1978): 102–16.

61 Cf. Velleius Paterculus, Roman History 1.16 (A.D. 30), cited and trans. in Harry Caplan, "The Decay of Eloquence at Rome in the First Century," in Harry Caplan, *Of Eloquence: Studies in Ancient and Mediaeval Rhetoric*, ed. Anne King and Helen North (Ithaca: Cornell University Press, 1970), p. 181: "Who can wonder enough that the most eminent geniuses in each art come together within the same narrow space of time? . . . Oratory burgeoned forth under Cicero, so that there are very few before his time who can give you pleasure, and none whom you can admire unless he had seen Cicero or had been seen by Cicero."

62 See Thomas M. Greene, *The Light in Troy: Imitation and Discovery in Renaissance Poetry* (New Haven: Yale University Press, 1982), p. 62. On the linguistic function of metonymy see Roman Jakobson, "Two Aspects of Language and Two Types of Aphasic Disturbances," in Roman Jakobson and Morris Halle, *Fundamentals of Language*, Janua Lingarum, Series Minor, 1 (The Hague: Mouton, 1956), pp. 69–96.

63 Quoted in Kennedy, *The Art of Rhetoric in the Roman World* p. 348.

64 Compare Petrarch's version of Seneca's dictum, where he echoes the Roman notion of textual imitation as lineality: "An imitator must take care to write something similar yet not identical to the original, and that similarity must not be like the image to its original in painting where the greater the similarity the greater the praise for the artist, but rather like that of a son to his father . . . We must see to it that if there is something similar, there is also a great deal that is dissimilar, and that the similar be elusive and unable to be extricated except in silent meditation, for the resemblance is to be felt rather than expressed. Thus we may appropriate another's ideas as well as his coloring but we must abstain from his actual words; for with the former, resemblance remains hidden, and with the latter it is glaring, the former creates poets, the second apes." *Letters on Familiar Matters: Rerum familiarum libri XVII–XXIV*, trans. Aldo S. Bernardo (Baltimore: Johns Hopkins University Press, 1985), 23.19, pp. 301–2.

65 From Fragment 3 of *On Imitation*, quoted in Kennedy, *The Art of Rhetoric in the Roman World*, p. 348.

66 Cf. Velleius Paterculus, *Roman History* 1.16, quoted in Caplan, *Of Eloquence*, p. 181: "Genius is nourished by emulation, and it is sometimes envy, sometimes esteem which enkindles imitation; and it is natural that that which is cultivated with greatest zeal rises to the highest point of perfection."

67 Gordon Williams, *Change and Decline: Roman Literature in the Early Empire* (Berkeley and Los Angeles: University of California Press, 1978), p. 192.

68 *Controversiae* 1, Pref. 6, in *Controversiae and Suasoriae*, ed. and trans. M. Winterbottom, 2 vols., Loeb Classical Library (Cambridge, Mass.: Harvard University Press, 1974).

69 Horace, *Satires, Epistles, and Ars poetica*, ed. and trans. H. Rushton Fairclough, Loeb Classical Library (Cambridge, Mass., Harvard University Press, 1926).

70 For further discussion of the interpretive problems of this passage and its reception-history in patristic and medieval theories of translation, see below, chapter 2, pp. 45–55, and chapter 6, pp. 168–78.

71 In view of the technical vocabulary in this passage, I have departed from the Loeb translation, basing my own translation on the commentary by C. O. Brink, *Horace on Poetry: The "Ars poetica,"* (Cambridge: Cambridge University Press, 1971), pp. 198–212.

72 On the structural affiliations of the *Ars poetica* with ancient rhetorics, especially of

its underlying scheme of matter, arrangement, and style with rhetorical *inventio*, *dispositio*, and *elocutio*, see C. O. Brink, *Horace on Poetry: Prolegomena to the Literary Epistles* (Cambridge: Cambridge University Press, 1963), pp. 3–40, 79–119.

73 *Horace on Poetry: The "Ars poetica,"* p. 211. On Horace's rhetorical theory of imitation see also Gian Biagio Conte, *The Rhetoric of Imitation: Genre and Poetic Memory in Virgil and Other Latin Poets*, trans. Charles Segal (Ithaca: Cornell University Press, 1986), pp. 23–31.

74 Greene, *The Light in Troy*, p. 62. On the linguistic function of metaphor, see Jakobson, "Two Aspects of Language and Two Types of Aphasic Disturbances." The use of the term "metaphor" here as a description of a linguistic function should not suggest that there was a historical identification between the Latin rhetorical term for metaphor, *translatio*, and the Latin word for translation, *translatio*. The fact that the same word, *translatio*, could mean both metaphor and translation has, of course, long teased critics, especially since in both its definitions, *translatio* signifies an accomplished transference, a carrying over from one sphere to another (Cf. Quintilian, *Institutio oratoria* 1.4.18 and 8.6.4). In rhetoric, *translatio* is also a term from *status* theory, where it represents a form of procedure in which the case requires a transfer to another court (*De inventione* 1.8.10 and 2.19.57–61). In all of these uses, *translatio* suggests a substitution of one thing for another. Moreover, rhetorical defintions of *translatio* as metaphor involve ideas of appropriation or usurpation (of place or position, cf. Cicero, *De oratore* 3.39.157 and 3.41.165) comparable to the idea of aggressive appropriation, which lies behind Roman rhetorical theories of translation. But despite the obvious etymological connection, there is no evidence that Roman theorists of translation deliberately conflated the meaning of *translatio* as rhetorical metaphor with that of *translatio* as translation. For further reflections on the idea of metaphor as substitution or appropriation, see Paul Ricoeur, *The Rule of Metaphor: Multidisciplinary Studies of the Creation of Meaning in Language*, trans. Robert Czerny, with Kathleen McLaughlin and John Costello, S. J. (Toronto: University of Toronto Press, 1977, rpt. 1984), pp. 16–24; and Patricia A. Parker, "The Metaphorical Plot," in David S. Miall, ed., *Metaphor: Problems and Perspectives* (Sussex: Harvester Press; Atlantic Highlands, New Jersey: Humanities Press, 1982), pp. 133–57.

75 Epistle 2.1 to Augustus, line 156 in Horace, *Satires, Epistles, and Ars poetica*, ed. Fairclough (my translation).

76 See George Steiner, *After Babel: Aspects of Language and Translation* (Oxford: Oxford University Press, 1975, rpt. 1977) p. 239.

77 Pliny the Younger, *Letters and Panegyricus*, ed. and trans. Betty Radice, 2 vols., Loeb Classical Library (Cambridge, Mass.: Harvard University Press, 1969).

78 Roland Barthes, "Science vs. Literature," *TLS*, Sept. 28, 1967, p. 897, cited in Struever, *The Language of History in the Renaissance*, p. 15, n. 10.

79 See Untersteiner, *The Sophists*, pp. 194–205.

80 *De inventione, De optimo genere oratorum, Topica*, H. M. Hubbell, ed. and trans., Loeb Classical Library (Cambridge, Mass.: Harvard University Press, 1949, rpt. 1976).

81 See chapter 2 below, section on the patristic model of translation and its influence.

82 Studies of Cicero's own translative practice seem to bear out his theoretical directive of textual reinvention through stylistic recasting. See David Payne Kubiak, "Cicero, Catullus, and the Art of Neoteric Translation," Diss. Harvard, 1979, abstract in *Harvard Studies in Classical Philology* 84 (1980): 337–8.

83 *Tusculan Disputations*, ed. and trans. J. E. King, Loeb Classical Library (Cambridge, Mass.: Harvard University Press, 1945, rpt. 1950).

84 The term "hermeneutical aggression" is borrowed here from Steiner, *After Babel*, ch. 5, "The Hermeneutic Motion."

2. FROM ANTIQUITY TO THE MIDDLE AGES I: THE PLACE OF TRANSLATION AND THE VALUE OF HERMENEUTICS

1 Struever, *The Language of History in the Renaissance*, p. 29.

2 Some of the standard studies of translation that deal with the historical transmission of ancient theoretical principles are: Steiner, *After Babel*; Louis Kelly, *The True Interpreter: A History of Translation Theory and Practice in the West* (Oxford: Basil Blackwell, 1979); W. Schwarz, *Principles and Problems of Biblical Translation: Some Reformation Controversies and their Background* (Cambridge: Cambridge University Press; 1955, rpt. 1970); Eugene A. Nida, *Towards a Science of Translating, with Special Reference to Principles and Procedures Involved in Bible Translating* (Leiden: Brill, 1964); Eric Jacobsen, *Translation: A Traditional Craft* (Copenhagen: Nordisk, 1958). See also the introductory discussions in Susan Bassnett-McGuire, *Translation Studies* (London and New York: Methuen, 1980).

3 Jacques Fontaine, *Isidore de Seville et la culture classique dans l'Espagne wisigothique*, 2 vols. (Paris: Etudes Augustiniennes, 1959), 1:212.

4 These rhetorical manuals, compendia, and commentaries (from approximately the later third century to Bede and Alcuin in the seventh and eighth centuries) are edited by Karl Halm, *Rhetores latini minores* (Leipzig: Teubner, 1863; rpt. Frankfurt: Minerva, 1964).

5 Fontaine, *Isidore de Seville* 1:212.

6 Pierre Hadot, *Marius Victorinus. Recherches sur sa vie et ses œuvres* (Paris: Etudes Augustiniennes, 1971) p. 77.

7 Fontaine, *Isidore de Seville* 1:224, conveniently provides some statistics on the treatment of invention in proportion to the other parts of rhetoric. Sulpitius Victor (*Institutiones oratoriae*, in Halm, *Rhetores latini minores*, pp. 311–52) gives two pages (pp. 320–1) over to *dispositio*, *elocutio*, and *actio*. The *Ars rhetorica* of Julius Victor (Halm, pp. 371–448), gives 58 pages to invention and 12 to the remaining parts: *dispositio* 7 lines, *elocutio* 9 pages, *memoria* ½ page, *pronunciatio* 2½ pages. Martianus Capella's section on rhetoric in the *De nuptiis Philologiae et Mercurii* (in Halm's collection pp. 449–92) gives 21 pages to invention as against ½ page to *dispositio*, 11 pages to *elocutio*, and one page each to *memoria* and *pronunciatio*. *Elocutio* takes up ⅛ of the treatises of Fortunatianus (*Artis rhetoricae libri III*, Halm, pp. 81–134) and Julius Victor, and ¼ of Martianus Capella's treatise. On these truncated rhetorics see also John Ward, "*Artificiosa Eloquentia* in the Middle Ages," Diss. Toronto, 1972 (2 vols.), 1:76–7.

8 Kennedy, *Classical Rhetoric and its Christian and Secular Tradition from Ancient to Modern Times* (Chapel Hill: University of North Carolina Press, 1980), p. 105; Ward, "*Artificiosa Eloquentia* in the Middle Ages" 1:76–94.

9 On Boethius and Martianus Capella, see Michael C. Leff, "The Topics of Argumentative Invention in Latin Rhetorical Theory from Cicero to Boethius," *Rhetorica* 1 (1983): 23–44; on Isidore's precedents among the *rhetores latini minores*, see Fontaine, *Isidore de Seville* 1:211–29; on Alcuin's dependence on Victorinus see Hadot, *Marius Victorinus*, pp. 21–2.

10 Items 1–5 in Halm, *Rhetores latini minores*, are classed together as "Scriptores de figuris sententiarum et elocutionis"; they are a group of relatively short texts concerned almost exclusively with figures and tropes. In the more comprehensive rhetorics of Fortunatianus and Julius Victor, where *elocutio* is treated, it has only a

secondary, ornamental force. On Asianist tendencies in late classical prose, see Eduard Norden, *Die antike Kunstprosa*, 2 vols., 4th edition (Leipzig: Teubner, 1923, rpt. 1958), 2:586–656.

11 See the excellent account of the autoteleology of topical invention in these minor rhetorics in Leff, "The Topics of Argumentative Invention," 35–44.

12 Victorinus, *Commentum in Ciceronis rhetoricam*, in Halm, p. 173, lines 6–7. See also Hadot, *Marius Victorinus*, pp. 99–100.

13 According to R. R. Bolgar, *The Classical Heritage and its Beneficiaries* (Cambridge: Cambridge University Press, 1954, rpt. 1977), pp. 33–42, rhetoric came to fulfill the same function as grammar, that of teaching *Latinitas* in the increasingly vernacular culture of the late Empire and early Middle Ages. This conclusion is based largely on the evidence that rhetoricians and grammarians taught very much the same subjects, and that schematized exercises grounded in rhetorical training (the *progymnasmata*) served a basic aim of linguistic instruction. Certainly *elocutio*, *dispositio*, *pronunciatio*, and *memoria* have been so subordinated to invention as to have lost any proper rhetorical underpinning, and have been virtually channeled into the service of grammatical instruction. But such rhetorically based exercises as the *progymnasmata* (a version of which is included in Halm's *Rhetores latini minores*) do not properly represent the range of rhetorical interests in late antiquity. It is more accurate to say that strict rhetorical study turned its attention almost entirely to inventional doctrine, and that grammatical study took over the other functions of discourse that had belonged to rhetoric.

14 Halm, *Rhetores latini minores*, p. 122, line 1.

15 *Ibid.* lines 11–19.

16 *Ibid.* lines 15–16.

17 *Cassiodori Senatoris Institutiones*, ed. R. A. B. Mynors (Oxford: Clarendon, 1937), p. 104.8–10. See also Fontaine, *Isidore de Seville* 2:224, n. 4, and Hadot, *Marius Victorinus*, p. 74, n. 9.

18 Martianus Capella, *De nuptiis Philologiae et Mercurii*, ed. Adolf Dick (Leipzig: Teubner, 1925), book 5, *passim.*

19 This section appears, in much the same form, under the title "The fortunes of 'non verbum pro verbo': or, why Jerome is not a Ciceronian," in Roger Ellis, ed., *The Medieval Translator: The Theory and Practice of Translation in the Middle Ages*, (Cambridge: D. S. Brewer, 1989, pp. 15–35).

20 This concern with meaning as a function within rather than beyond discourse was of course one of its hallmarks in antiquity, as in Plato's condemnation of the Sophists. Sextus Empiricus (second century A.D.) quotes Plato's definition of rhetoric in the *Gorgias* ("Rhetoric is the creator of persuasion by means of words, having its efficacy in the words themselves, and being persuasive, not instructive," *Gorgias* 453a) and goes on to explain: "and he added the phrase 'by means of words' probably because there are many things which effect persuasion in men without speech, such as wealth and glory and pleasure and beauty . . . It is not, however, always rhetoric when there is persuasion by words (for the art of medicine also and arts similar to it persuade by speech), but only if it is an art which has its efficacy dependent mainly on words alone, and that not like the rest . . . it employs persuasion not in order to instruct, like geometry, but to induce belief; for that is the special mark of rhetoric." *Adversus rhetores* 2–5, in R. G. Bury, ed. and trans., *Sextus Empiricus* 4, *Against the Professors*, Loeb Classical Library (Cambridge, Mass.: Harvard University Press, 1949), pp. 188–91.

21 On the secondary, albeit necessary, function of human language in the semiology of the early Church Fathers, see Marcia L. Colish, *The Mirror of Language: A*

Study in the Medieval Theory of Knowledge, rev. ed. (Lincoln: University of Nebraska Press, 1983), ch. 1, "Augustine: The Expression of the Word."

22 See G. R. Evans, *The Language and Logic of the Bible: The Earlier Middle Ages* (Cambridge: Cambridge University Press, 1984), pp. 6–7.

23 On the account of the origins of the Septuagint, see Schwarz, *Principles and Problems of Biblical Translation*, ch. 1.

24 Augustine, *De civitate Dei*, after the ed. of Bernard Dombert and Alphonse Kalb, *CCSL* 47–8 (Turnhout: Brepols, 1955), 18.43; trans. Henry Bettenson, *Concerning the City of God Against the Pagans* (Harmondsworth: Penguin, 1972), p. 822.

25 See Armand Strubel, "'Allegoria in factis' et 'allegoria in verbis'," *Poétique* 23 (1975): 342–57. On this "metaphysics" of origin in patristic thought, see also the discussion in R. Howard Bloch, *Etymologies and Genealogies: A Literary Anthropology of the French Middle Ages* (Chicago: University of Chicago Press, 1983), pp. 34–63.

26 *De doctrina christiana*, ed. William M. Green, *CSEL* 80 (Vienna: Hoelder-Pichler-Tempsky, 1963), 2.13.19; trans. D. W. Robertson, *On Christian Doctrine* (Indianapolis: Bobbs-Merrill, 1958), p. 46.

27 This notion of translation as a challenge to linguistic fragmentation, as promise of reconciliation between disparate languages, is echoed in Walter Benjamin's "messianic" notion of translation. See Benjamin, "The Task of the Translator," in Walter Benjamin, *Illuminations*, ed. Hannah Arendt, trans. Harry Zohn (New York: Schocken Books, 1969). See also Jacques Derrida, *The Ear of the Other: Otobiography, Transference, Translation*, ed. Christie V. McDonald, trans. Peggy Kamuf and Avital Ronell (New York: Schocken Books, 1985), pp. 91–161, "Roundtable on Translation," esp. p. 123.

28 *Praefatio in Pentateuchum, PL* 28:182A–183A. On this passage see Evans, *The Language and Logic of the Bible*, p. 7.

29 Kelly, *The True Interpreter*, pp. 180–1; but cf. Georges Cuendet, "Cicéron et Saint Jérôme traducteurs," *Revue des études latines* 11 (1933): 380–400, esp. 400: "Somme toute, Cicéron et saint Jérôme ont attent le but qu'ils s'étaient assignés: l'un a donné à la traduction l'éclat d'une œuvre originale, l'autre a réalisé une copie fidèle."

30 The term "dynamic equivalence" is from Kelly, *The True Interpreter*, p. 181.

31 Ed. and trans. Rackham.

32 See, for example, *De finibus*, 1.3.8.

33 *Eusibii Pamphili chronici canones latini vertit, adauxit, ad sua tempora produxit S. Eusebius Hieronymus*, ed. J. K. Fotheringham (London: Milford, 1923), p. 1, 12a–25b, and p. 3, 25a–p. 4, 5a.

34 Epistula 57, *Ad Pammachium de optimo genere interpretandi, CSEL* 54, S. Eusebii Hieronymi opera sec. 1, pars. 1, epistularum pars 1, I–LXX, ed. I. Hilberg (Vienna: Tempsky, 1910): 508–10. See also the edition with notes by G. J. M. Bartelink, *Liber de optimo genere interpretandi* (Epistula 57), *Mnemosyne*, supplement 61 (Leiden: Brill, 1980). In the quotation from the Eusebius preface I have emended Hilberg's reading "excidere" to "excedere," as in Fotheringham (p. 1) and Bartelink (p. 14). The translation from *De optimo genere oratorum* is from *De inventione, De optimo genere oratorum, Topica*, ed. and trans. Hubbell, p. 365.

35 Epistula 57, *CSEL* 54:511.

36 *Ibid.* 512.

37 Jerome's position on sacred translation is not without inconsistency, for here he also recommends idiomatic translation. See Epistula 106, *Ad Sunniam et Fretelam de psalterio, quae de LXX interpretum editione corrupta sint, CSEL* 55, *S. Eusebii*

Hieronymi opera sec. I, pars II, epistularum pars II, LXXI–CXX, ed. I. Hilberg (Vienna: Tempsky, 1912): 247–89. See also Pierre Courcelle, *Late Latin Writers and Their Greek Sources*, trans. Harry E. Wedeck (Cambridge, Mass.: Harvard University Press, 1969), pp. 54–7.

38 The history of translation theory is only one instance of the need to locate individual critical practices in larger discursive systems. See Michel Foucault, *The Archaeology of Knowledge*, trans. A. M. Sheridan Smith (New York: Harper Colophon, 1972), pp. 21–39.

39 Gregory the Great, Epistula 10, *MGH, Gregorii I Papae registrum epistolarum* 2, ed. L. M. Hartmann (Berlin: Weidmann, 1899): 258.

40 Bacon, *Opus tertium* 25.90, in Bacon *Opera inedita*, ed. J. S. Brewer (Rolls Series, 1859); Aquinas, *Contra errores Graecorum*, ed. P. Glorieux (Tournai: Desclée, 1957), p. 116.

41 Prologue to Wycliffite Bible, chapter 15, in Anne Hudson, ed., *Selections from English Wycliffite Writings* (Cambridge: Cambridge University Press, 1978), p. 68. The character "thorn" has been replaced with "th."

42 W. Schwarz, "The Meaning of *Fidus Interpres* in Medieval Translation," *Journal of Theological Studies* 45 (1944): 73–8.

43 Ed. Samuel Brandt, *CSEL* 48 (Vienna: Tempsky, 1906): 135.

44 *PL* 122:1032. I have followed Schwarz' reading of "fidi" for the *PL* reading of "infidi."

45 Schwarz, "The Meaning of *Fidus Interpres*," 75–6. On Boethius' introduction of Porphyry's *Isagoge* as signaling a shift in his own principles of translation towards increasing literalness, see J. Isaac, *Le Peri Hermeneias en occident de Boèce à Saint Thomas* (Paris: Vrin, 1953), pp. 17–20. On literal methods as the norm for Boethian and later translations of Aristotle, see Bernard G. Dod, "*Aristoteles latinus*," in Norman Kretzmann, Anthony Kenny, and Jan Pinborg, eds.; Eleonore Stump, assoc. ed., *The Cambridge History of Later Medieval Philosophy* (Cambridge: Cambridge University Press, 1982), pp. 45–79, esp. pp. 64–8.

46 Boethius, second commentary on the *Peri hermeneias*: "As those with whom the things are the same must have the same notions, but with those whose notions are the same the words are not the same, and of those who have the same words the same letters need not necessarily be formed, we must conclude that things and notions, being the same to everybody, are formed by nature, but the words and the letters, which are changed by the different institutions of people, are not by nature, but by institution." Hans Arens, ed. and trans., *Aristotle's Theory of Language and its Tradition*, Studies in the History of Linguistics 29 (Amsterdam: Benjamins, 1984), p. 165. Boethius, *Commentarii in librum Aristotelis Peri hermeneias, pars posterior, secundam editionem continens*, ed. Charles Meiser, (Leipzig: Teubner, 1880), pp. 22–3. See also Joseph Owens, "Faith, Ideas, Illumination, and Experience," in Kretzmann et al., eds., *The Cambridge History of Later Medieval Philosophy*, pp. 440–59, esp. 443–4.

47 It has long been recognized that Jerome's own practice in translating Scripture does not conform to this theory of literalism in biblical translation. See Schwarz, *Biblical Translation*, pp. 34–5. My concern here, however, is with the implications of his theoretical articulations.

48 According to Walter Ullmann, *Law and Politics in the Middle Ages* (Ithaca: Cornell University Press, 1975), p. 44, there was no general awareness in the Middle Ages of the character of the Vulgate as a translation, as its language carried the great political and moral weight of Rome. There is an analogy between the authority that the Vulgate achieved and Boethius' express purpose in translating

Greek philosophy so accurately as to preclude any future need to refer to the original texts.

49 "Ideoque solus eorum intellectus separatis verbis per periphrasin transfertur, ut eorum solummodo virtus intelligatur, quorum interpretatio de verbo ad verbum non exprimitur." *PL* 122:567 (and cited in Schwarz, "The Meaning of *Fidus Interpres* in Medieval Translation," 77). On Eriugena's activity as a translator see Maïeul Cappuyns, *Jean Scot Erigène: sa vie, son œuvre, sa pensée* (Paris, 1933; rpt. Brussels: Culture et Civilisation, 1969), pp. 128–79.

50 *Versus de ambiguis S. Maximi* II, *PL* 122:1235–6 (and cited in Schwarz, "The Meaning of *Fidus Interpres* in Medieval Translation," 77).

51 See Osmund Lewry, O.P., "Boethian Logic in the Medieval West," in Margaret Gibson, ed., *Boethius: His Life, Thought, and Influence*, (Oxford: Blackwell, 1981), p. 93.

52 Text in Dick, ed., *De nuptiis Philologiae et Mercurii*, pp. 85–6.

53 Translation from William Harris Stahl, Richard Johnson, and E. L. Burge, *Martianus Capella and the Seven Liberal Arts* 2, *The Marriage of Philology and Mercury* (New York: Columbia University Press, 1977): 67–8.

54 On analogous problems of the cultural reconstruction of ancient texts, see Peter Szondi, "Introduction to Literary Hermeneutics," *New Literary History* 10 (1978): 17–29.

55 See Robert A. Kaster, "Macrobius and Servius: *Verecundia* and the Grammarian's Function," *Harvard Studies in Classical Philology* 84 (1980): 219–62, and "Servius and *Idonei Auctores*," *American Journal of Philology* 99 (1978): 181–209. For further discussion of Servius' "philological humanism" see Christopher C. Baswell, "'Figures of Olde Werk': Visions of Virgil in Later Medieval England," Diss. Yale, 1983, esp. pp. 47–54. On the archaizing tendencies of classical scholarship in late antiquity, see Seth Lerer, *Boethius and Dialogue: Literary Method in the Consolation of Philosophy* (Princeton: Princeton University Press, 1985), pp. 15–93.

56 Fontaine, *Isidore de Seville* 1:32, 47, 157–85.

57 Latin text in Dick, ed., *De nuptiis Philologiae et Mercurii*, p. 150; English translation in Stahl et al., *The Marriage of Philology and Mercury*, 105.

58 The division between figures of speech and figures of thought was not even clear in classical Roman rhetoric. A good account of the problems raised by the often arbitrary distinctions can be found in A. D. Leeman, *Orationis Ratio: The Stylistic Theories and Practice of the Roman Orators, Historians, and Philosophers*, 2 vols. (Amsterdam: Hakkert, 1963), 1:33–42. On the similarly vexed question about grammatical as opposed to rhetorical treatment of the figures, see Robert A. Kaster, "The Grammarian's Authority," *Classical Philology* 75 (1980): 216–41, esp. 221–2. For a useful comparison between the *Rhetorica ad Herennium* and the *Barbarismus* of Donatus, see Murphy, *Rhetoric in the Middle Ages*, pp. 33–7.

59 Aquila Romanus, *De figuris sententiarum et elocutionis*, in Halm, *Rhetories latini minores*, pp. 22–37. For an account of Martianus' chapter on rhetoric, including his indebtedness to Aquila Romanus, see Hans-Werner Fischer, *Untersuchungen über die Quellen der Rhetorik des Martianus Capella*, (Inaugural-Dissertation, Breslau, 1936), esp. pp. 84–8. On his use of a number of grammatical works on style (including Donatus), see William Harris Stahl, Richard Johnson, and E. L. Burge, *Martianus Capella and the Seven Liberal Arts* 1, *The Quadrivium of Martianus Capella: Latin Traditions in the Mathematical Sciences, with a Study of the Allegory and the Verbal Disciplines* (New York: Columbia University Press, 1971): 115–21.

60 Cf. the distinction proposed by Donatus: "Schemata lexeos sunt et dianoeas, id est

figurae verborum et sensum. Sed schemata dianoeas ad oratores pertinent, ad grammaticos lexeos." *Ars maior* 3.5, in Heinrich Keil, ed., *Grammatici latini* 4 (Leipzig: Teubner, 1864): 367–402. On the influence of Donatus on later studies of the figures, see Ulrich Schindel, *Die lateinischen Figurenlehren des 5. bis 7. Jahrhunderts und Donats Vergilkommentar*, Abh. Akademie der Wissenschaften in Göttingen, Philologisch-Historische Klasse, 3rd series, 91 (Göttingen: Vandenhoeck and Ruprecht, 1975).

61 Kaster, "The Grammarian's Authority," 222.

62 "E quibus plurimae superius a Donato in schematibus artis Grammaticae adnotatae sunt. Vnde tantum illa hic interponi oportuit, quae in poemate aut numquam aut difficulter fiunt, in oratione autem libere." *Etymologiarum sive originum libri XX*, ed. W. M. Lindsay, 2 vols. (Oxford: Clarendon, 1911, rpt. 1962), 1:2.21.8–11. See also Fontaine, *Isidore de Seville*, 1:295–319. While classical theory had also made generic distinctions between the respective realms of grammar and rhetoric, assigning poetry to the former and prose to the latter, this was part of a larger scheme of hierarchical differentiation between the two disciplines. In Isidore, the division between the tropes more common in poetry and those more common in prose does not seem to arise from a categorical distinction between the competence of grammar and that of rhetoric.

63 *Etymologiarum*, ed. Lindsay, 1:2.17. See Franz Quadlbauer, *Die antike Theorie der Genera Dicendi im lateinischen Mittelalter*, Österreichische Akademie der Wissenschaften, Philosophisch-Historische Klasse, Sitzungsberichte 241. 2 (Vienna: Hermann Böhlaus, 1962), pp. 15–17.

64 Text in Halm, *Rhetories latini minores*, pp. 607–18. On the hermeneutical scope of Bede's grammatical-rhetorical analysis, see Armand Strubel, "'Allegoria in factis' et 'allegoria in verbis'."

65 Pierre Riché, *Education and Culture in the Barbarian West, Sixth through Eighth Centuries*, trans. John J. Contreni from the 3rd French edition (Columbia, South Carolina: University of South Carolina Press, 1976), pp. 193–206; and Pierre Riché, *Ecoles et enseignement dans le haut moyen âge* (Paris: Aubier Montaigne, 1979), p. 25. See also Ward, "*Artificiosa Eloquentia* in the Middle Ages," 1:116.

66 See the surveys in Marrou, *A History of Education in Antiquity*, pp. 314–50, Riché, *Ecoles et enseignement*, pp. 11–64. See also P. Riché, "L'Enseignement et la culture des laïcs dans l'occident pre-carolingien," *La scuola nell'occidente latino dell'alto medioevo*, Settimane di studio del centro italiano di studi sull'alto medioevo 19, 2 vols. (Spoleto: Presso la sede del centro, 1972), 1:231–53.

67 *Institutiones*, ed. Mynors, 1.6. See Henri de Lubac, *Exégèse médiévale: les quatre sens de l'écriture* 4 vols. (Paris: Aubier, 1959–64), 1:78–9; see also Leslie W. Jones, "The Influence of Cassiodorus on Mediaeval Culture," *Speculum* 20 (1945): 433–42.

68 *Etymologiae* 2.2. See Ward, "*Artificiosa Eloquentia* in the Middle Ages," 1:123.

69 *Disputatio de rhetorica et de virtutibus*, chs. 5 and 44, in Halm, *Rhetores latini minores*, pp. 526–7, 548–9. See also the discussion of the virtues in Wilbur Samuel Howell, ed. and trans., *The Rhetoric of Alcuin and Charlemagne* (Princeton: Princeton University Press, 1941), pp. 28, 31–2, 63–4; and see Ward, "*Artificiosa Eloquentia* in the Middle Ages" 1:122–40.

70 See John Ward, "From Antiquity to the Renaissance: Glosses and Commentaries on Cicero's *Rhetorica*," in James J. Murphy, ed., *Medieval Eloquence: Studies in the Theory and Practice of Medieval Rhetoric* (Berkeley and Los Angeles: University of California Press, 1978), pp. 42–4.

71 *De institutione clericorum*, *PL* 107:396–7 (ch. 20, "De rhetorica"). See James J. Murphy, "Saint Augustine and Rabanus Maurus: The Genesis of Medieval

Rhetoric," *Journal of Western Speech* 31 (1967): 88–96. See also Harry Caplan, "Classical Rhetoric and the Mediaeval Theory of Preaching," in Caplan, *Of Eloquence*, p. 116 (orig. publ. in *Classical Philology* 28 [1933]: 73–96).

72 Kennedy, *Classical Rhetoric and its Christian and Secular Tradition*, p. 179.

73 Barthes, cited Struever, *The Language of History in the Renaissance*, p. 15, n. 10.

74 The phrase is Struever's, *The Language of History in the Renaissance*, p. 15.

75 See Beryl Smalley, *The Study of the Bible in the Middle Ages* (Oxford: Blackwell, 1952; rpt. Notre Dame: University of Notre Dame Press, 1978), pp. 1–36, and esp. pp. 27 and 35.

76 Smalley, *The Study of the Bible in the Middle Ages*, p. 29. *Disputatio* is not developed as a real science of exegesis until the twelfth century: see G. R. Evans, *The Language and Logic of the Bible*, pp. 8–10, 125–63.

77 Ricoeur, "What is a Text," p. 159, and "Appropriation," p. 185, in Ricoeur, *Hermeneutics and the Human Sciences*, ed. Thompson.

78 Gadamer, *Truth and Method*, p. 274.

79 *Ibid.* pp. 345–60.

80 See Theodore Haarhoff, *The Schools of Gaul* (Oxford: Oxford University Press, 1920), p. 68: "The grammarian used his knowledge to expand the text, the rhetor his imagination." Cf. Eugene Vinaver, *The Rise of Romance* (Oxford: Oxford University Press, 1971), p. 22.

81 This is the view implied, for example, in Rosemond Tuve's term "imposed allegory." See *Allegorical Imagery: Some Mediaeval Books and Their Posterity* (Princeton: Princeton University Press, 1966). Cf. Susan Sontag, *Against Interpretation and Other Essays* (New York: Dell, 1966), p. 6.

82 See *Truth and Method*, p. 58.

3. THE RHETORICAL CHARACTER OF ACADEMIC COMMENTARY

1 Cf. Richard McKeon's remarks on rhetoric's displacement of philosophy: "The Roman rhetoricians . . . divided rhetoric into four distinctions or four questions, of which the first was a factual or a conjectural question, the second referred to names, the third involved a question of quality, and the last was a translative question. Where do these four questions come from? One does not have to speculate since Cicero tells us. They are the rhetorical translation of the four philosophical questions that Aristotle put at the opening chapter of the second book of the *Topics*. Rhetoric has assumed all of the task of philosophy by translating questions of fact into questions of how you establish the allegation of facts, and there are no facts that are discussed except alleged facts." *Arts libéraux et philosophie au moyen âge*. Actes du quatrième Congrès International de Philosophie Médiévale, 1967 (Montréal: Institut d'Etudes Médiévales; Paris: Vrin, 1969), p. 65 ("Questions et discussions").

2 R. B. C. Huygens associates it with Remigius: see *Accessus ad auctores; Bernard d'Utrecht; Conrad d'Hirsau, Dialogus super auctores*, ed. Huygens (Leiden: Brill, 1970), pp. 21 and 66, and Huygens' earlier edition of Conrad of Hirsau's *Dialogus super auctores*, Collection Latomus 17 (Latomus: Brussels, 1955), p. 11, n. 1. See also Huygens, "Remigiana," *Aevum* 28 (1954): 331, n. 6; Cora Lutz, "One Formula of *Accessus* in Remigius' Works," *Latomus* 19 (1960): 774–80. For the view that this prologue did not necessarily originate with Remigius, see Hubert Silvestre, "Le Schéma 'moderne' des *accessus*," *Latomus* 16 (1957): 684–9. One *accessus* to Virgil in a ninth-century German manuscript (Wolfenbüttel Gudianus, fol. no. 70) credits John Scotus Eriugena with devising this circumstantial prologue: see Lutz, "One Formula of *Accessus*," 777–8; for the text of this *accessus* see

Jacob Brummer, *Vitae Vergilianae* (Leipzig: Teubner, 1912), pp. 60–2 (Vita Gudiana I).

3 For the association of this prologue with Remigius, see Lutz, "One Formula of *Accessus*," 778, n. 5; Silvestre, "Le Schéma moderne," 685.

4 Text from Max Manitius, "Zur karolingischen Literatur," *Neues Archiv* 36 (1910): 74.

5 Cf. a prologue to the *Disticha Catonis* from a manuscript of the tenth or eleventh century: "In initio cuiuscumque libri tria sunt requirenda, persona, locus, tempus. Sed persona istius Catonis ignoratur, legimus enim duos Catones fuisse . . . Locus dinoscitur, quia scimus eum Romanum fuisse. Tempus vero: moderno tempore fuit, post Virgilium scilicet et Lucanum . . . " quoted in Manitius, "Zur karolingischen Literatur," 49–50. The fourfold scheme is exemplified in a prologue, attributed to Remigius, to Priscian's *De nomine*: "Quattuor in hoc loco requirenda sunt, locus persona tempus et causa scribendi. locus Roma, persona Priscianus, tempus sub Iuliano consule, causa scribendi ad instruendos pueros," quoted by Huygens, "Remigiana," 331–2; cf. A. Mancini, "Un commento ignoto di Remy d'Auxerre ai *Disticha Catonis*," *Rendiconti della R. Accademia dei Lincei* series 5, 11 (1902): 179.

6 *Commentum in Theodolum*, in Huygens, *Accessus ad auctores* p. 66.

7 See Richard William Hunt, "The Introductions to the 'Artes' in the Twelfth Century," in *Studia Mediaevalia in Honorem R. J. Martin* (Bruges: "De Tempel," 1948), pp. 85–112. The most comprehensive account of the development of the medieval *accessus ad auctores* is A. J. Minnis, *Medieval Theory of Authorship: Scholastic literary attitudes in the later Middle Ages* (London: Scolar Press, 1984).

8 According to Edwin A. Quain, "The Medieval *Accessus ad auctores*," *Traditio* 3 (1945): 215–64, the rhetorical circumstances are not the source of the main types of medieval *accessus*. Quain takes issue here with Gustavus Przychocki, "*Accessus Ovidiani*," *Rozprawy Akademii Umiejetnosci Wydzial Filologiczny*, ser. 3, vol. 4 (Krakow 1911), pp., 65–126, who had assumed a connection between the seven elements of Servius' prologue to Virgil (author, title, quality, intention, order, number of books, explanation) as cited by Conrad of Hirsau in the *Dialogus super auctores* (see Huygens, *Accessus ad auctores* p. 78), and the elements of the circumstantial prologue, also cited by Conrad of Hirsau (Huygens, p. 72). Przychocki had implied that "the ultimate source of the *accessus* lies in the rhetorical use of *circumstantiae*, which later writers had adapted until it took the form we know of the *accessus*" (Quain, 228). For Quain, "the form we know of the *accessus*" is that which came into use by the twelfth century, what Hunt has classified as the "type C" (*vita auctoris*, *titulus operis*, *intentio scribentis*, *materia operis*, *modus agendi*, *utilitas*, and *cui parti philosophiae supponatur*; see Hunt, "The Introductions to the 'Artes' in the Twelfth Century," pp. 94–7). This "type-C" prologue has its origins, as Quain shows, in ancient philosophical commentators. But Quain, like Przychocki, fails to recognize the circumstantial *accessus* as an altogether separate tradition. Hunt, however, does classify it separately, and recognizes its particular origins in rhetorical systems. It is largely a Carolingian form, and should not be confused with the later, more popular form whose origins Quain has traced.

9 What remains of Hermagoras' writing has been edited in Dieter Matthes, *Fragmenta* (Leipzig: Teubner, 1962). For more background see George Kennedy, *The Art of Persuasion in Greece* (Princeton: Princeton University Press, 1963), pp. 303–21.

10 Pseudo-Augustine, *De rhetorica*, in Halm, *Rhetores latini minores*, p. 141.

11 Pseudo-Augustine gives the terms *an sit*, *quid sit*, *quale sit*, *an induci in iudicium*

debeat; see Halm, *Rhetores latini minores*, p. 141. Cf. Cicero, *De inventione* 1.8.10–1.11.16, and Quintilian, *Institutio oratoria* 3.6.1–22. These are also the basic terms of philosophical inquiry: see Aristotle, *Posterior Analytics*, book 2, 89b2.

12 For C. Julius Victor's treatment, see Halm, *Rhetores latini minores*, p. 374; for Alcuin's version, see Halm, p. 527, or Howell, *The Rhetoric of Alcuin and Charlemagne*, p. 72.

13 See D. W. Robertson, "A Note on the Classical Origin of 'Circumstances' in the Medieval Confessional," *Studies in Philology* 43 (1946): 6–14; see also Karin Margareta Fredborg, "The Commentary of Thierry of Chartres on Cicero's *De inventione*," *Cahiers de l'Institut du moyen âge grec et latin* (Copenhagen) 7 (1971): 1–36.

14 Fredborg provides a helpful table of Cicero's attributes of the person and the act ("The Commentary of Thierry of Chartres on Cicero's *De inventione*," 18). The table is reproduced here with elements from the scheme of the seven circumstances italicized:

E persona:		*E negotio:*	
nomen	consilia	I	continentia cum negotio
natura	facta	II	in gestione negotii (*locus*, *tempus*, *occasio*, *modus*, *facultas*)
victus	casus		
fortuna	orationes	III	adiuncta negotio (maius, minus, par, simile, contrarium, disparatum, genus, pars, eventus)
habitus			
affectio			
studium		IV	consequentia negotium (accepted or not)

15 In later works, however, Cicero departed from Hermagoras' system in favor of Aristotle's system of topics. See *De oratore* 2.39.162–2.41.176, and *Topica* 2.8–4.25, 5.26–13.55.

16 For Quintilian, see *Institutio oratoria* 5.10.20–52; for Fortunatianus see Halm, pp. 102–3 and 115; for Martianus Capella, see Dick, ed., *De nuptiis Philologiae et Mercurii*, pp. 278–9, or Halm, pp. 188–9; for C. Julius Victor, see Halm, pp. 395 and 424; for Sulpitius Victor, see Halm, p. 323; for Victorinus, see Halm, pp. 213–14, and also pp. 206–7, where the interrogative forms *quis*, *quid*, *cur*, etc. are correlated with the topical forms *persona*, *factum*, *causa*, etc.

17 *PL* 64: 1205: "Rhetorica vero de hypothesibus, id est de quaestionibus circumstantiarum multitudine inclusis, tractat et disserit."

18 *PL* 64: 1212.

19 Boethius is concerned with examining the "whole discipline" of rhetoric, about which "we have received no tradition from ancient teachers. They gave precepts about particular issues, but did not essay the subject as a whole" (*PL* 64: 1207). See the notes to book 4 in Eleonore Stump, trans., *Boethius's De topicis differentiis* (Ithaca: Cornell University Press, 1978), pp. 141–55.

20 Michael Leff, "Boethius' *De differentiis topicis*, Book IV," in Murphy, ed., *Medieval Eloquence*, p. 24.

21 "On the Scope and Function of Hermeneutical Reflection," in Gadamer, *Philosophical Hermeneutics*, pp. 23–4.

22 *Remigii Autissiodorensis commentum in Martianum Capellam*, ed. Cora Lutz, 2 vols. (Leiden: Brill, 1962–5), 1:65.

23 *Commentum in Martianum*, ed. Lutz 2:107, 274.21 on *narratio*; and 2:110, 278.16, on artificial proof *ante rem* (all references to Remigius' glosses follow Lutz' system of referring the gloss to page and line number of Adolph Dick's edition of the *De nuptiis*). Cf. also the gloss at 278.19, where artificial proof *in re*

has twelve sources of argument, including difference, which uses the seven circumstances. Here Remigius supplies, as at 274.21, a list of the seven circumstances.

24 Thus at 278. 16 on proof *ante rem* he refers back to 274.21 on the *narratio*.

25 "Quibus auxiliis: id vero idcirco exponitur, quos fautores haberet, quia illi ita nobiles erant, quod neminem contra senatum iuvabant, ni opus laudabiliter posset ab eis defendi, et hoc dignitas operis erit." Mancini, "Un commento ignoto di Remy d'Auxerre ai *Disticha Catonis*," 180.

26 The *accessus* is printed in George Thilo and Hermann Hagen, eds., *Servii grammatici qui feruntur in Vergilii carmina commentarii* (Leipzig: Teubner, 1923) 1: LXXXV: "ut unde scripsit. de excidio uidelicet troiae et de erroribus aeneae quos passus est donec ueniret ad italiam." For the association with Remigius, see Lutz, "One Formula of *Accessus*," 780.

27 This is demonstrated in detail by Cora Lutz, "Remigius' Ideas of the Seven Liberal Arts," *Traditio* 12 (1956): 65–86. The following discussion is in large part indebted to the information presented in this article.

28 See John J. Contreni, "John Scottus, Martin Hiberniensis, the Liberal Arts, and Teaching," in Michael Herren, ed., *Insular Latin Studies* Papers in Mediaeval Studies 1 (Toronto: Pontifical Institute of Mediaeval Studies, 1981), p. 25.

29 On Eriugena, see Lutz, "Remigius' Ideas on the Classification of the Seven Liberal Arts"; and Gérard Mathon, "Les Formes et la signification de la pédagogie des arts libéraux au milieu du IXe siècle. L'enseignement palatin de Jean Scot Erigène," in *Arts libéraux et philosophie au moyen âge*, pp. 47–64. See also Contreni, "John Scottus."

30 Lutz, "Remigius' Ideas on the Classification of the Seven Liberal Arts," 70; see Eriugena, *De divisione naturae* 3. 29, *PL* 122:705.

31 Lutz, "Remigius' Ideas on the Classification of the Seven Liberal Acts," 77; cf. 474.10: "HANC IGITUR id est hoc TRIBARIUM SIVE TRIGEMINAM FEMINAM id est triplicem, SIVE TRES scilicet sunt, IN UNIUS HOMINIS VOCABULARUM id est putant eam esse phisicam, ethicam, et logicam." On Isidore's use of this system and its relationship to Platonist traditions, see Manuel C. Díaz y Díaz, "Les Arts libéraux d'après les écrivains espagnols et insulaires aux VIIe et VIIIe siècles," in *Arts libéraux et philosophie au moyen âge*, pp. 37–46; see also "Questions et discussions," pp. 65–70.

32 *Remigii . . . Commentum in Martianum* ed. Lutz, 2:25, at 160.1; cf. *Dunchad glossae in Martianum* ed. Cora E. Lutz, Philological Monographs 12 (Lancaster, Pennsylvania: American Philological Association, 1944), p. 22.

33 *Remigii . . . Commentum in Martianum* ed. Lutz, 2:26; cf. *Dunchad*, ed. Lutz, p. 23.

34 *Remigii . . . Commentum in Martianum* 2:26; cf. *Iohannis Scotti annotationes in Marcianum* ed. Cora E. Lutz (Cambridge, Massachusetts: The Mediaeval Academy of America, 1939), p. 94 (at 160.2).

35 E.g., at 171.10, his paraphrase of Eriugena at 171.10: "It is asked why the said liberal arts are not affections. The answer is that the liberal arts are inherent in the soul and are not understood to have come from elsewhere." This idea appears elsewhere in Eriugena's comments (e.g. at 170.14), which would account for why it becomes a governing principle in Remigius' commentary (e.g., 168.19, and 172.11 based on Eriugena at 172.13, where the example of justice as a quality is extended by analogy to learning).

36 *Remigii . . . Commentum in Martianum* ed. Lutz 1:112–13 (at 25.14).

37 See Huygens, *Accessus ad auctores*, "Accessus Prudentii 1," p. 19, lines 11–14, which considers author's name, title of the work, intention, material, and the part

of philosophy to which the work belongs; in the same volume, see also Bernard of Utrecht, p. 66, which investigates material, intention, and to what part of philosophy the work belongs. See also Mancini, "Un commento ignoto di Remy d'Auxerre ai *Disticha Catonis*," 179, citing an *accessus* from the eleventh century which lists the seven circumstances "apud antecessores nostros."

38 See H. Silvestre, "Aperçu sur les commentaires carolingiens de Prudence," *Sacris Erudiri* 9 (1957): 66, "Septem sunt consideranda in inicio cuiusque libri: persona, locus, tempus, scribentis intentio, titulis libri, qualitas carminis, cui parti philosophiae subiaceat" (from the eleventh century). See also Silvestre, "Le Schéma 'moderne' des *accessus*."

39 William M. Green, "Hugo of St. Victor: *De tribus maximis circumstantiis gestorum*," *Speculum* 18 (1973): 484–93. See also Hunt, "Introductions to the 'Artes'," pp. 93–4.

40 Conrad of Hirsau gives a terse definition of *intentio*: "Intentio est quid auctor intendat, quid, quantum, de quo scribere proponat" (*Dialogus super auctores*, lines 226–7, in Huygens, *Accessus ad auctores*, p. 78). In his expositions of individual authors, the statements of authorial intention often perform double service by indicating the utility (final cause) of the work as well. Thus, for example, the explanation of Aesop: "Ex ipsa materia patet auctoris intentio, quis per hoc opus variis compactum figmentis voluit et delectare hominumque naturam quasi rationis expertem ex brutorum animantium collatione ad se revocare. Causa finalis lectionis fructus est" (*Dialogus super auctores*, lines 449–53, in Huygens, *Accessus ad auctores* p. 86).

41 Huygens, *Accessus ad auctores* pp. 31–3.

42 On twelfth-century formats, see Hunt, "Introductions to the 'Artes'," pp. 93–5. The prologue to Ovid's *Heroides* uses an abbreviated version of this prologue type.

43 See Quain, "The Medieval *Accessus ad auctores*" and n. 8, above.

44 See Minnis, *Medieval Theory of Authorship*, p. 56.

45 All references are to Mancini, "Un commento ignoto di Remy d'Auxerre ai *Disticha Catonis*," 179–80.

46 See Richard Hazelton, "The Christianization of Cato: The *Disticha Catonis* in the Light of Late Mediaeval Commentaries," *Mediaeval Studies* 19 (1957): 157–73.

47 Hazelton, "The Christianization of Cato," 165–7, and n. 41.

48 On the relationship between the virtues and the study of rhetoric in the Middle Ages, see Philippe Delhaye, "L'Enseignement de la philosophie morale au XIIe siècle," *Mediaeval Studies* 11 (1949): 77–99.

49 Victorinus, in Halm, *Rhetores latini minores*, pp. 301–2; Alcuin, in Howell, ed., *The Rhetoric of Alcuin and Charlemagne*, pp. 142–55, or Halm, *Rhetores latini minores* pp. 547–50.

50 Text and translation from Marjorie Curry Woods, ed. and trans., *An Early Commentary on the Poetria nova of Geoffrey of Vinsauf* (New York and London: Garland Publ. Co., 1985), pp. 2–3. See also pp. xxii–xxv, and Marjorie Curry Woods, "Literary Criticism in an Early Commentary on Geoffrey of Vinsauf's *Poetria nova*," *Acta Conventus Neo-Latini Bononiensis*, ed. Richard Schoeck, Medieval and Renaissance Texts and Studies 37 (Binghamton, New York, 1985), pp. 667–73.

51 Woods, ed., *An Early Commentary on the Poetria nova* p. 7.

52 *Ibid.* pp. 8–9.

53 On this text and related issues, see Rita Copeland and Stephen Melville, "Allegory and Allegoresis, Rhetoric and Hermeneutics," forthcoming in *Exemplaria*

3.1 (1991), Peter Allen and Jeff Rider, eds., *Reflections in the Frame: New Perspectives on the Study of Medieval Literature.*

54 *The Commentary on the First Six Books on the Aeneid of Vergil Commonly Attributed to Bernardus Silvestris*, ed. Julian Ward Jones and Elizabeth Frances Jones (Lincoln: University of Nebraska Press, 1977), p. 1.

55 *Ibid.* p. 1.

56 *Ibid.* p. 3.

57 For detailed discussions of *integumentum* see: Edouard Jeauneau, "L'Usage de la notion d'*integumentum* à travers les gloses de Guillaume de Conches," *Archives d'histoire doctrinale et littéraire du moyen âge* 24 (1958), 35–100; Henri de Lubac, *Exégèse médiévale* 4: 182–262; Brian Stock, *Myth and Science in the Twelfth Century: A Study of Bernard Silvester* (Princeton: Princeton University Press, 1972), pp. 31–62; Winthrop Wetherbee, *Platonism and Poetry in the Twelfth Century: The Literary Influence of the School of Chartres* (Princeton: Princeton University Press, 1972), pp. 36–48; Peter Dronke, *Fabula: Explorations into the Uses of Myth in Medieval Platonism*, Mittellateinische Studien und Texte 9 (Leiden and Cologne: Brill, 1974); Haijo Jan Westra, ed., *The Commentary on Martianus Capella's De nuptiis Philologiae et Mercurii Attributed to Bernardus Silvestris*, Studies and Texts 80 (Toronto: Pontifical Institute of Mediaeval Studies, 1986), pp. 23–33.

58 William of Conches, *Glosae super Platonem*, ed. Edouard Jeauneau (Paris: Vrin, 1965), p. 57 (Prologue), pp. 58–61 (*accessus*). For an account of William's reading of the *Timaeus* as *integumentum*, see Jeauneau, "L'Usage de la notion d'*integumentum* à travers les gloses de Guillaume de Conches," 58–84.

59 *Commentary on the First Six Books of the Aeneid*, ed. Jones and Jones, p. 3.

60 A standard investigation of the paradoxical status of commentary in terms of modern critical theory is J. Hillis Miller, "The Critic as Host," in Harold Bloom et al., *Deconstruction and Criticism* (New York: Continuum, 1979, rpt. 1986), pp. 217–53.

61 Gerald L. Bruns, *Inventions: Writing, Textuality, and Understanding in Literary History* (New Haven: Yale University Press, 1982), p. 56.

62 *Truth and Method*, pp. 453–4.

63 *Inventions*, p. 56.

64 See Gadamer, *Truth and Method*, p. 359.

65 See Edouard Jeauneau, "Deux rédactions des gloses de Guillaume de Conches sur Priscien," *Recherches de théologie ancienne et médiévale* 27 (1960): 212–45, esp. 224–5. In his prologue to Plato, for example, William of Conches offers a specific distinction: "multos super Platonem commentatos esse, multos glosasse non dubitemus" (Jeauneau, ed., *Glosae super Platonem*, p. 57).

66 Marcus Boas, ed., *Disticha Catonis*, (Amsterdam: North-Holland Publishing Co., 1952). For example, at verse I.28, "Cum tibi sint nati nec opes, tunc artibus illos / instrue, quo possint inopem defendere uitam," Remigius provides almost word-by-word glosses: "Neque opes .i. non habes substantias artibus .i. diuersis quia uerae diuitiae sunt artes: non possunt amitti. Instrue .i. doce, ut uiuere possint. inopem .i. suam paupertatem." pp. 68–9.

67 "quia profundius philosophicam veritatem in hoc volumine declarat Virgilius, ideo non tantum summam, verum etiam verba exponendo in eo diutius immoremur." *Commentary on the First Six Books of the Aeneid*, ed. Jones and Jones, p. 28.

68 *Ibid.* p. 63.

69 In allegorical commentary, this kind of close exposition, or glossing, which rebuilds the text word by word, is also related to medieval concepts of verbal

polyvalence where, as Bernardus Silvestris puts it, "the same name may designate diverse properties, and conversely, diverse names may designate the same property" (see *Commentary on the First Six Books of the Aeneid*, ed. Jones and Jones, p. 9, lines 23–4). The implications of this for the practice of glossing among allegorical exegetes is discussed by Joseph A. Dane, "*Integumentum* as Interpretation: Note on William of Conches's Commentary on Macrobius (I, 2, 10–11)," *Classical Folia* 32 (1978): 201–15. On theoretical questions of allegory and polysemousness in classical and patristic semiotics, see Martin Irvine, "Interpretation and the Semiotics of Allegory in Clement of Alexandria, Origen, and Augustine," *Semiotica* 63 (1987): 33–71.

4. TRANSLATION AND INTERLINGUAL COMMENTARY: NOTKER OF ST. GALL AND THE *OVIDE MORALISÉ*

1 This double legacy is studied by Jean Pépin, "L'Herméneutique ancienne. Les mots et les idées," *Poétique* 23 (1975): 291–300. For the references to Philo I am indebted to Pépin's article. The rhetorical legacy of Aristotle's *Peri hermeneias* is studied in Friedrich Solmsen, "Demetrios *Peri hermeneias* und sein peripatetisches Quellenmaterial," *Hermes* 66 (1931): 241–67; rpt. in *Rhetorika: Schriften zur aristotelischen und hellenistischen Rhetorik*, ed. Rudolf Stark (Hildesheim: Georg Olms, 1968), pp. 285–311.

2 *De vita contemplativa* 3.28, in *Philo*, vol. 9, ed. and trans. F. H. Colson, Loeb Classical Library (London: Heinemann; Cambridge, Mass.: Harvard University Press, 1941). Cf. Colson's note on this passage: "I understand *hermeneia* to be here used as elsewhere . . . in the technical rhetorical sense of the language in which the thought is expressed as opposed to the thought itself, and so with the synonymous *lexis* or *phrasis* corresponding to the Latin *elocutio*" (pp. 128–9).

3 *De migratione Abrahami* 7.35, and 14.78, in *Philo*, vol. 4, ed. and trans. F. H. Colson and G. H. Whitaker, Loeb Classical Library (London: Heinemann; New York: Putnam, 1932).

4 Pépin, "L'Herméneutique ancienne," 293; see Philo, *De congressu quaerendae eruditionis gratia* 4.17, in *Philo*, vol. 4, ed. and trans. Colson and Whitaker.

5 Pépin, "L'Herméneutique ancienne," 292.

6 For the secondary meaning of "signification," see Lewis and Short, *A Latin Dictionary*, s.v. "interpretatio" I.B.2.

7 On the use of the term in Greek sources to mean translation (especially in the case of the Septuagint) see Pépin, "L'Herméneutique ancienne," 294 and references.

8 See Arno Reiff, *Interpretatio, Imitatio, Aemulatio: Begriff und Vorstellung literarischer Abhängigkeit bei den Römern* (diss. Cologne, 1959), pp. 27, 40–1, 70 and 90–1.

9 See Lewis and Short, *A Latin Dictionary*, s.v. *interpres* I.

10 See Roberto Busa, *Index Thomisticus: Sancti Thomae Aquinatis operum omnium indices et concordantiae* 12 (Stuttgart: Frommann-Holzboog, 1975), s.v. *interpres, interpretatio, interpretativus, interpretor*.

11 Cf. Quintilian, *Institutio oratoria* 1.1.35: "Protinus enim potest interpretationem linguae secretioris, quas Graeci γλωσσας vocant, dum aliud agitur, ediscere . . ."

12 *Summa super Priscianum*, excerpt printed in Thurot, *Notices et extraits*, p. 146. Cited also in R. W. Hunt, "The Lost Preface to the *Liber derivationum* of Osbern of Gloucester," *Mediaeval and Renaissance Studies* 4:2.267–82 (London: Warburg Institute, 1952); rpt. in R. W. Hunt, *Collected Papers on the History of Grammar in the Middle Ages*, ed. G. L. Bursill-Hall, Amsterdam Studies in the

Theory and History of Linguistic Science III [Studies in the History of Linguistics 5] (Amsterdam: John Benjamins, 1980), pp. 151–66.

13 Quoted in Hunt, "The Lost Preface to the *Liber derivationum*," pp. 271–2 (pp. 155–6).

14 Among earlier *loci classici* for this and related ideas, see, for example, Augustine, *De civitate dei* 7.14.

15 Joannes Balbus, *Catholicon*, s.v. *interpres* (Mainz, 1460; rpt. Westmead, Farnborough, Hants., England: Gregg International Publishers, 1971), unfol. The emendations are based on the edition of Georg Husner, Strasbourg, 1482. It is worth noting that the *Catholicon* also defines *translatio* as interlingual exposition: "translatio expositio sentencie per aliam linguam" (s.v. *translatio*; cf. *glosa*). This suggests that, historically, the dominant term is *interpretatio*, which can attract related terms, such as *translatio*, into its own field of meaning.

16 Vienna Österreichische Nationalbibliothek MS 4133, fols. 196rb–196va, from the transcription by Ralph Hanna III. I am grateful to Professor Hanna for bringing this text to my attention and supplying me with his own transcription of it. On the treatise by Ullerstan in this manuscript and the English tracts derived from it, see Anne Hudson, "The Debate on Bible Translation, Oxford 1401," *The English Historical Review* 90 (1975): 1–18.

17 *PL* 122: 1032. On this passage see ch. 2, n. 44.

18 See René Roques, "Traduction ou interprétation? Brèves remarques sur Jean Scot traducteur de Denys," in *The Mind of Eriugena*, eds. John J. O'Meara and Ludwig Bieler (Dublin: Irish University Press, 1973), pp. 59–77. Cf. *De divisione naturae* 5, *PL* 122: 1010: "Saepissime enim unam eandemque expositionis speciem absque ullo transitu in diversas figurationes sequentibus aut error aut maxima difficultas innascitur interpretandi: concatenatus quippe est divinae Scripturae contextus, daedalicisque diverticulis et obliquitatibus perplexus."

19 See Pierre Riché, "L'Enseignement et la culture des laïcs dans l'occident pre-Carolingian," in *La scuola nell'occidente latino dell'alto medioevo*. Settimane di studio del centro italiano di studi sull'alto medioevo 19 (Spoleto: Presso la sede de centro, 1972), vol. 1, pp. 231–53. See also Dag Norberg, "A quelle époque a-t-on cessé de parler latin en Gaule?" *Annales (Economies, sociétés, civilisations)* 21 (1966): 346–56.

20 See James J. Murphy, "The Teaching of Latin as a Second Language in the 12th Century," *Historiographia Linguistica* 7:1/2 (1980): 159–75; Brother Bonaventure, "The Teaching of Latin in Later Mediaeval England," *Mediaeval Studies* 23 (1961): 1–20; Bernhard Bischoff, "The Study of Foreign Languages in the Middle Ages," *Speculum* 36 (1961): 209–24, rpt. with some changes in Bischoff, *Mittelalterliche Studien: Ausgewählte Aufsätze zur Schriftkunde und Literaturgeschichte* vol. 2 (Stuttgart: Hiersemann, 1967), pp. 227–45.

21 On Old English glosses, see D. A. Bullough, "The Educational Tradition in England from Alfred to Aelfric: Teaching *Utriusque Linguae*," *La scuola nell'occidente latino dell'alto medioevo*, Settimane di studio del centro italiano di studi sull'alto medioevo 19, vol. 2, pp. 453–94; R. I. Page, "The Study of Latin Texts in late Anglo-Saxon England," part 2, "The Evidence of English Glosses," in Nicholas Brooks, ed., *Latin and the Vernacular Languages in Early Medieval Britain* (Leicester: Leicester University Press, 1982), pp. 141–65; and Helmut Gneuss, *Hymnar und Hymnen im englischen Mittelalter: Studien zur Überlieferung, Glossierung and Übersetzung lateinischer Hymnen in England* (Tübingen: Niemeyer, 1968), chs. 7–8. Among relevant studies of Old High German glosses and paraphrases, see Günter Glauche, "Die Rolle der Schulautoren im Unterricht von 800 bis 1100," in *La scuola nell'occidente latino dell'alto medioevo* vol. 2,

pp. 617–36; Rainer Reiche, *Ein rheinisches Schulbuch aus dem 11. Jahrhundert*, Münchener Beiträge zur Mediävistik und Renaissance-Forschung 24 (Munich: Arbeo-Gesellschaft, 1976); H. Götz, "Kontextübersetzung und Vokabelübersetzung in althochdeutschen Glossen," *Beiträge zur Geschichte der deutschen Sprache und Literatur* (Halle) 82 (1961, supplement vol.): 139–52; A. Schwarz, "Glossen als Text," *Beiträge zur Geschichte der deutschen Sprache und Literatur* (Tübingen) 99 (1977): 25–36; Stefan Sonderegger, "Frühe Übersetzungsschichten im Althochdeutschen," in *Philologia Deutsch: Festschrift zum 70. Geburtstag von Walter Henzen*, ed. Werner Kohlschmidt and Paul Zinsli (Berne: Francke, 1965), pp. 101–14; see also the useful historical overviews in J. K. Bostock, *A Handbook on Old High German Literature*, 2nd edition, K. C. King and D. R. McLintock, eds. (Oxford: Clarendon, 1976).

22 Text in Ernst Hellgardt, "Notkers des Deutschen Brief an Bischof Hugo von Sitten," in Klaus Grubmüller et al., eds., *Befund und Deutung. Zum Verhältnis von Empirie und Interpretation in Sprach- und Literaturwissenschaft* (Tübingen: Niemeyer, 1979), pp. 169–92 (the text of the letter is printed pp. 172–3).

23 The extant items from Notker's list are the translations of Boethius, Martianus Capella, Aristotle's *Categories* and *Peri hermeneias* (from the Boethian versions of these texts), and the Psalter. See the discussion in Hellgardt, "Notkers des Deutschen Brief," pp. 184–92. See also L. M. de Rijk, "On the Curriculum of Arts at St. Gall, 850–1000," *Vivarium* 1 (1963): 35–86. On the place of Notker's translations in the glossing tradition of the schools, see Nikolaus Henkel, *Deutsche Übersetzungen lateinischer Schultexte: Ihre Verbreitung und Funktion im Mittelalter und in der frühen Neuzeit*, Münchener Texte und Untersuchungen zur deutschen Literatur des Mittelalters 90 (Munich: Artemis, 1988), pp. 65–86.

24 The most important study on such hierarchies of prestige in medieval translation is Folena, "'Volgarizzare' e 'tradurre': idea e terminologia della traduzione dal medio evo italiano e romanzo all'umanesimo europeo."

25 For a comprehensive technical and historical study of Notker's translation of Martianus Capella, see Herbert Backes, *Die Hochzeit Merkurs und der Philologie: Studien zu Notkers Martian-Übersetzung* (Sigmaringen: Thorbecke, 1982).

26 James C. King, *Notker der Deutsche. Martianus Capella, "De nuptiis Philologiae et Mercurii." Die Werke Notkers des Deutschen* 4 (new ed. by James C. King and Petrus W. Tax of the series begun by Edward H. Sehrt and Taylor Starck), Altdeutsche Textbibliothek 87 (Tübingen: Niemeyer, 1979), p. 2, lines 3–7. I am grateful to T. A. Shippey and Hubert Heinen for advice on various points of translation from the Old High German.

27 All references to the Remigian sources of Notker's commentary are based on Lutz, ed., *Remigii Autissiodorensis commentum in Martianum Capellam*, checked against James C. King, ed., *Notker Latinus, Die Werke Notkers des Deutschen* 4A (Tübingen: Niemeyer, 1985), published as a supplement to the edition of Notker's translation of Martianus Capella.

28 King, ed., *Notker der Deutsche. Martianus Capella, "De nuptiis Philologiae et Mercurii,"* p. 3, lines 5–15.

29 Lutz, ed., *Remigii ... Commentum in Martianum* 1:67, 3.5; cf. King, ed., *Notker Latinus* 4A, p. 6.11.

30 Dick, ed., *De nuptiis Philologiae et Mercurii*, p. 3, line 13. Cf. King, ed., *Notker Latinus* 4A, p. 6. 12/13.

31 Dick, ed., *De nuptiis Philologiae et Mercurii*, p. 3, line 7.

32 King, ed., *Notker der Deutsche. Martianus Capella, "De nuptiis Philologiae et Mercurii,"* p. 4, lines 2–4. The lemma quoted from Martianus is line 10 of the poem. Cf. King, ed., *Notker Latinus* 4A, p. 7.3

33 See Kurt Mueller-Vollmer, ed., *The Hermeneutics Reader: Texts of the German Tradition from the Enlightenment to the Present* (New York: Continuum, 1985), Introduction, p. 40. In a study of Notker's translation of Martianus' hymn to the sun (*De nuptiis* book 2, lines 185–93), Peter Ganz also notes the breakdown of divisions between translation, commentary, and original text, pointing to the synthesis of classical and biblical strains in Notker's interpretation of the text: see "Der Sonnenhymnus des Martianus Capella bei Notker von St. Gallen," in Klaus Grubmüller, Ruth Schmidt-Wiegand, and Klaus Speckenbach, eds., *Geistliche Denkformen in der Literatur des Mittelalters*, Münstersche Mittelalter-Schriften 51 (Munich: Wilhelm Fink, 1984), pp. 139–51.

34 Dick, ed., *De nuptiis Philologiae et Mercurii*, p. 4, lines 5–6.

35 Lutz, ed., *Remigii ... Commentum in Martianum*, 1:70, 4.5. Cf. King, ed., *Notker Latinus* 4A, p. 11.10/11.

36 King, ed., *Notker der Deutsche. Martianus Capella, "De nuptiis Philologiae et Mercurii,"* p. 5, lines 9–12.

37 See D. H. Green, "The Primary Reception of the Works of Notker the German," *Parergon* n.s.2 (1984): 57–78, esp. 59–60.

38 See A. G. Jongkees, "Translatio studii: les avatars d'un thème médiéval," *Miscellanea Mediaevalia in Memoriam Jan Frederick Niermeyer* (Groningen: Wolters, 1967), pp. 41–51.

39 Brian Stock has explored this question for the eleventh and twelfth centuries: see *The Implications of Literacy: Written Language and Models of Interpretation in the Eleventh and Twelfth Centuries* (Princeton: Princeton University Press, 1983), esp. pp. 12–87 and 326–9.

40 Roger Wright, *Late Latin and Early Romance in Spain and Carolingian France*, ARCA Classical and Medieval Texts, Papers and Monographs 8 (Liverpool: Francis Cairns, 1982), esp. pp. ix–xii, 104–44 and 262.

41 *De vulgari eloquentia*, ed. Aristide Marigo (Florence: Felice le Monnier, 1938), 1.1.3, pp. 6–8.

42 *Il Convivio*, ed. G. Busnelli and G. Vandelli, 1 (Florence: Felice le Monnier, 1934) 1.5, pp. 34–6; translation from Robert S. Haller, trans., *Literary Criticism of Dante Alighieri* (Lincoln: University of Nebraska Press, 1973), p. 63.

43 Giles of Rome (Aegidius Romanus), *De regimine principum libri III*, (Rome, 1607, rpt. Aalen: Scientia Verlag, 1967), 2.2.7, p. 304. This passage is discussed by Serge Lusignan, *Parler vulgairement: les intellectuels et la langue française aux XIIIe et XIVe siècles* (Paris: Vrin; Montréal: University of Montréal Press, 1986), p. 43.

44 *Metalogicon*, ed. C. C. J. Webb (Oxford: Oxford University Press, 1929), 3.4.

45 *Il Convivio*, ed. Busnelli and Vandelli 1.5, p. 33; translation from Haller, *Literary Criticism of Dante Alighieri*, p. 62.

46 *De vulgari eloquentia*, ed. Marigo, 1.9.10–11, p. 72.

47 Thurot, *Notices et extraits*, p. 131; cf. citation and discussion in Lusignan, *Parler vulgairement*, pp. 41–3.

48 See Lusignan, *Parler vulgairement*, for a historical exploration of this problem along lines that are complementary with this study. See especially ch. 2 on medieval theories of the division of languages.

49 The major surveys for France are Jacques Monfrin, "Humanisme et traductions au moyen âge," *Journal des savants* 148 (1963): 161–90, which also contains briefer surveys for Italy and Spain; and Robert J. Lucas, "Mediaeval French Translations of the Latin Classics to 1500," *Speculum* 45 (1970): 225–53.

50 See Hunt, "Introductions to the 'Artes,'" p. 94. For the *accessus* of Arnulf of Orléans see Fausto Ghisalberti, *Arnulfo d'Orléans: un cultore di Ovidio nel secolo*

XII (Milan: Ulrico Hoepli, Libraio del R. Istituto di Scienze e Lettere, 1932), pp. 180–1. On the continuing and widespread use of this form, see the chart in Przychocki, "*Acccssus Ovidiani*", 105; and see the numerous examples of *Metamorphoses* prologues, mainly from the fourteenth century, in Fausto Ghisalberti, "Mediaeval Biographies of Ovid," *Journal of the Warburg and Courtauld Institutes* 9 (1946): 10–59, esp. 51–8.

51 See Ghisalberti, "Mediaeval Biographies of Ovid," 45 and 51, from the thirteenth and fourteenth centuries; and see the chart in Przychocki, "*Accessus Ovidiani*," 105.

52 See Przychocki, "*Accessus Ovidiani*," 99, and Ghisalberti, "Mediaeval Biographies of Ovid," 50–1. For Giovanni del Virgilio see Fausto Ghisalberti, "Giovanni del Virgilio espositore delle Metamorfosi," *Giornale Dantesco* 34, n.s. 4 (1933, Annuario Dantesco, 1931): 1–110 (prologue printed on pp. 13–19).

53 On the use of such terms in vernacular translations, and especially on vernacular equivalents of "utilitas," see Ian Johnson, "Prologue and Practice: Middle English Lives of Christ," in Ellis, ed., *The Medieval Translator: The Theory and Practice of Translation in the Middle Ages*, pp. 69–85, to which the present discussion of vernacular scholastic terminology is partly indebted. Johnson explores the question of translators' use of academic terminology in greater detail in "The Late-Medieval Theory and Practice of Translation with Special Reference to Some Middle English Lives of Christ," diss. University of Bristol, forthcoming.

54 All references to the text of the *Ovide moralisé* are to C. de Boer, *Ovide moralisé: Poème du commencement du quatorzième siècle*, 5 vols., [Verhandelingen der Koninklijke Akademie van Wetenschappen te Amsterdam, Afdeeling Letterkunde, Nieuwe Reeks, vols. 15, 21, 30 no. 3, 37, and 43] (Amsterdam: Johannes Müller, 1915–38).

55 I am grateful to William W. Kibler for advice on the translations from medieval French in this chapter and chapter 5.

56 See Huygens, *Accessus ad auctores*, pp. 30–3, "Accessus Ovidii epistolarum" II and III.

57 Huygens, *Accessus ad auctores* pp. 32 and 35.

58 See Minnis, *Medieval Theory of Authorship*, pp. 204–6.

59 Bruno Roy, ed., *L'Art d'amours: Traduction et commentaire de l'"Ars amatoria" d'Ovide* (Leiden: Brill, 1974), pp. 63–9.

60 See Minnis, *Medieval Theory of Authorship*, pp. 79–80, 102, 118, 164–5, and 173–5.

61 Joseph Engels, *Etudes sur l'Ovide moralisé* (Groningen: J. B. Wolters, 1945), p. 88.

62 The Copenhagen commentary on the *Ovide moralisé* echoes this theme and, like the *Ovide moralisé*, identifies the methods of interpreting pagan *fabula* with those of reading Scripture: "La saincte escripture doncques est acoustumée de user de telles et semblables fables, affin que d'icelles elle puisse extraire et conclure aucune verité" ("Le Commentaire de Copenhagen de l'*Ovide moralisé*," ed. J. Tr. M. van't Sant, Leiden thesis, 1929, rpt. C. de Boer, ed., *Ovide moralisé* vol. 5, appendix 2, p. 387).

63 Engels, *Etudes sur l'Ovide moralisé*, p. 87; Ghisalberti, *Arnulfo d'Orléans: un cultore di Ovidio nel secolo XII*, p. 182, note 1.

64 Ghisalberti, *Arnulfo d'Orléans*, pp. 181–2.

65 Michel Foucault, "What is an Author?" in Foucault, *Language, Counter-Memory, Practice: Selected Essays and Interviews*, ed. Donald F. Bouchard, trans. Donald F. Bouchard and Sherry Simon (Ithaca: Cornell University Press, 1977), pp. 113–38.

66 See Minnis, *Medieval Theory of Authorship*, pp. 94–103, 112–13, and 190–210.
67 The identification of the "Chrestiens" mentioned in book 6, line 2212, with Chrétien de Troyes is accepted by the editor, de Boer. For earlier scholarship see Gaston Paris, "Chrétien Legouais et autres traducteurs ou imitateurs d'Ovide," *Histoire littéraire de la France* 29 (Paris: Imprimerie nationale, 1885): 489–97.
68 *Metamorphoses*, ed. and trans. Frank Justus Miller, 3rd edition rev. by G. P. Goold, 2 vols., Loeb Classical Library (Cambridge, Mass.: Harvard University Press; London: Heinemann, 1977), 1:8–9.
69 Guillaume de Lorris and Jean de Meun, *Le Roman de la Rose*, ed. Felix Lecoy, vol. 2, *CFMA*, vol. 95 (Paris: Champion, 1979). All references will be to the Lecoy edition.
70 Translation from Charles Dahlberg, *The Romance of the Rose by Guillaume de Lorris and Jean de Meun* (Hanover, New Hampshire, and London: University Press of New England, 1971, rpt., 1983), p. 154. I have altered Dahlberg's translation slightly.
71 See Alex J. Denomy, "The Vocabulary of Jean de Meun's Translation of Boethius' *De consolatione philosophiae*," *Mediaeval Studies* 16 (1954): 20.
72 Boethius, *Philosophiae consolatio*, ed. Ludwig Bieler, *CCSL* 94 (Turnhout: Brepols, 1957). All references to the *Consolatio* are to this edition.
73 Text from V. L. Dedeck-Héry, ed., "Boethius' *De consolatione* by Jean de Meun," *Mediaeval Studies* 14 (1952): 165–275 (this citation from p. 198).
74 Translation from Dahlberg, p. 155.
75 Antoine Thomas and Mario Roques, "Traductions françaises de la *Consolatio philosophiae* de Boèce," in *Histoire littéraire de la France* 37 (Paris: Imprimerie nationale, 1938): 451.
76 Thomas and Roques, 454.
77 *Ibid.* 466.
78 *Ibid.* 487.
79 See de Boer's introduction, *Ovide moralisé*, vol. 1, p. 11.
80 The correspondence between the two versions of the *aetas aurea* are as follows: *Ovide moralisé* 466–8 and *Roman de la Rose* 8329–30; *OM* 487 and *RR* 8410–11; *OM* 490–9 and *RR* 8338–49; *OM* 509–12 and *RR* 8381–400.
81 Paule Demats, *Fabula: trois études de mythographie antique et médiévale* (Geneva: Droz, 1973), p. 68.
82 *Fabii Planciadis Fulgentii V.C. opera*, ed. Rudolph Helm (Leipzig: Teubner, 1898), pp. 43–6.
83 M. L. W. Laistner, "Fulgentius in the Ninth Century," in Laistner, *The Intellectual Heritage of the Early Middle Ages* (Ithaca: Cornell University Press, 1957), pp. 202–15.
84 On the multilevel exposition of the *Ovide moralisé*, cf. M. J. B. Richards, "Translation, Borrowing and Original Composition in Mediaeval Poetry: Studies in the *Metamorphoses*, the *Ovide moralisé*, and the *Book of the Duchess*," diss. Cambridge University, 1982, pp. 125–71.
85 John Ridewall, *Fulgentius metaforalis*, ed. Hans Liebeschütz (Leipzig: Teubner, 1926).
86 On Chartrian distinctions between the allegory of the poets and the allegory of the theologians, see Westra's introduction to *The Commentary on Martianus Capella's De nuptiis Philologiae et Mercurii Attributed to Bernardus Silvestris*, pp. 23–33.
87 Demats, *Fabula*, pp. 107–13.
88 *Ibid.* pp. 121–6.
89 See, for example, *The Commentary on Martianus Capella's De nuptiis Philologiae*

et Mercurii Attributed to Bernardus Silvestris, ed. Westra, pp. 23–5 and 45–7, for the distinction between allegory on the Bible and on poets.

5. TRANSLATION AND INTRALINGUAL RECEPTION: FRENCH AND ENGLISH TRADITIONS OF BOETHIUS' *CONSOLATIO*

1 Notable among recent publications is a collection of essays, *The Medieval Boethius: Studies in the Vernacular Translations of De consolatione philosophiae*, ed. A. J. Minnis (Cambridge: D. S. Brewer, 1987). This valuable collection appeared after the present chapter was written. But it has been possible to take account of the information provided in some of these essays and to incorporate further references in the notes to this chapter.

2 See Jacques Monfrin, "Les Traducteurs et leur public en France au moyen âge," *Journal des savants* 149 (1964): 5–20. On aristocratic ownership of manuscripts of the French revised "mixed" version of the *Consolatio*, see Glynnis M. Cropp, "*Le Livre de Boece de Consolacion*: From Translation to Glossed Text," in *The Medieval Boethius*, ed. Minnis, p. 69.

3 Vienna, Österreichische Nationalbibliothek MS 2642. See Thomas and Roques, "Traductions françaises de la *Consolatio*," pp. 423–32.

4 Pierre Courcelle, "Etude critique sur les commentaires de la *Consolation* de Boèce (IXe–XVe siècles), "*Archives d'histoire doctrinale et littéraire du moyen âge* 14 (1939): 95. The commentary by Adalbold of Utrecht is edited by Edmund T. Silk, "Pseudo-Johannes Scottus, Adalbold of Utrecht, and the Early Commentaries on Boethius," *Mediaeval and Renaissance Studies* (Warburg Institute) 3 (1954): 1–40.

5 "quels est la matere, quel entencion, quel profit, quel title," fol. 1a, quoted in Thomas and Roques, p. 424.

6 Fol. 33a, quoted in Thomas and Roques, p. 427.

7 Cited from MS Troyes 1381, fol. 82v and MS Orléans 274, fol. 34a in Jeauneau, "L'Usage de la notion d'*integumentum*," 37. Jeauneau also notes that another manuscript (Troyes 1101, fol. 15vb) adds a fourth mode to this list, *per fabulam*.

8 This portion of the translation is printed from the unique manuscript in Richard A. Dwyer, *Boethian Fictions: Narratives in the Medieval French Versions of the Consolatio philosophiae* (Cambridge, Mass.: The Mediaeval Academy of America, 1976), pp. 100–3. Cf. also Dwyer's discussion of the treatment of *integumentum* in the Burgundian translation of this metrum, pp. 26, 53–5.

9 Text from Dwyer, *Boethian Fictions*, p. 100.

10 "Est autem allegoria oratio sub historica narratione verum et ab exteriori diversum involvens intellectum, ut de lucta Iacob. Integumentum vero est oratio sub fabulosa narratione verum claudens intellectum, ut de Orpheo . . . Allegoria quidem divine pagine, integumentum vero philosophice competit." Westra, ed., *The Commentary on Martianus Capella's De nuptiis Philologiae et Mercurii Attributed to Bernardus Silvestris*, p. 45. Text also in Edouard Jeauneau, "Note sur l'Ecole de Chartres," *Studi Medievali*, 3rd ser. 5.2 (1964): 856.

11 See Jeauneau, "L'Usage de la notion d'*integumentum*," 45–7, for a transcription of this part of William of Conches' commentary from MS Troyes 1381, fol. 69r–v.

12 G. H. Bode, ed., *Scriptores rerum mythicarum latini tres Romae nuper reperti*, (Celle, 1934), Mythographer 1:76; Mythographer 2:44; Mythographer 3, pp. 211–12 (with extensive allegorization). Text of Fulgentius in Helm, ed., *Fulgentii opera*, pp. 77–9. For William's remarks on Fulgentius, see Jeauneau, "L'Usage de la notion d'*integumentum*," 47.

13 Text from Dwyer, *Boethian Fictions*, p. 102.

14 Text of William's commentary on 1 pr.1 in Charles Jourdain, "Des commentaires

inédits de Guillaume de Conches et Nicolas Triveth sur la Consolation de Boèce," *Notices et extraits de manuscrits de la Bibliothèque Impériale* 20.2 (1862): 72–4.

15 On classical studies at Orléans, see Hastings Rashdall, *The Universities of Europe in the Middle Ages*, new edition by F. M. Powicke and A. B. Emden (Oxford: Clarendon, 1936, rpt. 1987), 2:139–51.

16 Roberto Crespo, "Il prologo alla traduzione della 'Consolatio philosophiae' di Jean de Meun e il commento di Guglielmo d'Aragona," *Romanitas et Christianitas. Studi I. H. Waszink* (Amsterdam and London: North Holland Publishing Company, 1973), pp. 55–70. Crespo also recognized that William of Aragon's prologue was used in a Wallonian prose translation of the *Consolatio* made in the later thirteenth century (MS Troyes 898; see Thomas and Roques, pp. 433–6); see Crespo, pp. 61–2 for text and discussion.

17 Alastair Minnis, "Aspects of the Medieval French and English Traditions of the *De consolatione philosophiae*," in Gibson, ed., *Boethius: His Life, Thought, and Influence*, pp. 312–61; on the arguments in favor of William of Conches' commentary, see pp. 316–34.

18 Dedeck-Héry, "Boethius' *De consolatione* by Jean de Meun," 168.

19 This preface is printed (in modernized form) in A. W. Pollard, ed., *Fifteenth Century Prose and Verse* (London: Constable, 1903), pp. 203–8. See pp. 225–6 below for a discussion of Trevisa's prologue.

20 Oresme's preface to his translation from Latin into French of Aristotle's *Ethics* (1370) offers a justification of close translation in terms of the relative cultural status of Latin and French: "Et comme il soit ainsi que latin est a present plus parfait et plus habondant langage que françois, par plus forte raison l'en ne pourroit translater proprement tout latin en françois . . . Par quoy je doy estre excusé en partie se je ne parle en ceste matiere si proprement, si clerement et si ordeneement comme il fust mestier; car, avec ce, je ne ose pas esloingnier mon parler du texte de Aristote, qui est en pluseurs lieux obscur, afin que je ne passe hors son intencion et que je ne faille. Mais se Dieux plaist, par mon labeur pourra estre mieulx entendue ceste noble science et ou temps avenir estre bailliee par autres en françois plus clerement et plus complectement. Et, pour certain, translater telz livres en françois et baillier en françois les arts et les sciences est un labeur moult proffitable; car c'est un langage noble et commun a genz de grant engin et de bonne prudence" (*Le Livre de Ethiques d'Aristote*, ed. Albert Douglas Menut [New York: G. E. Stechert, 1940], pp. 100–1). On Bersuire as translator from Latin into French, see Jean Rychner, "Observations sur la traduction de Tite-Live par Pierre Bersuire (1354–1356)," *Journal des savants* 148 (1963): 242–67.

21 On the political conception of *translatio studii* in medieval France, see A. G. Jongkees, "Translatio studii: les avatars d'un thème médiéval," in *Miscellanea Mediaevalia in Memoriam Jan Frederik Niermeyer*.

22 Alexander Murray, *Reason and Society in the Middle Ages* (Oxford: Clarendon, 1978; rpt. 1985), pp. 251–5.

23 See Lusignan, *Parler vulgairement*, pp. 133–40; for an account of royal commission of translations and ownership of manuscripts, see Monfrin, "Les Traducteurs et leur public en France au moyen âge."

24 Léopold Delisle, *Recherches sur la librairie de Charles V*, 2 vols. (Paris: Champion, 1907), 1:82–119; see also Lusignan, *Parler vulgairement*, p. 136.

25 A recent study of this is John Fleming, *Reason and the Lover* (Princeton: Princeton University Press, 1984), esp. pp. 38–63. For an account of the glosses on Boethius that are common sources of the *Roman de la Rose* and *Li Livres de Confort de Philosophie*, see Minnis, "Aspects of the Medieval French and English Traditions," pp. 324–34.

26 Citations of Boethius' *Consolatio* are from the text of Bieler, *CCSL* 94; of the *Roman de la Rose* from the Lecoy edition; and of *Li Livres de Confort de Philosophie* from the edition by Dedeck-Héry.
27 Translation from Dahlberg, p. 102. In the first sentence, Dahlberg's translation has "above love," which I have emended to "about love."
28 Translation from Dahlberg, p. 104.
29 For example, the commentary edited by Edmund T. Silk, *Saeculi noni auctoris in Boetii consolationem philosophiae commentarius*, Papers and Monographs of the American Academy in Rome 9 (Rome: American Academy in Rome, 1935) gives a gloss quite similar to Jean's: "Quasi diceret, multum debes diligere aduersam fortunam, quae fecit te cognoscere qui tui sint amici, quod scire multo emisses dum eras in prosperitate" (pp. 111–12). Similarly, a version of William of Conches' commentary unpacks the syntax: "id est tempore prosperitatis cognoscere scilicet veros amicos a falsis," MS B.L. Royal 15. B.III, fol. 60v.
30 The manuscript is described in Dwyer, *Boethian Fictions*, p. 44.
31 See Minnis, "Aspects of the Medieval French and English Traditions," pp. 328–34.
32 MS B.N. fr. 812, fol. 14v: "Ce dit Cressus, 'Ja n'avendra, / Ne ja mon cueur ne le croira / Que si tres noble vision / Ait si malle exposicion'," quoted by Dwyer, *Boethian Fictions* p. 44. This corresponds, although in simplified terms, with Jean's lines 6578–84: "car sachiez que cist nobles songes, / ou fause glose volez metre, doit estre entenduz a la letre, / et je meïsmes l'i entens, / si con nos le verrons en tens. / Onc ausi noble vision / n'ot si vils exposicion." Cf. Minnis, "Aspects of the Medieval French and English Traditions," pp. 330–2, on Jean's possible reliance on William of Conches for the depiction of the daughter as an authoritative interpreter.
33 Quoted in Thomas and Roques, p. 450, from MS B.N. fr. 1096. See Thomas and Roques, pp. 450–2, and Dwyer, *Boethian Fictions*, pp. 13, 25–6, 68–9.
34 It is worth noting that another translation, written sometime after 1315, also implies a comparison with previous prose translations when, in a prologue, the translator explains his preference for rendering the *Consolatio* entirely in verse:

> Et l'ay tout rommanchiet en mettre,
> Car c'est plus bel qu'en prose mettre,
> Combien que c'en soit l'ordenanche
> Ou latin, ou il adevance
> Le mettre par devant la prose
> Si com il apert en la glose.

MS B.N. fr. 576, fol. 4v, quoted in Thomas and Roques, p. 455. At the end of this long translation, the translator identifies his birthplace as Meun; and the scribe, who gives the date of the copy as 1382, attributes the translation to Jean de Meun (fol. 82r, Thomas and Roques, p. 462), thus adding further to the intralingual nexus of Jean de Meun's translation. On this anonymous verse translation see J. Keith Atkinson, "A Fourteenth-Century Picard Translation-Commentary of the 'Consolatio Philosophiae'," in *The Medieval Boethius*, ed. Minnis, pp. 32–62.
35 On this second prose–verse translation, see Cropp, "*Le Livre de Boece de Consolacion*: From Translation to Glossed Text," in Minnis, ed., *The Medieval Boethius*, esp. pp. 86–7 for the list of manuscripts; and see G. M. Cropp, "A Checklist of Manuscripts of the Medieval French Anonymous Verse–Prose Version of the 'Consolatio' of Boethius," *Notes and Queries* n.s. 26 (1979): 294–6.
36 For textual comparisons of the first and second mixed versions with Jean de

Meun's version see Ernest Langlois, "La Traduction du Boèce par Jean de Meun," *Romania* 42 (1913): 331–69.

37 The most recent study of this is Glynnis M. Cropp, "Le Prologue de Jean de Meun et *Le Livre de Boece de Consolacion*," *Romania* 103 (1982): 279–83.

38 Glynnis M. Cropp, "Les Gloses du *Livre de Boece de Consolacion*," *Le moyen âge* 42 (1986): 367–81; see p. 367, n. 2 for a list of other manuscripts of this translation which contain a Latin commentary. See also Glynnis M. Cropp, "Les Manuscrits du *Livre de Boece de Consolacion*," *Revue d'histoire des textes* 12–13 (1982–83): 263–352.

39 I have examined the glossed version in MSS B.L., Add. 10341 and Add. 21602 (both fifteenth century). [Cropp, in Minnis, ed., *The Medieval Boethius*, p. 87, lists the latter as 21062.] This system of rubrics seems to be fairly standard among the manuscripts of the glossed version: see Cropp, "Les Gloses du *Livre de Boece de Consolacion*," 368.

40 For a transcription and brief account of the Orpheus meter, see Cropp, "Les Gloses du *Livre de Boece de Consolacion*," 379–80; the *aetas aurea* (2 m.5) is transcribed from MS B.N. fr. 575 in Thomas and Roques, pp. 452–4.

41 See Cropp, "*Le Livre de Boece de Consolacion*: From Translation to Glossed Text," in Minnis, ed., *The Medieval Boethius*, pp. 65 and 71–5; Cropp, "Le Prologue de Jean de Meun et *Le Livre de Boece de Consolacion*," 285–90; for texts of the French text and its Latin model see 291–8.

42 Dwyer, *Boethian Fictions*, p. 13; Cropp, "*Le Livre de Boece de Consolacion*: From Translation to Glossed Text," in Minnis, ed., *The Medieval Boethius*, p. 84n. and p. 87.

43 "Jusque cy souffist par tant comme il en appartient aus lais, et depuis ci jusques a la fin a esté pris de la translacion que fist maistre Jehan de Meun et est trop fort a entendre se n'est a gens bien lettrez," fol. 217r, quoted in Thomas and Roques, p. 438.

44 On this process of metrical experimentation, see Dwyer, *Boethian Fictions* pp. 67–71.

45 W. J. Sedgefield, ed., *King Alfred's Old English Version of Boethius* (Oxford: Oxford University Press, 1899); George Philip Krapp, ed., *The Paris Psalter and the Meters of Boethius* The Anglo-Saxon Poetic Records 5 (New York: Columbia University Press, 1932).

46 See Rita Copeland, "The Middle English 'Candet Nudatum Pectus' and Norms of Early Vernacular Translation Practice," *Leeds Studies in English*, n.s. 15 (1984): 57–81; more generally see Rosemary Woolf, *The English Religious Lyric in the Middle Ages* (Oxford: Clarendon, 1968), and Derek Pearsall, *Old English and Middle English Poetry* (London: Routledge and Kegan Paul, 1977), pp. 94–102 and 133–4.

47 The most complete study of the *Boece* and its response to its sources is by Tim William Machan, *Techniques of Translation: Chaucer's Boece* (Norman, Oklahoma: Pilgrim Books, 1985).

48 V. L. Dedeck-Héry, "The Manuscripts of the Translation of Boethius' *Consolatio* by Jean de Meung," *Speculum* 15 (1940): 432–43. At least one bilingual manuscript of Jean's translation, B.N.fr. 1098, contains the same commentary based on William of Conches, *Commentum domini Linconiensis*, which accompanies some of the manuscripts of the revised prosimetrum translation; see Cropp, "Les Gloses du *Livre de Boece de Consolacion*," 367.

49 On Cambridge University Library MS Ii.3.21, see Edmund T. Silk, "Cambridge MS. Ii.3.21 and the Relation of Chaucer's *Boethius* to Trivet and Jean de Meung," Diss. Yale, 1930. On the recently discovered fragment, University of Missouri MS

150, see George B. Pace and Linda E. Voigts, "A 'Boece' Fragment," *Studies in the Age of Chaucer* 1 (1979): 143–50.

50 Nigel Palmer has argued what would seem just the opposite case for vernacular translations of Boethius. See "Latin and Vernacular in the Northern European Tradition of the *De consolatione philosophiae*," in Gibson, ed., *Boethius. His Life, Thought, and Influence*, pp. 363–409: "In the Boethius translations however there is a growing tendency for the vernacular rendering to be treated as a commentary to the Latin rather than as a substitute" (pp. 365–6). Palmer argues from the evidence of the deployment of translations in manuscripts, as in Latin–French manuscripts of Jean de Meun's *Livre de Confort*, or as in the case of Oxford, Bodleian Library, MS Rawlinson G41, where parts of Jean's translation are used as marginal glosses to a Latin text. Palmer's argument is an important reminder of how "primary" translation operates under an official aim of exegetical service. But while such translations propose to serve the text they also carry the contestatory force that exegesis itself carries, but does not acknowledge.

51 On Renaut de Louhans see Dwyer, *Boethian Fictions* pp. 79–85. Chaucer's direct reliance on a complete copy of Trevet's commentary is verified in Mark J. Gleason, "Clearing the Fields: Towards a Reassessment of Chaucer's Use of Trevet in the 'Boece'," in Minnis, ed., *The Medieval Boethius*, pp. 89–105.

52 The following textual analysis is drawn from a similar analysis in my article, "Rhetoric and Vernacular Translation in the Middle Ages," *Studies in the Age of Chaucer* 9 (1987): 41–75; cf. pp. 58–60. Texts of Boethius and of Jean de Meun's translation as above; all citations of Chaucer are from *The Riverside Chaucer* 3rd edition, ed. Larry D. Benson (Boston: Houghton Mifflin, 1987). The text of Trevet's commentary is from E. T. Silk, ed., "Exposicio Fratris Nicolai Trevethi Anglici Ordinis Predicatorum super Boecio de consolacione," unpublished typescript.

53 In Cambridge University Library MS Ii.3.21, Trevet's gloss on this passage is not present in the Latin text or in the text of the *Boece*; see Silk, "Cambridge MS. Ii.3.21," pp. 486 and 493.

54 Text from John Walton, *Boethius: De consolatione philosophiae*, ed. Mark Science, EETS o.s. 170 (London: Milford, 1927). For the character "thorn" I have supplied the modern spelling, "th"; for the character "yogh" I have supplied the modern letter "y."

55 It is worth noting that Walton's invocation of Chaucer as "floure of rethoryk" recalls two of Chaucer's own invocations of recent predecessors whose works he is translating: the invocation of Petrarch at the start of *The Clerk's Tale*, "Fraunceys Petrak, the lauriat poete, / Highte this clerk, whos *rethorike* sweete . . . " (31–2); and the invocation of Graunson in the envoy of *The Complaint of Venus*, "To folowe word by word the curiosite / Of Graunson, *flour* of hem that make in Fraunce" (81–2). While the phrasing in all these cases may be conventional, there is an interesting contextual association between them: it points to the way that Walton identifies himself, not simply with Chaucer, but with the legacy of Chaucerian translation.

56 The 1525 printed edition of Walton's *Consolation* emends this line to read, "Though I hys makyng do conterfete," the "hys" referring presumably to Chaucer. It would appear that the sixteenth-century editor, Thomas Richard of Tavistock, acted on his perception of Walton's obvious dependence on the *Boece*, changing the line to foreground the historical relationship between the texts. See Science's introduction to his edition of Walton's text, p. li.

57 Ian R. Johnson, "Walton's Sapient Orpheus," in Minnis, ed., *The Medieval Boethius*, pp. 139–68 (quote from p. 163).

58 The following textual analysis draws partly from my article, "Rhetoric and Vernacular Translation in the Middle Ages," 58–9. References to all texts as above.

59 It is worth noting that in Cambridge University Library MS Ii.3.21, the gloss "approbo" is inserted above the word "probo" in Boethius' text. See Silk, "Cambridge MS. Ii.3.21," p. 486.

60 For a partial list of correspondences between the *Boece* and Walton's version, see the introduction to Science's edition of Walton, pp. lii–lviii. On correspondences in 2 m.5, see my "Rhetoric and Vernacular Translation in the Middle Ages," 68–74.

6. FROM ANTIQUITY TO THE MIDDLE AGES II: RHETORICAL INVENTION AS HERMENEUTICAL PERFORMANCE

1 Roland Barthes, "L'Ancienne Rhétorique," *Communications* (Ecole pratique des hautes études) 16 (1970): 198. In a lecture entitled "Reinventing Invention" (Cornell University, 1984), Jacques Derrida has made an interesting argument for invention as a form of *dispositio*, an arrangement of what is already there.

2 See the discussion in Silvia Gastaldi, *Discorso della città e discorso della scuola. Ricerche sulla "Retorica" di Aristotele* (Florence: La Nuova Italia, 1981), ch. 2, "Lo statuto concettuale della retorica aristotelica," esp. pp. 35–44.

3 See Karin Margareta Fredborg, "Petrus Helias on Rhetoric," *Cahiers de l'Institut du moyen âge grec et latin* 13 (1974): 31–41; and Fredborg, "The Commentary of Thierry of Chartres on Cicero's *De inventione*."

4 *De doctrina christiana*, 1.1, ed. Green, *CSEL* 80:8.

5 McKeon, "Rhetoric in the Middle Ages," 5–7; cf. Robert O. Payne, *The Key of Remembrance: A Study of Chaucer's Poetics* (New Haven: Yale University Press, 1963), pp. 45–6.

6 Gerald Press, "The Subject and Structure of Augustine's *De doctrina christiana*," *Augustinian Studies* 11 (1980): 99–124.

7 Prologue 1.1. *CSEL* 80:3. The translation of this passage is that of Press, "Subject and Structure," 112.

8 Press, "Subject and Structure," 107–12.

9 *Ibid.* 112–18.

10 *Ibid.* 117.

11 3.12.19–29. *CSEL* 80:91–2. Translation from Robertson, *On Christian Doctrine*, p. 91.

12 3.12.20. *CSEL* 80: 92; Robertson, trans., *On Christian Doctrine*, p. 91.

13 3.25.35, 37. *CSEL* 80:100–1; Robertson, trans., *On Christian Doctrine*, pp. 100–1.

14 John Ward's comprehensive study of medieval commentaries and glosses on Cicero's rhetoric, "*Artificiosa Eloquentia* in the Middle Ages," traces the dominance of dialectical study of rhetoric, especially in northern France from the eleventh to the thirteenth centuries. McKeon's article "Rhetoric in the Middle Ages" also provides a good account of the various phases of dialectical interest in rhetoric.

15 Ward, "*Artificiosa Eloquentia*" 1:52–3.

16 *De divisione naturae* books 1 and 4, *PL* 122: 475, 869–70.

17 Ward, "*Artificiosa Eloquentia*' 1:52–3, 200–8.

18 See Mary Dickey, "Some Commentaries on the *De inventione* and *Ad Herennium* of the Eleventh and Early Twelfth Centuries," *Mediaeval and Renaissance Studies* (Warburg Institute) 6 (1968): 1–41. See also Karin Margareta Fredborg, "The Commentaries on Cicero's *De inventione* and *Rhetorica ad Herennium* by

William of Champeaux," *Cahiers de l'Institut du moyen âge grec et latin* 17 (1976): 1–39.

19 *Commentarius super libros de inventione*, in Karin Margareta Fredborg, ed., *The Latin Rhetorical Commentaries by Thierry of Chartres* (Toronto: Pontifical Institute of Mediaeval Studies, 1988), pp. 49–51. See also Nicholas M. Häring, "Thierry of Chartres and Dominicus Gundissalinus," *Mediaeval Studies* 26 (1964): 271–86; Ward, "*Artificiosa Eloquentia*" 1:447–62, and 2:214–60.

20 For Eriugena, see *De divisione naturae* book 5, *PL* 122: 870, and for Eriugena and Martin of Laon, see Contreni, "John Scottus, Martin Hiberniensis, the Liberal Arts, and Teaching," in Herren, ed., *Insular Latin Studies*, pp. 23–44. See also Hugh of St. Victor's version of this in the *Didascalicon*, ed. C. H. Buttimer, Catholic University of America, Studies in Medieval and Renaissance Latin 10 (Washington, D.C.: Catholic University of America Press, 1939), book 2, chs. 28–30. On the scheme of Giles of Rome (a version of the Aristotelian scheme of theoretical and practical sciences), see Gilbert Dahan, "Notes et textes sur la poétique au moyen âge," *Archives d'histoire doctrinale et littéraire du moyen âge* 47 (1980): 177–8. For the classification under *eloquentia* by Ralph of Longchamp, see Martin Grabmann, *Die Geschichte der scholastischen Methode* (Freiburg, 1909; rpt. Darmstadt: Wissenschaftliche Buchgesellschaft, 1957) 2: 48–54. For an overview of these issues, see James A. Weisheipl, "Classification of the Sciences in Medieval Thought," *Mediaeval Studies* 27 (1965): 54–90.

21 See Douglas Kelly, "La Spécialité dans l'invention des topiques," in Lucie Brind'amour and Eugene Vance, eds., *Archéologie du signe* (Toronto: Pontifical Institute of Mediaeval Studies, 1983), pp. 101–25.

22 See Paolo Bagni, *La costituzione della poesia nelle artes del XII–XIII secolo*, Università degli Studi di Bologna, Studi e Ricerche n.s. 20 (Bologna: Zanichelli, 1968), esp. pp. 13–54.

23 Gundissalinus draws on Arabic classifications of the Aristotelian corpus: 'Secundum Alfarabium octo sunt partes logice: cathegorie, perhiermenias, analetica priora, analetica posteriora, thopica, sophistica, rethorica, poëtica," *De divisione philosophiae*, ed. Ludwig Baur, Beiträge zur Geschichte der Philosophie des Mittelalters 4, nos. 2–3 (Münster, 1903), p. 71. In the preface to his commentary on the *Posterior Analytics*, Aquinas gives a threefold division of the reasoning process: judicative, which leads to demonstrative proof; inventive, which involves judgment without certitude; and sophistic, which is fallacious reasoning. Under inventive logic, Aristotle's *Topics* is concerned with probable proof (belief or opinion), the *Rhetoric* with reasoning that produces suspicion rather than complete belief or opinion, and the *Poetics* with the process that invites judgment based on the "estimation" of something as represented through similitude (*Proemium* 6). See text in Raymundi M. Spiazzi, O.P. ed., *In Aristotelis libros peri hermeneias et posteriorum analyticorum expositio*, Leonine text (2nd edition, Turin: Marietti, 1964), p. 148.

24 Cf. Bagni's analysis of this problem, *La costituzione della poesia*, pp. 32–45.

25 Murphy, *Rhetoric in the Middle Ages*, pp. 135–6.

26 See above, chapter 3, pp. 76–82.

27 Traugott Lawler, ed. and trans., *The Parisiana poetria of John of Garland* (New Haven and London: Yale University Press, 1974), pp. xii–xv. All references will be to this edition.

28 For brief discussion and bibliography, see Lawler, ed., *Parisiana poetria*, p. xii and note 3.

29 Lawler, ed. and trans., *Parisiana poetria*, pp. 8–9.

30 *Ibid.* pp. 20–1. I have altered Lawler's translation slightly.

31 Huygens, *Accessus ad auctores* p. 32.

32 Lawler, ed. and trans., *Parisiana poetria*, pp. 28–31. I have altered Lawler's translation of the rubric; and for "libri disposicionem" he reads "the layout of the book," for which I have substituted the more general term "arrangement."

33 Paolo Bagni, "L'*inventio* nell'ars poetica latino-medievale," in Brian Vickers, ed., *Rhetoric Revalued* (Binghamton, New York: Center for Medieval and Early Renaissance Studies, 1982), pp. 99–114.

34 Douglas Kelly, "The Scope of the Treatment of Composition in the Twelfth- and Thirteenth-Century Arts of Poetry," *Speculum* 41 (1966): 261–78.

35 *Ars versificatoria* in Edmond Faral, ed., *Les Arts poétiques du XIIe et du XIIIe siècle* (Paris: Champion, 1924), pp. 110–11.

36 *Ibid.* pp. 118–51.

37 *Ibid.* p. 150: "Attributa vero, tam negotii quam personae, in hoc versiculo continetur: Quis, quid, ubi, quibus auxiliis, cur, quomodo, quando."

38 *Ibid.* p. 66.

39 *Ibid.* p. 135.

40 *Ibid.* p. 179.

41 *Ibid.* pp. 179–80.

42 Cf. Bagni, "L'*inventio* nell'ars poetica latino-medievale," in Vickers, ed., *Rhetoric Revalued* p. 102: "Sembra tuttavia insufficiente l'opposizione tra *sententiae conceptio* e *verborum excogitatio* per potersi riferire, qui, alla categoria dell'*inventio*."

43 *Ars versificatoria*, in Faral, *Les Arts poétiques* p. 180.

44 *Ibid.* p. 184.

45 Cf. D. Kelly, "The Scope of the Treatment of Composition in the Twelfth- and Thirteenth-Century Arts of Poetry," 268: "In fact, there is nothing in the *Ars versificatoria* to suggest that Matthew even thought that *inventio* and *dispositio* in any form were relevant to his instruction. These two steps in composition are not taken up in elementary versification; indeed there is no need for them, since Matthew supplies his students with the *materia* all ready for ornamentation." As Kelly notes, the treatise does not aim to cover invention as a separate consideration. But while this passage does not represent a systematic treatment of invention, it does represent the only real reference in the treatise to the basic concern of invention, that is, finding what there is to say and selecting from among the possibilities that present themselves. Whether it is a teacher who performs this inventional function for a student or a writer who performs it for himself does not change the assumption in medieval rhetorical poetics of a traditional textual framework for invention.

46 *Ars versificatoria*, in Faral, *Les Arts poétiques* p. 180.

47 *Documentatum de modo et arte dictandi et versificandi*, in Faral, *Les Arts poétiques*, p. 309.

48 *Ibid.* p. 310.

49 Cf. Karin Margareta Fredborg, "'Difficile est proprie communia dicere' (Horace, *A.P.* 128), Horatsfortolkningens bidrag til middelalderens poetik," in *Studier i antik og middelalderlig filosofi og idehistorie*, Museum Tusculanum 40–3 (Copenhagen: Museum Tusculanum, 1980), pp. 583–97, esp. p. 590. I am grateful to Gudni Elisson for translating this article from the Danish.

50 See above, ch. 2, pp. 45–55.

51 Brink, *Horace on Poetry: The "Ars poetica,"* pp. 204 and 432–40.

52 Otto Keller, ed., *Pseudacronis scholia in Horatium vetustiora* 2 (Leipzig: Teubner, 1904): 330.

53 See Brink, *Horace on Poetry: The "Ars poetica,"* pp. 204–10.

54 See *ibid.* pp. 205–7 for the implications of the Pseudo-Acronian reading, and for his own argument about *communia* and *proprie* as roughly equivalent to logical categories of generalities and particulars.
55 On the proscriptive force of *difficile*, see *ibid.* p. 204.
56 H. J. Botschuyver, ed., *Scholia in Horatium codicum Parisinorum latinorum 7972, 7974, 7971* (Amsterdam: Bottenburg, 1935), p. 432. Hereafter this edition is cited as Botschuyver 1935.
57 For example, H. J. Botschuyver, ed., *Scholia in Horatium in codibus Parisinis latinis 17897 et 8223 obvia, quae ab Heirico Autissiodorensi profecta esse videntur* (Amsterdam: Bottenburg, 1942), pp. 464–5 (hereafter cited as Botschuyver 1942); J. Zechmeister, ed., *Scholia Vindobonensia ad Horatii Artem poeticam* (Vienna, 1877), p. 13. Cf. also MS Zurich, Zentralbibl. 76 (twelfth century), ff. 16vb–17ra, as printed in Fredborg, "'Difficile est proprie communia dicere,'" p. 595: "COMMUNIA idest contracta. Quod enim ab aliquo dictum non est, id omnibus communiter licet."
58 Cf. the discussion of these departures in Geoffrey and other commentators in Fredborg, "'Difficile est proprie communia dicere,'" p. 590.
59 f. 22v.
60 MS Copenhagen, Kgl. Bibl., Ny kgl. Saml. 213b 4°, f. 10r, printed by Fredborg, "'Difficile est proprie communia dicere,'" p. 595. Fredborg also lists (p. 596, n. 9) nine other manuscripts, located throughout Europe and dating from the twelfth through the fourteenth centuries, in which this commentary is found.
61 As one commentary puts it, to gloss the term *proprie*: "id est appropriare sibi" (MS B. L. Burney 178, f. 52v.).
62 Keller, ed., *Pseudacronis scholia* 2:331. Cf. Botschuyver 1935, p. 433: "UNDE PEDEM PROFERRE PUDOR VETET AUT OPERIS LEX ut verbum e verbo non transferas, ne incidas in obscuritatem aliquam, quam non possis transferre."
63 MS B.N.lat. 7973, f.52r.
64 MS B.N.lat. 8216, f.79r.
65 MS B.N.n.a.lat. 350, f.33v.
66 Botschuyver 1942, p. 465.
67 See above, chapter 4, p. 89.
68 *Documentum de modo et arte dictandi et versificandi*, in Faral, *Les Arts poétiques*, pp. 311–12.

7. TRANSLATION AS RHETORICAL INVENTION: CHAUCER AND GOWER

1 Another important area for an exploration of the intersections of vernacularity, rhetoric, and hermeneutics is the social and textual practices of the Wycliffite movement. See, for example, Margaret Aston, "Wyclif and the Vernacular," in Anne Hudson and Michael Wilks, eds., *From Ockham to Wyclif*, Studies in Church History Subsidia 5 (Oxford: Blackwell, 1987), pp. 281–330.
2 This reading of *De vulgari eloquentia* is indebted to Colish, *The Mirror of Language*, pp. 175–83.
3 This paragraph draws on the arguments of Marianne Shapiro, "On the Role of Rhetoric in the *Convivio*," *Romance Philology* 40 (1986): 38–64.
4 Cf. the discussion of medieval ethical justifications of literary pleasure in Glending Olson, *Literature as Recreation in the Later Middle Ages* (Ithaca: Cornell University Press, 1982), pp. 19–38 and 93–109.
5 On Dante's use of the vernacular in the *Convivio* for academic exegesis and the historical and stylistic implications for the work, see Cesare Segre, *Lingua, stile e società: Studi sulla storia della prosa italiana* (Milan: Feltrinelli, 1963), pp. 227–70.
6 In modern critical discussions the point of departure for such a critique is

Gramsci's notion of the "organic intellectual." See Antonio Gramsci, "La formazione degli intelletuali," in *Gli intelletuali e l'organizzazione della cultura*, Opera di Antonio Gramsci, 3 (Turin: Giulio Einaudi, 1955), pp. 3–19.

7 On *Troilus and Criseyde* and *Knight's Tale* see David Wallace, *Chaucer and the Early Writings of Boccaccio* (Cambridge: D. S. Brewer, 1985); on *Romaunt of the Rose*, see Caroline D. Eckhardt, "The Art of Translation in *The Romaunt of the Rose*," *Studies in the Age of Chaucer* 6 (1984): 41–63; on the *Book of the Duchess* as a tissue of quotation from Machaut, Froissart, and *Le Roman de la Rose*, see James I. Wimsatt, *Chaucer and the French Love Poets: The Literary Background of the Book of the Duchess* (Chapel Hill: University of North Carolina Press, 1968), pp. 155–62. See also R. A. Shoaf, "Notes Toward Chaucer's Poetics of Translation," *Studies in the Age of Chaucer* 1 (1979): 55–66.

8 See, for example, John M. Fyler, *Chaucer and Ovid* (New Haven: Yale University Press, 1979), pp. 96–123.

9 For further reflection on these issues as they pertain to Chaucerian poetics, see Robert O. Payne, "Making His Own Myth: The Prologue to Chaucer's *Legend of Good Women*," *Chaucer Review* 9 (1975): 197–211. Cf. Jesse M. Gellrich, *The Idea of the Book in the Middle Ages: Language Theory, Mythology, and Fiction* (Ithaca: Cornell University Press, 1985), pp. 202–23, esp. p. 207.

10 On the question of sources see *The Riverside Chaucer*, p. 1059. On the influence of hagiographies, see Lisa J. Kiser, *Telling Classical Tales: Chaucer and the Legend of Good Women* (Ithaca: Cornell University Press, 1983), pp. 101–11.

11 See chapter 3 above, pp. 76–80.

12 See chapter 3 above, pp. 77–8 for a discussion of this *accessus*.

13 Huygens, *Accessus ad auctores* p. 32.

14 The most important study of Chaucer's debt to Ovidian scholia is M. C. Edwards, "A Study of Six Characters in Chaucer's *Legend of Good Women* with Reference to Medieval *Scholia* on Ovid's *Heroides*," B.Litt. thesis, Oxford, 1970. See also Sanford Brown Meech, "Chaucer and an Italian Translation of the *Heroides*," *PMLA* 45 (1930): 110–28; and Meech, "Chaucer and the *Ovide moralisé* – a Further Study," *PMLA* 46 (1931): 182–204. The commentary on the *Heroides* in MS Munich Clm. 19475 is edited by Ralph Hexter, *Ovid and Medieval Schooling. Studies in Medieval School Commentaries on Ovid's Ars amatoria, Epistulae ex Ponto, and Epistulae Heroidum*, Münchener Beiträge zur Mediävistik und Renaissance-Forschung, 38 (Munich: Arbeo-Gesellschaft, 1986), pp. 229–302.

15 See especially Payne, *The Key of Remembrance*, pp. 91–111.

16 See James I. Wimsatt, *The Marguerite Poetry of Guillaume de Machaut*, University of North Carolina Studies in the Romance Languages and Literatures 87 (Chapel Hill: University of North Carolina Press, 1970), esp. pp. 30–9.

17 Compare the opposition in Chaucer between "making" and "poetry." See Winthrop Wetherbee, *Chaucer and the Poets: An Essay on Troilus and Criseyde* (Ithaca: Cornell University Press, 1984); Glending Olson, "Making and Poetry in the Age of Chaucer," *Comparative Literature* 31 (1979): 272–90.

18 *Middle English Dictionary*, ed. Hans Kurath and Sherman M. Kuhn, part D.1 (Ann Arbor: University of Michigan Press, 1961), s.v. "declaren," 1.a.

19 On this as a conventional posture of the compiler, see Minnis, *Medieval Theory of Authorship*, pp. 190–8.

20 See "Accessus Boetii," Huygens, *Accessus ad auctores*, p. 47; see also Conrad of Hirsau on Boethius, *Dialogus super auctores*, Huygens, pp. 105–10.

21 Eva Matthews Sanford, "The Manuscripts of Lucan: *Accessus* and Marginalia," *Speculum* 9 (1934): 290.

22 See text in Huygens, esp. Ovid, p. 114, Prudentius, p. 97, and Virgil, p. 120.

23 Ghisalberti, "Giovanni del Virgilio, espositore delle 'Metamorfosi,'" 14–17. Cf. Ghisalberti, "Medieval Biographies of Ovid," 36: "In those prefaces which have the character of true lives, we find the indispensable catalogue of the works." We find such canonical inventories in Arnulf of Orleans and throughout later Ovidian commentaries. See also B. Nogara, "Di alcune vite e commenti medioevali di Ovidio," *Miscellanea Ceriani* (Milan: Ulrico Hoepli, 1910), pp. 415–31.

24 It is worth noting that these two lines of G, 341–2, render some small but significant changes on the corresponding lines in F by substituting terms more specific to a textual culture for the more general terms in F: F reads "He myghte *doon yt*, gessyng no malice," for which G reads "He may *translate* a thyng . . . "; and in F the line "But for he useth *thynges* for to make" is altered in G to "he useth *bokes* for to make."

25 A. J. Minnis, "The Influence of Academic Prologues on the Prologues and Literary Attitudes of Late-Medieval English Writers," *Mediaeval Studies* 43 (1981): 375–6.

26 See Minnis, *Medieval Theory of Authorship*, pp. 100–2, 193–4.

27 Robert Worth Frank, Jr., *Chaucer and the Legend of Good Women* (Cambridge, Mass.: Harvard University Press, 1972), pp. 199–206 and *passim*; Kiser, *Telling Classical Tales*, pp. 99–101; Peter L. Allen, "Reading Chaucer's Good Women," *Chaucer Review* 21 (1987): 419–34.

28 For a reading of the textual struggle with the authority of Virgilian traditions in the "Legend of Dido" and the *House of Fame*, see Baswell, "'Figures of Olde Werk': Visions of Virgil in Later Medieval England," pp. 227–334.

29 Lewis and Short, *A Latin Dictionary*, s.v. *tenor* II.

30 See Meech, "Chaucer and an Italian Translation of the Heroides," 112, n. 7.

31 The two *accessus* (one general and one on Medea) are from the same manuscript, Munich Clm. 19475, ff. 1r, 28r, cited from Edwards, "A Study of Six Characters in Chaucer's *Legend of Good Women*, pp. 29 and 72. The general *accessus* is also edited by Huygens, *Accessus ad auctores* pp. 29–30.

32 See Conrad Mainzer, "John Gower's Use of the 'Mediaeval Ovid' in the *Confessio Amantis*," *Medium Aevum* 41 (1972): 215–29; Derek Pearsall, "Gower's Narrative Art," *PMLA* 81 (1966): 475–84 (esp. 481–2, on Benoit de Sainte-Maure as a source for Gower's version of Jason and Medea).

33 See Charles Runacres, "Art and Ethics in the 'Exempla' of *Confessio Amantis*," in A. J. Minnis, ed., *Gower's Confessio Amantis: Responses and Reassessments* (Cambridge: D. S. Brewer, 1983), pp. 106–34; also Kurt O. Olsson, "Rhetoric, John Gower, and the Late Medieval *Exemplum*," *Medievalia et Humanistica* n.s. 8 (1977): 185–200.

34 *Medieval Theory of Authorship*, pp. 177–90; see also Minnis, "'Moral Gower' and Medieval Literary Theory," in Minnis, ed., *Gower's Confessio Amantis*, pp. 50–78, esp. 67 ff. More recently, James Simpson, in "Ironic Incongruence in the Prologue and Book 1 of Gower's *Confessio Amantis*," *Neophilologus* 72 (1988): 617–32, has argued that the philosophical or ethical framework of the *Prologus* is ironically, and deliberately, at odds with the thematics of love derived from Ovid which Gower treats in the text of the poem. Simpson only considers book 1; see, however, my discussion below of the more broadly discursive implications of book 7.

35 All quotations of *Confessio amantis* are from *The English Works of John Gower* ed. G. C. Macaulay, 2 vols., EETS e.s. 81–2 (London: Kegan Paul, Trench, Trübner, 1900–1).

36 Gloss at book 1, line 60, p. 37.

37 Winthrop Wetherbee has noted the deflection of the tables from their ostensibly illustrative purpose as moral *exempla*, arguing that their presentation often

subverts their purported moral intent, partly because the figure of Genius as teller does not represent a one-dimensional moral vision; see "Genius and Interpretation in the *Confessio Amantis*," in Arthur Groos, ed., *Magister Regis: Studies in Honor of Robert Earl Kaske* (New York: Fordham University Press, 1986), pp. 241–60. Cf. Simpson, "Ironic Incongruence," 623–7.

38 See Minnis, "'Moral Gower' and Medieval Literary Theory," in Minnis, ed., *Gower's Confessio Amantis*, pp. 67–78.

39 Gloss at *Prologus* lines *34 ff., pp. 3–4.

40 See Malcolm B. Parkes, "The Influence of the Concepts of *Ordinatio* and *Compilatio* on the Development of the Book," *Medieval Learning and Literature: Essays Presented to Richard William Hunt*, ed. J. J. G. Alexander and M. T. Gibson (Oxford: Clarendon, 1975), pp. 115–41.

41 Parkes, "The Influence of the Concepts of *Ordinatio* and *Compilatio*," pp. 125–9.

42 See Judson Boyce Allen, *The Ethical Poetic of the Later Middle Ages: A Decorum of Convenient Distinction* (Toronto: University of Toronto Press, 1982), ch. 3, "Poetic Disposition and the Forma Tractatus," pp. 117–78.

43 *Summa theologiae*, vol. 1, ed. Bernard Klumper (Quaracchi: Collegii S. Bonaventurae 1924), Tractatus introductorius, quaestio i, cap. 4, art.1, ad secundum (p. 8); cf. Parkes, 'The Influence of the Concepts of *Ordinatio* and *Compilatio*," p. 119.

44 See George Cary, *The Medieval Alexander* (Cambridge: Cambridge University Press, 1956), esp. pp. 105–10 and 163–225.

45 Gundissalinus divides practical science into "civilis racio" (the arts of speech), "ordinacio familiaris" (economics), and ethics or morals. Rhetoric, grammar, and poetics comprise "civilis racio" (*De divisione philosophiae*, p. 16). Giles of Rome also follows a version of the Aristotelian scheme of the sciences, with divisions into mechanical, practical (moral), and speculative (theoretical): here, grammar, logic, and rhetoric represent "instrumental" arts under speculative science (see Dahan, "Notes et textes sur la poétique au moyen âge," 177). Cf. Vincent of Beauvais, who presents the *artes sermocinales* as the intellectual tools of the primary divisions of the sciences, theoretical, practical, and mechanical; see *Speculum historiale* (Douai, 1624, rpt. Graz: Akademische Druck, 1965), 1.53–5.

46 *Li Livres du Trésor de Brunetto Latini*, ed. Francis J. Carmody, University of California Publications in Modern Philology (Berkeley and Los Angeles: University of California Press, 1948), pp. 18–22.

47 *Trésor*, ed. Carmody, p. 17.

48 *Trésor*, 2.1, ed. Carmody, p. 175.

49 Cf. Margaret T. Gibson, "The *Artes* in the Eleventh Century," *Arts libéraux et philosophie au moyen âge*, pp. 121–6.

50 *Trésor*, 1.4, ed. Carmody, pp. 20–1.

51 *Trésor*, 3.1, ed. Carmody, p. 317.

52 Carmody, introduction, pp. xxv–xxvi. For background on Brunetto's treatment of rhetoric in the *Trésor* in relation to his earlier rhetorical studies, the *Rettorica*, a vernacular version and exposition of part of the *De inventione*, and his translations of three of Cicero's orations, see Bianca Ceva, *Brunetto Latini: l'uomo e l'opera* (Milan: Ricciardi, 1965), pp. 64–81, 124–55, and Thor Sundby, *Della vita e delle opere di Brunetto Latini*, trans. Rodolfo Renier (Florence: Le Monnier, 1884), pp. 187–94.

53 John H. Fisher, *John Gower, Moral Philosopher and Friend of Chaucer* (London: Methuen, 1965), pp. 185 and 191.

54 On Gower's knowledge of formal rhetoric and his indebtedness to Brunetto, see James J. Murphy, "John Gower's *Confessio Amantis* and the First Discussion of Rhetoric in the English Language," *Philological Quarterly* 41 (1962): 401–11.

55 *The English Works of John Gower*, 2:273.
56 See Elizabeth Porter, "Gower's Ethical Microcosm and Political Macrocosm," in Minnis, ed., *Gower's Confessio Amantis*, pp. 135–62.
57 Russell Peck, ed., *Confessio Amantis* (New York: Holt, Rinehart and Winston, 1966; rpt. Toronto: University of Toronto Press, 1980), p. xx.
58 See Runacres, "Art and Ethics in the 'Exempla' of *Confessio Amantis*," and Porter, "Gower's Ethical Microcosm and Political Macrocosm." On the manipulation of sources in the individual tales see Russell Peck, *Kingship and Common Profit in Gower's Confessio Amantis* (Carbondale: Southern Illinois University Press, 1978).
59 *De regimine principum* 1.1.1, pp. 2–3.
60 For a different view of "division," focusing on some internal thematics of the poem, the conflict between love and ethics, and on more strictly poetic questions of structure, see Hugh White, "Division and Failure in Gower's *Confessio Amantis*," *Neophilologus* 72 (1988): 600–16.
61 See Lusignan, *Parler vulgairement*, pp. 51–3.
62 See Arno Borst, *Der Turmbau von Babel: Geschichte der Meinungen über Ursprung und Vielfalt der Sprachen und Völker*, 2.2 (Stuttgart: Anton Hiersemann, 1959): 730–3.
63 Lusignan, *Parler vulgairement*, p. 52.
64 *Der Turmbau von Babel* 2.2:730–921.
65 *The English Works of John Gower*, 1:1.
66 Derek Pearsall, "Gower's Latin in the *Confessio Amantis*," in A. J. Minnis, ed., *Latin and Vernacular: Studies in Late-Medieval Texts and Manuscripts* (Cambridge: D. S. Brewer, 1989), pp. 13–24.
67 Cf. Allen's discussion of *forma tractatus* as part of an "ethical poetic"; see *The Ethical Poetic of the Later Middle Ages*, pp. 117–78.

AFTERWORD

1 *Poets and Princepleasers: Literature and the English Court in the Late Middle Ages* (Toronto: University of Toronto Press, 1980) pp. 161 and 140–67.
2 Prologue to Wycliffite Bible, ch. 15, in Hudson, ed., *Selections from English Wycliffite Writings*, pp. 68 and 71. Modern English "th" has been substituted for the character "thorn."
3 Cited from Pollard, ed., *Fifteenth Century Prose and Verse*, p. 207.
4 See above, ch. 2, p. 51.
5 Ralph Hanna III, "*Compilatio* and the Wife of Bath: Latin Backgrounds, Ricardian Texts," in A. J. Minnis, ed., *Latin and Vernacular: Studies in Late-Medieval Texts and Manuscripts* (Cambridge: D. S. Brewer, 1989), p. 10.
6 See the notes to the poem by Denton Fox, ed., *The Poems of Robert Henryson* (Oxford: Clarendon, 1981), pp. 391–425. Citations of the text are from this edition.

Bibliography

PRIMARY SOURCES

Anonymous works are listed, where possible, by conventional title, otherwise by editor. Collections of anonymous texts are listed by editor (e.g., Brummer, ed., *Vitae Vergilianae*). See p. xiv for the list of standard abbreviations of series and collections.

Alcuin. *Disputatio de rhetorica et de virtutibus*, in Halm, ed., *Rhetores latini minores*, pp. 523–50.

The Rhetoric of Alcuin and Charlemagne, ed. and trans. Wilbur Samuel Howell. Princeton: Princeton University Press, 1941.

Alexander of Hales. *Summa theologiae* 1, ed. Bernard Klumper. Quaracchi: Collegii S. Bonaventurae 1924.

Alfred. *King Alfred's Old English Version of Boethius*, ed. W. J. Sedgfield. Oxford: Oxford University Press, 1899).

Aquila Romanus. *De figuris sententiarum et elocutionis liber*, in Halm, ed., *Rhetores latini minores*, pp. 22–37.

Aquinas, St. Thomas. *Contra errores Graecorum*, ed. P. Glorieux. Tournai: Desclée, 1957.

In Aristotelis libros peri hermeneias et posteriorum analyticorum expositio (Leonine text), ed. Raymundi M. Spiazzi, O.P. 2nd edition. Turin: Marietti, 1964.

Arens, Hans, ed. and trans. *Aristotle's Theory of Language and its Tradition*. Studies in the History of Linguistics 29. Amsterdam: Benjamins, 1984.

Aristotle. *The Complete Works of Aristotle: The Revised Oxford Translation*, ed. Jonathan Barnes. Bollingen Series 71. Princeton: Princeton University Press, 1984.

Arnulf of Orléans. *Arnulfo d'Orléans: un cultore di Ovidio nel secolo XII*, ed. Fausto Ghisalberti. Milan: Ulrico Hoepli, Libraio del R. Istituto di Scienze e Lettere, 1932.

Augustine, St. *De civitate Dei*, after the ed. of Bernard Dombert and Alphonse Kalb. *CCSL* 47–8. Turnhout: Brepols, 1955.

Concerning the City of God Against the Pagans, trans. Henry Bettenson. Harmondsworth: Penguin, 1972.

De doctrina christiana, ed. William M. Green. *CSEL* 80. Vienna: Hoelder–Pichler–Tempsky, 1963.

On Christian Doctrine, trans. D. W. Robertson, Jr. Indianapolis: Bobbs-Merrill, 1958.

Pseudo-Augustine. *Liber de rhetorica*, in Halm, ed., *Rhetores latini minores*, pp. 135–51.

Bacon, Roger. *Opera inedita*, ed. J. S. Brewer. Rolls Series, 1859.

Bede. *Liber de schematibus et tropis*, in Halm, ed., *Rhetores latini minores*, pp. 607–18.

Bibliography

Bernardus Silvestris. *The Commentary on the First Six Books of the Aeneid of Vergil Commonly Attributed to Bernardus Silvestris*, ed. Julian Ward Jones and Elizabeth Frances Jones. Lincoln: University of Nebraska Press, 1977.

The Commentary on Martianus Capella's De nuptiis Philologiae et Mercurii Attributed to Bernardus Silvestris, ed. Haijo Jan Westra. Studies and Texts 80. Toronto: Pontifical Institute of Mediaeval Studies, 1986.

Bode, G. H., ed. *Scriptores rerum mythicarum latini tres Romae nuper reperti*. Celle, 1934.

Boethius. *Commentarii in librum Aristotelis Peri hermeneias, pars posterior, secundam editionem continens*, ed. Charles Meiser. Leipzig: Teubner, 1880.

De differentiis topicis PL 64: 1173–216.

Boethius' De topicis differentiis, trans. Eleonore Stump. Ithaca: Cornell University Press, 1978.

In Isagogen Porphyrii, ed. Samuel Brandt. *CSEL* 48. Vienna: Hoelder-Pichler-Tempsky, 1906.

Philosophiae consolatio, ed. Ludwig Bieler. *CCSL* 94. Turnhout: Brepols, 1957.

Botschuyver, H. J., ed. *Scholia in Horatium codicum Parisinorum latinorum 7972, 7974, 7971*. Amsterdam: Bottenburg, 1935.

ed. *Scholia in Horatium in codibus Parisinis latinis 17897 et 8223 obvia, quae ab Heirico Autissiodorensi profecta esse videntur*. Amsterdam: Bottenburg, 1942.

Brummer, Jacob, ed. *Vitae Vergilianae*. Leipzig: Teubner, 1912.

Brunetto Latini. *Li Livres du Trésor de Brunetto Latini*, ed. Francis J. Carmody. University of California Publications in Modern Philology. Berkeley and Los Angeles: University of California Press, 1948.

Cassiodorus. *Cassiodori Senatoris Institutiones*, ed. R. A. B. Mynors. Oxford: Clarendon, 1937.

Chaucer, Geoffrey. *The Riverside Chaucer*, 3rd edition, ed. Larry D. Benson. Boston: Houghton Mifflin, 1987.

Cicero. *Brutus, Orator*, ed. and trans. H. M. Hubbell. Loeb Classical Library. Cambridge, Mass.: Harvard University Press, 1939.

De finibus bonorum et malorum, ed. and trans. H. Rackham. Loeb Classical Library. London: Heinemann, 1914.

De inventione, De optimo genere oratorum, Topica, ed. and trans. H. M. Hubbell. Loeb Classical Library. Cambridge, Mass.: Harvard University Press, 1949; rpt. 1976.

De officiis, ed. and trans. Walter Miller. Loeb Classical Library. Cambridge, Mass.: Harvard University Press, 1938.

De oratore, ed. and trans. E. W. Sutton and H. Rackham. Loeb Classical Library, 2 vols. Cambridge, Mass.: Harvard University Press, 1942; rpt. 1976.

Tusculan Disputations, ed. and trans. J. E. King. Loeb Classical Library. Cambridge, Mass.: Harvard University Press, 1945; rpt. 1950.

Pseudo-Cicero. *Ad Herennium*, ed. and trans. Harry Caplan. Loeb Classical Library. Cambridge, Mass.: Harvard University Press, 1954.

Conrad of Hirsau. See Huygens, ed., *Accessus ad auctores*.

Dante Alighieri. *De vulgari eloquentia*, ed. Aristide Marigo. Florence: Felice le Monnier, 1938.

Il Convivio, ed. G. Busnelli and G. Vandelli. 2 vols. Florence: Felice le Monnier, 1934–7.

Literary Criticism of Dante Alighieri, trans. Robert S. Haller. Lincoln: University of Nebraska Press, 1973.

Dionysius of Halicarnassus. *Dionysius of Halicarnassus: The Three Literary Letters*, ed. and trans. W. Rhys Roberts. Cambridge: Cambridge University Press, 1901.

Bibliography

Disticha Catonis, ed. Marcus Boas. Amsterdam: North-Holland Publishing Co., 1952.

Donatus, Aelius. *Ars maior*, in Heinrich Keil, ed., *Grammatici latini* 4: 353–402. Leipzig: Teubner, 1864.

Donatus, Tiberius Claudius. *Interpretationes Vergilianae*, ed. Heinrich Georges, 2 vols. Leipzig: Teubner, 1905–12; rpt. Stuttgart: Teubner, 1969.

Dunchad. See Martin of Laon.

Faral, Edmond, ed. *Les Arts poétiques du XIIe et du XIIIe siècle*. Paris: Champion, 1924.

Fortunatianus. *Artis rhetoricae libri III*, in Halm, ed., *Rhetores latini minores*, pp. 81–134.

Fulgentius. *Fabii Planciadis Fulgentii V.C. opera*, ed. Rudolph Helm. Leipzig: Teubner, 1898.

Geoffrey of Vinsauf. *Documentum de modo et arte dictandi et versificandi*, in Faral, ed., *Les Arts poétiques du XIIe et du XIIIe siècle*, pp. 263–320.

Giles of Rome (Aegidius Romanus). *De regimine principum libri III*. Rome. 1607; rpt. Aalen: Scientia Verlag, 1967.

Giovanni del Virgilio. "Giovanni del Virgilio espositore delle Metamorfosi," ed. Fausto Ghisalberti. *Giornale Dantesco* 34, n.s. 4 (1933, Annuario Dantesco, 1931): 1–110.

Goetz, G. *Corpus glossariorum latinorum* 3. Leipzig: Teubner, 1892.

Gower, John. *The English Works of John Gower*, ed. G. C. Macaulay. 2 vols. EETS e.s. 81–2. London: Kegan Paul, Trench, Trübner, 1900–1.

Confessio amantis, ed. Russell Peck. New York: Holt, Rinehart and Winston, 1966; rpt. Toronto: University of Toronto Press, 1980.

Gregory the Great. Epistula 10. *MGH, Gregorii I Papae registrum epistolarum* 2, ed. L. M. Hartmann. Berlin: Weidmann, 1899.

Guillaume de Lorris and Jean de Meun. *Le Roman de la Rose*, ed. Felix Lecoy. 3 vols. *CFMA* 92, 95, and 98. Paris: Champion, 1970–82.

The Romance of the Rose by Guillaume de Lorris and Jean de Meun, trans. Charles Dahlberg. Hanover, New Hampshire and London: University Press of New England, 2nd edition, 1983.

Gundissalinus, Dominicus. *De divisione philosophiae*, ed. Ludwig Baur. Beiträge zur Geschichte der Philosophie des Mittelalters 4, no. 2–3. Münster, 1903.

Halm, Karl, ed. *Rhetores latini minores*. Leipzig: Teubner, 1863; rpt. Frankfurt: Minerva, 1964.

Henryson, Robert. *The Poems of Robert Henryson*, ed. Denton Fox. Oxford: Clarendon, 1981.

Hermagoras. *Fragmenta*, ed. Dieter Matthes. Leipzig: Teubner, 1962.

Hilgard, A., ed. *Grammatici graeci* 1, part 3. Leipzig: Teubner, 1901.

Horace. *Satires, Epistles, and Ars poetica*, ed. and trans. H. Rushton Fairclough. Loeb Classical Library. Cambridge, Mass.: Harvard University Press, 1926.

Hudson, Anne. *Selections from English Wycliffite Writings*. Cambridge: Cambridge Univerity Press, 1978.

Hugh of St. Victor. *Didascalicon*, ed. C. H. Buttimer. Catholic University of America, Studies in Medieval and Renaissance Latin 10. Washington, D.C.: Catholic University of America Press, 1939.

Huygens, R. B. C., ed. *Accessus ad auctores; Bernard d'Utrecht; Conrad d'Hirsau, Dialogus super auctores*. Leiden: Brill, 1970.

ed. Conrad of Hirsau, *Dialogus super auctores*. Collection Latomus 17. Brussels: Latomus, 1955.

Hyginus. *Fabularum liber*. Basel, 1535; rpt. New York: Garland, 1976.

Isidore of Seville. *Etymologiarum sive originum libri XX*, ed. W. M. Lindsay. 2 vols. Oxford: Clarendon, 1911; rpt. 1962.

Jean de Meun. "Boethius' *De consolatione* by Jean de Meun," ed. V. L. Dedeck-Héry. *Mediaeval Studies* 14 (1952): 165–275.

Le Roman de la Rose. See Guillaume de Lorris and Jean de Meun.

Jerome, St. Epistula 57, *Ad Pammachium de optimo genere interpretandi*. In *S. Eusebii Hieronymi opera* sec. I, pars. I, epistularum pars I, I–LXX, ed. I. Hilberg. *CSEL* 54. Vienna: Tempsky, 1910.

Liber de optimo genere interpretandi (Epistula 57), ed. G. J. M. Bartelink. *Mnemosyne*, supplement 61. Leiden: Brill, 1980.

Epistula 106, *Ad Sunniam et Fretelam de psalterio, quae de LXX interpretum editione corrupta sint*. In *S. Eusebii Hieronymi opera* sec. I, pars. II, epistularum pars II, LXXI–CXX, ed. I. Hilberg. *CSEL* 55. Vienna: Tempsky, 1912.

Eusibii Pamphili chronici canones latini vertit, adauxit, ad sua tempora produxit S. Eusebius Hieronymus, ed. J. K. Fotheringham. London: Milford, 1923.

Praefatio in Pentateuchem. *PL* 28: 177–84.

Joannes Balbus. *Catholicon*. Mainz, 1460; rpt. Westmead, Farnborough, Hants., England: Gregg International Publishers, 1971.

Catholicon. Strasbourg, 1482.

John of Garland. *Integumenta Ovidii*, ed. Fausto Ghisalberti. Testi e documenti inediti o rari 2. Messina and Milan: Principato, 1933.

The Parisiana poetria of John of Garland, ed. and trans. Traugott Lawler. New Haven and London: Yale University Press, 1974.

John of Salisbury. *Metalogicon*, ed. C. C. J. Webb (Oxford: Oxford University Press, 1929).

John Scotus Eriugena. *Iohannis Scotti annotationes in Marcianum*, ed. Cora E. Lutz. Cambridge, Mass.: The Medieval Academy of America, 1939.

De divisione naturae. *PL* 122: 441–1022.

De caelisti hierarchia.*PL* 122: 1029–70.

Versus de ambiguis S. Maximi. *PL* 122: 1235–6.

Julius Victor. *Ars rhetorica*, in Halm, ed., *Rhetores latini minores*, pp. 371–448.

Keller, Otto, ed. *Pseudacronis scholia in Horatium vetustiora*. 2 vols. Leipzig: Teubner, 1902–4.

Krapp, George Philip, ed. *The Paris Psalter and the Meters of Boethius*. The Anglo-Saxon Poetic Records 5. New York: Columbia University Press, 1932.

"Longinus". *On Sublimity*, trans. D. A. Russell, in D. A. Russell and M. Winterbottom, eds., *Ancient Literary Criticism: The Principal Texts in New Translations*. Oxford: Clarendon, 1972, pp. 460–503.

Martianus Capella. *De nuptiis Philologiae et Mercurii*, ed. Adolf Dick. Leipzig: Teubner, 1925.

The Marriage of Philology and Mercury, trans. William Harris Stahl and Richard Johnson, with E. L. Burge. *Martianus Capella and the Seven Liberal Arts* 2. New York: Columbia University Press, 1977.

(Martin of Laon). *Dunchad glossae in Martianum*, ed. Cora E. Lutz. Philological Monographs 12. Lancaster, Pennsylvania: American Philological Association, 1944.

Matthew of Vendôme. *Ars versificatoria*. In Faral, ed., *Les Arts poétiques du XIIe et du XIIIe siècle*, pp. 106–93.

Notker of St. Gall. *Notker der Deutsche. Martianus Capella, "De nuptiis Philologiae et Mercurii,"* ed. James C. King. *Die Werke Notkers des Deutschen* 4 (new edition by James C. King and Petrus W. Tax of the series begun by Edward H.

Sehrt and Taylor Starck). Altdeutsche Textbibliothek 87. Tübingen: Niemeyer, 1979.

Notker Latinus, ed. James C. King. *Die Werke Notkers des Deutschen* 4A. Tübingen: Niemeyer, 1985 (published as a supplement to the edition of Notker's translation of Martianus Capella).

"Notkers des Deutschen Brief an Bischof Hugo von Sitten," ed. Ernst Hellgardt. In Klaus Grubmüller et al., eds., *Befund und Deutung. Zum Verhältnis von Empirie und Interpretation in Sprach- und Literaturwissenschaft*. Tübingen: Niemeyer, 1979, pp. 169–92.

Oresme, Nicole. *Le Livre de Ethiques d'Aristote*, ed. Albert Douglas Menut. New York: G. E. Stechert, 1940.

Ovid. *Heroides and Amores*, trans. Grant Showerman. 2nd edition rev. G. P. Goold. Loeb Classical Library. Cambridge, Mass.: Harvard University Press, 1977.

Metamorphoses, ed. and trans. Frank Justus Miller, 3rd edition rev. by G. P. Goold. 2 vols. Loeb Classical Library. Cambridge, Mass.: Harvard University Press, 1977.

Ovide moralisé: Poème du commencement du quatorzième siècle, ed. C. de Boer. 5 vols. Verhandelingen der Koninklijke Akademie van Wetenschappen te Amsterdam, Afdeeling Letterkunde, Nieuwe Reeks, 15, 21, 30 no. 3, 37, and 43. Amsterdam: Johannes Müller, 1915–38.

Petrarch, Francis. *Letters on Familiar Matters: Rerum familiarum libri XVII–XXIV*, trans. Aldo A. Bernardo. Baltimore: Johns Hopkins University Press, 1985.

Philo Judaeus. *De congressu quaerendae eruditionis gratia*, and *De migratione Abrahami*, ed. and trans. F. H. Colson and G. H. Whitaker, *Philo*, vol. 4. Loeb Classical Library. London: Heinemann; New York: Putnam, 1932.

De vita contemplativa, ed. and trans. F. H. Colson, *Philo*, vol. 9. Loeb Classical Library. Cambridge, Mass.: Harvard University Press, 1941.

Pliny the Younger. *Letters and Panegyricus*, ed and trans. Betty Radice. 2 vols. Loeb Classical Library. Cambridge, Mass.: Harvard University Press, 1969.

Priscian. *Praeexercitamina ex Hermogene versa*, in Halm, ed., *Rhetores latini minores*, pp. 551–60.

Quintilian. *Institutio oratoria*, ed. and trans. H. E. Butler. 4 vols. Loeb Classical Library. Cambridge, Mass.: Harvard University Press, 1920.

Rabanus Maurus. *De institutione clericorum. PL* 107: 297–420.

Remigius of Auxerre. *Remigii Autissiodorensis commentum in Martianum Capellam*, ed. Cora Lutz. 2 vols. Leiden: Brill, 1962–5.

Ridewall, John. *Fulgentius metaforalis*, ed. Hans Liebeschütz. Leipsig: Teubner, 1926.

Roy, Bruno, ed. *L'Art d'amours: Traduction et commentaire de l'"Ars amatoria" d'Ovide*. Leiden: Brill, 1974.

Rutherford, William G., ed. *A Chapter in the History of Annotation, being Scholia Aristophanica: vol. III*. London: Macmillan, 1905.

van't Sant, J. Tr. M., ed. "Le Commentaire de Copenhagen de l'*Ovide moralisé*," printed in de Boer, ed., *Ovide moralisé*, vol. 5, appendix 2, from Leiden thesis, 1929.

Seneca the Elder. *Controversiae and Suasoriae*, ed. and trans. M. Winterbottom. 2 vols. Loeb Classical Library. Cambridge, Mass.: Harvard University Press, 1974.

Seneca the Younger. *Ad Lucilium epistulae morales* 2, ed. and trans. Richard M. Gummere. Loeb Classical Library. London: Heinemann, 1920.

Servius. *Servii grammatici qui feruntur in Vergilii carmina commentarii*, ed. George Thilo and Hermann Hagen. 2 vols. Leipzig: Teubner, 1923.

Sextus Empiricus. *Adversus rhetores*, R. G. Bury, ed. and trans., *Sextus Empiricus* 4, *Against the Professors*, Loeb Classical Library. Cambridge, Mass.: Harvard University Press, 1949.

Silk, Edmund T., ed. *Saeculi noni auctoris in Boetii consolationem philosophiae commentarius*. Papers and Monographs of the American Academy in Rome 9. Rome: American Academy in Rome, 1935.

Suetonius. *De grammaticis et rhetoribus*, ed. Giorgio Brugnoli. Leipzig: Teubner, 1963.

Sulpitius Victor. *Institutiones oratoriae*, in Halm, ed., *Rhetores latini minores*, pp. 311–52.

Thierry of Chartres. *Commentarius super libros de inventione*, ed. Karin Margareta Fredborg, *The Latin Rhetorical Commentaries by Thierry of Chartres*. Toronto: Pontifical Institute of Mediaeval Studies, 1988.

Trevet, Nicholas. "Exposicio Fratris Nicolai Trevethi Anglici Ordinis Predicatorum super Boecio De consolacione," ed. Edmund T. Silk. Unpublished typescript.

Trevisa, John. "Dialogue between a Lord and Clerk upon Translation, from Trevisa's Translation of Higden's *Polychronicon*," ed. A. W. Pollard, *Fifteenth Century Prose and Verse*. London: Constable, 1903, pp. 203–8.

Victorinus. *Explanationum in Ciceronis rhetoricam libri II*, in Halm, ed., *Rhetores latini minores*, pp. 153–304.

Vincent of Beauvais. *Speculum historiale*. Douai, 1624; rpt. Graz: Akademische Druck, 1965.

Walton, John. *Boethius: De consolataione philosophiae*, ed. Mark Science. EETS o.s. 170. London: Milford, 1927.

William of Conches. *Glosae super Platonem*, ed. Edouard Jeauneau. Paris: Vrin, 1965.

Woods, Marjorie Curry, ed. and trans. *An Early Commentary on the Poetria nova of Geoffrey of Vinsauf*. New York and London: Garland, 1985.

Zechmeister, J., ed. *Scholia Vindobonensia ad Horatii Artem poeticam*. Vienna, 1877.

SECONDARY SOURCES

It should be noted that many of the critical and historical sources in the following list contain some of the important primary materials used in this book.

Allen, Judson Boyce. *The Ethical Poetic of the Later Middle Ages: A Decorum of Convenient Distinction*. Toronto: University of Toronto Press, 1982.

Allen, Peter L. "Reading Chaucer's Good Women," *Chaucer Review* 21 (1987): 419–34.

Amos, Flora Ross. *Early Theories of Translation*. New York: Columbia University Press, 1920; rpt. New York: Octagon Books, 1973.

Arts libéraux et philosophie au moyen âge. Actes du quatrième Congrès International de Philosophie Médiévale, 1967. Montréal: Institut d'Etudes Médiévales; Paris: Vrin, 1969.

Aston, Margaret. "Wyclif and the Vernacular." In Anne Hudson and Michael Wilks, eds., *From Ockham to Wyclif*. Studies in Church History Subsidia 5. Oxford: Blackwell, 1987, pp. 281–330.

Atkins, J. W. H. *Literary Criticism in Antiquity* 2. Cambridge: Cambridge University Press, 1934.

Atkinson, J. Keith. "A Fourteenth-Century Picard Translation-Commentary of the 'Consolatio philosophiae'." In Minnis, ed., *The Medieval Boethius*, pp. 32–62.

Backes, Herbert. *Die Hochzeit Merkurs und der Philologie: Studien zu Notkers Martian-Übersetzung*. Sigmaringen: Thorbecke, 1982.

Bibliography

Bagni, Paolo. *La costituzione della poesia nelle artes del XII–XIII secolo*. Università degli Studi di Bologna. Studi e Ricerche n.s. 20. Bologna: Zanichelli, 1968.

"L'*inventio* nell'ars poetica latino-medievale." In Brian Vickers, ed., *Rhetoric Revalued*. Binghamton, New York: Center for Medieval and Early Renaissance Studies, 1982, pp. 99–114.

Barthes, Roland. 'L'Ancienne Rhétorique." *Communications* (Ecole pratique des hautes études) 16 (1970): 172–229.

Barwick, Karl. *Probleme der stoischen Sprachlehre und Rhetorik*. Abh. der sächsischen Akademie der Wissenschaften zu Leipzig. Philologisch-historisch Klasse 49.3. Berlin: Akademie, 1957.

Bassnet-McGuire, Susan. *Translation Studies*. London and New York: Methuen, 1980.

Baswell, Christopher C. "'Figures of Olde Werk': Visions of Virgil in Later Medieval England." Diss. Yale, 1983.

Benjamin, Walter. "The Task of the Translator." In Walter Benjamin, *Illuminations*, ed. Hannah Arendt. Trans. Harry Zohn. New York: Schocken Books, 1969.

Bernstein, Richard J. "From Hermeneutics to Praxis." In Robert Hollinger, ed., *Hermeneutics and Praxis*. Notre Dame: University of Notre Dame Press, 1985, pp. 272–96.

Bischoff, Bernhard. "The Study of Foreign Languages in the Middle Ages." *Speculum* 36 (1961): 209–24; rpt. with some changes in Bernhard Bischoff, *Mittelalterliche Studien: Ausgewählte Aufsätze zur Schriftkunde und Literaturgeschichte* 2. Stuttgart: Hiersemann, 1967: 227–45.

Bloch, R. Howard. *Etymologies and Genealogies: A Literary Anthropology of the French Middle Ages*. Chicago: University of Chicago Press, 1983.

Bolgar, R. R. *The Classical Heritage and its Beneficiaries*. Cambridge: Cambridge University Press, 1954; rpt. 1977.

Brother Bonaventure, "The Teaching of Latin in Later Mediaeval England." *Mediaeval Studies* 23 (1961): 1–20.

Bonner, Stanley F. *The Literary Treatises of Dionysius of Halicarnassus: A Study in the Development of Critical Method*. Cambridge: Cambridge University Press, 1939.

Education in Ancient Rome: From the Elder Cato to the Younger Pliny. Berkeley and Los Angeles: University of California Press, 1977.

Borst, Arno. *Der Turmbau von Babel: Geschichte der Meinungen über Ursprung und Vielfalt der Sprachen und Völker*. 4 vols. Stuttgart: Hiersemann, 1957–63.

Bostock, J. K. *A Handbook on Old High German Literature*. 2nd edition. K. C. King and D. R. McLintock, eds. Oxford: Clarendon, 1976.

Brind'amour, Lucie, and Eugene Vance, eds. *Archéologie du signe*. Toronto: Pontifical Institute of Mediaeval Studies, 1983.

Brink, C. O. *Horace on Poetry: Prolegomena to the Literary Epistles*. Cambridge: Cambridge University Press, 1963.

Horace on Poetry: The "Ars poetica." Cambridge: Cambridge University Press, 1971.

Bruns, Gerald L. *Inventions: Writing, Textuality, and Understanding in Literary History*. New Haven: Yale University Press, 1982.

Bullough, D. A. "The Educational Tradition in England from Alfred to Aelfric: Teaching *Utriusque Linguae*." In *La scuola nell'occidente latino dell'alto medioevo*, Settimane di studio del centro italiano di studi sull'alto medioevo 19. 2: 453–94.

Busa, Roberto. *Index Thomisticus: Sancti Thomae Aquinatis operum omnium indices et concordantiae*. Stuttgart: Frommann-Holzboog, 1975.

Bibliography

Cahn, Michael. "Reading Rhetoric Rhetorically: Isocrates and the Marketing of Insight." *Rhetorica* 7 (1989): 121–44.

Caplan, Harry. *Of Eloquence: Studies in Ancient and Mediaeval Rhetoric*, ed. Anne King and Helen North. Ithaca: Cornell University Press, 1970.

Cappuyns, Maïeul. *Jean Scot Erigène: sa vie, son œuvre, sa pensée*. Louvain and Paris, 1933; rpt. Brussels: Culture et Civilisation, 1969.

Cary, George. *The Medieval Alexander*. Cambridge: Cambridge University Press, 1956.

Ceva, Bianca. *Brunetto Latini: l'uomo e l'opera*. Milan: Ricciardi, 1965.

Clark, Donald Lemen. "Imitation: Theory and Practice in Roman Rhetoric." *Quarterly Journal of Speech* 37 (1951): 11–22.

Colish, Marcia L. *The Mirror of Language: A Study in the Medieval Theory of Knowledge*. Rev. ed. Lincoln: University of Nebraska Press, 1983.

Conte, Gian Biagio. *The Rhetoric of Imitation: Genre and Poetic Memory in Virgil and Other Latin Poets*. Trans. Charles Segal. Ithaca: Cornell University Press, 1986.

Contreni, John J. "John Scottus, Martin Hiberniensis, the Liberal Arts, and Teaching." In Michael Herren, ed., *Insular Latin Studies*. Papers in Mediaeval Studies 1. Toronto: Pontifical Institute of Mediaeval Studies, 1981, pp. 23–44.

Copeland, Rita. "The Middle English 'Candet Nudatum Pectus' and Norms of Early Vernacular Translation Practice." *Leeds Studies in English*, n.s. 15 (1984): 57–81.

"Rhetoric and Vernacular Translation in the Middle Ages." *Studies in the Age of Chaucer* 9 (1987): 41–75.

and Stephen Melville. "Allegory and Allegoresis, Rhetoric and Hermeneutics." Forthcoming in *Exemplaria* 3.1 (1991). Peter Allen and Jeff Rider, eds., *Reflection in the Frame: New Perspectives on the Study of Medieval Literature*.

Courcelle, Pierre. "Etude critique sur les commentaires de la *Consolation* de Boèce (IXe–XVe siècles)." *Archives d'histoire doctrinale et littéraire du moyen âge* 14 (1939): 5–140.

"La Culture antique de Remi d'Auxerre." *Latomus* 7 (1948): 247–54.

Late Latin Writers and Their Greek Sources. Trans. Harry E. Wedeck. Cambridge, Mass.: Harvard University Press, 1969.

Cousin, Jean. *Etudes sur Quintilien*. 2 vols. Paris: Boivin, 1935–6; rpt. Amsterdam: Schippers, 1967.

Crespo, Roberto. "Il prologo alla traduzione della 'Consolatio philosophiae' di Jean de Meun e il commento di Guglielmo d'Aragona." *Romanitas et Christianitas. Studi I. H. Waszink*. Amsterdam and London: North Holland Publishing Company, 1973, pp. 55–70.

Cropp, Glynnis M. "A Checklist of Manuscripts of the Medieval French Anonymous Verse–Prose Version of the 'Consolatio' of Boethius." *Notes and Queries* n.s. 26 (1979): 294–96.

"Le Prologue de Jean de Meun et *Le Livre de Boece de Consolacion*." *Romania* 103 (1982): 279–83.

"Les Manuscrits du *Livre de Boece de Consolacion*." *Revue d'histoire des textes* 12–13 (1982–3): 263–352.

"Les Gloses du *Livre de Boece de Consolacion*." *Le Moyen âge* 42 (1986): 367–81.

"*Le Livre de Boece de Consolacion*: From Translation to Glossed Text." In Minnis, ed., *The Medieval Boethius*, pp. 63–88.

Cuendet, Georges. "Cicéron et Saint Jérôme traducteurs." *Revue des études latines* 11 (1933): 380–400.

Curtius, Ernst Robert. *European Literature and the Latin Middle Ages*. Trans.

Willard R. Trask. Princeton: Princeton University Press, 1953. Bollingen edition 1973.

Dahan, Gilbert. "Notes et textes sur la poétique au moyen âge." *Archives d'histoire doctrinale et littéraire du moyen âge* 47 (1980): 171–239.

Dane, Joseph A. "*Integumentum* as Interpretation: Note on William of Conches's Commentary on Macrobius (I, 2, 10–11)." *Classical Folia* 32 (1978): 201–15.

Dedeck-Héry, V. L. "The Manuscripts of the Translation of Boethius' *Consolatio* by Jean de Meung." *Speculum* 15 (1940): 432–43.

Delhaye, Philippe. "L'Enseignement de la philosophie morale au XIIe siècle." *Mediaeval Studies* 11 (1949): 77–99.

Delisle, Léopold. *Recherches sur la librairie de Charles V.* 2 vols. Paris: Champion, 1907.

Demats, Paule. *Fabula: trois études de mythographie antique et médiévale*. Geneva: Droz, 1973.

Denomy, Alex J. "The Vocabulary of Jean de Meun's Translation of Boethius' *De consolatione philosophiae*." *Mediaeval Studies* 16 (1954): 19–34.

Derrida, Jacques. *Of Grammatology*. Trans. Gayatri Chakravorty Spivak. Baltimore: Johns Hopkins University Press, 1976.

"Reinventing Invention." Lecture, Cornell University, 1984.

The Ear of the Other: Otobiography, Transference, Translation. Ed. Christie V. McDonald. Trans. Peggy Kamuf and Avital Ronell. New York: Schocken Books, 1985.

Díaz y Díaz, Manuel C. "Les Arts libéraux d'après les écrivains espagnols et insulaires aux VIIe et VIIIe siècles." In *Arts libéraux et philosophie au moyen âge*, pp. 37–46.

Dickey, Mary. "Some Commentaries on the *De inventione* and *Ad Herennium* of the Eleventh and Early Twelfth Centuries." *Mediaeval and Renaissance Studies* (Warburg Institute) 6 (1968): 1–41.

Dilthey, Wilhelm. "The Rise of Hermeneutics." Trans. Fredric Jameson. *New Literary History* 3 (1972): 229–44.

Dod, Bernard G. "*Aristoteles latinus*." In Kretzmann et al., eds., *The Cambridge History of Later Medieval Philosophy*, pp. 45–79.

Dronke, Peter. *Fabula: Explorations into the Uses of Myth in Medieval Platonism*. Mittelateinische Studien und Texte 9. Leiden and Cologne: Brill, 1974.

Dwyer, Richard A. *Boethian Fictions: Narratives in the Medieval French Versions of the Consolatio philosophiae*. Cambridge, Mass.: The Mediaeval Academy of America, 1976.

Eckhardt, Caroline D. "The Art of Translation in *The Romaunt of the Rose*." *Studies in the Age of Chaucer* 6 (1984): 41–63.

Eden, Kathy. *Poetic and Legal Fiction in the Aristotelian Tradition*. Princeton: Princeton University Press, 1986.

"Hermeneutics and the Ancient Rhetorical Tradition." *Rhetorica* 5 (1987): 59–86.

Edwards, M. C. "A Study of Six Characters in Chaucer's *Legend of Good Women* with Reference to Medieval *Scholia* on Ovid's *Heroides*." B.Litt thesis. Oxford, 1970.

Ellis, Roger, ed. *The Medieval Translator: The Theory and Practice of Translation in the Middle Ages*. Cambridge: D. S. Brewer, 1989.

Engels, Joseph. *Etudes sur l'Ovide moralisé*. Groningen: J. B. Wolters, 1945.

Evans, G. R. *The Language and Logic of the Bible: The Earlier Middle Ages*. Cambridge: Cambridge University Press, 1984.

Fantham, Elaine. "Imitation and Evolution: The Discussion of Rhetorical Imitation in Cicero's *De oratore* 2. 87–97 and Some Related Problems of Ciceronian Theory." *Classical Philology* 73 (1978): 1–16.

"Imitation and Decline: Rhetorical Theory and Practice in the First Century after Christ." *Classical Philology* 73 (1978): 102–16.

Fischer, Hans-Werner. *Untersuchungen über die Quellen der Rhetorik des Martianus Capella*. Inaugural-Dissertation. Breslau, 1936.

Fisher, John H. *John Gower, Moral Philosopher and Friend of Chaucer*. London: Methuen, 1965.

Fleming, John. *Reason and the Lover*. Princeton: Princeton University Press, 1984.

Folena, Gianfranco. "'Volgarizzare' e 'tradurre': idea e terminologia della traduzione dal medio evo italiano e romanzo all'umanesimo europeo." In *La traduzione: saggi e studi*. Trieste: Lint, 1973, pp. 57–120.

Fontaine, Jacques. *Isidore de Seville et la culture classique dans l'Espagne wisigothique*. 2 vols. Paris: Etudes Augustiniennes, 1959.

Foucault, Michel. *The Archaeology of Knowledge*. Trans. A. M. Sheridan Smith. New York: Harper Colophon, 1972.

"What is an Author?" In Michel Foucault, *Language, Counter-Memory, Practice: Selected Essays and Interviews*, ed. Donald F. Bouchard. Trans. Donald F. Bouchard and Sherry Simon. Ithaca: Cornell University Press, 1977, pp. 113–38.

Frank, Robert Worth, Jr. *Chaucer and the Legend of Good Women*. Cambridge, Mass.: Harvard University Press, 1972.

Fredborg, Karin Margareta. "The Commentary of Thierry of Chartres on Cicero's *De inventione*." *Cahiers de l'Institut du moyen âge grec et latin* 7 (1971): 1–36.

"Petrus Helias on Rhetoric." *Cahiers de l'Institut du moyen âge grec et latin* 13 (1974): 31–41.

"The Commentaries on Cicero's *De inventione* and *Rhetorica ad Herennium* by William of Champeaux." *Cahiers de l'Institut du moyen âge grec et latin* 17 (1976): 1–39.

"'Difficile est proprie communia dicere' (Horace, *A.P.* 128), Horatsfortolkningens bidrag til middelalderens poetik." In *Studier i antik og middelalderlig filosofi og idehistorie*. Museum Tusculanum 40–3. Copenhagen: Museum Tusculanum, 1980, pp. 583–97.

Frede, Michael. "Principles of Stoic Grammar." In J. M. Rist, ed., *The Stoics*. Berkeley and Los Angeles: University of California Press, 1978, pp. 27–75.

Fyler, John M. *Chaucer and Ovid*. New Haven: Yale University Press, 1979.

Gadamer, Hans-Georg. *Truth and Method*. Trans. Garrett Barden and John Cumming. New York: Crossroad, 1975.

"On the Scope and Function of Hermeneutical Reflection." In Hans-Georg Gadamer, *Philosophical Hermeneutics*. Trans. and ed. David E. Linge. Berkeley and Los Angeles: University of California Press, 1976, pp. 18–43.

Ganz, Peter. "Der Sonnenhymnus des Matrianus Capella bei Notker von St. Gallen." In Klaus Grubmüller, Ruth Schmidt-Wiegand, and Klaus Speckenbach, eds., *Geistliche Denkformen in der Literatur des Mittelalters*. Münstersche Mittelalter-Schriften 51. Munich: Wilhelm Fink, 1984, pp. 139–51.

Gastaldi, Silvia. *Discorso della città e discorso della scuola. Ricerche sulla "Retorica" di Aristotele*. Florence: La Nuova Italia, 1981.

Gellrich, Jesse M. *The Idea of the Book in the Middle Ages: Language Theory, Mythology, and Fiction*. Ithaca: Cornell University Press, 1985.

Ghisalberti, Fausto. "Mediaeval Biographies of Ovid." *Journal of the Warburg and Courtauld Institutes* 9 (1946): 10–59.

Gibson, Margaret T. "The *Artes* in the Eleventh Century." In *Arts libéraux et philosophie au moyen âge*, pp. 121–6.

ed. *Boethius: His Life, Thought, and Influence*. Oxford: Blackwell, 1981.

Glauche, Günter. "Die Rolle der Schulautoren im Unterricht von 800 bis 1100." In *La scuola nell'occidente latino dell'alto medioevo*. Settimane di studio del centro italiano di studi sull'alto medioevo 19. 2: 617–36.

Gleason, Mark J. "Clearing the Fields: Towards a Reassessment of Chaucer's Use of Trevet in the 'Boece'." In Minnis, ed., *The Medieval Boethius*, pp. 89–105.

Gneuss, Helmut. *Hymnar und Hymnen im englischen Mittelalter: Studien zur Überlieferung, Glossierung und Übersetzung lateinischer Hymnen in England*. Tübingen: Niemeyer, 1968.

Gombrich, E. H. "The Debate on Primitivism in Ancient Rhetoric." *Journal of the Warburg and Courtauld Institutes* 29 (1966): 24–38.

Götz, H. "Kontextübersetzung und Vokabelübersetzung in althochdeutschen Glossen." *Beiträge zur Geschichte der deutschen Sprache und Literatur* (Halle) 82 (1961, supplement vol.): 139–52.

Grabmann, Martin, *Die Geschichte der scholastischen Methode*. 2 vols. Freiburg, 1909; rpt. Darmstadt: Wissenschaftliche Buchgesellschaft, 1957.

Gramsci, Antonio. "La formazione degli intelletuali." In *Gli intelletuali e l'organizzazione della cultura*. Opere di Antonio Gramsci 3. Turin: Giulio Einaudi, 1955, pp. 3–19.

Green, D. H. "The Primary Reception of the Works of Notker the German." *Parergon* n.s. 2 (1984): 57–78.

Green, Richard Firth. *Poets and Princepleasers: Literature and the English Court in the Late Middle Ages*. Toronto: University of Toronto Press, 1980.

Green, William M. "Hugo of St. Victor: *De tribus maximis circumstantiis gestorum*." *Speculum* 18 (1973): 484–93.

Greene, Thomas M. *The Light in Troy: Imitation and Discovery in Renaissance Poetry*. New Haven: Yale University Press, 1982.

Grube, G. M. A. *The Greek and Roman Critics*. London: Methuen, 1965.

Guillemin, A. "L'Imitation dans les littératures antiques et en particulier dans la littérature latine." *Revue des études latines* 2 (1924): 35–57.

Haarhoff, Theodore. *The Schools of Gaul*. Oxford: Oxford University Press, 1920.

Hadot, Pierre. *Marius Victorinus. Recherches sur sa vie et ses œuvres*. Paris: Etudes Augustiniennes, 1971.

Hanna, Ralph, III. "*Compilatio* and the Wife of Bath: Latin Backgrounds, Ricardian Texts." In Minnis, ed., *Latin and Vernacular*, pp. 1–11.

Häring, Nicholas M. "Thierry of Chartres and Dominicus Gundissalinus." *Mediaeval Studies* 26 (1964): 271–86.

Hazelton, Richard. "The Christianization of Cato: The *Disticha Catonis* in the Light of Late Mediaeval Commentaries." *Mediaeval Studies* 19 (1957): 157–73.

Henkel, Nikolaus. *Deutsche Übersetzungen lateinischer Schultexte: Ihre Verbreitung und Funktion im Mittelalter und in der frühen Neuzeit*. Münchener Texte und Untersuchungen zur deutschen Literatur des Mittelalters 90. Munich: Artemis, 1988.

Hexter, Ralph. *Ovid and Medieval Schooling. Studies in Medieval School Commentaries on Ovid's Ars amatoria, Epistulae ex Ponto, and Epistulae Heroidum*. Münchener Beiträge zur Mediävistik und Renaissance-Forschung 38. Munich: Arbeo-Gesellschaft, 1986.

Hoy, David Couzens. *The Critical Circle: Literature, History, and Philosophical Hermeneutics*. Berkeley and Los Angeles: University of California Press, 1978; rpt. 1982.

Hudson, Anne. "The Debate on Bible Translation, Oxford 1401." *The English Historical Review* 90 (1975): 1–18.

Hunt, Richard William. "The Introductions to the 'Artes' in the Twelfth Century." In *Studia Mediaevalia in Honorem R. J. Martin, O.P.*. Bruges: "De Tempel," 1948, pp. 85–112.

"The Lost Preface to the *Liber derivationum* of Osbern of Gloucester." *Mediaeval and Renaissance Studies* (Warburg Institute) 4.2 (1952): 267–82. Rpt. in R. W. Hunt, *Collected Papers on the History of Grammar in the Middle Ages*, ed. G. L. Bursill-Hall. Amsterdam Studies in the Theory and History of Linguistic Science III [Studies in the History of Linguistics 5]. Amsterdam: John Benjamins, 1980, pp. 151–66.

Huygens, R. B. C. "Notes sur le *Dialogus super auctores* de Conrad de Hirsau et le *Commentaire sur Théodole* de Bernard d'Utrecht." *Latomus* 13 (1954): 420–8.

"Remigiana." *Aevum* 28 (1954): 330–44.

Irvine, Martin. "Interpretation and the Semiotics of Allegory in Clement of Alexandria, Origen, and Augustine." *Semiotica* 63 (1987): 33–71.

Grammatica and Textual Culture: Literary Theory in the Early Middle Ages. Cambridge: Cambridge University Press, forthcoming.

Isaac, J. *Le Peri Hermeneias en occident de Boèce à Saint Thomas.* Paris: Vrin, 1953.

Jacobsen, Eric. *Translation: A Traditional Craft.* Copenhagen: Nordisk, 1958.

Jakobson, Roman. "Two Aspects of Language and Two Types of Aphasic Disturbances." In Roman Jakobson and Morris Halle, *Fundamentals of Language*. Janua Linguarum, Series Minor 1. The Hague: Mouton, 1956, pp. 69–96.

Jeauneau, Edouard. "L'Usage de la notion d'*integumentum* à travers les gloses de Guillaue de Conches." *Archives d'histoire doctrinale et littéraire du moyen âge* 24 (1958): 35–100.

"Deux rédactions des gloses de Guillaume de Conches sur Priscien." *Recherches de théologie ancienne et médiévale* 27 (1960): 212–45.

'Note sur l'Ecole de Chartres." *Studi Medievali*, 3rd ser., 5.2 (1964): 821–65.

Johnson, Ian R. "Walton's Sapient Orpheus." In Minnis, ed., *The Medieval Boethius*, pp. 139–68.

"Prologue and Practice: Middle English Lives of Christ." In Ellis, ed., *The Medieval Translator*, pp. 69–85.

"The Late-Medieval Theory and Practice of Translation with Special Reference to Some Middle English Lives of Christ." Diss. University of Bristol (forthcoming).

Jones, Leslie W. "The Influence of Cassiodorus on Mediaeval Culture." *Speculum* 20 (1945): 433–42.

Jongkees, A. G. "Translatio studii: les avatars d'un thème médiéval." In *Miscellanea Mediaevalia in Memoriam Jan Frederick Niermeyer*. Groningen: Wolters, 1967, pp. 41–51.

Jourdain, Charles. "Des commentaires inédits de Guillaume de Conches et Nicolas Triveth sur la Consolation de Boèce." *Notices et extraits de manuscrits de la Bibliothèque Impériale* 20.2 (1862): 40–82.

Kahn, Victoria. *Rhetoric, Prudence, and Skepticism in the Renaissance*. Ithaca: Cornell University Press, 1985.

Kaster, Robert A. "Servius and *Idonei Auctores*." *American Journal of Philology* 99 (1978): 181–209.

"Macrobius and Servius: *Verecundia* and the Grammarian's Function." *Harvard Studies in Classical Philology* 84 (1980): 219–62.

"The Grammarian's Authority." *Classical Philology* 75 (1980): 216–41.

Kelly, Douglas. "The Scope of the Treatment of Composition in the Twelfth- and Thirteenth-Century Arts of Poetry," *Speculum* 41 (1966): 271–78.

"La Spécialité dans l'invention des topiques." In Brind'amour and Vance, eds., *Archéologie du signe*, pp. 101–25.

Bibliography

Kelly, Louis. *The True Interpreter: A History of Translation Theory and Practice in the West*. Oxford: Basil Blackwell, 1979.

Kennedy, George. *The Art of Persuasion in Greece*. Princeton: Princeton University Press, 1963.

The Art of Rhetoric in the Roman World: 300 B.C.–A.D. 300. Princeton: Princeton University Press, 1972.

Classical Rhetoric and its Christian and Secular Tradition from Ancient to Modern Times. Chapel Hill: University of North Carolina Press, 1980.

Kinneavy, James L. "*Kairos*: A Neglected Concept in Classical Rhetoric." In Jean Dietz Moss, ed., *Rhetoric and Praxis: The Contribution of Classical Rhetoric to Practical Reasoning*. Washington, D.C.: The Catholic University of America Press, 1986, pp. 79–105.

Kiser, Lisa J. *Telling Classical Tales: Chaucer and the Legend of Good Women*. Ithaca: Cornell University Press, 1983.

Kretzmann, Norman, Anthony Kenny, and Jan Pinborg, eds.; Eleonore Stump, assoc. ed. *The Cambridge History of Later Medieval Philosophy*. Cambridge: Cambridge University Press, 1982.

Kubiak, David Payne. "Cicero, Catallus, and the Art of Neoteric Translation." Diss. Harvard, 1979. Abstract in *Harvard Studies in Classical Philology* 84 (1980): 337–8.

Kurath, Hans, Sherman M. Kuhn, and John Reidy, eds. *Middle English Dictionary*. Ann Arbor: University of Michigan Press, 1952– in progress.

Laistner, M. L. W. *The Intellectual Heritage of the Early Middle Ages*. Ithaca: Cornell University Press, 1957.

Langlois, Ernest. "La Traduction du Boèce par Jean de Meun." *Romania* 42 (1913): 331–69.

Leeman, A. D. *Orationis Ratio: The Stylistic Theories and Practice of the Roman Orators, Historians, and Philosophers*. 2 vols. Amsterdam: Hakkert, 1963.

Leff, Michael C. "Beothius' *De differentiis topicis*, Book IV." In Murphy, ed. *Medieval Eloquence*, pp. 3–24.

"The Topics of Argumentative Invention in Latin Rhetorical Theory from Cicero to Boethius." *Rhetorica* 1 (1983): 23–44.

Lerer, Seth. *Boethius and Dialogue: Literary Method in the Consolation of Philosophy*. Princeton: Princeton University Press, 1985.

Lewis, Charlton T. and Charles Short. *A Latin Dictionary*. Oxford: Clarendon, 1879.

Lewry, Osmund, O.P. "Boethian Logic in the Medieval West." In Gibson, ed., *Boethius: His Life, Thought, and Influence*, pp. 90–134.

de Lubac, Henri. *Exégèse médiévale: les quatre sens de l'écriture*. 4 vols. Paris: Aubier, 1959–64.

Lucas, Robert J. "Mediaeval French Translations of the Latin Classics to 1500." *Speculum* 45 (1970): 225–53.

Lusignan, Serge. *Parler vulgairement: les intellectuels et la langue française aux XIIIe et XIVe siècles*. Paris: Vrin; Montréal: University of Montréal Press, 1986.

Lutz, Cora E. "Remigius' Ideas of the Seven Liberal Arts." *Traditio* 12 (1956): 65–86.

"The Commentary of Remigius of Auxerre on Martianus Capella." *Mediaeval Studies* 19 (1957): 137–56.

"One Formula of *Accessus* in Remigius' Works." *Latomus* 19 (1960): 774–80.

Machan, Tim William. *Techniques of Translation: Chaucer's Boece*. Norman, Oklahoma: Pilgrim Books, 1985.

Mainzer, Conrad. "John Gower's Use of the 'Mediaeval Ovid' in the *Confessio Amantis*." *Medium Aevum* 41 (1972): 215–29.

Mancini, A. "Un commento ignoto di Remy d'Auxerre ai *Disticha Catonis.*" *Rendiconti della R. Accademia dei Lincei* series 5, 11 (1902): 175–98.

"Ancora sul commento di Remigio d'Auxerre ai *Disticha Catonis.*" *Rendiconti della R. Accademia dei Lincei* series 5, 11 (1902): 369–82.

Manitius, Max. "Zur karolingischen Literatur." *Neues Archiv* 36 (1910): 43–75.

Mariétan, Joseph. *Problème de la classification des sciences d'Aristote à St-Thomas.* Paris: Alcan, 1901.

Marrou, Henri. "'Doctrina' et 'disciplina' dans la langue des Pères de l'Eglise." *Bulletin du Cange* 9 (1934): 5–25.

A History of Education in Antiquity. Trans. George Lamb. New York: Sheed and Ward, 1956.

Mathon, Gérard. "Les Formes et la signification de la pédagogie des arts libéraux au milieu du IXe siècle. L'enseignement palatin de Jean Scot Erigène." In *Arts libéraux et philosophie au moyen âge*, pp. 47–64.

McKeon, Richard. "Literary Criticism and the Concept of Imitation in Antiquity." *Modern Philology* 34 (1936–7): 1–35. Rpt. in R. S. Crane, ed., *Critics and Criticism* (Chicago: University of Chicago Press, 1952), pp. 117–45.

"Rhetoric in the Middle Ages." *Speculum* 17 (1942): 1–32. Rpt. in R. S. Crane, ed., *Critics and Criticism* (Chicago: University of Chicago Press, 1952), pp. 260–96.

Meech, Sanford Brown. "Chaucer and an Italian Translation of the *Heroides.*" *PMLA* 45 (1930): 110–28.

"Chaucer and the *Ovide Moralisé* – a Further Study." *PMLA* 46 (1931): 182–204.

Metzger, Thérèse and Mendel Metzger. *Jewish Life in the Middle Ages: Illuminated Hebrew Manuscripts of the Thirteenth to Sixteenth Centuries.* Trans. Rowan Watson. New York: Alpine Fine Arts, 1982.

Miller, J. Hillis. "The Critic as Host." In Harold Bloom et al., *Deconstruction and Criticism* (New York: Continuum, 1979; rpt. 1986), pp. 217–53.

Minnis, A. J. "Aspects of the Medieval French and English Traditions of the *De consolatione philosophiae.*" In Gibson, ed., *Boethius: His Life, Thought, and Influence*, pp. 312–61.

"The Influence of Academic Prologues on the Prologue and Literary Attitudes of Late-Medieval English Writers." *Mediaeval Studies* 43 (1981): 342–83.

ed. *Gower's Confessio Amantis: Responses and Reassessments.* Cambridge: D. S. Brewer, 1983.

"'Moral Gower' and Medieval Literary Theory." In Minnis, ed., *Gower's Confessio Amantis*, pp. 50–78.

Medieval Theory of Authorship: Scholastic Literary Attitudes in the Later Middle Ages. London: Scolar Press, 1984.

ed. *The Medieval Boethius: Studies in the Vernacular Translations of De consolatione philosophiae.* Cambridge: D. S. Brewer, 1987.

ed. *Latin and Vernacular: Studies in Late-Medieval Texts and Manuscripts.* Cambridge: D. S. Brewer, 1989.

Monfrin, Jacques. "Humanisme et traductions au moyen âge." *Journal des savants* 148 (1963): 161–90.

"Les Traducteurs et leur public en France au moyen âge." *Journal des savants* 149 (1964): 5–20.

Morse, Ruth Karen. "Uses of Antiquity: The Legends of Jason and Medea with special reference to Raoul Lefèvre and William Caxton." Diss. Cambridge, 1977.

Mueller-Vollmer, Kurt, ed. *The Hermeneutics Reader: Texts of the German Tradition from the Enlightenment to the Present.* New York: Continuum, 1985.

Bibliography

Munk Olsen, Birger. *L'Etude des auteurs classiques latins aux XIe et XIIe siècles.* 2 vols. Paris: Editions du Centre National de la Recherche Scientifique, 1982–5.

Murphy, James J. "John Gower's *Confessio Amantis* and the First Discussion of Rhetoric in the English Language." *Philological Quarterly* 41 (1962): 401–11.

"Saint Augustine and Rabanus Maurus: The Genesis of Medieval Rhetoric." *Journal of Western Speech* 31 (1967): 88–96.

Rhetoric in the Middle Ages: A History of Rhetorical Theory from St. Augustine to the Renaissance. Berkeley and Los Angeles: University of California Press, 1974.

ed. *Medieval Eloquence: Studies in the Theory and Practice of Medieval Rhetoric.* Berkeley and Los Angeles: University of California Press, 1978.

"The Teaching of Latin as a Second Language in the 12th Century." *Historiographia Linguistica* 7: 1/2 (1980): 159–75.

Murray, Alexander. *Reason and Society in the Middle Ages.* Oxford: Clarendon, 1978; rpt. 1985.

Nida, Eugene A. *Towards a Science of Translating, with Special Reference to Principles and Procedures Involved in Bible Translating.* Leiden: Brill, 1964.

Nogara, B. "Di alcune vite e commenti medioevali di Ovidio." *Miscellanea Ceriani.* Milan: Ulrico Hoepli, 1910, pp. 415–31.

Norberg, Dag. "A quelle époque a-t-on cessé de parler latin en Gaule?" *Annales (Economies, Sociétés, Civilisations)* 21 (1966): 346–56.

Norden, Eduard. *Die antike Kunstprosa vom VI. Jahrhundert v. Chr. bis in die Zeit der Renaissance.* 2 vols. 4th edition. Leipzig: Teubner, 1923. Rpt. Stuttgart: Teubner, 1958.

Olson, Glending. "Making and Poetry in the Age of Chaucer." *Comparative Literature* 31 (1979): 272–90.

Literature as Recreation in the Later Middle Ages. Ithaca: Cornell University Press, 1982.

Olsson, Kurt O. "Rhetoric, John Gower, and the Late Medieval *Exemplum.*" *Medievalia et Humanistica*, n.s. 8 (1977): 185–200.

Owens, Joseph, "Faith, Ideas, Illumination, and Experience." In Kretzmann et al., eds., *The Cambridge History of Later Medieval Philosophy*, pp. 440–59.

Pace, George B. and Linda E. Voigts. "A 'Boece' Fragment." *Studies in the Age of Chaucer* 1 (1979): 143–50.

Page, R. I. "The Study of Latin Texts in Late Anglo-Saxon England," part 2, "The Evidence of English Glosses." In Nicholas Brooks, ed., *Latin and the Vernacular Languages in Early Medieval Britain.* Leicester: Leicester University Press, 1982, pp. 141–65.

Palmer, Nigel. "Latin and Vernacular in the Northern European Tradition of the *De consolatione philosophiae.*" In Gibson, ed., *Boethius. His Life, Thought, and Influence*, pp. 363–409.

Paris, Gaston. "Chrétien Legouais et autres traducteurs ou imitateurs d'Ovide." *Histoire littéraire de la France* 29: 455–525. Paris: Imprimerie nationale, 1885.

Parker, Patricia A. "The Metaphorical Plot." In David S. Miall, ed., *Metaphor: Problems and Perspectives.* Sussex: Harvester Press; Atlantic Highlands, New Jersey: Humanities Press, 1982, pp. 133–57.

Parkes, Malcolm B. "The Influence of the Concepts of *Ordinatio* and *Compilatio* on the Development of the Book." In J. J. G. Alexander and M. T. Gibson, eds., *Medieval Learning and Literature: Essays Presented to Richard William Hunt.* Oxford: Clarendon, 1975, pp. 115–41.

Payne, Robert O. *The Key of Remembrance: A Study of Chaucer's Poetics.* New Haven: Yale University Press, 1963.

"Making His Own Myth: The Prologue to Chaucer's *Legend of Good Women*." *Chaucer Review* 9 (1975): 197–211.

Pearsall, Derek. "Gower's Narrative Art," *PMLA* 81 (1966): 475–84.

Old English and Middle English Poetry. London: Routledge and Kegan Paul, 1977.

"Gower's Latin in the *Confessio Amantis*." In Minnis, ed., *Latin and Vernacular*, pp. 13–25.

Peck, Russel. *Kingship and Common Profit in Gower's Confessio Amantis*. Carbondale: Southern Illinois University Press, 1978.

Pépin, Jean. "L'Herméneutique ancienne. Les mots et les idées." *Poétique* 23 (1975): 291–300.

Porter, Elizabeth. "Gower's Ethical Microcosm and Political Macrocosm." In Minnis, ed., *Gower's Confessio Amantis*, pp. 135–62.

Press, Gerald. "The Subject and Structure of Augustine's *De doctrina christiana*." *Augustinian Studies* 11 (1980): 99–124.

Przychocki, Gustavus. "*Accessus Ovidiani*." *Rozprawy Akademii Umiejetnosci Wydzial Filologiczny*, ser. 3, vol. 4. Krakow 1911, pp. 65–126.

Quadlbauer, Franz. *Die antike Theorie der Genera dicendi im lateinischen Mittelalter*. Österreichische Akademie der Wissenschaften, Philosophisch-Historische Klasse, Sitzungsberichte, 241.2. Vienna: Hermann Böhlaus, 1962.

Quain, Edwin A. "The Medieval *Accessus ad auctores*." *Traditio* 3 (1945): 215–64.

Rashdall, Hastings. *The Universities of Europe in the Middle Ages*. 3 vols. New edition by F. M. Powicke and A. B. Emden. Oxford: Clarendon, 1936; rpt. 1987.

Reiche, Rainer. *Ein rheinisches Schulbuch aus dem 11. Jahrhundert*. Münchener Beiträge zur Mediävistik und Renaissance-Forschung 24. Munich: Arbeo-Gesellschaft, 1976.

Reiff, Arno. *Interpretatio, Imitatio, Aemulatio: Begriff und Vorstellung literarischer Abhängigkeit bei den Römern*. Diss. Cologne, 1959.

Richards, M. J. B. "Translation, Borrowing and Original Composition in Mediaeval Poetry: Studies in the *Metamorphoses*, the *Ovide moralisé*, and the *Book of the Duchess*." Diss. Cambridge, 1982.

Riché, Pierre. "L'Enseignement et la culture des laïcs dans l'occident pre-carolingien." In *La scuola nell'occidente latino dell'alto medioevo*. Settimane di studio del centro italiano di studi sull'alto medioevo 19. 1: 231–53.

Education and Culture in the Barbarian West, Sixth through Eighth Centuries. Trans. John J. Contreni from the 3rd French edition. Columbia, South Carolina: University of South Carolina Press, 1976.

Ecoles et enseignement dans le haut moyen âge. Paris: Aubier Montaigne, 1979.

Ricoeur, Paul. *The Rule of Metaphor: Multidisciplinary Studies of the Creation of Meaning in Language*. Trans. Robert Czerny, with Kathleen McLaughlin and John Costello, S. J. Toronto: University of Toronto Press, 1977; rpt. 1984.

Hermeneutics and the Human Sciences. Ed. and trans. John B. Thompson. Cambridge: Cambridge University Press, 1981; rpt. 1984.

de Rijk, L. M. "On the Curriculum of Arts at St. Gall, 850–1000." *Vivarium* 1 (1963): 35–86.

Robertson, D. W. "A Note on the Classical Origin of 'Circumstances' in the Medieval Confessional." *Studies in Philology* 43 (1946): 6–14.

Robins, R. H. *Ancient and Medieval Grammatical Theory in Europe*. London: Bell, 1951.

Roques, René. "Traduction ou interprétation? Brèves remarques sur Jean Scot traducteur de Denys." In *The Mind of Eriugena*, eds. John J. O'Meara and Ludwig Bieler. Dublin: Irish University Press, 1973, pp. 59–77.

Runacres, Charles. "Art and Ethics in the 'Exempla' of *Confessio Amantis.*" In Minnis, ed. *Gower's Confessio Amantis*, pp. 106–34.

Rychner, Jean. "Observations sur la traduction de Tite-Live par Pierre Bersuire (1354–1356)." *Journal des savants* 148 (1963): 242–67.

Sanford, Eva Matthews. "The Manuscripts of Lucan: *Accessus* and Marginalia." *Speculum* 9 (1934): 278–95.

Schindel, Ulrich. *Die lateinischen Figurenlehren des 5. bis 7. Jahrhunderts und Donats Vergilkommentar.* Abh. Akademie der Wissenschaften in Göttingen, Philologisch-Historische Klasse, 3rd ser., 91. Göttingen: Vandenhoeck and Ruprecht, 1975.

Schwarz, A. "Glossen als Text." *Beiträge zur Geschichte der deutschen Sprache und Literatur* (Tübingen) 99 (1977): 25–36.

Schwarz, W. "The Meaning of *Fidus Interpres* in Medieval Translation." *Journal of Theological Studies* 45 (1944): 73–8.

Principles and Problems of Biblical Translation: Some Reformation Controversies and their Background. Cambridge: Cambridge University Press, 1955. Rpt. 1970.

La scuola nell'occidente latino dell'alto medioevo. Settimane di studio del centro italiano di studi sull'alto medioevo 19. 2 vols. Spoleto: Presso la sede del centro, 1972.

Segre, Cesare. *Lingua, stile e società. Studi sulla storia della prosa italiana.* Milan: Feltrinelli, 1963.

Sehrt, Edward H., ed. *Notker-Glossar: Ein Althochdeutsch-Lateinisch-Neuhochdeutsches Wörterbuch zu Notker's des Deutschen Schriften.* Tübingen: Niemeyer, 1962.

Self, Lois S. "Rhetoric and *Phronesis*: The Aristotelian Ideal." *Philosophy and Rhetoric* 12 (1979): 130–45.

Shapiro, Marianne. "On the Role of Rhetoric in the *Convivio*," *Romance Philology* 40 (1986): 38–64.

Shapiro, Susan E. "Rhetoric as Ideology Critique: the Gadamer–Habermas Debate Reinvented." *Journal of the American Academy of Religion*, forthcoming.

Shoaf, R. A. "Notes Towards Chaucer's Poetics of Translation." *Studies in the Age of Chaucer* 1 (1979): 55–66.

Silk, Edmund T. "Cambridge MS. Ii.3.21 and the Relation of Chaucer's *Boethius* to Trivet and Jean de Meung." Diss. Yale, 1930.

"Pseudo-Johannes Scottus, Adalbold of Utrecht, and the Early Commentaries on Boethius." *Mediaeval and Renaissance Studies* (Warburg Institute) 3 (1954): 1–40.

Silvestre, Hubert. "Aperçu sur les commentaires carolingiens de Prudence." *Sacris Erudiri* 9 (1957): 50–74.

"Le Schéma 'moderne' des *accessus.*" *Latomus* 16 (1957): 684–9.

Simpson, James. "Ironic Incongruence in the Prologue and the Book 1 of Gower's *Confessio Amantis.*" *Neophilologus* 72 (1988): 617–32.

Smalley, Beryl. *The Study of the Bible in the Middle Ages.* Oxford: Blackwell, 1952. Rpt. Notre Dame: University of Notre Dame Press, 1978.

English Friars and Antiquity in the Early Fourteenth Century. Oxford: Oxford University Press, 1960.

Solmsen, Friedrich. "Demetrios *Peri hermeneias* und sein peripatetisches Quellenmaterial." *Hermes* 66 (1931): 241–67. Rpt. in Rudolf Stark, ed., *Rhetorikia: Schriften zur aristotelischen und hellenistischen Rhetorik.* Hildesheim: Georg Olms, 1968, pp. 285–311.

Sonderegger, Stefan. "Frühe Übersetzungsschichten im Althochdeutschen." In

Werner Kohlschmidt and Paul Zinsli, eds., *Philologia Deutsch: Festschrift zum 70. Geburtstag von Walter Henzen*. Berne: Francke, 1965, pp. 101–14.

Sontag, Susan. *Against Interpretation and Other Essays*. New York: Dell, 1966.

Stahl, William Harris, Richard Johnson, and E. L. Burge. *Martianus Capella and the Seven Liberal Arts* 1, *The Quadrivium of Martianus Capella: Latin Traditions in the Mathematical Sciences, with a Study of the Allegory and the Verbal Disciplines*. New York: Columbia University Press, 1971.

Steiner, George. *After Babel: Aspects of Language and Translation*. Oxford: Oxford University Press, 1975. Rpt. 1977.

Stock, Brian. *Myth and Science in the Twelfth Century: A Study of Bernard Silvester*. Princeton: Princeton University Press, 1972.

The Implications of Literacy: Written Language and Models of Interpretation in the Eleventh and Twelfth Centuries. Princeton: Princeton University Press, 1983.

Strubel, Armand. "'Allegoria in factis' et 'allegoria in verbis'." *Poétique* 23 (1975): 342–57.

Struever, Nancy. *The Language of History in the Renaissance: Rhetoric and Historical Consciousness in Florentine Humanism*. Princeton: Princeton University Press, 1970.

Sundby, Thor. *Della vita e delle opere di Brunetto Latini*. Trans. Rodolfo Renier. Florence: Le Monnier, 1884.

Szondi, Peter. "Introduction to Literary Hermenteutics." *New Literary History* 10 (1978): 17–29.

Thomas, Antoine and Mario Roques. "Traductions françaises de las *Consolatio philosophiae* de Boèce." *Histoire littéraire de la France* 37: 419–88. Paris: Imprimerie nationale, 1938.

Thurot, Charles. "Extraits de divers manuscrits latins pour servir à l'histoire des doctrines grammaticales au moyen âge." *Notices et extraits des manuscrits de la Bibliothèque Nationale et autres bibliothèques* 22.2. Paris, 1869; rpt. Frankfurt: Minerva, 1964.

Todorov, Tzvetan. *Theories of the Symbol*. Trans. Catherine Porter. Ithaca: Cornell University Press, 1982.

Trimpi, Wesley. *Muses of One Mind: The Literary Analysis of Experience and its Continuity*. Princeton: Princeton University Press, 1983.

Tuve, Rosemond. *Allegorical Imagery: Some Mediaeval Books and Their Posterity*. Princeton: Princeton University Press, 1966.

Ullmann, Walter. *Law and Politics in the Middle Ages*. Ithaca: Cornell University Press, 1975.

Untersteiner, Mario. *The Sophists*. Trans. Kathleen Freeman. Oxford: Blackwell, 1954.

Vance, Eugene. "Chaucer, Spenser, and the Ideology of Translation." *Canadian Review of Comparative Literature* 8 (1981): 217–38.

Vinaver, Eugene. *The Rise of Romance*. Oxford: Oxford University Press, 1971.

Wallace, David. *Chaucer and the Early Writings of Boccaccio*. Cambridge: D. S. Brewer, 1985.

Ward, John. "*Artificiosa Eloquentia* in the Middle Ages." 2 vols. Diss. Toronto, 1972.

"From Antiquity to the Renaissance: Glosses and Commentaries on Cicero's *Rhetorica*." In Murphy, ed., *Medieval Eloquence*, pp. 25–67.

Weisheipl, James A. "Classification of the Sciences in Medieval Thought." *Mediaeval Studies* 27 (1965): 54–90.

Wetherbee, Winthrop. *Platonism and Poetry in the Twelfth Century: The Literary Influence of the School of Chartres*. Princeton: Princeton University Press, 1972.

Bibliography

Chaucer and the Poets: An Essay on Troilus and Criseyde. Ithaca: Cornell University Press, 1984.

"Genius and Interpretation in the *Confessio Amantis*." In Arthur Groos, ed., *Magister Regis: Studies in Honor of Robert Earl Kaske*. New York: Fordham University Press, 1986, pp. 241–60.

White, Hugh. "Division and Failure in Gower's *Confessio Amantis*." *Neophilologus* 72 (1988): 600–16.

Williams, Gordon. *Change and Decline: Roman Literature in the Early Empire*. Berkeley and Los Angeles: University of California Press, 1978.

Wimsatt, James I. *The Marguerite Poetry of Guillaume de Machaut*. University of North Carolina Studies in the Romance Languages and Literatures 87. Chapel Hill: University of North Carolina Press, 1970.

Chaucer and the French Love Poets: The Literary Background of the Book of the Duchess. Chapel Hill: University of North Carolina Press, 1968.

Woods, Marjorie Curry. "Literary Criticism in an Early Commentary on Geoffrey of Vinsauf's *Poetria nova*." In Richard Schoeck, ed., *Acta Conventus Neo-Latini Bononiensis*. Medieval and Renaissance Texts and Studies 37. Binghamton, New York, 1985, pp. 667–73.

Woolf, Rosemary. *The English Religious Lyric in the Middle Ages*. Oxford: Clarendon, 1968.

Wright, Roger. *Late Latin and Early Romance in Spain and Carolingian France*. ARCA Classical and Medieval Texts, Papers and Monographs 8. Liverpool: Francis Cairns, 1982.

Zetzel, James. *Latin Textual Criticism in Antiquity*. Diss. Harvard, 1972; rpt. Salem, New Hampshire: Ayer Company, 1981.

1. Index of names and titles

1. Index of names and titles

1. Index of names and titles

1. Index of names and titles

2. General index

2. General index

2. General index

2. General index

2. General index